Lt. Col. Sir William Hillary, Bt., 1771 - 1847.
Resident of Douglas, Isle of Man, from 1808 and Founder of the National Lifeboat Institution for the Preservation of Life from Shipwreck in 1824. (later to become known as the RNLI.)

The Ramsey Lifeboats
1829 - 1991

W. N. Seybold

ISBN 0 9517945 0 7 THE RAMSEY LIFEBOATS 1829-1991 (PBK)
Published in the Isle of Man in 1991 by the RNLI Ramsey Station, c/o
Capt. W. N. Seybold, "Cair Vie", 36 Ballaterson Fields, Ballaugh, I.O.M.

Printed by Nelson Press Co. Ltd., Douglas, Isle of Man.

Cover photograph by B. P. Grenfell. The RNLB *James Ball Ritchie* of Ramsey assisting to refloat the mfv St. Britwin at the Point of Ayre, Isle of Man, on the 18th April, 1988. (See Chapter 9, page 164)

CONTENTS

FOREWORD

By His Grace the Duke of Atholl

Member of the RNLI Committee of Management and a former Chairman;

Member of the Executive Committee: Member of the Search and Rescue Committee;

Member of the Public Relations Committee.

It is always difficult to write a book such as this, knowing how much to put in and what to leave out, and I certainly do not envy Captain Seybold his task; however I consider that he has done an excellent job. While the book might be thought to be a history of the Isle of Man's Lifeboat Service, it undoubtedly concentrates on the Ramsey Station, and gives a most interesting account of not only the services undertaken by the boats but also of the personalities involved.

The Isle of Man could well be described as the foundation stone of the RNLI for it was in Douglas where Sir William Hillary lived and was a member of the crew and where he floated his idea of a lifeboat service covering the whole of Britain, and which eventually was accepted in 1824; nonetheless although Ramsey is only 12 miles from Douglas, it was not until 1868 that that station came under the umbrella of the RNLI. Captain Seybold in my view quite rightly does not start his story with the coming of *The Two Sisters* to Ramsey (she was the first lifeboat operated under the aegis of the RNLI there) but with the events leading up to her arrival and the work of the pre-RNLI lifeboat. This makes it perfectly clear why it was necessary for a lifeboat to be stationed at Ramsey. Each of Ramsey's lifeboats is then detailed, and her exploits described; which gives a continuing indication of the development of the Lifeboat Service, and of the myriads of improvements which have taken place since *The Two Sisters* took up station. Of course the improvements in design and equipment must not allow us to overlook the extremely important part that the crews and shore-helpers have played, and Captain Seybold in this book certainly pays due homage to them, and one is left in no doubt about their competence and great gallantry.

The book acknowledges the extremely important part played by the fund-raisers (the Ladies' Guilds), and also pays tribute to the Chairman, Honorary Secretary and Honorary Administrative Officer of the Ramsey Branch, and gives the reader an idea of the organisation behind a lifeboat station, although I am afraid that Captain Seybold somewhat diminishes the part played by the Station Committee, no doubt due to understandable reticence on his part.

I am sure that all who have had the opportunity of reading this book will find it rewarding and will enjoy not only the tales of heroism, but also reading about the technology which is incorporated into the modern lifeboat. In short, this book has something to enthrall anyone who is interested in the sea, the Lifeboat Service or the Isle of Man's fascinating marine history, and I recommend those who cannot buy it, to beg, borrow or steal it.

Atholl.

LIST OF ILLUSTRATIONS

LIST OF ILLUSTRATIONS cont'd

ACKNOWLEDGMENTS

After four-and-a-half years' work on this history, my list is a long one. It would not have been possible to collate so much information or obtain the large number of photographs without the help of many people from both near and far. I wish to express my thanks and appreciation to all those listed below and apologise in advance for any omissions.

Incorporated in this book are facts from Keith Grimble Groves' original history of the Station, published in 1968, which deals mainly with Committee matters. The lifeboat records of an Archivist, the late Grahame Farr, were supplied by the RNLI at Poole and have been invaluable in tracing the services carried out. His booklet on the Early Manx Lifeboats gives interesting details on Ramsey. The present Lifeboat Enthusiasts' Society Honorary Archivist, Jeff Morris, has supplied information and up-to-date photographs of the latest Ramsey Boat.

Mr. Robert Kelly's book on Sir William Hillary, "For Those in Peril", has given us an insight into his career and makes fascinating reading for those further interested in the Lifeboat Service.

Dennis Learoyd and William Corlett supplied extensive press cuttings, notes and photographs from their private collections on the local lifeboats. Brian Grenfell has given invaluable assistance in making available his own portfolio of recent lifeboat photographs, also with copying, enlarging and processing, and he kept an up-to-date record of recent lifeboat events for the book. His cover photograph has been especially appreciated. Stan Basnett, Dennis Reed, Albert Lowe, Barry Ramsey, Roger Oram, Gilbert Hampton, David Smith, Philip Monekton and Graham Cooke have all kindly processed and supplied their own photographs. A. Christian, J. Woolnough, J. Cottier, Director P. E. Neumann of FotoFlite and Curator D. Brierley of the San Diego Maritime Museum have kindly lent or donated from their collections of photographs.

D. Clarey, Wm. Kneale, D. Power, A. Shimmin, K. Horsley, T. Muir, Parkinsons Ltd., and the Clerk to the Ramsey Commissioners have all given general historical information on Ramsey life, the shipyard and lifeboat matters.

The M.O.D. Hydrographic Office has kindly given permission for the reproduction of two Admiralty charts in Chapter One. The Manx Museum and National Trust has given permission to reproduce several photographs. I also have to thank Librarian-Archivist Miss A. Harrison and Miss M. Critchlow and the staff at the Museum Library for all their assistance during my hours of labour there. The Editors of the Courier Group and Independent Newspapers also gave permission for the use of their articles and thanks go to reporters S. Wooley, E. Richmond and P. McPherson. The Editors of the Daily Telegraph, the Liverpool Daily Post and Echo, the Western Morning News papers, Sea Breezes, Motor Boat and Yachting and the Lifeboat magazines all gave permission for the use of lifeboat material and the reproduction of photographs and plans.

Archivists E. Hanna and S. Campelton of the Isle of Man Postal Authority gave assistance with advertising the book and Project Manager D. Border of FBM Ltd. gave prompt help with information and photographs of the new *Ann and James Ritchie*. Personnel at the RNLI Poole Headquarters who helped throughout the project were E. Wake-Walker, Mrs. S. Woodroffe, Mrs. H. Deane, Mrs. Cull and also M. Floyd and, in Manchester, D. Jones.

ACKNOWLEDGMENTS cont'd

Local lifeboatmen both past and present who assisted me with information and photographs were T.A. Corlett, R. Christian, J. Kneale, Coxswain J. Kinnin, 2nd Coxswain R. Stanfield, Mechanic J. Martin and Crewman K. Holland. All members of the Branch Executive Committee gave me help and support, which included Chairman Ewan Corlett, Neil Luck, Michael Brew, John Sands and Steven Spencer. Bill Clague of the Committee gave general help and assisted with proof-reading. Edna Corlett, Hilary Sands, Mary Page and Jane Forth of the Ladies' Guild all assisted me with various items.

P. Gilbertson, T. Peace and J. Shaw of the Nelson Press turned the manuscript into print and were always helpful and patient.

Most sincere and grateful thanks go to two people in particular. To local Historian Constance Radcliffe for her unfailing assistance in checking facts, providing information, proof reading and continual moral support. Also to John Swale, publisher of "Sea Breezes", who spent countless hours editing and then giving me professional advice on the layout and general production of the History.

To my wife, Maureen, and to all those friends who have supported me during this first venture as an author, I express my deep gratitude and admiration for their patience over these past years. I am not an easy patient. (So they tell me!)

THE HISTORY FUND

Finally I must thank all the friends of the Ramsey RNLI, both on the Island and in the UK, for their financial assistance in the project. This book could not have been published without their generosity. Their donations to the History Fund enabled the initial work at the Printers to proceed.

A long list of individual names is omitted with regret but, simply, it continues to grow daily and therefore I could not possibly guarantee a complete one.

All who buy this book also contribute directly to the funds of the RNLI.

INTRODUCTION

The years since the first history of the Ramsey Lifeboats was completed in 1968 have seen very marked changes in the world shipping scene which have, of course, been felt to a great extent by the United Kingdom and also here in the Isle of Man. Gone are the days of intense coastal traffic around the shores of the British Isles; the demise of the Commonwealth trade and thus the British Merchant Navy; the building of the UK motorways and the increased use of the airways for both passenger and freight use, have all seen to that. Nowadays our Isle of Man coastal shipping consists mainly of passing ferries, fishing vessels, yachts and pleasure craft and a limited number of our own freight and passenger vessels and oil company tankers.

Moreover , modern navigational aids both ashore and afloat have made seagoing and navigation a more exact science and also safer. Radar has considerably tamed the hazards of fog and making landfalls. Decca, Loran, vhf D/F and Satnav have enabled vessels so fitted to pinpoint their positions at any given time. Satcom and vhf radio have now made telephonic communications at sea commonplace. New materials have been introduced by the builders of smaller craft and the RNLI has been in the forefront of designing and producing lighter and faster lifeboats for all methods of launching.

The last "Oakley" Class lifeboat stationed in Ramsey served from 1970 to the beginning of this year, 1991. She has now been semi-retired and placed in the reserve fleet of the RNLI.

The old Norbury Boathouse was demolished in April, 1990, after one hundred years of service to the Station. Now the New Norbury Boathouse, a large new tractor and a brand new "Mersey" Class fast-carriage lifeboat are all in operation and should serve the RNLI and the Ramsey Station for very many years to come.

But two things do remain the same: the weather and the willingness of men to put to sea in almost any conditions to save human lives. We may not see the great disasters and rescues of years gone by any more, but we shall always have unpredictable weather with the dangers it brings to the ever-growing number of pleasure craft; engine and equipment failures; ropes around propellers; swimmers and surfers in trouble and calls for urgent medical help. So long as the perils of the sea threaten life so shall the lifeboats and the men who man them remain "on call".

W. N. Seybold

Ballaugh, Isle of Man, July 1991.

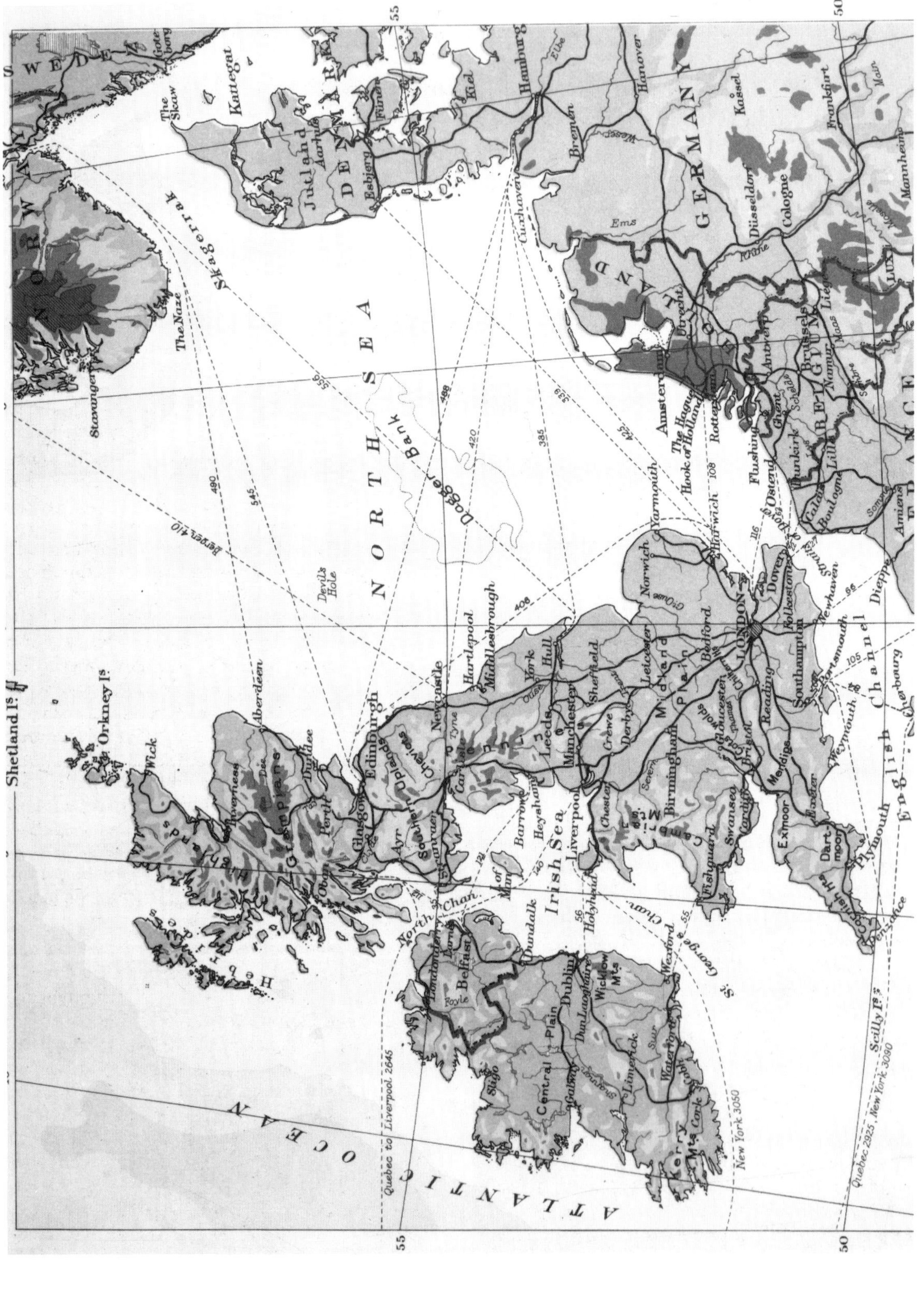

MAP OF IOM - UK - CONTINENT

CHAPTER 1

The Early Days in Ramsey; Sir William Hillary and the first Lifeboat on station, 1829-1851

FOR all inhabited islands, large or small, the seas surrounding them govern their ways of life. So it is with the Isle of Man. Lying in the Northern latitudes of the Irish Sea and part of the British Isles, it is a self-governing nation which boasts one of the oldest parliaments in the world. Tynwald, as the governing body is called, celebrated its Millennium in 1979. The Queen holds the position of Lord of Mann.

The Island covers an area of some 230 square miles with its main 36 mile axis lying NNE to SSW and its shores present the mariner with anything from low gravel beaches in the North to sheer rock cliffs in the South. Douglas is the Island's capital and main centre for business and commerce. It is also the centre for the bulk of the population of the Island, which is gradually increasing and had reportedly reached about 68,000 in 1989.

The town and small port of Ramsey lies in the centre of Ramsey Bay with a geographical position of 54-19N 04-23W and some 12 miles North of Douglas on the Island's North East Coast. It is the second most important commercial port and has been for over 100 years now. But Ramsey Bay as a sheltered anchorage for shipping goes back hundreds of years and still today sees trawlers, small coastal vessels and yachtsmen gaining shelter from all gales from the South through West to the North.

Ramsey saw some of its greatest changes in the mid-nineteenth century and during those years shipping in its various forms led such changes. In the 1790's the Ramsey town population was only 920 out of a total Island figure of some 28,000. People were mainly employed in agriculture, fishing and related industries in the North of the Island. The first smoke-house for the still-famous Manx Herring was erected in Peel in 1769 and the Island exported grain, potatoes and hides to the mainland from those early years. Boat-building went on from very early times and often from countryside locations. Brewing, tanning, paper-making, mining, flour-milling, flax-processing and ship-building all followed on and Ramsey ships not only took their cargoes to Douglas and other Island ports, but had their own export routes to Liverpool, Cumbrian and many smaller Irish Sea ports. In the mid-1800's in fact, a steam vessel from Ramsey could make the short passage to Douglas in just over one hour whereas by road and horse-drawn vehicle it took over four hours!

As a port Ramsey has always suffered from the fact that the berths dry out at low water. The harbour lies at the seaward end of the Sulby River which, of course, is part tidal. The building of the South Pier, or breakwater, was commenced in the late 1700's but although there were planned improvements for the port from 1792, money was always short and thus progress slow. The North Pier was erected in stages between 1829 and 1864 and then in 1876 further work was undertaken to extend the length of South Pier by 570 feet. This took two years. Meanwhile, the long Queen's Pier at the Southern end of the promenade, which led South from the harbour entrance, was opened in 1886. This provided a proper landing stage for the packet steamers of the day and catered for the expanding tourist industry.

Shipwrecks abound around the Island's coasts and a recent survey has put the number at 500; and those are only the accountable ones! Naturally, the area from Douglas Bay South to Castletown and around the Calf of Man and Kitterland Sound account for a large majority of these, with vessels coming from Liverpool and the South intending to make their first landfall in the South of the Island. Castletown was the original capital of the Island. But Northern shores and the approaches to Ramsey Bay have also taken their toll of shipping. The Ramsey Lifeboat area covers the coasts from Jurby Head on the North-West Coast of the Island; round to the Point of Ayre, our most Northerly point; down through Ramsey Bay to Maughold Head and Southwards to Laxey Bay where its limits meet the Douglas Lifeboat area. It thus covers about 22 miles of coast and offshore waters.

The greatest dangers that still remain within these Northern waters are the shallows off the Point of Ayre. These are the Whitestone Bank which is but one mile off the Point itself and further East the Bahama Bank, Ballacash Bank and the King William Banks. Perhaps the most dangerous of these is the Whitestone Bank with a patch of water only one foot deep at low water, but all of them the causes of groundings and disasters in the past. Early records of these are scant and no official records were kept until the eighteenth century. Even then only brief references were made in Parish Registers or early newspapers. Such an entry in the Kirk Bride Parish Register of 1774 states:

"John Curphey, a mariner of Braddan, murdered on board the NELLY, sloop of Liverpool, by Robert Halsal, Master. Curphey, who was thrown into the hatch by the Master in a fit of temper, was buried in the churchyard."

Another entry of 1793 states briefly:

"Brig BELLA of Workington wrecked on King William's Sand"

However, the Great Storm of 1787 is better documented and it stands out in Manx maritime history and, very possibly more than any other shipwreck, made people realise that the need for the organised saving of life at sea was becoming imperative. On this particular night, the 21st September, 1787, the Manx herring fleet was lost off Douglas Bay. Up to 60 boats were totally wrecked and newspapers reported that 161 fishermen had died. The Irish Sea was as deceiving as ever. It had been a flat calm all day with sunny skies and some four hundred wooden fishing vessels were out fishing off the East Coast. That night the wind veered and a storm from the South forced its way into Douglas Bay, causing a short steep sea. The fleet made for the shore; most for Douglas but some of the larger boats preferred to risk running before the gale and attempted to make Ramsey. Crowds of relatives and onlookers on Douglas beach held lanthorns to guide their men back. The harbour entrance, however, was lit by only one single lanthorn and this was soon extinguished in the storm. The disaster ahead then became apparent as many boats were smashed to pieces on St. Mary's Isle (or Conister Rock) which lies at the very entrance to the harbour. Other boats were torn apart in the surf as they attempted to make the beach itself. The tragedy was incalculable and it must have affected over half the families on the Island at the time.

THE FIRST LIFEBOATS

It is considered nowadays that the very first boat to be maintained solely as a lifeboat was stationed at Formby on the Lancashire Coast, just North of Liverpool, in 1777. But men of the North-East Coast of England were aware of distress at sea much earlier than this. In 1721 when the Bishop of Durham died he bequeathed a sum of money to provide a sanctuary for sailors who survived shipwreck. It was established at Bamburgh Castle on the Northumberland Coast between Berwick and Tynemouth. It was administered by the Crewe Trust, a body of gentlemen headed by Dr. John Sharp, a local archdeacon. This Trust also invented a system of distress signals.

During the latter half of the eighteenth century Lionel Lukin from Dunmon in Essex was experimenting with boats to try and perfect an "unimergible" one. This he eventually succeeded in doing in 1786 by converting a local coble. Three years later, on the 15th March, 1789, South Shields witnessed one of their worst early maritime disasters when the full-rigged ship ADVENTURE, registered in its home port of Newcastle, was blown on to the Hurd Sands at the very mouth of the River Tyne. The surf was raging and no boat could possibly reach the wreck in the conditions prevailing. Thus, as on the night of the Manx herring fleet disaster only two years earlier, relatives of the seamen and onlookers saw the crew gradually drop from their last stand in the rigging into the boiling sea never to be seen alive again.

Thus, more impetus to save life at sea was heralded. Yet another group of men known as the Gentlemen of Lawe House, and this time from South Shields itself, offered a two-guinea prize for the best lifeboat design. William Woodhave, a house painter of the town, shared half the prize. His design was a boat 30 feet in length and with a beam of 10 feet. Propulsion was by oars and it used cork for added buoyancy. Henry Greathead shared the rest of the prize. He was a boat-builder from the same area but neither of their designs were considered satisfactory in their own right. The Lawe House Gentlemen therefore improved these plans and Greathead was commissioned to build the resulting design. It was a lifeboat aptly named *Original*. This version served for over 40 years and became accepted as the standard boat. It was a lifeboat of this design, although somewhat smaller with only eight oars, which was the first one ever stationed in Douglas. This was in the year 1803 and was financed by the Governor of the Isle of Man, the Duke of Atholl. In those days it cost £130 and that included the freight from Liverpool. It lasted only eleven years as it was kept on the open beach and was inevitably destroyed in a gale. The formation of the "National Institution for the Preservation of Lives and Property from Shipwreck" was still a decade away.

SIR WILLIAM HILLARY

The name of Sir William Hillary is synonymous with the NIPLS, later to become the Royal National Lifeboat Institution. The name of Sir William Hillary is also synonymous with Douglas and the Isle of Man, for it was here in Douglas Bay that his attention was forcibly drawn to the plight of seafarers drowning at sea but within yards of the safety of the shore. This was in 1822.

Hillary was born of elderly parents on the 4th January, 1771. He lived in a Quaker environment on a small farmstead in Wensleydale, Yorkshire. His early years of manual labour gave him the physique and stamina that would be called upon in later years in the Isle of Man. The family had Quaker connections in London and through these in the 1790's, Hillary was nominated and appointed to the post of equerry to the sickly Prince Augustus Frederick, the sixth son of King George III. The Prince, in search of warmer climes for health reasons, travelled to Mediterranean shores and thus Hillary spent some years living abroad in Italy and Malta. He seemingly became quite wealthy and was called upon to assist with diplomatic work which caused him to return to England. He gave up the position in 1798 and returned to live in Liverpool for a short period. Here his elder brother Richard owned a house although he lived in Jamaica where he owned plantations and exported produce to Liverpool.

By 1800 William's wealth was depleted and he married the wealthy heiress Frances Elizabeth Disney Ffytche from a large estate in Essex. The union was very unpopular with her family as she was officially betrothed to another and so they had to elope to marry. In 1805 Hillary was made a Baronet for his earlier services to King and Country, but it did not save his marriage which broke up in 1808. His wife remained in the family home in Essex with their two children, son Augustus and daughter Elizabeth Mary, but Hillary looked elsewhere to begin a new life.

Hillary to the Isle of Man

Richard Hillary had meanwhile died in Jamaica and so William inherited the proceeds of the sale of the lands. He did not wish to go that far away to live. Instead he chose the Isle of Man and in the same year, 1808, made the passage on the weekly packet boat from Whitehaven to Douglas. He settled in well, acquiring initially a house on Prospect Hill. The Island suited him and reminded him of his earlier country life in the Yorkshire Dales. He made friends and entered the commercial world, later re-marrying and living in Fort Anne overlooking Douglas Harbour and Bay. His new wife was Amelia (Emma) Tobin, a Manx lady of Irish descent.

In the early 1820's small packet paddle steamers were running a service from Liverpool to Greenock, calling en route at Douglas. Their arrivals were heralded by a bugler who marched through the town summoning intending passengers. This often happened during the early hours of the morning. On one such Monday, the 6th October, 1822, instead of bugle notes, Douglas was awakened by the noise of cannon fire in the Bay. From his house Hillary could just make out the misty outline of the Royal Navy cutter Vigilant, obviously in trouble in gale conditions. It later became known that numerous vessels had, during the previous day, anchored in the Bay to shelter from a WNW'ly gale. This had backed to the South during the night and so was blowing into the Bay and putting the ships on a lee shore, making the anchorage a dangerous one instead of a safe one. This was appreciated by the Vigilant's commander, Lt. Reid, and he weighed anchor to make for the greater safety of the open sea. Whilst undertaking this manoeuvre a fully loaded sloop, being driven by the gale, crossed the Vigilant's bow. In taking evasive action the Royal Navy vessel grounded on St. Mary's Isle and the heavy seas were threatening to break her up.

There had been no lifeboat available since the wrecking of the *Atholl* in 1814, but Sir William was soon on the scene and borrowed a small rowing boat belonging to a hotel proprietor and, together with some retired Naval officers, pulled out to seaward of the Vigilant. Their intention was to drop down on to the stricken vessel and put a tow line aboard and physically tow her off the rocks and into Douglas Harbour. Quite amazingly this is what they achieved. Although Vigilant had lost her rudder and suffered other damage, once her crew cut away her mast and lightened her as much as possible, she was able to float off under tow. A rocket-line from the harbour entrance was also put aboard once she was within range and thus other tow lines were able to be manhandled by the many willing onlookers watching events from the shore.

This was not the end of the rescue, however, as other vessels were dragging their anchors towards the beach. Hillary called for fresh volunteers who were at first reluctant to go until Sir William offered cash rewards at his own expense. They successfully towed the laden schooners Content of Dundalk and Eliza of Irving into port. The sloop Merchant of Fraserburgh was not so fortunate, however, as she was driven ashore and lost. Her crew jumped overside and made the beach, mercifully.

The following day the gale had still not abated and there were still ships out at anchor and in danger, but too far out for rocket-lines to reach them. Hillary and further volunteers pulled a mile out into the Bay, this time towing hawsers with them. These were passed to three of the ships which were then hauled into port manually by teams of men on the shore. At the end of this storm Sir William and his crews were accredited with saving 84 lives and several ships.

Within two months of the Vigilant rescue another shipwreck took place on the Isle of Man. Not only was this connected with this previous episode but had consequences which were far-sighted at that time and far-reaching for the future.

This was the disaster of H.M. brig Racehorse in December, 1822. This ship had sailed from

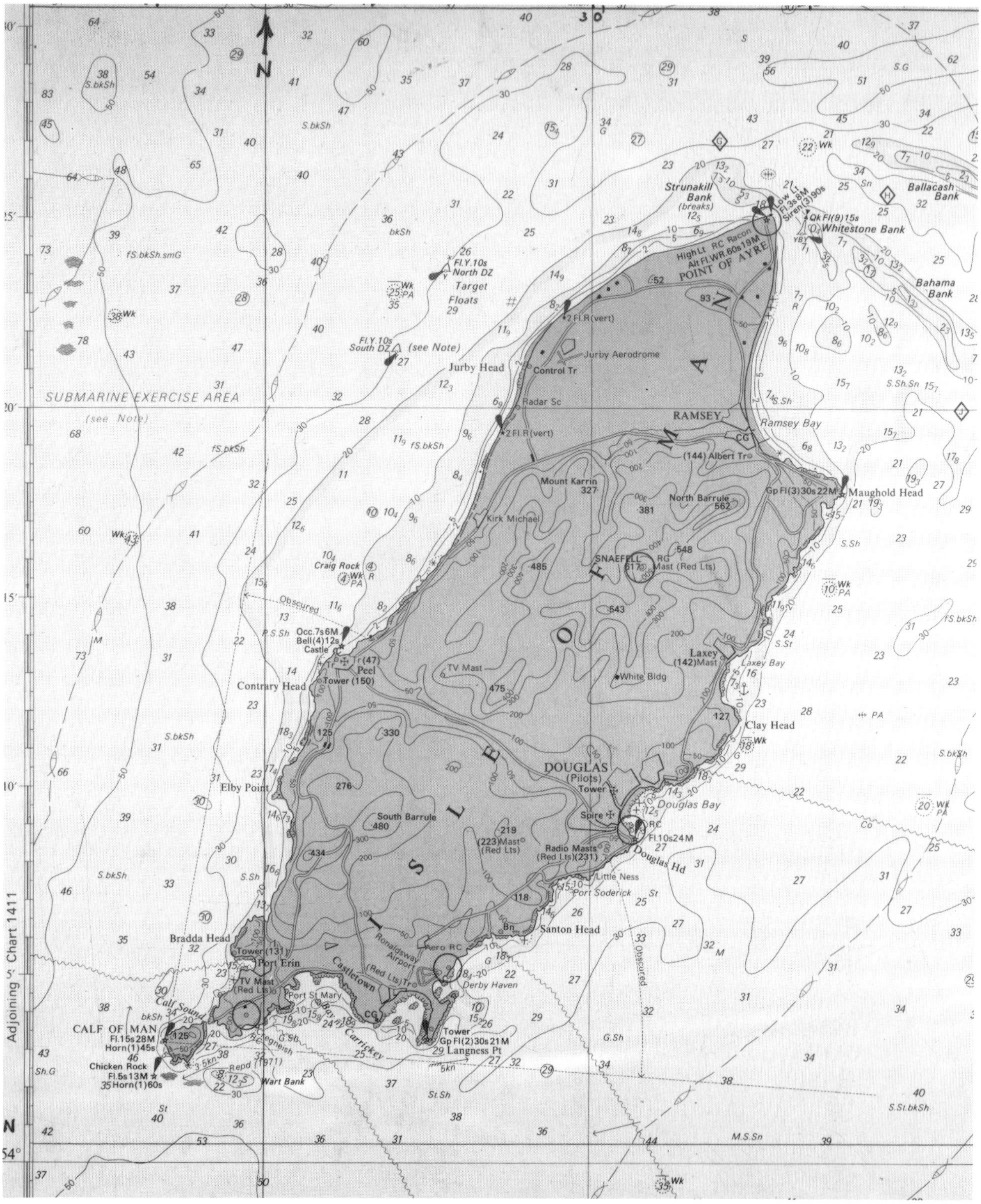

The Isle of Man.

The Northern coasts of the Isle of Man showing the Ramsey Lifeboat area from Jurby Head in the West to Laxey in the East.

D. Reed

Ramsey Bay in the 1970s looking SE towards Maughold Head. The Norbury Lifeboathouse is just to the left of the church tower, centre right.

D. Reed

Ramsey Harbour at low water in the 1970s. The Boathouse is adjacent to the slipway, bottom right.

Milford Haven bound for Douglas under the command of Capt. W.B. Suckling. Her task was to provide assistance to the Vigilant and it is known that she was carrying extra stores and supplies, presumably for such work. On the passage North the weather was fair and it seems that on making his landfall off the Island, the ship's pilot (navigator) mistook the shore lights of Castletown for those of Douglas. It was 5.30 a.m. and well before dawn. The Captain ordered sail to be shortened and made for what he presumed were the lights of Douglas Harbour. Instead he struck the rocks off Langness. There follows a gallant but tragic story of rescue by the citizens of Castletown who made for the wreck in small boats. Owing to the tidal and sea conditions off Langness however, only one boat persisted in getting alongside the Racehorse. This boat then made five trips between the brig and the nearby shore, ferrying crew members to safety. But on the very last run she was overturned and six crew members of the Racehorse were lost together with three of their rescuing Manxmen.

(It is interesting to note that only recently this wreck has been officially identified and local divers have brought up artifacts which are now in the care of the Manx Museum and National Trust).

Sir William Hillary soon had news of this disaster and of the plight of the Castletown families who had lost their menfolk. One, Robert Quayle, left a widow and eight children. Thomas Hall, another, left a widow and two daughters. The third death was of Norris Bridson who, although a bachelor, maintained his sister and her two boys. Hillary's mind immediately went back to the earlier Vigilant rescue. Here he had had to offer cash rewards in order to crew the rescue boats. In Castletown men had willingly gone to the aid of the seamen in trouble but by some of them giving up their lives by so doing, had left their families without provision. And this was the conflict in the minds of such men; in order to offer their services for such rescues, they were abdicating their responsibilities towards their own families. Why should such a decision have to be made?

To alleviate the problems immediately on hand Sir William wrote to Naval friends of his and obtained small pensions for the dependent families. This would not have happened, however, had the vessel been purely a commercial one and not belonging to the Navy. But, most importantly, the seeds were sown. Hillary realised that a properly funded national organisation was very urgently needed not only to provide funds for pensions in the event of the loss of rescuers' lives, but to provide adequately designed boats and to organise their regular maintenance and manning.

Formation of the NILPS

"An Appeal to the British Nation on the Humanity and Policy of forming a National Institution for the Preservation of Lives and Property from Shipwreck". This was Sir William's first move to motivate King and Country to form such a body. The appeal was first published in February, 1823, and directed to the First Lord of the Admiralty and later to John William Croker, Secretary to the Admiralty. After only a vague answer from the authorities in September of that year, a second edition was printed in November 1823. This time it was circulated to politicians, diplomats and many men of high office in London. This was successful and resulted in the famous meeting at the Tavern in Bishopsgate, London, on the 4th March, 1824. Many eminent men attended including Parliamentarians, social reformers, and churchmen such as the Archbishops of Canterbury and York: the Bishops of London, Durham and Bath & Wells. William Wilberforce of the slave trade abolition campaign attended and so did Capt. Manby of rocket-line fame. It was here that the "National Institution for the Preservation of Life from Shipwreck", the NIPLS, was born. (It later became the Royal National Lifeboat Institution in 1854). King George IV agreed to be Patron; the Prime Minister, President; and the Dukes of Sussex, York, Clarence, Cambridge and Gloucester, Vice-Presidents. Thomas Wilson was elected the first Chairman rather than Hillary, as the latter was at a disadvantage with his home being in Douglas and its attendant communications problems with London. London's loss, however, was Douglas's gain as future events were to prove.

Capt. Manby's name became well-known. He was the inventor of the Manby rocket-line throwing gear which had already been distributed around the UK coasts. This was the very earliest of life-saving devices which was the origin of the breeches buoy whereby seamen could be brought ashore from wrecks or grounded vessels by means of endless ropes and harness. No doubt the men who manned these appliances were the fore-runners of the Rocket Brigade of 1864 and later again to become the present day Coastguard and Marine Rescue Service.

The Isle of Man Branch

In June, 1824, Hillary returned to Douglas full of enthusiasm and plans to immediately set up an Isle of Man District Association of the NIPLS with lifeboats and mortars situated at seven key points around our coasts. At a first meeting on the 13th August it was acknowledged that initially only one boat and mortar could be entertained for the Island. It was, after all, an Institution to be subscribed to voluntarily

B.P. Grenfell

The Point of Ayre Lighthouse; the scene of so many incidents.

B.P. Grenfell

The Point of Ayre looking North towards Wigtown Bay, Scotland.

throughout and funds had to be raised locally from the start. However, a 20 ft. Plenty type lifeboat was initially ordered from headquarters for Douglas. Sir William did admit that they had previously ordered a North-country type of boat in April, for the money was at hand for that already. This was to be the *True Blue* which arrived that year and replaced the original *Atholl*, destroyed in 1814. A year later the *Nestor* took up her station "officially".

The Isle of Man District Association was well supported by Lt. Governor Smelt, the Duke of Atholl, the Lord Bishop, the Deemsters and other officers in Council and members of the House of Keys. Nearly 100 original subscribers were listed at that time. It was officially inaugurated on the 6th January, 1826, with its first Station at Douglas. This was followed in due course by Castletown in 1827, Peel in 1828 and Ramsey in 1829. Rocket-line throwing apparatus was also provided at the four ports.

The First Ramsey Lifeboat 1829-1851

It is reported that the Ramsey Station was set up in 1829 although records of its Committee and the Boat itself appear to be almost non-existent. There is conflicting evidence of the first boat destined to be for Ramsey.

The earlier history of our lifeboats states that Hillary applied for a Ramsey Boat in 1828 and that Palmer, the designer, of Nazing Park, London, was asked to order one of his boats from Harton the boat-builder of Commercial Road, East End of London. This gentleman reported the boat ready on the 15th November, 1828, and it was forwarded that month to the Isle of Man aboard H.M. cutter Industry. On the 20th February, 1829, it was reported that the boat had arrived here and a final statement issued was worded:

> "that on the 11th June boat tried and has given the greatest satisfaction."

A lifeboat historian, on the other hand, deduced that the boat was built locally in Douglas by Robert Oates. It was of a Palmer design: 26 ft. overall and with 8 oars. The cost was £55 of which £50 was subscribed by the Institution. This report (or story!) continues by stating that whilst she was being fitted out in Douglas on the 14th January, 1830, the Glasgow sloop Eclipse went ashore in Douglas Bay. Four of her crew managed to row ashore in their small boat but, after the wind freshened, could not return for the Master and the two remaining seamen. Sir William Hillary appeared on the scene once again and, together with Coxswain Issac Vondy and 12 men, took the new boat which still lacked some buoyancy air cases, double-banked the oars and "pulled mightily" for the Eclipse. Although the lifeboat became full of water, they gained their objective, took off the three men and returned safely. The lifeboat crew was rewarded locally and Sir William was awarded a second "Gold Boat" by the Institution which constituted a third service bar to his original Gold Medal.

Whatsoever the origins of the boat, certainly one of the first times such a boat is mentioned was in an advertisement in the Manx Advertiser of the 23rd August, 1827. It read:

> "To raise funds to provide a Lifeboat for Ramsey, a ball will be held. Tickets available at Mrs. Ryde's Mitre Hotel. Tickets 10/6d each."

A press report of later years in the Ramsey Courier of 1896 states that about 1830:

> "A kind of shed was erected at the back of the Harbour Board Office, now owned by the Insular Harbour Board. This shed was built as a Lifeboat Shelter and in it was stored the First Lifeboat that there is any account of being possessed by Ramsey".

It goes on to state that its origins were uncertain and although doubtless it was constructed on up-to-date principles, it was a very primitive affair. She was high and narrow as if her chief feature should be to keep her from shipping water over the gunwale. She was fitted with crude kinds of delivery tubes and had copper tanks under her seats. The boat had no actual self-righting capabilities. The statement continues:

> "However, her sea-going qualities were never put to the test – not in Ramsey, at any rate – because she was never launched either for practice or service. I understand that there were neither Committee, Coxswains nor Crew appointed in connection with this Lifeboat and she was placed in a most awkward position for launching. Here she was allowed to lie until shed, boat and carriage fell to pieces – a monument to the listlessness and neglect of the seafaring population of Ramsey of that day".

The writer further comments that the services of a lifeboat were sorely needed in those days (the 1830's) as there were very many sailing fishing craft in Ramsey and cargo ships. Also, 1833 saw the first ship-building in the port on a large scale with Taggarts opening up on the North shore of the Sulby River. Although this yard had a chequered career in the 19th century, it built some important vessels and in the 1870's employed between 300 and 400 people.

There is no doubt, therefore, that the local Lifeboat Committee failed to function as did the Lifeboat itself. The only RNLI entry relating to Ramsey was that in 1845 John Cowin of Port-e-Vullen was awarded the Silver Medal for rescuing six persons from the schooner Hazlewood. This was the result of a collision between the Hazlewood and the Mary of Douglas. They both ran ashore near Ramsey and both Masters were drowned. It is not thought that Cowin was acting as part of the lifeboat crew as, surely, mention of this would have been made.

During the first five years of the Institution's existence 45 lifeboats were provided around

Years	Builder	Type Cost	Name Donor	Len. Brdh Oars	Station	Disposal
1803-1814	Greathead, S.Shields	NC £200	ATHOLL Duke of Atholl	31' 10½' 10	Douglas 1803-14	Wrecked on beach, Dec.1814
1824-p1851	(? Wake) Sunderland	NC £115	TRUE BLUE Lloyds+local subscriptions	29' 10'	Douglas 1824-p1851	Unserviceable by 1851
1825	Plenty, Newbury	Pl £100	NESTOR RNIPLS	20' 6¾' 6	Douglas 1825	Wrecked (service) 19 Oct.1825
1826-p1851	Plenty, Newbury	Pl £130	? RNIPLS	22½' 6¼' 6	Castletown 1826-p1851	Out p.1851
1828-p1836	Taylor, Limehouse	Pa £55	? RNIPLS	26' 6¼' 6	Peel 1829-1836	Wrecked and replaced 1836
1829-p1851	Rt.Oates, Douglas	Pa £50	? RNIPLS	28' 6¾ 12	Douglas 1830 Ramsey 1830-p1851	Unserviceable 1851
1836-p1843	Wm. Corlett, Peel	? £55	? Hy.Hutchinson	26' 6¼' 6	Peel 1836-p43	Out by 1843

Unfortunately the Annual Reports of the Isle of Man District Association did not at any time list the life-boats they operated- unlike those of similar bodies. In the 10th Report of 1836 they mention the new Peel life-boat, the gift of Henry Hutchinson and others. They also describe another as 'destined for Ramsey, having had a complete repair at Douglas, and we can only assume this was the Ramsey boat of 1829 having been overhauled.

The Northumberland Report, of 1851, in which the list of Life-boats around our coasts was collected from many sources, some of which are known to have been obsolete and inaccurate, mentions all the boats - Douglas, Peel and Ramsey, as being unserviceable.

Abbreviations for Types of Life-boat used above -
NC = North country; Pa = Palmer; Pl = Plenty.

ii

THREE TYPES OF EARLY MANX LIFEBOATS

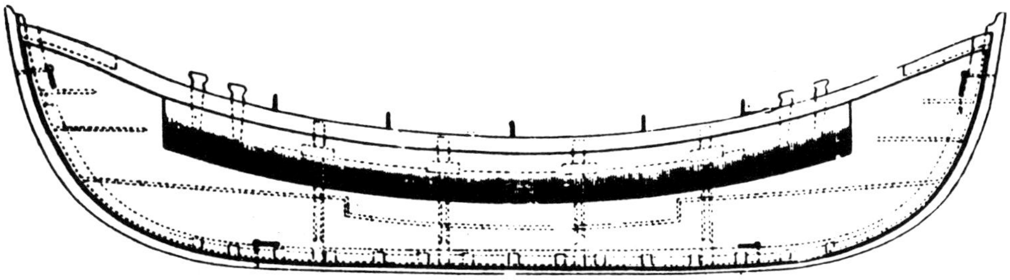

The first Douglas life-boat - ATHOLL - of 1803, was of the original Greathead, or North-Country type as this plan. The replacement - TRUE BLUE - of 1824, was similar in outward appearance, but had internal air-cases instead of relying on cork applied to the outside of the hull.

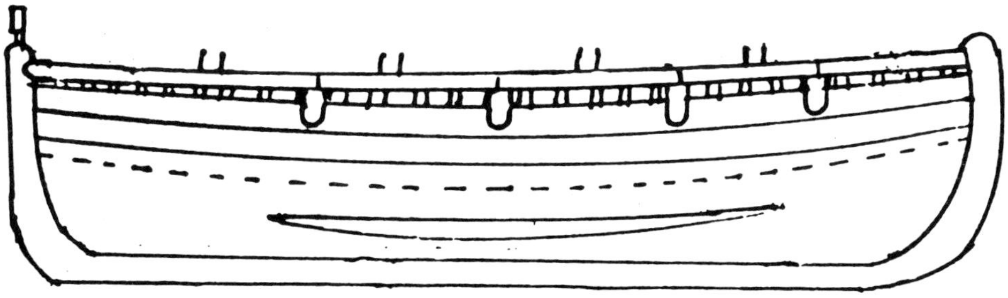

The NESTOR of 1825, and the apparently un-named life-boat at Castletown of 1826 were of the type designed and built by William Plenty, of Newbury, They incorporated such large air compartments that they were in effect a boat within a boat, and were further strengthened by a liberal layer of cork on the bottom. The top strakes were omitted to allow water to roll out with the motion of the boat. (See 'Papers on Life-boat History,' No.1)

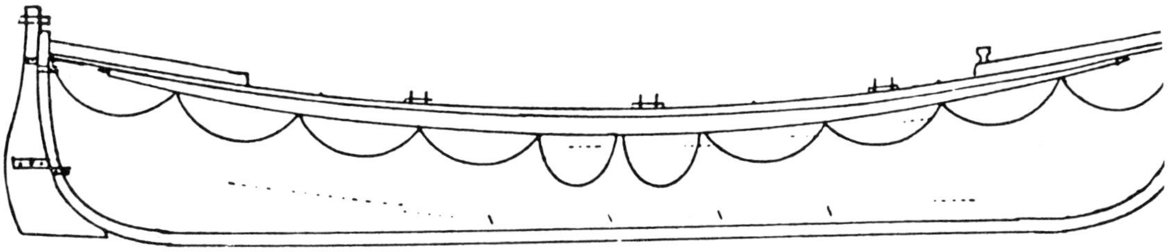

Because the Plenty type were so difficult to repair the Institution adopted the Palmer type which was more like ordinary boats with the addition of removeable internal air cases. The construction was so straightforward that any skilled boat-builder could build and repair this type. The two boats provided in 1828-9 by the RNIPLS were of this type, and the Peel-built boat of 1836 was probably similar. (See 'Papers on Life-boat History,' No.2)

i

Manx Museum and National Trust archives

Douglas Harbour entrance c. 1890, showing Conister Rock and its Tower of Refuge, initiated by Sir William Hillary in 1832.

A. Christian collection

Four notable Ramsey Lifeboatmen with a total service of over 160 years.
L to R: Harry Sharpe (1888-1928) - Bowman 1918-1928 - Sea Gallantry Medal; Oscar Corlett (1875-1931 - 2nd Coxswain 1890-1901 - Chief Launcher 1901-1931; Keppel Gawne, a Crewman for about 40 years; Harry Corkish - Coxswain 1903-1925 - Crewman for about 40 years. These men together attended a Birmingham RNLI fund raising event which brought in over £10,000.

the UK coasts and four were stationed in the Isle of Man. This was a relatively high percentage which was justified by the fact that between 1821 and 1846 no fewer than 144 ships were wrecked around the Island and 172 lives were lost. No doubt the number of boats put into local service was also due to Hillary living here!

After the initial impetus and publicity given to forming the Institution, however, public interest waned and so did the funds. By 1849 numerous district associations had ceased to exist and their boats lay decayed and unserviceable. So Ramsey was by no means alone in this respect. The NIPLS Committee in London, by then under the Presidency of Algernon, Duke of Northumberland, and known as the "Good Sailor Duke", therefore renewed its efforts in 1851 to provide more lifeboats. They set up a special Committee to award a prize for the best model of a lifeboat and the committee also made available information on the conditions of current lifeboats on station around the coasts. Against Ramsey the report read:

> "A Lifeboat provided in 1828 at a cost of £55: built by Harton on Palmer's plan, 28ft by 6ft 9ins, rowing twelve oars. Kept in shed near Boathouse; condition unserviceable."

Death of Hillary

One could be quite certain that such conditions would not have existed had Sir William Hillary still been alive. He died on the 5th January, 1847, and was buried in St. George's Churchyard in Douglas. There is a bronze memorial plaque to his memory on the wall of the promenade leading to the present boathouse. It is on the site of the old boathouse and shows a life-size portrait of Hillary in profile together with a lifeboat under full sail. It may well be noted that one of the first men to climb Mount Everest, the New Zealander Sir Edmund Hillary, is said to be a member of this same Hillary family. Courage and adventurous spirit obviously manifested itself once again down the line.

During his period of involvement in rescues from shipwrecks in the Isle of Man, Sir William Hillary and his crews were accredited with being involved in rescues from 29 ships and in saving 509 lives. Apart from being the first President of the District Association, he often acted as Cox or Crew Member in the Douglas Lifeboat. He was awarded three Gold Medals by the Institution for his deeds.

On the 20th November, 1830, the Royal Mail Steam Packet ST. GEORGE went ashore on the reef of St. Mary's Isle (Conister Rock) at the entrance to Douglas Harbour. Sir William and a volunteer crew put off in the lifeboat and attempted a rescue. The work was so hazardous that, though momentarily in peril of being washed overboard by seas breaking over the reef, the Captain of the ST. GEORGE entreated them not to attempt his rescue. Hillary and his crew persisted, however, and at a cost of ten oars broken or lost; air-tight cases and the boat's upper-works damaged and four crew washed overboard but recovered, the rescue succeeded. Hillary had been one of those washed overboard from the boat and he had sustained six broken ribs. But all 22 crew members of the ST. GEORGE and the 18 lifeboatmen landed safely ashore.

After this particular rescue Hillary collected funds and had John Welch build the famous Tower of Refuge on Conister Rock in order to warn seamen of the danger and to provide shelter "from the fury of the waves". He had personally witnessed the loss of far too many lives on the shores of Douglas Bay.

Today, seafarers and passengers to the port; citizens of the Island and tourists are still well reminded of the foundation of the RNLI and William Hillary. The Tower still guards the entrance to Douglas Harbour; by day it flies the Royal National Lifeboat Institutions's ensign; by night it is floodlit overall by scores of lights. A far cry from that one single lanthorn of centuries ago!

Note. There are two preserved documents in Ramsey originally owned by the Town Commissioners but now in the care of private residents. These are dated between 1835 - 1845 and two of them give some proof that the first Ramsey Lifeboat lay neglected without either shelter, a Crew or a Committee.

A third document is a letter written in Sir William Hillary's own hand in 1845, two years before he died, to the Royal National Institution of a rescue by seven Ramsey boatmen. (Not Lifeboatmen).

The above documents are laid out from page 207 at the back of this book.

Manx Museum and National Trust Archive

pxx.81.5 Creighton, c.1845 (based on Drinkwater 1826).

CHAPTER 2

The Two Sisters 1868-1890 and 1894

41 service launches and 147 lives saved

THE new era in Ramsey's history began in 1830 when John Taggart set up his shipyard within the limits of Ramsey Harbour and larger wooden vessels could then be constructed.

Around the Island's coasts, however, ships and crews continued to be lost. During the 20 years 1822-1842, 105 ships were wrecked and 152 lives taken. The value of such ships was estimated at £207,902 and included three steam packet boats; three barques; 32 brigs and 27 schooners. Thirteen of these ships were lost in the immediate vicinity of Ramsey Bay and six of them in 1834 alone. But it seems that the First Lifeboat, its Crew and Committee failed to operate. RNLI records show that the Ramsey Station was considered officially to be closed from 1843.

In September, 1847, Queen Victoria visited Ramsey Bay in the Royal Yacht. Whilst passing over the Bahama Bank, North-East of Ramsey, she asked why there was not a light or bell on such a dangerous bank? Shortly afterwards the Bahama Bank Lightship took up station there and remained in local waters until the 25th June, 1915. She was tendered from the harbour for part of her life.

Ramsey's population slowly grew and in the 1850's it reached 2607 in the town but up to 9444 when including the surrounding rural areas. This accounted for about one fifth of the total Island population. Furthermore the tourist industry was expanding rapidly and was bringing up to 30,000 visitors a year to the Island. Ramsey had her fair share in this and in June, 1854, 100 tourists a day were landing in the port. Originally the main bulk of the visitors came from the Liverpool and Manchester area which was served by the famous Liverpool and Manchester Railway. This network was then extended Southwards to the U.K. Midlands and so widened the scope for potential holidaymakers to the Island.

Ramsey Ships

1853 saw the start of service of the packet steamer Manx Fairy between Ramsey and Liverpool. She was owned originally by the Ramsey (Isle of Man) Steam Packet Company and was set up in direct competition with the earlier Douglas-based Isle of Man Steam Packet Company which ran the Mona's Queen to Liverpool. Unfortunately the Manx Fairy had a short and chequered career and the service did not last after 1861. The Isle of Man Steam Packet Company, however, is still our main Island carrier to this day, although now partly owned by Sea Containers.

The 1850's and 1860's also put Ramsey firmly on the ship-building map and this industry became one of the largest employers in the town. T.C. Gibson of London, who owned the shipyard, supplied capital for a patent slip-way to be built in 1856 when Mr. Patterson had taken lease of the yard. The way was then clear for much larger vessels to be built than hitherto.

In 1857 the notable ship Manxman was built. She was the first Manx ship built of iron and was a screw steamer of 125 ft. overall with a 40 h.p. engine. In 1862 the timber schooner Jane was launched and was possibly the very first purpose-built oil tanker ever built. She had iron oil tanks for her bulk cargoes and plied on the USA to Liverpool trade initially. But the most famous of all was undoubtedly the iron-hulled ship Euterpe. This ship was launched in November, 1863, and was the fore-runner of four similar vessels of considerable size. The Euterpe was a full-rigged sailing ship of 1246 nett register tons with a hull length of 220ft. O.A.; a beam of 35ft. and a depth of 23ft. She was owned by Messrs. Wakefield Nash & Co., of Liverpool, who were Manxmen, and at first was engaged in trading to India. Next she entered the UK to New Zealand immigrant trade whilst under ownership of the Shaw Savill Company. Later she changed hands again; this time to the Alaska Packers of San Francisco. She was renamed the Star of India in line with company policy and served for many years on the Alaska to California salmon trade until she was retired in 1923. She sailed as a barque for this company and is rigged as such to this day. Yes; she is still afloat and after years of careful restoration by the Maritime Museum and citizens of San Diego, she is now the centre-piece of their museum. On the 4th July, 1976, she was taken to sea again off the port for a brief cruise and again in 1984, 1986

By courtesy of her owners, the San Diego Maritime Museum, California

The STAR OF INDIA (ex EUTERPE) in San Diego Bay, 1989.

and 1989. The STAR OF INDIA can well lay claim to being the oldest iron-hulled sailing ship still afloat and in a seaworthy condition. Several residents of Ramsey have been aboard her in recent years, including one of the present Directors of that same shipyard, Mr. Wm. Kneale and the Ramsey RNLI Branch Chairman, Dr. E.C.B. Corlett, who was much involved in the rebuilding of the yard in 1962/63.

SHIPWRECKS CONTINUE

In 1861, and again in 1867, shipwrecks took place off Ramsey which once more prompted the local population that there was urgent need to obtain a new Lifeboat and to set up a reliable Committee to oversee its installation and running.

In February, 1861, during a memorable Easterly gale, no less than eight Whitehaven traders were driven ashore on the South Ramsey beach near the Prince of Wales Hotel.

> "It was a fearful night with sleet and snow accompanied by a gale force wind and very heavy seas. Once word got around that 15 vessels were trying to make the harbour, the beach and piers were soon crowded; in fact it might be said that the whole town was on the scene. Amongst the spectators were wives and children and other relatives of the men whose lives were placed in danger. The excitement was intense and altogether the scene was one never to be forgotten by those who witnessed it. There was neither a Rocket Brigade nor a serviceable Lifeboat in Ramsey in those days, but there was no scarcity of stout and willing hearts. Although there were nearly 30 men in danger, they were all landed safely without so much as one of them being hurt. Capt. T. Brayden, the Harbour Master at the time, was one of the first on the scene and he rendered a grand service in assisting to save the lives of his brother sailors.
>
> It was after this incident that the town's-people of Ramsey decided that it was high time that a Lifeboat Station should be re-established."

In 1864 the UK Board of Trade established a Rocket Brigade (Life Saving Corps) in Ramsey. This consisted of First and Second Officers and 23 men. They were equipped with rockets and line-throwing equipment and did sterling service in the ensuing years; very soon to be joined by the first operational Ramsey Lifeboat. [1]

A year later, Capt. Robertson, a representative of the RNLI, paid a visit to the Lt. Governor of the Isle of Man (later to become Lord Loch). His Excellency stated that in his opinion Ramsey greatly needed a Lifeboat owing to the number of vessels which frequently took shelter in the roadstead. RNLI Headquarters agreed to send Capt. Robertson to Ramsey in order to confer with the Rev. George Paton on this matter. This was done – incidentally on the chaplain's own wedding day – and thus the wheels were put in motion for the order of a suitable boat.

On the 31st December, 1867, the Workington barque I.O. came ashore near the "Old Swan", Ramsey. She was fully loaded and outward bound from Liverpool to the West Indies. When she ran ashore before a strong SE'ly gale the crew spilled barrels of oil over the ship's side to calm the seas enough to launch their long boat. This they did and were saved but their ship became a total loss. It is said that some 50 years after this incident calico and cotton goods from her cargo could be found in and around Ramsey! Be that as it may, this further wreck confirmed yet again the immediate need for a local lifeboat.

RNLI TAKE OVER

In 1868 the RNLI took over formal jurisdiction of the Ramsey Station and, at long last, on Wednesday, 18th November of that year, the new Boat arrived. She was *The Two Sisters* and arrived in the port under tow from the I.O.M. Steam Packet Company's MONA'S QUEEN after a passage from Whitehaven. RNLI's Capt. Robertson (later to become Admiral Robertson McDonald) was in charge of the operation and the event caused much excitement and enthusiasm in the port. All shops closed and the Provisional Lifeboat Committee, Rocket Brigade and a large crowd of residents welcomed the Boat and saw it safely landed upon its carriage and taken around to the shipyard. The new Boathouse was not yet ready for another year, so the Boat was kept at the shipyard in the meantime.

At this event it is noted that the following names were included in the list of the provisional Lifeboat Committee: The Rev. G. Paton; the High Bailiff; the Rev. W.B. Christian, Chairman; Capt. Brown and Mr. Teare. Mr. A. Dumbell, Hon. Secretary, was off the Island at the time. Capt. Goldsmith was mentioned as Commander of the Rocket Brigade.

The Lifeboat herself was built by a Mr. Forest of Limehouse, London, and she had had her initial trials in the Regent's Canal Dock nearby. She was 33ft. long with an 8ft. beam and rowed 10 oars double-banked. She was self-righting and self-ejecting and had two masts. Her probable rig was fore and aft sails for jib and

[1] Other archives state that the first Ramsey Volunteer Life Corps was originated by the Church in the mid-1860s and led by Mr. Jackson of HM Customs Service in 1867. It was equipped with the Manby rocket-line gear. In 1886 it came under the jurisdiction of the Admiralty in London and became the Ramsey Rocket Brigade and the Rev. John Kewley of St. Paul's was named as its Captain. In 1923 responsibility was transferred to the UK Board of Trade and control of the Brigade passed to HM Coastguard. The name changed to the Life Saving Apparatus Team (LSA). In 1972 the Team became the Coastguard Rescue Company and finally in the 1980s the Coastguard and Marine Rescue Service. 1989 saw the closure of the Coastguard Section on the Island by the UK Government and the remaining 75 men of the Auxilliary Marine Rescue Service came under the control of the Isle of Man Government.

B.P. Grenfell

Booth Kelly's Shipyard, Ramsey, 1990. This site saw the building of the full rigged ship EUTERPE in 1863. (She became the STAR OF INDIA in 1906).

mizzen and a main lug sail. Mr. James Ryder, a member of the Manchester Corporation, provided the funds for this boat through the Manchester RNLI Branch and it was thus named *The Two Sisters* after his daughters. It cost £297 and came with its own new carriage.

This time the Committee and Crew were properly organised and at last we have records, through the Minutes Books kept, of the deliberations of the meetings held; the composition of the Boat's Crews and of some of the services undertaken. Regrettably, the books do not give a comprehensive list of the services. Details of the rescues of those times have had to be gleaned from newspaper reports, RNLI records and other material handed down through the years.

The initial entry in the first Minutes Book was made on the 11th December, 1868, and refers to the first Lifeboat service carried out that day, only three weeks after its delivery from London. The first crew was also listed and gave the following names:-

1st Coxswain, Thomas Kaighin; 2nd Coxswain, Robert Fell; Launcher, Robert Kermeen and Crew Members William Christian, William Corkhill, William Kinnan, John Thompson, Thomas Crennell, Joseph Hewson, James Weir, John Maxwell, William Corkish, John Galbreath and John Cowell.

These family names occur again and again right to this day and the tradition that generations of the same local families provide members of the crews is an RNLI one. Ramsey is certainly no exception. The local names of Christian, Cottier, Crix, Garrett, Kaighin, Kinnin, Martin and Starkey and others are frequently mentioned throughout the years. In 1887 there were three Kaighins in the crew; three Kinnins in 1926 and three Christians in 1933. In 1991 James Kinnin is Cox and amongst the Crew and Shore-side personnel are two Crowes, three Clagues, three Faraghers and certainly the inevitable Christian!

The William Kinnan mentioned on the first service was the first of many members of his family who have served for several generations in the Ramsey lifeboats. In 1967 F.W. Kinnin, Asst. Coxswain, was the grandson of that first Kinnan in 1868 and thus that family had a record of having a crew member serving throughout the first 100 years and so it continues to James Kinnin, our present Coxswain.

The Two Sisters Lifeboat made a name for herself throughout the Island on her very first service as it occurred the same day as a Tynwald Committee was meeting in the Ramsey Court House to discuss improvements to the harbour there.

At about 1.30 p.m., with the wind rising from the ENE, proceedings were interrupted by an announcement that a schooner was ashore in the Bay and that the Rocket Brigade members at the meeting were required immediately. The Court House cleared rapidly with everyone hastening to the promenade there to see two schooners already ashore, with three other ships in imminent danger of the same fate. Capt. Goldsmith and his Rocket Brigade succeeded in getting two rocket-fired lines aboard two ships from the South Pier. Their third rocket to the brigantine JANE of Workington missed its mark and this was the last one left in their outfit. Only earlier that day they had telegraphed to Douglas for more rockets which had not yet arrived. Some five months previously they had applied to the UK Board of Trade for a new supply which was still awaited.

Thus the call to launch *The Two Sisters* was made as matters in the Bay were getting serious for the JANE and also the schooner PRUDENCE of Aberystwyth. Their crews had taken to the rigging and were clinging on for their lives. Lifeboat Committee Hon. Secretary, the Rev. George Paton, in later years reflected:

> "On that occasion an enquiry was being held in the Court House on the question of accommodation for Ramsey Harbour. I remember I was helping in the launch and some way out in the water, a voice behind me exclaiming; "The parson is the best of us". Looking round I recognised the Governor, later to become Lord Loch, and His Honour Deemster Drinkwater who were both deep in water and bending on to the launching rope as stoutly as any of the launchers there. The Lifeboat was not a moment too soon at the wrecks as the Master of one of the schooners, who was too weak to get into the rigging, had been washing about on the deck and was insensible when passed into the Boat. He soon recovered under treatment he received in the 'Neptune', later the Prince of Wales Hotel."

The afternoon ended with the crew of *The Two Sisters* saving the four-man crew of each vessel and bringing them ashore to cheering crowds who had watched the rescues. The PRUDENCE later became a total loss. Coxswain Thomas Kaighin must have been well pleased with his first service and the enthusiasm of his Crew, launchers and helpers.

Methods of handling the lifeboat carriage seem to have varied in those early years. Certainly at first, whilst the boat was kept in the shipyard, its carriage was either man-handled or horse-drawn to the most suitable place nearest the ship in distress. Man-handling at the launch was most common, no doubt because when the maroons were fired to summon the crew, most of the townspeople turned out to assist or watch, and many willing hands were available. It would have taken time to team up horses and no doubt this method was used more for recovering the boat after a service. The carriage was physically pushed into the water from the beach and the boat released off this. In later years and for a long period thereafter a haul-off warp was used (especially in the winter or in a strong on-shore Easterly wind). This was initially made fast to the South Pier and later to a moored buoy off the concrete slip which was built. Another warp was also used from the Queen's Pier for some years. Carriage wheels sinking into the sand was always an early problem but later this was alleviated with the invention of the "Slipper Sand Shoes". These were flexible wooden boards attached to the wheel rims of the carriage to spread its weight over the sand.

When *The Two Sisters* first arrived in Ramsey the officers of the Rocket Brigade were under the impression that they would be in charge of the Lifeboat. This was dispelled during the first meeting convened to appoint a Boat's Crew and their own Committee. There is evidence of some early bad feeling between the two life-saving services and in those days some volunteers insisted on being both in the Rocket Brigade and the Lifeboat's Crew! Obviously this was a non-starter as events soon proved that each service complemented the other. But at least it showed enthusiasm for saving life at sea and there was no lack of such volunteers in 1868 - just as in 1991! Very soon, however, a firm liaison grew up between the two services and that has continued to this day, notwithstanding the recent changes in the local H.M. Coastguard and Marine Rescue presence on the Island.

THE COMMITTEE

It seems that the first full-scale Lifeboat Committee meeting was held in Dumbells Bank in January, 1869. The Rev. W.B. Christian of Milntown (MHK for Ramsey) was officially elected Chairman together with the Rev. George Paton of St. Paul's, Ramsey, as Hon. Secretary & Treasurer and Members A. Dumbell, R. Teare, Capt. Brown, T. Corkhill, D. Joughin, W.T. Kaighin and Dr. Clucas. His Excellency the Lt. Governor was elected President of the Branch, a tradition which was kept up for some 100 years thereafter.

The very first Ramsey Boathouse was provided for the original non-operational boat in 1829 at a cost of £10. This was positioned at the North end of Shore Road (now Queen's Promenade) right on the shore and some 30 ft. seawards of

Keith Groves' History

The Two Sisters Lifeboat in 1869 in front of her boathouse which was a few yards North of the present lifeboat slipway. Coxswain Thomas Kaighin and 2nd Coxswain Robert Fell.

the old Coastguard lookout tower. This house fell into decay as did its Boat. In 1869 it was resolved to build a new Boathouse immediately at a cost of £145. This was re-positioned with "the North wall of the house being parallel to the wall of the Steam Packet Company's yard". There is an iron post at the seaward end of what is now Mezeron's warehouse which was probably at the front corner of this second Boathouse, being used in those days as a bollard to which the hauling tackle was attached when the Lifeboat was hauled up from the shore.

The new Boathouse was in use by the 29th September, 1869, when the naming ceremony of the Boat took place. Mr. Ryder and his daughters were invited to perform this ceremony but owing to their illness Mrs. Christian of Milntown named the boat *The Two Sisters*. A quarterly practice and public demonstration of the Boat was held at the same time, showing her self-righting qualities. Crew Members and the launchers were each paid five shillings for their services on that day. The Rocket Brigade was also in attendance.

On the 19th December of that same year the Boat was taken out in a SW'ly gale on exercise and it was reported that the launch went well and that the Boat behaved splendidly under sail. That time the Crew Members were paid five shillings and the Launchers two shillings each.

The 1870's saw much activity for *The Two Sisters* and began with the John Bell service on the 6th February, 1870. During the evening of that Sunday the schooner John Bell of Barrow was seen at anchor in Ramsey Bay, South of the harbour, with sails torn and yards broken. As the tide was full at the time it was expected that she would make for the harbour, but she remained at anchor and was soon seen to be dragging on to a lee shore. She held after a while but as night fast approached, Hon. Sec. the Rev. Paton deemed it wise to request Coxswain Thomas Kaighin to launch the Lifeboat. It was obvious to all that the ship was in a dangerous position as she was fully loaded with iron ore. The Rocket Brigade also proceeded to the North Shore in case the John Bell parted her anchor cables before the Lifeboat reached her. The latter was seen ploughing her way through the heavy seas (no doubt in a SSE'ly gale) and at times could be seen atop white crested waves; at other times lost from view in the troughs. After 15 minutes the Lifeboat was seen to leave the ship and head for the harbour. By this time the tide had changed and the wind did not assist them and they fought gamely for one and a half hours to make port. Eventually they had to beach the Boat instead. However, they safely landed the ship's Skipper, his wife and son, four crewmen and a boy. Ironically, the John Bell was brought safely into Ramsey Harbour the following morning.

A somewhat similar rescue took place on Saturday, 8th October, 1870. At about 2 a.m. a nightwatchman observed a schooner in trouble in breakers North of the harbour. He fired the signal gun summoning the Rocket Brigade. Although they got a line aboard, the crew declined to come ashore by that means. At 5 a.m. the Lifeboat was launched to take off the crew of the wreck. They had a hard pull but succeeded in saving the ten-man crew. The ship was the schooner Gipsy of Glasgow and was on passage from Glasgow to Liverpool when all her sails carried away and her crew was forced to run her ashore. The cargo of pig iron, paraffin and ale had to be unloaded immediately as the wreck would have been awash at the next high water.

On the 18th December of the same year the Lifeboat was out for some six hours on a rescue of the Ramsey smack Pearl, en route from Ramsey to Douglas with a cargo of sand. Three men were saved and the ship sank.

The William - 1871

There were four rescues in 1871 and 12 seamen saved: *The Two Sisters* and her Crew were proving their mettle. One of the longest services of that year took place on the 5th February. A schooner entering Ramsey reported that a vessel was in distress about four miles West of the Point of Ayre Lighthouse and approximately two miles off the shore (a position some 10 miles from Ramsey). The schooner's Master had offered to take off the crew of the distressed vessel as they had been riding the weather there for some two days and were constantly manning their bilge pumps. However, the crew of the William had declined their help although the opinion in Ramsey was that she would soon sink. *The Two Sisters* was launched in heavy surf from a strong ESE wind and was soon lost to sight. At 4 a.m. the next morning the Rev. Paton reported that he had gone to Rue Point, a distance of some nine miles, and signalled to the Lifeboat asking whether or not they had found the William. They had not. Local opinion was then divided as to whether the Lifeboat would make for the shelter of Peel Harbour on the Island's West Coast or return to Ramsey on the next flood tide. The latter was correct and she arrived at 9 p.m. that Sunday night, together with two crewmen and a boy. They were in a very exhausted state after pumping for 36 hours. Their ship had been on a passage from Garston to Belfast with coal and reportedly sank not long after the rescue.

The 20th August, 1871, saw a service to the Preston schooner Rapid and on the 29th October one to the Pausillippo of Ramsey. Five seamen were saved in all.

A reward of £20 was given for the William service and the Minutes Book shows that in 1871 £67 had been received by the Committee for salvage. At this time a payment of five shillings per man was made to the Lifeboat's Crew for each service call-out and two shillings to each Launcher. This was a reasonable sum for in those days five shillings purchased up to 10lbs of meat or 15 loaves of bread or four gallons of beer!

Discipline was strict and reports show that at least one early member of the Crew was dismissed because of a felony conviction. Some others who did not attend the naming ceremony were to be struck off the Crew List if they did not give a good reason for their absence. One member was dismissed for being a habitual drunkard. Later a Coxswain was reprimanded for over-sleeping and on another occasion there was a reprimand for a dirty boat. But volunteers were not short and it was considered an honour to be made a member of the Crew.

As one can quite imagine, rivalry existed between the Boat's Crew and the Rocket Brigade as each Service wished to make the rescues. It is even suggested (probably quite true!) that on one occasion at least, the Rocket Brigade tried to get a vessel in distress nearer to the shore so that they could get their lines aboard, whereas the Lifeboat's Crew considered this made it too dangerous for them to get their Boat alongside to effect the rescue!

1872 and 1873 were quieter years on the local maritime rescue front but three lives were saved from the schooner MARY of Douglas during the period.

1874 was a different story and four services were made saving some 13 lives. Two of them were very local and short but Thursday, the 26th November, was busy. During the dark evening and in a strong Easterly wind with heavy seas, the Rocket Brigade's heavy-weather lookout sighted up to six small vessels either ashore or riding very low in Ramsey Bay. They fired the signal gun which summoned both the Brigade team and the Lifeboat Crew. The Boat was launched and after two hours returned with the crew of four from the Preston yacht MARIA, plus two passengers. The yacht held her anchor and was berthed the next morning.

At 10 p.m. that same night Capt. Brayden, the Harbour Master, observed a light flashing from the direction of Dog Mills and considered that a vessel could be in distress. Both Life-saving Services were called out and the Lifeboat launched in almost storm-force conditions. She was very much in danger of being driven ashore herself. Once again the rescue succeeded

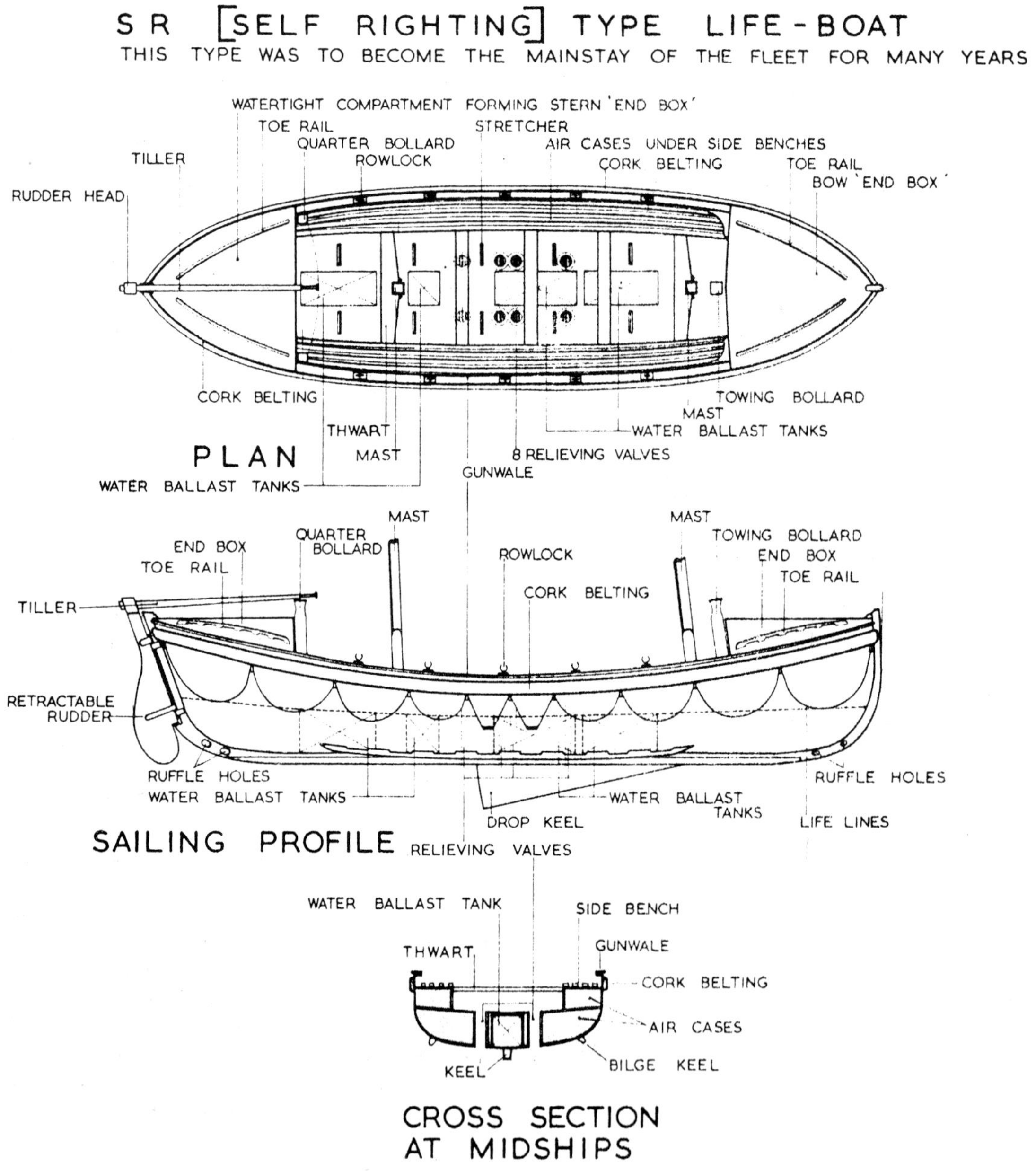

RNLI, Poole

The early self-righting type lifeboats. All of the first four Ramsey lifeboats were of similar design to this.

and *The Two Sisters* returned with the three-man crew of the smack LAUREL. The owner, Mr. Cowley, was among them and, although he had done everything in his power to prevent disaster, his vessel became a total loss.

Another busy year was 1880 and 19 lives were saved. One service of note was on the 25th October at about 12.30 p.m. The brig VICTOIRE of Irving showed distress signals whilst some two miles East of Ramsey. A NE'ly gale was blowing and reportedly:

> "A more arduous launch was never before undertaken by the Lifeboat, Crew and Helpers. With great difficulty and after some heart-stopping moments she was finally launched. Sail had to be set before this and for the first time the haul-off warp from the pier head was used. However the service was splendidly rendered and the adaptability of the Lifeboat to all emergencies was never better proved. The crew of five was saved and the vessel herself was later brought into harbour by part of the Lifeboat Crew themselves".

Only two days later on the 27th October an almost carbon-copy service was executed in similar circumstances with a NNE'ly gale blowing. This time the crew of five of the brig WILLIAM HILL of Dundalk was brought ashore and later the ship herself brought in by some of the Lifeboat Crew. Another report stated that the ship only required a pilot and was not signalling distress. Whatever the case, the crew-men were "rescued", whether they liked it or not!

Later on the 27th the schooner GEORGE was about to enter harbour when her tiller broke. She was driven ashore just North of the harbour. As the Lifeboat was not available immediately the Rocket Brigade was called out and within half an hour had rescued her crew of three.

On November 14th, 1880, the schooner ADA of Beaumaris was seen making for the harbour entrance. For some reason she struck the beach just South of the Port and opposite the Albert Hotel. Both Lifeboat and Rocket Brigade Crews were soon on the scene. The rocket-line fell short and after ploughing through some heavy seas the Lifeboat got alongside and took off three men. Just as they were leaving the casualty they were informed that there was a fourth man aboard who had gone to search for his dog. He was also taken off and later it was found that the dog had made his own way ashore – obviously the first off!

1881 saw the Rev. George Paton elected as Chairman of the Committee after his previous service as Hon. Secretary. This post he then held until his death in 1900.

THE SERVICES CONTINUE

The 14th October, 1881, saw the rescue of the schooner EULALA of Dumfries in distress whilst at anchor in the Bay during a gale. The crew of four was saved by *The Two Sisters*. This rescue was overshadowed, however, by the loss of four Douglas lifeboat-men and some of the crew of the barque LEBU on the same day when their boat capsized whilst returning from her distress call.

On a lighter note for 1881, the services of the 26th November were different, to say the least. The Lifeboat was first launched to go to the aid of the schooner WONDER in trouble in the Bay. Owing to onshore gale conditions, the I.O.M. Steam Packet Company's ss MONA, commanded by Capt. Brew, towed the Lifeboat out. The service was not needed, however, and she returned only to be called out a second time and

TYPICAL SAIL PLAN OF SR TYPE LIFE-BOAT: DRG. NO 8A

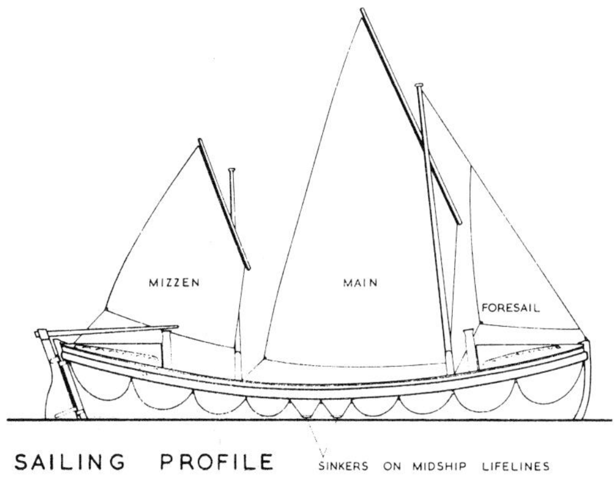

RNLI, Poole

again Capt. Brew organised a tow. This time it was to the steamship SHANNON, some six miles out with engine trouble. Yet again the service was not required as the ship got under-way just as the Lifeboat arrived. Whilst returning empty-handed for a second time, *The Two Sisters* was hailed by the Master of a schooner with a request to take off his wife and land her in Ramsey. Soon after leaving the schooner in the Lifeboat the said lady requested to go back to her ship as she had forgotten her shawl and umbrella! Ever obliging, the Boat's Crew did so and were towed back into Ramsey by the ss MONA. Capt. Brew was awarded the RNLI Silver Medal for his services.

The 26th March, 1882, saw assistance being given to the schooner COUNTESS OF CAITHNESS of Gloucester, out from Inverness. During a violent Northerly gale the ship was sighted in distress off Gob Ny Rona, South of Ramsey. The Lifeboat was launched and went alongside the schooner. Five Lifeboatmen were put aboard the ship and she was then sailed safely to Douglas.

1883 saw three services and the one on the 6th March is documented. This concerned the trawler EMERALD ISLE of Whitehaven. At 6.30 p.m. a strong NE'ly gale was blowing and the trawler

RNLI, Poole

Crew of *The Two Sisters* in 1887.
L to R back row: J. White, R. Corkish, R. Kinnin, C. Godfrey. Centre row: H. Clarke, O. Corlett, T. Kaighin (Coxswain), R. Garrett (2nd Cox), K. Gawne, W. Christian Front row: J. Kaighin, R. Kaighin, W. McCormick.

was driven aground as she was attempting to make the harbour. It was seen that her crew was in danger and the Rocket Brigade mustered quickly. They fired a rocket-line but it missed the ship's hull, hit the rigging and slid down the lee side. In the meantime the Lifeboat was launched and soon got alongside the EMERALD ISLE which by this time was in a very dangerous position. They plucked her crew off and had made very little progress back when a huge wave hit the Lifeboat and Lifeboatman John White was thrown out of the Boat. Very luckily he managed to get a hold of one of the grab lines which were becketted (looped) around the Boat's gunwale. He was quickly pulled back aboard by many willing hands. In the meantime the Lifeboat had been thrown back against the stern of the fishing vessel; her large steering oar was smashed together with four of the pulling oars. But the Crew was undaunted and eventually made the safety of the shore to the cheers of onlookers on the shoreline. Four men had been saved. Two days later the EMERALD ISLE was found still afloat and, despite the battering by wind and wave, was brought into port.

The other two services that year concerned the flat FLORA of Runcorn in April when three men were saved and in September assistance was given to the barque HEREWARD.

1883 saw the retirement of Robert Fell who had served as 2nd and 1st Coxswain for 14 years since the arrival of *The Two Sisters*. He was awarded the RNLI Silver Medal for his gallant services and was succeeded as Coxswain by Thomas Kaighin, the son of the 1868 Cox of the same name. John Cowell took over as 2nd Cox at this time and later, in 1886, he was succeeded by Robert Garrett.

THE FISHING INDUSTRY

It is interesting to note that these years saw the fishing industry at its peak in Ramsey. In 1883 90 fishing vessels totalling 609 tons and of all sizes were using the port and employing 219 men and boys. This was about a tenth of the Island's fishermen and ranked Ramsey as the third most important centre. Together with people employed in trades related to fishing and their dependents, probably a quarter of the Island's population relied on this industry for its livelihood. Cod, herring, mackerel, eels and shellfish provided the bulk of the catches and the annual yield for the port that same year was calculated to be nearly £11,000.

The following three years seem to have been quiet for the Lifeboat according to the records, with only one service a year.

An old photograph from 1884 shows the Ramsey schooner FANNIE aground just South of the South Pier on the 9th October. She was returning from Whitehaven with coal and it appears that she struck the bottom three times before ending up on the beach in a leaking condition. (Not surprising!) She had a crew of five but there was no emergency.

On the 31st of that month the Lifeboat was called out on service to the Dundalk wherry DANIEL YORKE. Four seamen were saved.

A year later on the 2nd October, 1885, the Norwegian brig PROFESSO of Tvedestrand came into Ramsey Bay and anchored. Later an onshore gale blew up and she became in danger of being driven ashore as her anchor dragged. The crew cut away both masts but she still continued to drag. The Lifeboat was then launched and she took off the crew and the Ramsey Pilot. The ship was then more securely anchored (presumably the Lifeboat's Crew doing this) and later was safely towed into port by the steamship ELLAN VANNIN.

1886

1886 saw a double service on October 5th and 6th. On the first day, just after 8 a.m., the Skipper and Mate of the schooner FANNIE arrived in Ramsey to report that their ship was aground South of Ramsey between Port Mooar and Port Cornaa. The Lifeboat was launched in thick fog and found the ship but she was high and dry by that time. Nothing could be done and so the ship was left to the elements. She very soon became a complete wreck.

Later in the day the schooner VULCAN of Douglas ran aground at the Dhoon. She was taken in tow by a boat manned by four men from Ramsey Harbour and later escorted into harbour by the Lifeboat as well.

No doubt both of these incidents were entirely due to the foggy conditions and even to this day fog is still the seaman's greatest danger. Radar has greatly helped to make such weather conditions safer in modern times and there are few groundings of this kind now. However, radar-assisted collisions do occur as the human element can never be entirely eliminated.

The following year, 1887, a total of 14 lives were saved. The first service on the 11th March was to the schooner ISABELLA STUART registered in Ardrossan. Yet again a vessel at anchor off Ramsey in a NE'ly onshore gale was in difficulties and the Lifeboat was launched soon after 11 p.m., distress signals having been seen. Four Lifeboatmen were put aboard the ship to assist and then the Lifeboat towed the vessel into harbour, arriving at 2 a.m. the next morning. The ISABELLA STUART was on passage from Mull to Liverpool with a cargo of timber.

November 1st, 1887, saw the Lifeboat out in gale conditions to the schooner KATTIE DARLING of Chester (some reports give her name as KITTY DARLING) and the brigantine PROTHESA of Teignmouth. An old Ramsey Courier of May, 1896, gave a vivid account of similar launchings of the Lifeboat for such rescues:

> "The launching of the Lifeboat at low water before the Tipping Sand Slippers were utilised, or the haul-off warp laid down, was an undertaking of extreme difficulty, not to say risk, during a gale of inshore wind. Any one who knows what Ramsey beach is like, can picture to themselves the almost superhuman efforts that were necessary to be put forth to get a Lifeboat afloat under the conditions I have named. Yet on more than one occasion I have seen *The Two Sisters* transported on her carriage to the water's edge, the masts erected in the Boat and close-reefed canvas set on her; the oars manned and then the Boat has been launched into the boiling surf. With no aid beyond that of the oars and sails, the Crew have been compelled to work the Lifeboat off a dead lee shore, through broken water which extended for more than half a mile seawards. Had the Crew been able to head on to the sea, the damage would have been minimised to a great extent, but under the circumstances rowing was out of the question and the only way progress could be made was by short tacks. As *The Two Sisters* was not very keen in windward work nor yet particularly active in seas, you may reckon the number of tacks that had to be made. Besides being in danger of being battered on to a beach, the heavy breakers followed one another in such quick succession that the brave old *Two Sisters* was almost continually full of water. No sooner had she ejected the water shipped from one sea than she was filled by another. However, by dint of perseverance and indomitable pluck, the Crew got the Lifeboat through the broken water and ultimately saved the vessel and crew. On two days in succession there were similar undertakings with like results. On the latter occasion the Lifeboat was launched to go to the assistance of a brig which was riding in a dangerous position in the bay. After surmounting almost insurmountable difficulties, the Boat reached the brig in question and the Lifeboat Crew succeeded in bringing the ship into harbour."

TALK OF REPLACEMENT

Several other valuable services were performed by the old Boat when it became rumoured that *The Two Sisters* was to be replaced by a new boat of modern type. This rumour turned out to be true, although the Crew could not see that there was the slightest necessity for a change, as the old one seemed good enough for years to come ....

How right the Crew was in this supposition, as events soon proved.

Old RNLI records show that the rescues of the 1st November, 1887, to the two ships saved 10 lives, but that *The Two Sisters* sustained damage. She broached-to when a line to the drogue (sea anchor) gave way and the Boat was thrown high up on to the beach on top of an immense wave. No one was lost. This was at least the second time the Boat had been damaged in the past few years. In 1881 she was repaired by

G.D. Learoyd collection
The schooner FANNIE aground off Ramsey South Pier in 1884.

Woolfe's boat-builders after being damaged during the EULALIE service in the October.

There is no doubt that there was now serious talk of a replacement Lifeboat. The first Minutes Book shows that the matter was discussed by the Committee in May, 1887. The current RNLI North West District Inspector, Lt. Tipping, was also in favour of getting a more modern boat and succeeded in talking the Crew around to the idea. Although the new Boat arrived in Ramsey late in 1888 – the *Mary Isabella* (the first) – it was by no means the end of *The Two Sisters*.

The *Mary Isabella* proved unsatisfactory upon her first two services in February, 1889, and so, whilst alterations were put in hand, *The Two Sisters* continued her invaluable work.

The end of 1889 saw a service to the pleasure boat VOLUNTEER of Ramsey and assistance was rendered. On the 24th December the year ended with another call-out; this time to the schooner JAMES WILLIAMSON. A message from the Northern village of Andreas to the Ramsey authorities stated that a large three-masted schooner was ashore half a mile off Rue Point, on the Northern shores of the Isle of Man, and that seas were breaking over her.

At 10 a.m. *The Two Sisters* was launched and reached the casualty at 12.15 p.m., only to find the crew of the JAMES WILLIAMSON safely ashore. They had managed this by floating a lifebuoy ashore where local farmers had bent on another line and had hauled all four crew members to safety through the surf. The Captain, however, was severely injured and suffering from exhaustion.

THE LAST YEAR

The last full year that saw *The Two Sisters* on Station was 1890 and proved to be one of the busiest years in her career, no doubt due to adverse weather in the early and later winter months.

On the 14th January, 1890, at 11.45 a.m. the Lifeboat was launched in a SSW'ly gale to go to the assistance of a half-decked boat which was riding heavily at anchor in Ramsey Bay. Just as the launch took place, a large schooner parted her anchor cable and signalled for help. On reaching the smaller vessel the Lifeboat's Crew could only persuade one member of the three-man crew to leave his ship. The remaining two were warned by the Coxswain that once the Lifeboat had aided the schooner she would not be able to return to their half-decker. They still stayed aboard but after an hour called for help which could not be given. Meanwhile the Lifeboat got alongside the schooner W.M.J., registered in Briton Ferry and took off the crew of four.

Later in the day at 3.45 p.m. the Lifeboat was out again and this time brought in seven further men, crews of the fishing cutter OTTER of Port St. Mary (Isle of Man) and the cutter HAMILTON of Ramsey.

The remaining two crew-men aboard the first vessel attended, the Peel cutter ZEALOT, rode out the gale at anchor and survived to tell the tale.

A press report of the above rescues makes vivid reading:

> "....1890 was only young when, on the 14th January, the most exciting scenes almost ever witnessed in Ramsey were enacted. It was blowing a "living" gale from the SSW and Ramsey Bay was full of shipping. The principal part of the vessels were trawl boats – several of them being the very finest in the Channel – and so suddenly and violently did the storm come on, that masters and crews of these vessels scarce knew what to do with their craft. All had double reefs tied down and would have certainly gone in for a third reef, but they were unable to take it in. Stout canvas was blown into ribbons; large trawlers were run for the harbour at low-water, the crews being glad to stick them on terra-firma anywhere. One trawler lost a man and taken altogether, it was a day long to be remembered. In the height of the storm the Lifeboat was called out and the old *Two Sisters* was launched about noon. She made two or three trips on that occasion, rescuing the crews of four vessels – 12 men in all. It was not until one o'clock the next morning that the Lifeboat got back to her station".

The 7th November saw the steam dredger WALTER BIBBY of Preston show distress signals from her position one and a half miles SE of the harbour. The Lifeboat was launched in very heavy seas and had great difficulty in getting the 15 crew of the dredger off owing to her very heavy rolling. The men were landed at Port Lewaigue just South of Ramsey as the Lifeboat could not return to her Station. The tug HERCULES was actually in charge of the dredger but was helpless to render assistance herself and was later berthed in the harbour.

The final service of 1890 was one of the most remarkable and earned further official distinction for the Ramsey Crew. This took place on the 11th November during a SE'ly gale which was accompanied by driving sleet.

> "The Coastguard on duty noticed what he took to be a flare shown from a vessel on Ramsey beach. It was visible for so short a time, however, that it was impossible to locate the position of the vessel, or even to be very certain as to whether there was a vessel at all. To make sure, the sound signal was fired and almost in a twinkling the Lifeboat Crew and the Rocket Brigade turned out, together with hundreds of townspeople. It was the early hours of the morning. The Brigade made for the North Shore but owing to the darkness of the night, nothing could be seen. The Lifeboat was hauled down on to the sands, the tide having ebbed to seaward of the piers. Here a halt was made as there were no further indications of the stranded ship. After an hour or so a flare was shown and

this left no doubt in the minds of those on shore that help was needed. The Rocket Brigade commenced to blaze away but with no success. The vessel was a long way off and her flare disappeared almost instantly, making the darkness doubly dark. A more awkward state of tide could scarcely be hit upon, as sand bank after bank seemed to impede progress. There was only one single haul-off warp at that time, so instead of the Boat being hauled off by people on the shore, those in the Boat had to haul themselves. When fairly afloat, the Crew (who were accompanied by Mr. E.C. Kerr, Hon. Sec.) found the sea much heavier than they had bargained for. The haul-off warp was led in over the roller in the stem of the Boat, and was held down by an iron clamp. In hauling out through a nasty bar of broken water, the clamp gave way, with the result that the Boat came broadside onto the sea and at the same time she was struck by a heavy sea which had the effect of throwing the Boat on her beam ends and the Crew into her lee side. One Crew Member was washed overboard but quickly regained the Boat. Had it not been that some of the Crew happened to be thrown across the legs of the others, no doubt more of them would have been thrown into the sea, but they soon recovered and after a desperate struggle got the Boat into deep water. It was still pitch dark and the distressed vessel could not be located so the anchor was let go and a sharp lookout kept. As soon as there was sufficient daylight to discover the stranded vessel, the Lifeboat's anchor was weighed and she was taken alongside of the schooner MARGARET of Belfast. And not a moment too soon. She was full of water with the seas making a clean breach over her. The crew, three in number, were huddled together on the main boom and barely out of reach of the seas. To get at these unfortunate men, the Lifeboat had to be taken over the vessel's deck – a risky undertaking. This was done and although the Lifeboat went clean through the schooner's main rail and bulwark, the boat only sustained a slight scratch, and a gallant rescue was effected".

The old Boat was then presented to the Ramsey Commissioners and placed on view in Mooragh Park. Unfortunately she fell into a state of disrepair and was eventually sold for breaking up in 1901.

Coxswain Robert Garrett and Mr. Kerr were both awarded the RNLI Silver Medal for these last two services. Mr. Garrett had taken over as Coxswain that year from Thomas Kaighin (the second) and Oscar Corlett was appointed Second Cox.

The next Lifeboat, *Mary Isabella* (1) took over station in 1891 but one final service is attributed to *The Two Sisters* on 30th January, 1894, when she gave assistance to the Fiume registered barque CELESTINA.

Manx Museum and National Trust Archives

The Island's five lifeboats at Douglas c1932. Thought to be during the Centenary celebrations of Sir William Hillary and the building of the Tower of Refuge.

CHAPTER 3

Mary Isabella (1) 1888-1896

27 service launches and 86 lives saved

ON the 30th August, 1888, the new Lifeboat to be named *Mary Isabella* was sent by rail from Portsmouth to Liverpool for her passage to Ramsey. She was similar to the Palmer design and was 37ft. long and had an 8 ft. beam. She rowed 10 oars, double-banked, and possessed all the latest equipment. Her builders were Hansen & Sons of Cowes, Isle of Wight, and she had a drop-keel which was to facilitate sailing to windward. The *Mary Isabella* was four feet longer than *The Two Sisters* but otherwise just a more modern version of the earlier Lifeboat.

On first sighting the new Boat in Liverpool the Lifeboatmen sent over to collect her were not impressed. They considered her decking too low and this proved correct. As soon as she took a full crew aboard, sea water flowed up through the delivery-tubes and washed about the men's feet – and this in still-water conditions.

The *Mary Isabella* was inaugurated on the 6th September, 1888, but the naming ceremony was marred by one of her carriage wheels collapsing just as the procession commenced. Later in the ceremony a heavy downpour took place just as the choir of St. Paul's Church was participating and everyone had to scurry for shelter. It was not surprising, therefore, that the Boat was at first looked upon as unlucky, even though later on in the day when she sailed in competition with *The Two Sisters* she showed her sailing superiority, especially when beating to windward.

The cost of the new Boat was £420. This sum, together with the cost of its equipment and a new carriage, was paid for by an anonymous person through the Manchester RNLI Branch and the good offices of Mr. and Mrs. Norbury whose business was in the North West but who lived at Port Lewaigue, near Ramsey, from 1894. During that same year Mr. and Mrs. Norbury also donated a sum of £1,000 to the RNLI – £700 for a Boat and £300 towards the cost of a new Boathouse for Ramsey.

In late 1889 the "Norbury Boathouse" was built and it was a particularly fine one with a crew assembly (recreation) room on the first floor and a coxswain's flat above this on the second floor. A new slip-way was also built on the beach opposite the Boathouse and the total cost came to £1,731. The old Boathouse site was sold to the Ramsey Town Commissioners in 1890 for £300 and the old house for £22 10s. The Norbury Boathouse survived until March, 1990, when it was demolished only to make way for one to take a new breed of boat.

The first services made by the new Lifeboat were both in February, 1889. On the 8th she rescued the crew of four from the Peel cutter PATRICK and on the 13th she saved the schooner BRILLIANT, also of Peel, although her crew had scrambled ashore at Dog Mills.

However, the sea-keeping qualities of the *Mary Isabella* were unsatisfactory. This was investigated by the RNLI District Inspector after the initial two services. It was recorded that the Crew wanted the Boat to be deeper with the deck and waist raised some 4" to 6". They also wanted a newer pattern drop-keel fitted and to be 1ft. further forward; and attention to the valves of the delivery-tubes which were not operating properly. In April, 1889, the Boat was sent back to London for tests and alterations. Meanwhile *The Two Sisters* remained on Station for the rest of the year until the altered *Mary Isabella* finally took up station in January, 1891, and in time for a year of storms.

During 1890 Robert Garrett took over from Thomas Kaighin (the second) as Coxswain and Oscar Corlett was appointed 2nd Coxswain.

The 31st January, 1891, saw the new *Mary Isabella* back out on service and she is accredited with saving the four-man crew of the Belfast schooner LEONA at Jurby Head on the North West Coast of the Island.

Later in the year, at midnight on October 8th/9th, both the Rocket Brigade and Lifeboat Crews were called out with the news that a barque was ashore at Port Mooar, some four miles South of Ramsey. The Rocket Brigade reached the distress at about 2 a.m. and succeeded in getting their first rocket-line across the ship between her main and mizzen masts, from a difficult position on cliffs above the ship. However, the gale-force Southerly wind caught the whip line and it fouled on rocks above the shoreline. Cliff ladders were used and Coastguards Dawes, James McCormick and Walter Clarke went down to clear the line but

J. Kneale

The old Norbury Boathouse showing the original Coxswain's top-floor flat as built in 1889.

found it impossible in the gale. By this time the Lifeboat arrived on the scene but those on shore thought that it would be impossible for it to get alongside the COLUMBA owing to the rocky shore and prevailing conditions. However, after several attempts, the Lifeboat managed to drop down alongside the barque and take off the nine-man crew. It was a very tricky and courageous operation as the barque was light-ship and high out of the water and constantly heaving around. During the transfer of the nine men from ship to Lifeboat one man did go down between the two vessels but was retrieved and no-one suffered injury other than exposure. The ship was registered in Khristiansand, Norway, and had actually been under tow from the tug FLYING HUNTRESS, en route from Glasson Dock (near Lancaster) to Ardrossan, when the towing hawser parted in the gale. The Captain had just managed to let go both anchors as they drifted ashore. But his ship survived and was brought into Ramsey the next day. The tug also made Ramsey, reporting damage to her paddle wheels.

THE GREAT STORM OF 1891

"The Great Storm of 1891 commenced on the morning of Tuesday, 13th October, at the dawn of which there was little or no wind. As the morning wore on the glass fell fast and early in the afternoon the wind began to freshen from the SSE with a rising sea".

So commences a Press article of the day dealing with a decade historically known for its severity of weather around the British Isles. It continued:

"The sailing trawler INDUSTRY (R. Leadbetter, Master) arrived in Ramsey Bay followed shortly afterwards by the schooners ECLIPSE and NORTH BARRULE.

The wind quickly increased in violence, so much so that large trees were uprooted in various parts outside the town, and great damage done. The sea was a complete mass of foam and nothing could be seen but broken water. The crew of the trawler INDUSTRY let go their anchor under the shelter of Maughold Head but the anchor would not hold and the vessel ran for the port where she arrived safely, although striking heavily whilst making the harbour entrance. Nothing could be seen of the two schooners and it was a most trying time for the wives and relatives of the unfortunate men aboard. (Both were local ships). The Lifeboat Crew and the Rocket Brigade were at their posts the whole time but it was considered entirely out of the question to launch the Lifeboat off the beach – should she be wanted – in the face of such a storm, and accordingly it was decided that she should be launched into the harbour and taken to sea by a tug.

Somewhere towards darkness the wind flew around to the SW and piped loud and long. Still nothing could be seen of the schooners and it was presumed that they had gone round to the Point of Ayre. At about 10 o'clock word arrived in the town to the effect that the FAYAWAY had gone ashore two and a half miles North of Ramsey and that the crew, T. Corlett and Caesar Clarke, had been able to get ashore as best they could. They had then walked on into Ramsey to report the matter.

Somewhere about eleven o'clock at night the sound of rockets of the Lifeboat and Rocket Brigade were heard almost simultaneously, and there was a quick muster. It seems that a steamer had arrived in the Bay showing flares and in a very few minutes the *Mary Isabella* was speeding away under reefed lugsails in the direction from whence the signals came. After running seaward for about a mile and a half or so, the Lifeboat fell in with a schooner lying across the bows of a steamer.

A portion of the Lifeboat's Crew went aboard the vessel in order to save her, and the *Mary Isabella* returned to port with the other portion of her Crew and the Captain of the schooner in question, who along with his colleagues had had an awful time of it. The schooner was the MARY AGNES of Dumfries and she was safely brought into harbour the next day.

At the break of the following morning a vessel was observed at anchor about six miles NE from the harbour. There was a fresh gale blowing from the SW and the Lifeboat proceeded to the spot.

The craft was in a sorry plight, nearly all her spars being broken and much of her canvas blown away. The Lifeboatmen put things in order and the tug FLYING HUNTRESS towed her into harbour. She was the schooner UNITY of Chester and the Captain and crew were glad to reach a haven of safety.

Early in the morning, to the great relief of many all-night watchers, the schooners ECLIPSE and NORTH BARRULE were seen coming up the Bay from the direction of the Point of Ayre, round about where they had spent a fearful night. Considerable damage was done to the vessels but the captains and crews seemed to be deeply thankful that their lives had been spared.

During the day the following vessels were brought into Ramsey Harbour disabled by the storm: brigantine LYNWOOD; schooners ECLIPSE, NORTH BARRULE, LILY GARTON, MARY AGNES, UNITY; trawlers DAISY, RANGER, ANNA MARIA and the smack FAYAWAY.

An idea may be gathered from the foregoing of what Ramsey Harbour resembled on the occasion in question – a veritable maritime hospital."

The Lifeboat Crew put in a claim for £50 salvage for the UNITY service but at a court case was only awarded £5. This is possibly the first time an Isle of Man Lifeboat Crew got as far as the courts in such an action.

1891 saw the Lifeboat Committee meet in the new Norbury Boathouse and that continued for 100 years. Before this date they had met at Dumbells Bank, the Court House or the old School.

1892

The next year, 1892, was a relatively quiet one with only two services. One on the 2nd July took place at 5.45 p.m. when the *Mary Isabella* went out to the Ramsey schooner MARY JANE, showing distress signals some three miles out. The crew of three was taken off and the local steamship MANX MAID towed the ship into port. On the 12th August late in the evening the Lifeboat went to the assistance of the Peel registered trawler ROYAL FERN. She had gone aground near the Cranstal Coastguard Station, some four miles North of Ramsey. However, with the help of local farmers Teare and Kissack, fishermen Brew and Crennell and Coastguard Dawes, the ship was re-floated and the *Mary Isabella* later escorted her back to Ramsey.

In 1892 a new carriage made by Bristol, the UK firm, arrived for the Lifeboat. It appears that the altered *Mary Isabella* was exceptionally heavy for her size and therefore required a heavier carriage. Alterations were also made to the slip-way at a cost of £132.

The next service was on the 17th April, 1893. This was to the Lancaster schooner ANNIE, which was in distress some three miles off Ramsey. Her crew of three was taken off. The ship was on passage from Belfast to Barrow with pit props. After a quiet summer, the 22nd November saw the *Mary Isabella* out to the Ardrossan schooner JEAN MCCRAE which was towed into port. Four days later, on the 26th, there was a service to the steamship MACRAE of Glasgow where assistance was given to save the vessel.

LIFEBOAT STRANDED

But the 10th December, 1893, was a day of storms and an incident to the Lifeboat which could have had disastrous results.

The day was a Sunday and the wind rose shortly before dawn. By 10 a.m. it was blowing violently from the SSE. Reports state that there were two Norwegian brigs, a brigantine and a three-masted schooner anchored and sheltering in Ramsey Bay.

At about 10.30 a.m. the brigantine SULTANA REINA of Liverpool showed a distress signal from her rigging. (Usually the ensign flown inverted, by day). She was on passage from Rochester to Belfast with cement. The Lifeboat Crew was summoned by the gun and within ten minutes the Boat was launched into a foaming sea with considerable difficulty even with the aid of the haul-off warp and many willing hands. After tacking towards the Queen's Pier, the *Mary Isabella* was turned and stood off towards the brigantine which lay further North and about two miles from land. Running almost with the wind the Lifeboat reached the ship in a little over a quarter of an hour. As she was dragging her anchors the crew of six was taken off and a start made to return to port. Nearby lay one of the Norwegian brigs, the CORMORANT, but as she was further seaward and the crew did not ask for help, the Lifeboat commenced her difficult passage back to Ramsey. She was then tied up in the harbour, as seemed prudent in the conditions. At noon both brigs carried away their anchor cables almost simultaneously and the Lifeboat was soon under-way again on a second errand of mercy. Large crowds cheered her as huge waves which rolled into the harbour mouth were breasted; she was under close-reefed sails and reached off until she was well in the wake of the nearest brig, the CORMORANT, which was being driven North by the gale. Seeing this, her Master hoisted a topsail and caused his ship to run aground at Dog Mills. She was fully laden with bran. Meanwhile the *Mary Isabella* struck her canvas and scudded after the CORMORANT under bare masts. Seeing the distressed ship go aground and then broach-to on to the sea, Lifeboat Coxswain Garrett realised

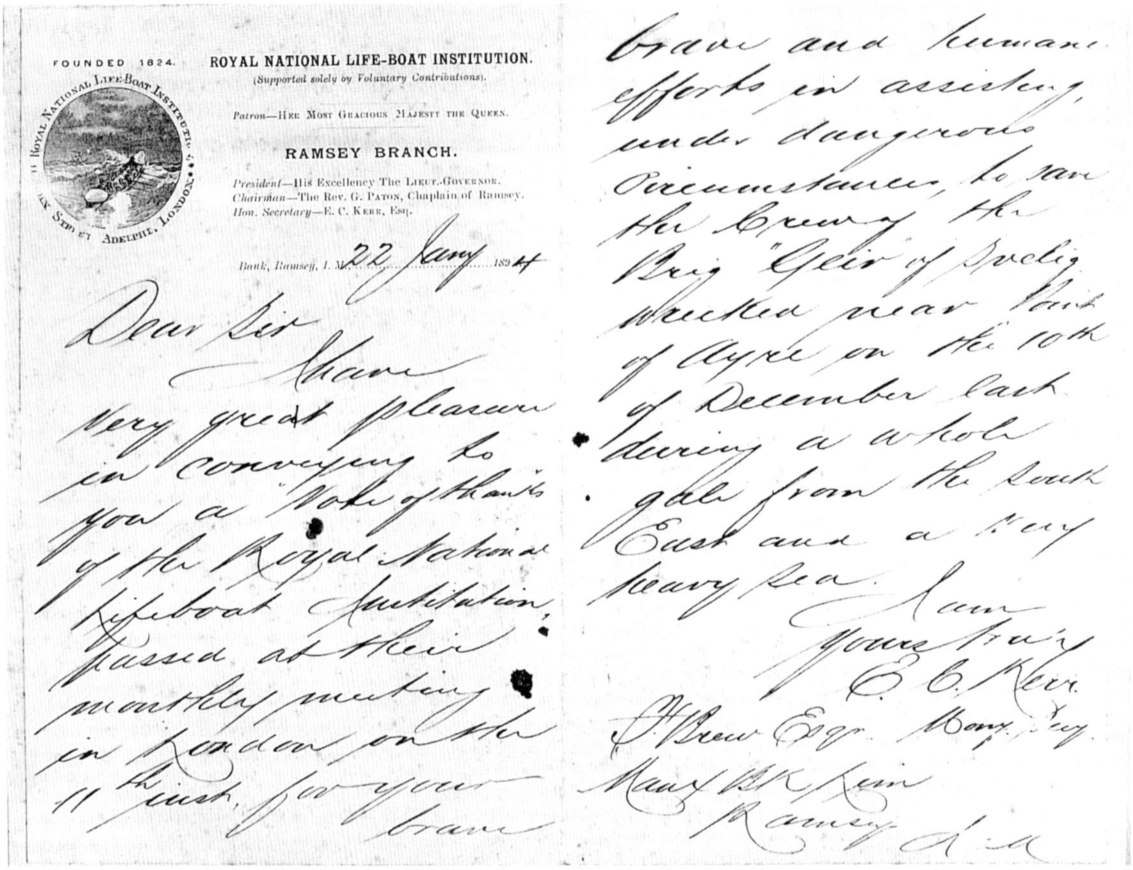

FOUNDED 1824. ROYAL NATIONAL LIFE-BOAT INSTITUTION.
(Supported solely by Voluntary Contributions).
Patron—Her Most Gracious Majesty the Queen.
RAMSEY BRANCH.
President—His Excellency The Lieut.-Governor.
Chairman—The Rev. G. Paton, Chaplain of Ramsey.
Hon. Secretary—E. C. Kerr, Esq.

Bank, Ramsey, I. M. 22 Jany 1894

Dear Sir

I have very great pleasure in conveying to you a "Vote of thanks" of the Royal National Lifeboat Institution, passed at their monthly meeting in London on the 11th inst, for your brave and humane efforts in assisting, under dangerous circumstances, to save the Crew of the Brig "Geir" of Svelvik wrecked near Point of Ayre on the 10th of December last during a whole gale from the South East and a very heavy sea.

I am
Yours truly
E. C. Kerr

J. Brew Esqr. Hony Secy

Dr. E.C.B. Corlett collection

Letter from the RNLI Ramsey Hon. Secretary E.C. Kerr to Mr. John Brew, in 1894.

that the only thing he could do was to attempt to get under the lee of the brig in order to take off her crew. The Lifeboat therefore dropped her own anchor to prevent going ashore, hoping to drop down on the Cormorant. But the anchor dragged and she herself was driven ashore some fifty yards North of the big ship. Spectators lined the shore and were aghast to see a mountainous wave break over the Lifeboat and put her on her beam ends. Six of the crew were thrown out, including Coxswain Garrett. Three of them were driven ashore together with the Boat, but Robert Garrett was not so fortunate and was dragged back off the beach three times before the gallant efforts of the shore spectators rescued him, exhausted, from the waves. Thanks once again to many willing hands, no lives were lost. The Lifeboat suffered no damage and sat upright on the beach as if nothing had happened.

In the meantime the crew of the Cormorant was still in a precarious position. The Rocket Brigade was called and soon got a line aboard. But then it transpired that the Norwegian crew was unfamiliar in rigging a breeches-buoy. Coastguard Davies pluckily volunteered to be hauled aboard the ship and set up the gear himself. The crewmen were all saved and the crowd cheered lustily when Mr. Davies was hauled back onshore. The Rocket Brigade then proceeded further along the Bride coast-road Northwards to where the three-masted schooner Dairy Maid of Fleetwood had run ashore. By this time though, the tide was on the ebb and their services were not needed. The crew preferred to remain on board as the vessel was on a sandy bottom and they expected to float off on the next tide.

Almost simultaneously with the running ashore of the Cormorant, the other Norwegian brig Gier, laden with timber from Sundsvall for Castletown, ran ashore further North at Ballavarkish, some three miles South of the Point of Ayre. This vessel had a crew of eight and became a total wreck very quickly. Before she struck the shore one of her masts had been carried away and, within a short time of grounding, the second mast went overboard and several of the crew barely escaped being crushed to death by falling spars. A number of people from Ramsey, seeing that their services were not needed by the Dairy Maid, proceeded to the Gier and a gentleman named Mark Joughin, with a rope secured around his waist, went into the water and succeeded in getting hold of a second rope which was thrown to him by the imperilled crew. Thus communication between ship and shore was established and the crew came ashore by this rope, hand over hand, being assisted by a human chain of anxious helpers which included J.H. Cruickshank (later to become High Bailiff), W.H. Kneale and John Brew. Board of Trade medals were awarded for this rescue.

The gale went down more quickly than it rose and from 3 o'clock the wind fell rapidly away and the SULTANA REINA, which had ridden out the storm safely, was brought into Ramsey Harbour on the Monday morning.

It is to be noted that when the maroons were fired for the GIER rescue all the local churches and chapels emptied and the Rev. J.K. Kewley, who later became Archdeacon, was himself First Officer of the Rocket Brigade at the time. Later the RNLI, Norwegian and U.K. Governments made awards to a number of shore rescuers. Among these, the aforesaid John Brew was awarded a Board of Trade Bronze Medal and a Citation from the RNLI. He was a Ramsey butcher and the grandfather of the present Chairman of the Ramsey RNLI Branch Committee, the well-known naval architect, Dr. E.C.B. Corlett.

The final service in 1893 was to the schooner NOT FORGOT of Connah's Quay (near Chester), on passage from Belfast to Dublin with moulding sand. She became distressed near the Point of Ayre, somewhat off her course, and the *Mary Isabella* took off her crew of three. The ship was towed to the Queen's Pier, Ramsey, by ss ASTOR and she remained there for several weeks awaiting better weather.

Services in 1894 show only six on record and they came in batches of two at a time.

The first two took place on the 30th January. During this night and in weather said to be the worst ever known locally, the *Mary Isabella* was launched to go to the aid of the Ramsey ship MARGARET ANNIE in trouble off the Cranstal, some four miles North of the port. Unbeknown to the Boat's Crew, however, the ship was beached in the meantime and the crew safely taken ashore into local houses.

During the day, at 1.45 p.m., the previous Lifeboat, *The Two Sisters*, made her very last service run; this to the Fiume registered (now Rijeka, Yugoslavia) barque CELESTINA, under the command of Capt. Antonio Antich. She was on passage from the River Plate, (Argentine), to Ayre with bone meal and in trouble of some kind off the Bahama Bank. The Lifeboat took the Master off and landed him in Ramsey in order that he could communicate with agents. The Glasgow tug DEFIANCE assisted the ship thereafter.

On the 7th February, soon after noon, the Peel nicky (a popular type of local lug-sail fishing vessel) ANNIE JANE was dismasted near Maughold Head. The *Mary Isabella* was launched to go to her aid but the steam tug BRITANNIC from Hull was sheltering in the Bay and got to her first. The BRITANNIC took both the ANNIE JANE and the Lifeboat in tow to return them to the harbour, but en-route the Dublin smack DOLPHIN showed distress signals and so the *Mary Isabella* took aboard her crew and thus four seamen were landed safely.

Saturday, 22nd December, ended the year's

Dr. E.C.B. Corlett collection

Bronze Board of Trade Medal awarded to Mr. John Brew, 1894.

Manx Museum and Naional Trust archives

The schooner GEM aground off the old Boathouse, Ramsey, in 1895. Also E.C. Kerr Branch Hon. Secretary (1881-1907) and Lifeboatmen.

K.G. Groves' History

Launching the *Mary Isabella* over the harbour wall during a blizzard in 1895 for a service to the schooner MARGARET AND ELIZABETH.

Lifeboat work with one of the year's worst storms. This time the gale came from the NW during the early hours of the morning. Soon after daybreak the chimney stack to the kitchen of the Coxswain's flat above the Boathouse was torn clean from its fixings and, throughout the town and countryside, roofs were stripped, trees uprooted and a great amount of damage done. The sea was a white mass of seething foam. Soon after 9 a.m. a distress signal was seen flying from a yard of a schooner lying hard at anchor off the piers. The maroons were sounded and very shortly the *Mary Isabella* was away with only her small mizzen set. She was lost to sight in the surf almost immediately and not seen again for two hours when she landed the crew of three from the schooner MARGARET JONES of Caernafon. While this took place the ship herself drifted away "Not under command" and damaged the Chester schooner EXCELSIOR which was at anchor. Once again the Lifeboat went out and took her crew of four off but the gale prevented her from making harbour and so, at 4 p.m., the Coxswain decided to put the wind astern and make for the port of Laxey, nearly nine miles to the South. This was accomplished and the survivors landed safely.

During this interval the schooner AGNES was driven aground off Ballaugh on the Island's NW coast; by sea a distance of 16 miles from Ramsey and eight miles North of Peel. The Rocket Brigade went there by train and then lugged their equipment some two miles down to the beach and for many hours attempted to get their rocket-lines aboard the ship, but failed. As the Ramsey Lifeboat was unavailable, the Peel Lifeboat *John Monk* was launched and effected the rescue of all 12 crew members. On returning to Ramsey the *Mary Isabella* was informed of the AGNES stranding and again set out, prepared to sail the 16 miles to Ballaugh. However, during the early hours of Sunday the 23rd, the *Mary Isabella* met the Peel Lifeboat off the Point of Ayre with the crew of the AGNES aboard. Both Lifeboats made back for Ramsey and many men, dead-beat, arrived safely on dry land that Sunday morning.

THE BLIZZARD OF 1895

1895 saw the last full year's service for the *Mary Isabella* (1) and it was one not without incident! The first "nail in her coffin" was probably the snow blizzard of the 7th February and the subsequent unusual launch and damage to the Boat.

The snow started falling on the morning of the 6th and by afternoon it was lying thick around the streets of Ramsey. A gale from the SE rose by this time, piling up the snow and whipping it into a blizzard. The fishing fleet had put to sea in the morning but quickly returned when they saw conditions worsening. By the time they made the harbour approaches, however, there was insufficient water for them and they had to shelter as best they could beside the Queen's Pier. During the following hours of darkness, fishermen reported a ship aground directly in front of the Norbury Boathouse. Conditions were so bad in the blizzard that it was impossible to confirm this from the shore. Nevertheless the Lifeboatmen were summoned and considered that to launch the Boat was the only way to effect a rescue. This was vainly attempted and many hours were spent as huge seas rolled on to the beach and freezing snow blinded the crew, launchers and helpers. The haul-off warp would not function for some reason and so the attempt was eventually abandoned until daybreak.

As the day dawned the gale became fiercer but it was certainly possible to see that – yes, indeed – a schooner lay aground close by the Boathouse. And that had been the problem of the dark hours, too. She lay right across the haul-off warp and thus prevented it from running. There was no sign of the ship's crew and although the schooner had superficial damage she did not appear to be breaking up. It was still imperative to get alongside the ship and so, after considerable deliberations by all concerned, it was decided to haul the Lifeboat and carriage to the quayside and tip them to launch the *Mary Isabella* off into the harbour. This took some considerable effort owing to the heavy snow and even a lamp-post had to be dismantled which was in the way of the launching site. The Boat suffered a considerable hole in her bow from this method but it was quickly and temporarily tacked over with a sheet of tin and the Boat taken out to the MARGARET AND ELIZABETH of Liverpool. The ship's two crewmen then suddenly appeared, quite unharmed; they had been sheltering amongst the top-sails and quickly boarded the Lifeboat which returned them to the harbour.

The full damage to the *Mary Isabella,* upon closer inspection, amounted to 13 of her planks being stove in and it took local boat-builders three days of continuous work to make her fully sea-worthy again.

THE LAST SERVICES

The month of November, 1895, saw the Lifeboat at sea on services for the last time off Ramsey. On the 10th the Wigtown schooner ELLEN AND MARY (38 tons: Capt. Nish) was in distress in a gale only one and a half miles NE of the port. The *Mary Isabella* was launched, picked up the crew of three and put them aboard the ANNIE HERON lying in the harbour. That was at 6 p.m. An hour later she was out again; this time to the brig GLOBE of Whitehaven, also in trouble in the Bay. This time the Master

T.H. Midwood — Ramsey RNLI collection

The Isle of Man Steam Packet Co's ss Tynwald in Ramsey c.1890.

T.H. Midwood — Ramsey RNLI collection

The Isle of Man Steam Packet Co's ss Snaefell; Ramsey c.1890.
(The very tall thin figure in the background left is recognised as the late T.A. Corlett [Senior], father of T.A. Corlett, Lifeboat Mechanic and Assistant Mechanic, 1956-64!).

T.H. Midwood

Ramsey RNLI collection

The Isle of Man Steam Packet Co's ss PEVERIL: Ramsey c.1890.

and his wife and five crewmen were taken off. The ship was bound from the Mersey to Limerick with 395 tons of coal. The Coxswain's wife, Mrs. Garrett, looked after the Captain's wife whilst the crew – soon to be joined by others – took up residence in the assembly room of the Norbury Boathouse. Finally that busy evening, the Lifeboat went out again to the schooner HARVEST HOME of Preston. She had timber from Coleraine for Garston. The crew of four was taken off and joined the others in the assembly room.

On the 15th November, soon after midday, the Norwegian brigantine SOMERSET was observed lying in the Bay with a pilot on board and showing a distress signal. She was on a ballast passage from Conway to Tonsberg. The Lifeboat took off all her crew of nine as requested.

Finally, on the 23rd of the month, the old Ramsey schooner GEM was stranded on the beach opposite the Lifeboat Station. The crew of four was taken off to safety.

At a Committee Meeting of the Branch on the 15th May, 1895, a letter from the RNLI Headquarters was read out to all present. A new class of boat was proposed for Ramsey. She would be 37ft in length and 9ft in breadth, and carry two drop-keels. She would have no water ballast and would be similarly rigged to the present Boat except that the mizzen lug would be jib-headed and the foremast shorter and stepped in a tabernacle.

This new Lifeboat was to carry the same name as her predecessor, namely *Mary Isabella*. She was to serve the Station for twice the length of time and save nearly twice the number of lives.

D. Reed

East Quay, Ramsey, c.1948, showing fishing vessels MASTER FRANK and GOWAN HILL and the stern of the Ramsey Steamship Co's BEN ELLAN.

B.P. Grenfell

East Quay, Ramsey, 1988, with B.C. MERCURIUS and Mezeron Co's SILVER RIVER and COLBY RIVER.

CHAPTER 4

Mary Isabella (2) 1896-1915

48 service launches and 153 lives saved

THE new *Mary Isabella* (the second one of this same name) was named by Mrs. Norbury in Ramsey on the 7th May, 1896, whilst berthed at the Queen's Pier.

Three weeks earlier the old *Mary Isabella* was towed out of Ramsey by the ss MANX MAID, a locally owned ship, under the command of Capt. Burrows. The old boat was manned by Coxswain R. Garrett, Assistant Cox Oscar Corlett, Bowman Wm. McCormick, W. Christian and R. Corkish. The celebrated footballer Arthur Corkill also went along for the passage. She was towed to Whitehaven for her return to London. The new *Mary Isabella* was also towed from Whitehaven by the ss ELLAN VANNIN, on the 20th April, her new carriage having been delivered to Ramsey earlier.

For the first time we have quite a full description of the carriage and Boat from Press articles and the one in the Ramsey Courier gives a good picture of the latest in RNLI Lifeboats of the time:

"The carriage is built on the most modern principle. The framework is constructed of oak and ash and all the fittings are of galvanised steel; the wheels are made with English elm tyres, oak spokes and galvanised steel nave. The old Tipping Sand Plates have been utilised and the only complaint about the carriage seems to be that it is too strong – a very good fault, surely?

The new *Mary Isabella* was built by the celebrated yacht builders Hansen & Sons of Cowes, Isle of Wight, from the very latest and most improved designs. From a general observation of the exterior of the new Boat, one cannot help in the first instance being impressed by her noble appearance all over; the beauty and symmetry of her lines; the absence of all inward curves, or of anything to produce friction; the perfect regularity of every section from the stem to the sternpost; and perhaps, what is of most importance, she shows stability at every point. Instead of being wall-sided like the old *Mary Isabella*, she comes up with a graceful sweep from the bilge to the gunwale – thus giving great canvas carrying powers. She appears to be slightly fuller forward than the old Boat, but this may be accounted for by the extra breadth of beam of the new craft. She is, however, very fine aft, without being in any way hollowed out. In short, in model the new Lifeboat seems to possess all the qualities necessary to develop speed and stability.

So much for the *Mary Isabella's* general appearances. She is 37ft o'all (the same length as the old Boat), and 9ft 3ins. beam (15 ins. more than the old boat), which means that besides giving the Boat more power, so as to enable her to stand up to her canvas better, it also means that her crew, as weather ballast, will be so much further from the centre of the Boat. This will produce a far greater effect in counteracting the force of the wind on the sails than was possible in the old Boat, owing to her narrowness of beam. It was in this respect only, that the old Boat showed any failure – that she was rather tender under canvas.

The new Boat rows ten oars, the same as the old one, with the difference that owing to the increased beam, the crew will be enabled to use 15ft oars instead of 13ft ones. The new *Mary Isabella* is rigged the same as the old one, namely, with two lugs and a jib, with the difference that instead of the mizzen lug being square-headed and lashed to a yard, it is a triangular or leg-of-mutton sail.

In the old *Mary Isabella* the bollard for towing purposes or for securing the cable when at anchor, could not be used when the foremast was erected. In the new *Mary Isabella* the bollard is secured to the after end of the forward air drum, whilst the mast is fixed in a "tabernacle". This tabernacle consists of two galvanised steel bitts, which are secured to the deck. These bitts stand about a foot high and are just sufficiently far apart to admit the heel of the mast working between them. The heel of the mast is shod with galvanised steel and through it is a bolt about a foot from the bottom which ships near the top of the tabernacle, thus placing the mast, as it were, on a hinge. By this means the mast can be placed on end with the aid of the jib tack, without the slightest difficulty or danger in any weather. Once the mast is erected, another bolt is inserted at the bottom of the tabernacle and the mast is secured.

The new Boat has an iron keel of about 30cwt under her, which is similar to the old Boat. But unlike the old *Mary Isabella*, which was fitted with a centre-board of 12ft length and which could be lowered down square, or either end at will, the new Boat has two centre-boards each 9ft long and hinged at the fore end. The forward centre-board has a drop of 2ft 4ins. and the after one a drop of 2ft 4ins. The drop-keels are fin-shaped and are very simply worked. All you have to do is to knock out a pin and the keel falls until brought up by an india-rubber buffer which is attached to a wire lanyard of the proper length. These keels weigh about 3 cwt. each and one man can handle either

Manx Museum and National Trust archives

Said to be the crew of the *Mary Isabella* (2) c.1896. So far as can be ascertained, those identified are:- Back row L to R: --, Corkish, Walter Martin, "Ha" Gawne, Harry Corkish, Partridge, Tom Corkish, Charlie Godfrey, --, Joe Cottier, R. Kinnin, Willie Corkish. Front row: Keppel Gawne, Bill (Danjou) Christian, Oscar Corlett (2nd Cox), Jimmy Cottier, Robert Garrett (Cox), --, W. McCormick (Bowman), Wm. Christian (nick-named "Billie the Charmer").

of them. In beating up to windward, the advantage of having two drop keels is clearly apparent, more especially in making short tacks, because it stands to reason that by pulling up the after drop-keel and leaving the other one down, the boat will stay twice as handy. Again, in heavy running, the after drop-keel would undoubtedly assist the steering of the Boat. The new Boat draws about six inches less with the drop-keels up than the old one, but about the same with them down.

The new *Mary Isabella* has considerably more sheer – that is, somewhat lower at one particular place in the waist than the old Boat – but she averages a greater freeboard all over than the latter craft, and as such will carry her crew better.

The old Boat was fitted with tanks below the deck for holding water ballast, bilge and other pumps. This Boat has nothing below the decks but air compartments, having no pumps of any description. The only tanks she has run along each side of the Boat under the fore-and-aft seats. These are made of pine and covered with canvas bedded in white lead. It is by doing away with the water tanks that the new Boat is said to be a ton lighter than the old one, although considerable larger. The new *Mary Isabella* has four delivery valves, each of which measure from the deck to the bottom of the Boat, 1ft 8ins., and are supposed, in the event of the Boat shipping sufficient sea-water to fill her, to clear the Boat of water in the short space of one minute. She is so constructed that even supposing a large hole was made in her she would still float, and what is more, carry her crew.

There are several improvements to the steering gear and one addition to the new Boat. Alongside of where the coxswains stand is fitted a neat hardwood watertight box, constructed to hold a metal case for biscuits and also a couple of quart "medicine" bottles and two drinking cups. May the Lifeboatmen never have to go to sea with that box empty!

The *Mary Isabella* has enormous air space, and I am informed by a gentleman who was present, that in undergoing a most severe stability test, the Boat was capsized with all her gear onboard and with the air valves left open so as to allow the water free scope to run into all compartments. Yet notwithstanding all this the grand Boat righted almost as quickly as it was engulfed. The Ramsey men seem highly pleased with the new arrival and Coxswain Garrett and his Crew also speak very highly on the way in which the new Boat behaved whilst being towed astern of the ss Fenella which was proceeding at full speed."

The First Service

The first service of the new Lifeboat took place on the 17th September, 1896, when she was called out to the Ramsey fishing smack GRACE DARLING. The ship was in distress some three to four miles off the harbour piers and the *Mary Isabella* (2) took off her crew of five. Later in the year saw the "Great Storm of 1896" on the 7th and 8th October and the Boat's second service then called upon her finest sea-keeping qualities and also the skill of her Crew.

"The Big Snow" in February, 1885, was followed in Ramsey by the "Great Storm of 1896". The first indication that a storm was on the way was at about 5 p.m. on Wednesday, 7th October. A telegram warning ordered "Hoist South cone: depression approaching from Ireland". Already a fresh SSW wind had backed SE and grown stronger. As darkness fell anxiety was felt for the fishing fleet still at sea, but it soon arrived back and made the harbour with the exception of the half-decker, TWO BROTHERS (Capt. J. White). This vessel eventually made port safely in company with the NERBUDDA of Ramsey and the MARIA JANE of Peel, at about 9 p.m. At the same time two barques were observed to be riding at anchor in the Bay and a close lookout was then kept on them from the Boathouse and the Rocket Brigade Depot.

During the night sections of Ramsey were flooded in spite of barricades; footpaths carried away and piles of shingle washed up on to the promenade. This was only a foretaste of what was to come.

LIFEBOAT LAUNCHED

At daylight on Thursday morning the barometer had fallen to 28.00 ins. (948.2 mbs.) and after a lull with the heavy rain easing up, the wind picked up again from the SSW and blew with fresh fury. It was then seen that one of the barques had been battered and only the stump of her mizzen mast was standing. At 9.25 a.m. the new *Mary Isabella* (2) was summoned and, with Coxswain R. Garrett at the helm, was launched in hurricane force conditions. The Lifeboat was thrown around in spectacular fashion as she sailed out to the barque, some two and a half miles East of the harbour. The barque turned out to be the GIOVANNI of Lillesand, Sweden.

Later in the day wild rumours started to spread amongst the spectators on the waterfront that someone aboard the Lifeboat had been killed. This emanated from the observation that the Boat could, at times, be seen flying a flag at half-mast. At 3.15 p.m., however, the Lifeboat was seen pulling away from the barque. At this time there was a strong lee tide running and so the *Mary Isabella* (2) was brought alongside the Queen's Pier. There was great relief then when it was found out that there had been no mishap and there was cheering when the 13 crew members of the GIOVANNI were landed. She was en-route from Fleetwood to Savannah and only had 380 tons of salt ballast aboard.

It transpired that the half-masted ensign aboard the Lifeboat was meant as a signal for aid from any steamer in the vicinity. The anchor of the *Mary Isabella* (2) had become foul of the barque's own anchor cable. It was decided by the Coxswain, in spite of the extreme peril involved, to hold on to their anchor instead of slipping it, until the tide slackened. This was an ordeal for both the rescuers and the rescued as seas were constantly washing over them whilst they waited. The quart bottle of brandy which was carefully rationed out proved a welcome stimulant under such circumstances!

At half-ebb the Lifeboat sailed under her smallest canvas back to the harbour. There was Press criticism after this event about the lack of assistance from powered steamers, but it is not clear whether any such vessel was ever in the area at the time or if the flag signal was even understood.

At the end of this year the Lifeboat Committee met and proposed that the Coxswain's annual salary be raised to £10 and that of the Asst. Coxswain's to £3. This move was on account of the previous payments being abolished in the new RNLI Rules.

1897

The next year, 1897, was a busy one for the *Mary Isabella* (2) and saw no less than six services.

The first, on the 28th March, was to the brigantine UTO of Lillesand. She lost her anchor in the Bay and her crew of six was landed.

On the 16th June, in gale conditions, the schooners MAID OF IRVINE of Belfast and FURNESS ABBEY of Lancaster dragged their anchors and requested assistance. Their three-man crews were taken off.

The 17th August, 1897, saw the cutter yacht LUCINDA of Beaumaris lying at anchor in the Bay for some 36 hours. As the Lifeboat was out on exercise, she made contact and landed the crew of two. Apparently the yacht had been cruising around the Scottish Coast for a month and the crew was exhausted.

On this same day the steamship BELGIAN KING of Newcastle was seen passing the Point of Ayre Lighthouse "showing flags". The Lifeboat was informed, went alongside her and took a telegram ashore for the Master.

The 28th November saw the schooner NELSON of Belfast aground on Cor Stack, a pinnacle of rock close to Maughold Head Lighthouse. The *Mary Isabella* (2) rescued Capt. Martin, his crew of four and the ship's dog.

Finally, on the 14th December, the crew of three was landed from the schooner GLYNAERON of Beaumaris (Anglesey) when she requested assistance whilst lying at anchor in the Bay in a SE gale.

On the 29th April, 1897, the Ramsey boat NELLIE was fishing off the Bahama Bank when she was struck by a tremendous sea. She sank with all hands and no rescue was possible. Her crew was W. McCormick; his son R. McCormick; W. Partridge and H. Gawne. William McCormick was Bowman of the *Mary Isabella* (2) at the time and after his death W.F. Martin took his place in the Lifeboat.

At a Committee Meeting on the 2nd July, 1897, the desirability was discussed of having a small surf boat for the Station. This came up again at their December meeting but the idea was shelved until the work in progress on the harbour piers was completed.

The Crew also met at the end of the year and they agreed to using the Lifeboat for salvage purposes providing their claims were met by the officer in charge of the vessel or by an arbitrator appointed by the Board of Trade. This was instead of a court of law settling disputes as had been the case to that date. The following year new Salvage Regulations were posted in the Norbury Boathouse.

1898

1898 was yet another busy year for the Lifeboat and eight services were recorded with the saving of some 32 lives.

On the 13th April the ketch NEWLANDS (Capt. Davis) registered in Newport, Monmouthshire, was on a passage from Belfast to the Point of Ayr on the River Dee estuary near Chester. The Lifeboat was launched to take off the Master, his two crewmen and two Ramsey boatmen. Presumably she was sheltering in the Bay during an on-shore gale.

The brigantine PARKSIDE of Dundalk (Capt. Cheshire) got into difficulties in strong winds on the 11th May. She had a cargo of timber aboard from Londonderry to Garston (Liverpool) but not enough dead-weight ballast. The *Mary Isabella* (2) took off the crew of five.

The busiest day of 1898 was the 23rd November which was accompanied by a very bad Easterly gale. The Ramsey Courier newspaper of the day reported:-

> "Very early morning (2.30 a.m.) on the 23rd November in a terrific Easterly gale, signals of distress were seen from a vessel at anchor in the Bay. The Rocket Brigade and the Lifeboat Crew mustered. It was low water and so an attempt was made to launch the Lifeboat with the aid of the haul-off warp. It wouldn't work. The Boat therefore had to be dragged along the beach on its carriage to the Queen's Pier, where a second haul-off warp was made fast. It took two hours from the first maroon being fired to finally launching the Boat. Soon the *Mary Isabella* (2) got alongside the schooner WILLIAM THOMPSON of Dumfries, took off the crew of four and then ran before the gale and was skilfully brought over the bar in mountainous seas to the safety of the harbour.
>
> Immediately following this service, further excitement took place on the seafront. A steamer was observed approaching the harbour but making very heavy weather of it. As she neared the entrance she was steering badly and broached-to on top of an unusually big sea. By the skin of their teeth they missed hitting the piers and berthed safely.
>
> At 8.10 a.m. a Duddon schooner entered Ramsey and reported another vessel was flying distress signals out in the Bay. The storm was by now hurricane-force but again the Lifeboat went out and safely returned with the ship's crew of five from the Whitehaven schooner BESSIE ARNOLD.
>
> The final service was at 11.10 a.m. that day when the only steamship still registered in Ramsey, the MANX MAID, came to anchor in the Bay and hoisted distress signals. The Lifeboat responded and brought ashore her crew of five. Thus 14 seamen were landed in 10 hours."

The final services of 1898 were on the 27th December when the Stranraer schooner TWIN SISTERS developed windlass trouble in the Bay during a SW'ly gale and called for assistance. She was on passage from Liverpool to Drummore in Ireland. This was at 3 p.m. and the Lifeboat was launched. On her way to the TWIN SISTERS the Lifeboat spotted a distress signal flying from the Aberdovey schooner ANNIE WARREN (78 tons) which was sheltering whilst en-route from Plymouth to Preston. The *Mary Isabella* (2) took off her crew of five first and landed them on the Queen's Pier. She then proceeded to pick up the three-man crew of the other schooner. Yet a third ship, the schooner RETURN registered in Greenock and on passage from London to Whitehaven, requested help at about the same time and her crew of five was also landed.

1899

The New Year of 1899 opened up with continued winter gales and it wasn't long before the *Mary Isabella* (2) was out assisting ships once more. Both on the 2nd January and 12th the crew of the TWIN SISTERS was landed yet again! That made it three times for them within three weeks – surely a "record" even to this day?

On the 28th March in late afternoon the schooner MAXIM of Drogheda rounded Maughold Head with her sails in ribbons and ran ashore near the Lifeboat slipway. She was on her final passage in ballast from her home port to Liverpool to become a hulk. Her crew of four was landed by the *Mary Isabella* (2).

The year was then quiet until late October when more gales produced further maritime drama off the coasts of the Isle of Man. The 31st October to the 9th November, 1899, may well have been the peak of Ramsey Bay's shipping dramas of the era, due, as usual, to severe weather conditions around the North Channel and the Irish Sea.

The Cordillera Episode

On Tuesday, 31st October, the large barque CORDILLERA registered in Buenos Aires (Argentina) was seen to anchor in the vicinity of the Bahama Bank, NNE of Ramsey. This ship was built in Nova Scotia in 1873 and was currently Norwegian owned with a Norwegian Master. She was on passage from Saint John, New Brunswick, to Newry, Ireland, with a cargo of timber and had been out for some 51 days in stormy conditions. Her anchorage position was perilous in the SW wind and two stern trawlers, the STAG of Ramsey and the LADY LOCH of Douglas, offered to tow her into safer waters in Ramsey Bay. Their offer was declined but when the half-decker FORRESTER contacted her Captain he agreed to send a message ashore asking for a tug to be sent from Liverpool.

The tug KNIGHT OF ST. GEORGE was dispatched on the 1st November, arriving in Ramsey Bay on the 2nd. Also with her came the tug PRAIRIE COCK on a "no cure no pay" basis – pay which they certainly earned in the end. In the meantime on the 31st the weather grew worse and a close watch from the shore was being kept on the ship and also on the schooner CONCORD of Dublin and the three-masted schooner VICTORIA of Porth Madog in Cardigan Bay.

As darkness fell the wind increased from the South, gradually veering SW, and so it was not surprising when the maroons were fired calling for the launching of the *Mary Isabella* (2). Everyone ashore guessed that it was the big barque in trouble. As expected, when the Lifeboat reached her it was found that she had already parted her best anchor cable and was holding on, but labouring heavily, to her second anchor which was not expected to hold. The CORDILLERA's crew of 11 was successfully transferred to the Lifeboat and landed in Ramsey.

On Thursday, 2nd November, the tug KNIGHT OF ST. GEORGE towed out a large open boat with the Captain of the barque and nine of his crew. One hand, a Limerick man, had declined to go and stayed in Ramsey. Four local boatmen also went along and, with great difficulty in the SW swell, all managed to board the CORDILLERA.

The tug, with the assistance of the PRAIRIE COCK, managed to tow the ship into a snug anchorage near the Queen's Pier.

The tug Skipper actually wanted to bring the ship into harbour but her Master, being Norwegian, would hear none of it and refused to give up that easily. By that time there were 12ft. of water in her hold and his idea was to ship ten extra men to man the pumps and then carry on to Newry. But it was not to be, as another gale blew up from the SW. During this time her Master was ashore conducting some business and had taken four of his crew with him. That left five hands aboard, as the local boatmen had also come ashore.

Again the CORDILLERA started to drag her anchor. People were surprised because this anchor had held well when off the Bahama Bank. The Captain and his four men could only watch helplessly from the shore. The gale gradually increased to storm force and shortly before 11 a.m. the anchor cable parted. The Bay was crowded with shipping and the CORDILLERA at once drifted down on the steamship SPINEL of Glasgow, which had been anchored in her lee. The steamship's crew rushed up to their foc'sle as the two ships met, but the impact was not severe and, taking advantage of the situation, the Chief Mate of the CORDILLERA and three hands jumped on to the deck of the SPINEL. The fourth man, Durham, was not so fortunate and was left behind – he later said that he felt like Robinson Crusoe having to remain alone in his ship!

The tug PRAIRIE COCK then manoeuvred close enough to get a line aboard the barque to seaman Durham but he was unable to make a hawser fast. However, three tug men managed to jump aboard and between them they got a tow rope around the foremast. The KNIGHT OF ST. GEORGE also got a rope aboard but neither tug could get into a proper towing position owing to the fierceness of the weather. By this time all three were drifting North, getting perilously near the Point of Ayre.

Mary Isabella Launched

During the morning the Lifeboatmen had been watching events and soon the maroons were fired and the *Mary Isabella* (2) was away within three minutes of the summons; it was a high water launch. Once at sea the Crew realised that they were carrying too much canvas and they had to reduce sail as the Boat was almost swamped. It was not too long before they got alongside the CORDILLERA and took off all four men aboard her. In shoving off, however, one of the barque's braces fouled the Lifeboat's mast and almost sucked her under. The son of John Garrett, Coxswain, clambered aboard the ship in his heavy oilskins and cords and cut away the offending rope with an axe. Fortunately for them, the Lifeboat's Sampson Post took the full weight of the crushing and it was smashed to pieces. In order to get away from the barque's side the Lifeboatmen had to use their oars as the suction of the large ship and the ebb tide running North were so strong. After getting clear and using the smallest possible canvas, it was found that working to windward was impossible so the anchor had to be let go where they were. The sea was terrific and the Lifeboat shipped tons of water but they could do nothing but hold on at anchor.

Whilst the Lifeboat's Crew and the rescued were in this dangerous position the two tugs were fighting a losing battle as they were being carried still nearer to the Point of Ayre. The

F. Henry A. Christian collection

Launching the *Mary Isabella* (2) using the haul-off warp c.1890. Hon. Sec. E.C. Kerr watching proceedings. Cox Robert Garrett.

W.S. Basnett collection

Down she goes. Another launch of the *Mary Isabella* (2).

PRAIRIE COCK's tow parted and fouled her propeller, putting her broadside on to the sea which even got into her engine room. It looked as if they would have to signal the Lifeboat. For a time, however, their engineer managed to keep the engine going ahead and astern until at last he got her going "slow ahead"; they did not even dare to stop then to take the Lifeboat in tow.

After reaching harbour it took four men several hours with cold chisels to get their screw clear.

The KNIGHT OF ST. GEORGE also carried away her tow and so the CORDILLERA was again abandoned – twice within three days. The tug then picked up the *Mary Isabella* (2) and towed her to Ramsey, dropping her South of her Station as the tide had fallen back. In the meantime feelings were running very high ashore as nobody knew if they had carried out the rescue successfully or not. When, after much difficulty owing to heavy cross seas, the Boat was beached and the crowd ashore realised that the rescue had been achieved, their excitement knew no bounds and they were ready to carry the Boat and her Crew to her House but were prevented from doing so by the seas crashing on the beach. Feelings about a rescue had never been known to run so high before.

ANOTHER ATTEMPT

On Saturday morning early, the 4th November, the steam trawler ROSE ANN of Douglas and the tug PRAIRIE COCK left harbour to search for the CORDILLERA. In the meantime the four men from her who had jumped aboard the SPINEL were landed. At 10 a.m. the barque was sighted by the Point of Ayre Lighthouse Keeper, hull down and in the tow of a steamship. When the Skipper of the KNIGHT OF ST. GEORGE heard this, he also left harbour as soon as he floated and proceeded North. At 4 p.m. it was reported from the Lighthouse that the barque was in too close upon the Point. It appears that at first light of day the ROSE ANN had come up on the barque, put four men aboard and then commenced towing at about 7 a.m., some 14 miles NE of the Point of Ayre. The tow parted. In the meantime the PRAIRIE COCK arrived and took over the tow, joined later by the KNIGHT OF ST. GEORGE. Already it had started to blow hard yet again from the SW, but this time neither tug would let go! They spent an anxious night in Ramsey Bay which again was crowded with shipping, but they dared not enter the harbour during the hours of darkness.

Sunday morning saw the weather fine away and allowed the tugs to make preparations to enter harbour, which they did at noon: the PRAIRIE COCK ahead and the KNIGHT OF ST. GEORGE astern of their charge. Owing to her exceptional draft, Capt. Clarke, the Harbour Master, berthed the CORDILLERA at the Steam Packet berth. She was by then drawing 18ft, her hold having 16ft of water in it. She lay in this berth for two days whilst local carpenter John Dodd and her own ship's carpenter patched her up to enable her to berth in the inner harbour. At this time she was the largest laden vessel to ever enter Ramsey, having aboard some 375 standards of timber (1100 tons) which was eventually discharged in the port. Even with all her battering she did not appear to be in bad condition, despite her sails having carried away. Her cargo was valued at £4,000 and at first her salvage was reckoned at £1,000, with a claim which would be put in by the ROSE ANN.

MORE CASUALTIES

This same day another Norwegian brigantine, the BERTHA of Tonsberg, was sighted in Ramsey Bay with a heavy list. She was loaded with timber which was assigned to Mr. R. Cowley of Ramsey and when brought in by local boatmen, her Master stated that they had had a very bad passage from Sundsvall, Sweden, having left there on the 2nd October. Whilst she was in the North Channel on Friday, 2nd November, she was caught in the worst of the gale and lost a man overboard and a lot of deck cargo as well. Further to the South in Ramsey Bay another large barque was sighted which proved to be the FIN, bound from Pictou, Nova Scotia, to Preston. She was 28 days out and also had a cargo of timber. A small boat was noticed coming ashore from her and having a stiff pull. In it were her Master and four men and they landed at the Queen's Pier. The Master had come ashore to send a telegram to Preston for a pilot and to report losing an anchor the previous night. He also stated that he nearly lost the ship near the Chickens (Southern Coast of the Isle of Man) on the previous Friday and had to carry extra canvas to save her from being wrecked.

SIXTEEN MEN SAVED

On the night of 8th November, the Portuguese barque AFRICA of Lisbon (726 tons and Capt. Riberio) left the shelter of Ramsey Bay whilst on her passage from Liverpool to Bahia in Brazil with general cargo. She returned to the Bay on the 9th in a strong SSE breeze under lower and upper top-sails. As darkness fell she fired a blue flare, which, as the weather wasn't too bad, was answered by some local boatmen in their own boat. The Master told them that they were not required but by midnight the strong breeze had turned into a SE'ly gale. The *Mary Isabella* (2) was launched and took off all 15 men and a Trinity House pilot.

The "Ramsey Courier" of the 22nd December, 1899, gives a full account of the final service of the year which took place on Saturday night, 16th December, to the Aberystwyth schooner RUBY. Four men were saved.

"There are two Coxwains, one Bowman and 25 enrolled men who can be picked as Crew Members. This night the Crew was R. Garrett, Cox; Oscar Corlett, Asst. Cox; W. Martin, Bowman; and W. Christian, W. Corkish, Jas. Cottier and J. White. The shore gang consisted of a signalman, a man in charge of the flares and a till-man to navigate the Lifeboat carriage.

The methods of launching; if the tide is up and the wind off the land, the carriage is run down the slipway and the Boat slipped off it directly into the sea. If the wind is on-shore, the haul-off warp must be used each time. The haul-off warp is a long rope rove through a large block laid down below the low-water mark. One end is made fast at the Lifeboat slip and the other at the slip opposite the Albert Hotel (the site of the present-day swimming pool). Here the bight of the warp is passed through a bull's eye at the bottom of the sea wall and the three parts of rope fastened to the promenade railings in such a way that the rope can be got at at all stages of the tide. Further, this end is the hauling part."

A strong S'ly wind arose on Friday night the 15th December and several vessels, including a number of Fleetwood trawlers, arrived in port. The weather worsened on Saturday and more Lancashire fishermen put in for shelter and also the Trinity House steamship STELLA. The wind was South and a moderate gale. A steamship and a schooner anchored in the Bay. During the afternoon the wind veered SSE and freshened, throwing a heavy sea into the Bay. The schooner was riding it heavily and it seemed that she might well need assistance before the night was over.

Groups of Fleetwood fishermen full of drink became a nuisance in the town by evening, accosting people and being rowdy. By 10 p.m. the West Quay became somewhat of a battlefield with a few belligerent local people also involved.

At 10 p.m. the schooner showed distress flares for the Lifeboat. The wind was still a SSE gale but the seas appeared heavier than the wind warranted. The maroons were was set off and the Crew mustered immediately, but the signal also caused many of the revellers to muster at the Boathouse full of "Dutch" courage and prepared to become unwanted "heroes of the hour". As the Boat was being hauled out with the Crew aboard, the large crowd presented a problem which the Police were unable to deal with. One man reportedly got aboard the Lifeboat and lay across the cable saying: "You'll never be in want of a man as long as I'm about." The Coxswain certainly wasn't in need of this gentleman and he was summarily ejected! Others tugged at the carriage and ropes and one pulled the steering pole of the carriage away from the official steersman and one of the fore wheels banged into the door-frame of the Boathouse. Mr. Kerr, Hon. Secretary, implored the crowd to keep clear, but to no avail.

The *Mary Isabella* (2) was finally hauled on to the Promenade. The haul-off warp had to be used and was made fast to the Boat, and the other end, near the Albert Hotel, cast adrift. When hauling commenced, however, nothing happened and it appeared that the warp was fouled near the bull's eye. Mr. Kerr and Capt. Gawne did their utmost to clear it, but the sea was too rough for them and they were beaten back. The haulers again tried their luck but first pulled the Promenade railings down and then the warp parted. It became apparent that the Crew would have to pull themselves off on the "standing" part of the rope. The Lifeboat was therefore run down the slip but the shore-gang member who was to slip the Boat from the carriage did so too soon and the carriage up-ended and the Boat's bow slipped off and hit the concrete slip. Just as this happened some breakers tumbled on to the beach and lifted the Boat and carriage and tipped them over the lee side of the slip. A launcher was also swept off the carriage and tossed around like a cork, but luckily someone plucked him out of the water. As the carriage became submerged the Boat floated off but broadside on to the seas which broke right over her.

On shore there was great excitement and also apprehension amongst the large crowd of spectators, as the occurance was plainly visible in the moonlight. After working with a tremendous will, the Crew managed to extricate the Boat from the wheels of the carriage and move out to seaward. However, with a strong North-running current and the onshore gale, the Boat started to drift down on to the stonework of the South Pier. The First Officer of the Rocket Brigade, Mr. C.B. Heyes, seeing imminent danger to the Lifeboatmen, fired their muster signal and members immediately took their gear on to the Pier. The Lifeboat was getting very close to it and they hoisted their fore-lug, making every effort to ease the Boat around the end of the pier. The shore crowd, including the High Bailiff, held their breath. Suddenly a call: "She's clear!" was heard, and true enough, the *Mary Isabella* (2) was clear of danger. She hoisted sail and sped away to the schooner RUBY, taking off and landing her crew of four on the Queen's Pier at 1 a.m. on Sunday, 17th. The launch had taken 21 minutes instead of five. The ship herself was on passage from Stranraer to Liverpool with a cargo of oilcake and foodstuffs with its Owner-Master, Capt. Jones.

COMMITTEE MATTERS

In 1900 the Rev. George Paton died, after being in office as Honorary Secretary, and later as Chairman, for 31 years. The Committee passed a resolution of condolence to his family and at the same time elected his son, the Rev. Edward Paton, as a member of the Committee. He was curate of St. Paul's, Ramsey, but only served the Lifeboat for a year as he was then posted to London. High Bailiff Cruikshank was elected the next Chairman and served as such for 16 years.

During the meetings held in 1900 it was seen that the Lifeboat Committee was sensitive about lifeboat work being given to local men. The Secretary was requested to point out to the RNLI in London that repairs to the Boathouse had been carried out by a Douglas firm and that in future such work should be done by local tradesmen.

A discussion also took place over a bill for £620 from the vendor of the land which formed the yard to the Boathouse. The Committee had had no Bill of Sale for this land and so the vendor was still at liberty to dispose of it at a higher price than he had requested from the Committee. It was now 10 years since the yard had first been used and no rent had been asked for or paid. The Hon. Secretary was therefore empowered to offer W. Walker & Co. £100 as rent, but a year later they gave up the land to the owner.

After the turn of the century life became somewhat quieter for the Ramsey Lifeboatmen, no doubt due to the increase of steam-powered ships and possibly to less adverse weather conditions and, of course, two World Wars. During the next four decades up to a maximum of three services a year were recorded, apart from the routine exercises which were gradually increased from quarterly ones to monthly ones as at present. After the Second World War, however, as coastal shipping generally increased the new motor lifeboats were kept busy and so it continued for a further 30 years until the steep decline in merchant shipping in the 1970's.

Three services were completed in 1900.

On the 3rd August the fishing smack QUEEN of Douglas got into difficulties and the Lifeboat rendered assistance to her.

The 4th October saw the *Mary Isabella* (2) launched at 5.30 a.m. to help the Norwegian barque TOPDAL of Mandal (536 tons) which was dragging her anchor off the Bahama Bank. Her crew of 8 was taken off. The ship had a cargo of pitchpine from Apricolo for Whitehaven and had been a week awaiting sufficient water in her discharging port.

Near the end of the year, on the 17th December, the schooner RHEIDOL VALE of Aberystwyth (75 tons) requested that her crew be landed after being at anchor in Ramsey Bay for several days during gale conditions. She was on a short passage from Belfast to Porthmadog.

Five days later on the 22nd, the Lifeboat was out for seven hours searching off the Point of Ayre. The Lighthouse Keeper had reported seeing a vessel showing distress signals. Nothing was ever found but it may have been the barque CUMBRIA which disappeared without trace about the same time.

On the 18th August, 1901, the ss CORNELIAN whilst light-ship and on a passage from her home port of Glasgow, stranded in fog between Cranstal and the Point of Ayre. She floated off on the rising tide and so needed no assistance.

During 1902 the Lifeboat Committee agreed with the Ramsey Commissioners to recover *The Two Sisters* Lifeboat which had been in retirement and on show in Mooragh Park. She had fallen into disrepair and was put up for sale or for breaking up.

The schooner ELLESMERE of Runcorn got into difficulties in the Bay on the 8th February, 1902. The Lifeboat was launched in the forenoon and landed her crew of three. Later Lifeboatmen brought the ship into Ramsey.

Later in the year, on the 11th November, the Spanish steamship AVILES, from Santander to Harrington with a cargo of iron-ore, had rudder problems and anchored in the Bay. She put a small boat over the side with two men in order to inspect the trouble but they began to drift away on the tide. A second boat with a crew of four was then lowered from the ship to go to their aid. This was unsuccessful as they, too, had to contend with the tide and both boats were seen being pulled vigorously towards the harbour entrance. The *Mary Isabella* (2) was launched as a precaution and escorted the team of rowers safely ashore.

During the following year of 1903 the Liverpool schooner ELIZABETH went aground on Ramsey's North Shore. She had a cargo of freestone and was en-route from Bristol to Dublin. The Lifeboat was launched but the water was too shallow for her to get near the ship. The Rocket Brigade waded out to get a line aboard and took off three seamen and a boy.

An entry in the Branch Minutes Book records a routine visit of the area RNLI Inspector in August, 1903. He recommended that the following work should be undertaken:-

1. The painting of the Lifeboat as soon as possible.
2. The drogue to be used in practices.
3. The cracks in the slip-way to be attended to.
4. A w.c. for use of the Coxswain's family to be added to the premises.
5. A rack to be made for drying oilskins.
6. Two duck lamps to be purchased.

In 1904 Mrs. Elizabeth Cowle of Andreas, near Ramsey, left a legacy of £500 to be used for the purposes decided by the local Lifeboat Committee. Another gift of £100 from Mrs. Teare of "Eden Cottage", Ramsey, was donated and both sums were invested in an Endowment Fund set up for the first time. It is still in

W.S. Basnett collection

Crew of the *Mary Isabella* (2) in the late 1890s. Some of the men identified: H. Corkish, E. Corlett, F. Corlett, O. Corlett, J. Crix, J. Garrett, P. Sharpe.

operation to this day and has regularly received funds to assist the Branch. At the end of the year it was reported to the Committee that a figure of £350 had been agreed upon with W. Walker & Co. for the purchase of the Boathouse yard.

During the early evening of the 29th January, 1904, the Lifeboat was launched to take off the four-man crew of the Barrow registered schooner USEFUL, anchored in the Bay. The following afternoon a steam trawler put four men aboard the ship in order to commandeer her, considering her a "derelict". The USEFUL's Master saw what was happening from the shore and immediately went out with his crew to order the men off his vessel. They complied and the schooner was taken to a better anchorage!

On the 10th November, the schooner ELIZABETH ELLEN FISHER of Fleetwood (90 tons) lost her main-sail whilst on passage from Whitehaven to Strangford Lough with coal. The *Mary Isabella* (2) was launched at 3.30 a.m. and landed her crew of four.

THE CONQUEROR DISASTER

1905 brought tragedy to Ramsey Bay for six Liverpool mariners of the tug CONQUEROR. Although the Lifeboat was not launched and the Rocket Brigade failed to effect a full rescue (through no fault of their own), the disaster became a controversial talking point on the Island for many years to come. The "Isle of Man Times" of the 21st January that year gave a very full account of the incident and subsequent inquest and painted a vivid picture of the circumstances:

> "The tug CONQUEROR owned by the Alexandra Towing Company of Liverpool entered Ramsey Bay about noon on Saturday, 14th January, under sail and she came to anchor. (En-route from Liverpool to the Orkney Islands). A boat went out in answer to her signals and learned that her boiler had given way and she was unable to raise steam. The Skipper wanted a telegram sent to his owners requesting help.
>
> The sea and wind began to rise and by Saturday evening it was blowing a gale from the ESE. This continued throughout Sunday and the Rocket Brigade and Lifeboat Crew were in readiness all Sunday night to render assistance should it be needed. On Monday morning she was still holding on to her anchor. At about a quarter to twelve, however, her single cable parted and she hoisted the distress signal. At noon the signal gun for the Rocket Brigade was fired. Meanwhile the tug began to drift towards the North Shore. A rush was made to get the rocket cart out but some delay was experienced and it was about a quarter of an hour

before they got started. The CONQUEROR drifted North to leeward and eventually struck the shore just North of the Ramsey Hydro (now the Grand Island Hotel), and some 300 yards from land. Fortunately the beach is sandy and as soon as this happened a small boat was launched from the tug with one crew-man in it. After sheltering under the lee of the doomed vessel, it made for the shore. There were tremendous seas rolling in and every moment the spectators, of whom there were hundreds, expected to see the boat capsize. She was, however, splendidly managed and although the seas broke over her continually, she was not swamped and at last made the shore. The sailor jumped into the tide and was caught hold of by two men who brought him to safety. He turned out to be Wm. Wilson, the Cook – a boy of 17.

The sea on the beach was very heavy and the terrific wind driving before it blinding sheets of spray, and, what was worse, fine sand. It made standing on the shore a difficult job. The ship was lying partly broadside on to the sea, thus forming a sort of breakwater, with comparatively smooth water inside. She was in about 6ft or 8ft of water which, within 100 yards of her, shallowed to 2ft or 3ft. If the crew could have, as soon as they grounded, or at any time within two hours afterwards, launched their port boat, there was no reason why they could not have got safely ashore. Or they could have jumped over with lifebelts and either swum or have been washed ashore.

Rocket Brigade Attempt a Rescue

Soon after the tug struck, the Rocket Brigade arrived on the scene. Their first rocket, considering the wind and the distance of the wreck, was a good shot, just missing the bow of the vessel and being carried to leeward. Two more attempts in quick succession were made to get a line aboard, but both rockets were delivered too low and were beaten into the tide close inshore. A fourth rocket was fired from a point further North and it reached the tug amid cheers, dropping near her stern. The CONQUEROR in the meantime, had been severely knocked about, being lifted by the seas and bumped on to the shore. So bad was the shaking which she received that her funnel went overboard. It was low water when she struck and the rising tide commenced to break over her in great sheets which eventually filled the ship.

One member of the crew of the tug went up the mast and got hold of the rocket-line, and all hands aboard commenced hauling on it. After ten minutes or so, from some cause or another, they gave it up and went up on to the bridge and into the wheelhouse. The Coastguards signalled to them to haul out but they did not appear to understand. Time after time the Rocket Brigade signalled to them in every possible way to resume hauling, but they appeared to take no notice. First Officer Taylor had the whips carried to windward to see if they were foul and then dropped them into the tide so that the crew could haul them on board as they were washed to the lee, but again without success. The Rocket Brigade were all by this time up to their ankles or waists in water. It went on until 3 p.m. when word was sent round to the Lifeboat to try and effect a rescue.

The Lifeboatmen were standing-by at the Boathouse when the signal went off and the Boat was ready almost at once. A good deal of discussion seemed to take place as to what should be done. To launch the Boat from the slip-way or from the Queen's Pier seemed possible enough but for some inexplicable reason the Boat was taken on her carriage over to to the North Shore to the scene of the disaster. She was launched and an attempt made to haul her off to the wreck by the rocket line which was still attached to the vessel. The rope, as was to be expected, either parted or pulled away, and the Boat was hurled back on to the beach. Another attempt was made to get the Boat out using oars but it was entirely impossible.

Darkness set in and the fate of the men on the tug became almost hopeless. They had ben waiting for help for five hours and seeing that all assistance from the shore was impossible, they apparently made up their minds to risk jumping, one by one, into the sea and trusting to be washed up. Hundreds of willing hands were waiting to secure them."

Four men, including her Master, Capt. Brown, reached the dry land safely but six perished in those breakers crashing on the shore.

The Inquiry

It was conjectured later that had the Lifeboat been launched at the time the first distress flag was seen, she could have been alongside the CONQUEROR before the tug grounded. The only possible way was for the *Mary Isabella* (2) to go to sea and then drop down on to the tug using a kedge anchor. However, the Coxswain thought this impossible but taking the Boat around to the North Shore seemed to be a mistake considering the conditions there.

At the inquest Capt. Brown of the tug explained that his crew had refused his orders to continue hauling the rocket-line whip.

At the next Lifeboat Committee Meeting on the 31st January, 1906, the Hon. Secretary, Mr. E.C. Kerr, explained that originally the rescue was a Rocket Brigade one and that the Lifeboat was not launched until they were told that no progress was being made in getting the men off the ship. This happened at 2.00 p.m., but the Crew did not think that they could launch from the Queen's Pier area and so they elected to attempt to do so from the North Shore. Mr. Kerr agreed with this decision. At the meeting, however, the Chairman and Committee were of the opinion that the Lifeboat should have been launched from near the Queen's Pier and the Crew agreed later that, had there been no Rocket Brigade, then the launch would have been attempted from the Pier. Further discussion on the topic took place at the March Committee Meeting and a report to the area RNLI Inspector on the reasons for not launching the Lifeboat in the normal manner was read out and agreed upon.

Other matters discussed by the Lifeboat Committee in 1906 included the sum of £315

Ramsey RNLI collection

Ramsey Harbour during the construction of the Swing Bridge, c.1890.

From a painting by Elmer Keene

D. Reed collection

Ramsey Harbour by moonlight in the early 1900s.

which Headquarters in London had earmarked for the purchase of the plot of land adjoining the boathouse. (The full price was £350). The Endowment Fund was reported to stand at £600 with most of the amount invested in the Isle of Man Railways. The Committee also decided to look into the matter of insuring the Crew for injury and the following sums were allotted: £1 per week pension for total disablement and half this sum for partial disablement; £100 to the next of kin as a result of a death amongst the crew; and the crew to receive 5/- each for Christmas out of the Endowment Fund.

In mid-January, 1906, the Lifeboat was launched when it was reported that flares had been seen out in the Bay. It turned out to be a wild-goose chase as it was only a steam trawler cleaning her fish at night with the aid of flares. This was a procedure much discouraged by the authorities but still carried on from time to time.

Personal Compensation

Late the same year the Committee received a claim for £20 compensation from a Mr. John Kerr of Hale in Cheshire. It appertained to an unusual occurrence. Mrs. Kerr had been sitting on the North Shore at Ramsey on Lifeboat Day during August. She had been struck on the thigh by the buffer of a rocket fired from the Boathouse area, some 500 yards away and on the other side of the harbour. The Committee did not accept liability but offered £10 in good faith. This was later followed by a repeat of the offer plus any medical expenses incurred. The rocket manufacturers ultimately agreed to pay £15 in compensation.

At the end of the year the steam trawler Crown of Fleetwood struck rocks at Traie ny Unaig, South of Ballafayle-e-Callow. The crew of 10 landed in a small boat and made their way to Corteen's, Ballacannell. An attempt to salvage the ship was made the following year but it was unsuccessful and later she turned over in a gale and disappeared.

The 20th February, 1907, produced a day of WNW gales. Overnight the wind veered a little to the NW and brought snow. Over 20 steamships were at anchor and sheltering in Ramsey Bay and also the Barrow schooner Isabella. She was on a short passage from Belfast to Connah's Quay, near Chester. After spending three days at anchor she requested the Lifeboat to take off her crew of four. After the gales the ship was brought into the harbour.

The year 1907 brought the retirement of Mr. E.C. Kerr as Honorary Secretary to the Branch, on the grounds of ill-health. He received a Resolution of Thanks from the Institution for his 26 years of service. His place was first taken by Mr. W.L. Corlett for three years and then in 1910 by Mr. D. Vondy.

1908 was a quiet year and only one launch was recorded. This was on the 28th June to the Runcorn schooner Guiding Star. Her crew of four was taken off.

At a Committee Meeting some three weeks earlier it was agreed to sell a plot of land adjoining the Boathouse for £150. This included the right to build up against the Boathouse gable. Towards the end of the following year the minutes of meetings contained references to Coxswain J. Corkish being incapacitated and to the death of another J. Corkish in the steamship Ellan Vannin sinking. A year later the Committee approved a payment of £12 to Assistant Cox W. Martin for acting as Cox during the disablement of Mr. Corkish.

On the 8th January, 1910, the Belfast schooner Glide was moored in Ramsey Bay to two anchors. They became foul and the steam trawler Trent, registered in Fleetwood, tried to assist. In doing so she carried away part of the Glide's bowsprit. The Lifeboat was called out to take off the crew of four but later that night the wind got up and the Lifeboat returned to the schooner to put men aboard to man her bilge pumps.

This ship was eventually wrecked near Peel in February, 1915. A court decided that the ship had been unseaworthy and the plaintiff, a David Crawford who was a tile manufacturer of Carty, was awarded the cargo of tiles which defendants George Flack and Frank Fawcett had seized for salvage charges. These two gentlemen were also ordered to return the £9 freight fee.

The Manchester Connection

Later in 1910, on the 18th August, the Lighthouse Keeper at the Point of Ayre reported sighting a yacht dragging her anchor nearby and without masts or sails. The *Mary Isabella* (2) was launched in the early evening. The yacht was the Sea Bird of Caernarfon and en-route from Lamlash on the Clyde to North Wales. She had been cruising around the Scottish Coast for some weeks with her owners, two Manchester businessmen. On their way South they had encountered fierce SW'ly gales and ended up in a distressed condition off the Island's North Coast. The Lifeboat took off the crew of three and returned to Ramsey after some considerable difficulty, landing them at the pier at 4 a.m. the next morning. Later, after the gale, the yacht was retrieved.

Two years later, during Manchester's Lifeboat Day, those same businessmen saw some of their rescuers and their Boat being paraded down the city's Market Street. No doubt their thoughts went back to that evening in August when their first sight of this Lifeboat was of her in a smother of white horses in the tide-race off the Point of Ayre and coming to their assistance.

Manx Museum and National Trust archives

Mary Isabella (2). Crew, Launchers and Officers c.1910.

Back row, L to R: J. Crix, A. Palmer, T. Cowle, T. Wilson, E. Corlett, J. McCormick, J. Kerruish, I. Gawne, J. Graham, J. Killey, C. Kneale, F. Cannell. Centre row: P. Sharpe, J. Christian, O. Corlett, W. Corkish, J. Crix, W. Martin (2nd Cox), W. Christian, J. Garrett, F. Corlett, W. Clarke. Front row: J. Gawne, C. Godfrey, J. Crix (Bowman), J.M. Cruickshank, J.P. (Chairman), Harry Corkish (Cox), D. Vondy (Hon. Sec.), W. Christian, J. Cottier.

Ramsey RNLI collection

Launching the *Mary Isabella* (2) on a service in the early 1900s.

One can imagine their thoughts of thankfulness to the men of RNLI on that occasion!

The Ramsey Lifeboat has always had the closest association with Manchester. Both *The Two Sisters* and the *Mary Isabella* (1) (as has been mentioned), were paid for by generous donations received through the Manchester RNLI Branch. In 1911 James Grimble Groves, one-time Member of Parliament for South Salford and who was Hon. Treasurer of the Manchester and Salford Branch, was invited to join the Ramsey Committee. He had a summer residence in Port-e-Vullen, near the port, which later became a permanent family residence. It was Mr. Groves who, in 1912, arranged for representatives of the crew to go to Manchester on Lifeboat Day when they manned the Boat standing in it with their oars held upright as they were drawn by horses and paraded through the main streets.

Services in 1911

The year 1911 provided four services for the Crew of the *Mary Isabella* (2). On the 21st February the Barrow schooner Claggan was sheltering in Ramsey Bay whilst on passage from Dublin to Peel. She dragged her anchor and the Lifeboat took off her crew of three and a terrier pup.

In the late afternoon of the 29th October, the ketch x.l. of Castletown was in difficulty off the port and the *Mary Isabella* (2) took off her four-man crew.

The early hours of Saturday morning, the 12th November, saw the Ramsey trawler Faithful in trouble off Ramsey. She was returning from fishing in severe gale conditions when her rudder-head collapsed and she had no alternative but to anchor. The Isle of Man Steam Packet's Fenella was also in the Bay, waiting to berth when wind and tide allowed. Capt. Tanner of this ship saw distress flares from the Faithful and took the Fenella close by but was unable to assist in the conditions and he, too, set off rocket flares to summon the Lifeboat to the Faithful. The Boat was soon on its way after a very difficult launch in which helper John Graham was twice swept off his feet by the seas. The trawler's crew of three was landed safely and the ship survived the night and was berthed after the gale on the Sunday.

Help for Lightship

The fourth "service" of 1911 on the 1st September was actually counted as an exercise, but turned out to be an errand of mercy.

In the forenoon of that day flag signals were observed flying from the Bahama Bank Lightship requesting a boat. As it was low water and there were no suitable boats afloat, Mr. Vondy, Hon. Secretary, decided that, as an exercise was due anyway, the Lifeboat should answer the signal. There was a strong WSW breeze blowing and a new haul-off warp, which had only recently been put in place, was used in the launch. The Boat returned at noon with a Seaman Wulford who required medical assistance. It turned out that he had a heart disease and was in a weakened condition. After initial treatment he was sent home to Holyhead via Douglas. That afternoon visitors to the Island who had watched the proceedings insisted upon taking collection boxes out. They included the Hon. Secretary of the Blackpool Lifeboat; the Secretary and Chairman of the Bradford Branch and a member of the Manchester Demonstration Team. They collected £2.16s.6d. The local Committee afterwards wrote to Trinity House asking for "expenses" to cover the service and suggested a payment for the Crew as well. There was no record of the outcome. Sadly, Mr. Wulford died later, on the 4th November.

Also in 1911 a new acetylene beach light was provided for night launches and recoveries. The Lifeboatmen were also issued with new kapok-filled life-jackets. These replaced the original standard-issue cork slab ones and were considerably lighter and more comfortable to wear and had been gradually introduced to stations over the past four years.

In 1912 the Rev. M.W. Harrison and Mr. A.H. Teare were elected to the Committee. They were both destined to hold future office as Chairman and Secretary of the Branch.

1912

During this year only two services were recorded.

The first, on the 17th July, was to the Port St. Mary (Isle of Man) schooner Jessie Sinclair. Although she was sheltering in the Bay and did not request assistance, obviously it was considered ashore that she was in danger as both the Rocket Brigade and Lifeboat Crews turned out and the *Mary Isabella* (2) was launched shortly before 2 a.m. Records show that the Lifeboat assisted in saving the ship and her crew of four and the Committee directed the Chairman, Mr. Cruikshank, to attend to the claim against the ship's owners put in by the Branch Secretary for salvage expenses.

The Lifeboat was out again on the stormy night of the 26th November when the schooner Princess Louise signalled for help in the Bay. She was on passage from Garston to Rosstrevor, and the Lifeboat had considerable difficulty getting alongside. Her crew of four was taken off.

The Ladies' Auxiliary

Afloat, 1913 saw no services but ashore there was considerable Committee activity with an increase in members and agreement to form a Ladies' Auxiliary. Mrs. Harrison was, in effect, the Founder and the first officers were Mrs. Cruickshank, President; Mrs. Norbury, Vice

G.D. Learoyd collection

A rough day for launching – using the haul-off warp.

R. Stanfield collection

Thought to be the accident on the 1st September, 1913, when the axle of the carriage fractured and a bystander was injured.

President; Mrs. Mark Harrison, Chairman; Miss Paton and Miss Garrett, joint Honorary Secretaries. The Auxiliary later became the Ladies' Lifeboat Guild and Mrs. Harrison was re-elected Chairman until her death in 1954. The Ladies' fund-raising work has been the backbone of the shore activities of the Branch from their inception to the present day.

During a launching exercise in 1913 a serious accident befell two members of the public who were watching proceedings. One of the main axle arms of the carriage carried away and a wheel fell on a visitor, Mr. Haworth, and a local boy, Master Stowell. Mr. Howarth received an ex-gratia payment from the Institution of £100.

Most of 1914 was quiet for the Lifeboat Crew until the 15th November. At 6 a.m. the Duddon schooner CONISTON sent up a flare off Ramsey and the Rocket Brigade and Lifeboat Crews were summoned. The *Mary Isabella* (2) was launched and took off the ship's crew of four. The following month on the 30th December, the J.H. BARROW was seen to be flying the distress flag a mile off the Queen's Pier. The Lifeboat was launched and took off her crew of five and a dog. The ship was a schooner registered in Lancaster and was proceeding to Glasgow with a cargo of bricks and fire-clay.

LOSS OF THE NEW LEADER

It was the 18th March, 1915, before the next service and this was to take off the four-man crew of the Ramsey ketch NEW LEADER. The day dawned with the barometer falling, a storm-force NxE gale with blinding snow showers and the Bay a mass of "white horses" Several steamers were sheltering and also the ketch NEW LEADER which was very close inshore. One steamship at anchor got under-way, leaving the steam trawler ADVENTURE and the NEW LEADER still at anchor on a dead lee shore. The ketch began to ride heavily and had both anchors out. She was about half a mile SE of the harbour entrance. Shortly after 9 a.m. she showed distress signals and the Lifeboat Crew mustered quickly in answer to the maroons. One substitute crewman, Robert Kneale (of the half-decker MAJESTIC), was asked to go out for the first time as some of the fishermen crew were away in Whitehaven. The haul-off warp was used and the launch was swift and efficient. The *Mary Isabella* (2) soon made the NEW LEADER but found it very difficult to get alongside her as she had dragged her anchors and was very near to the pier extension. The tide, wind and sea were also all running together. After two attempts a rope was passed from the ketch to the Lifeboat but, as weight came on it, it parted. The Lifeboat made several more attempts and eventually got alongside and snatched off the Master, Jas. Lace, and his crew of three and landed them safely. Later in the morning the snow ceased and the ADVENTURE and the steamship FENELLA berthed but the wind did not drop and the NEW LEADER continued to drag shore-wards. At 4 p.m. her cables parted and she stranded just abeam of the entrance to Ballure Glen. By the following morning the ketch became totally submerged and a total loss. Her passage had been from Ayr to Ramsey with seeds for Cowleys and coal for the salt works. She was 58 nett register tons, built in Jersey in 1873, and owned by Mr. J.D. Clucas, C.P.

The 28th October saw the next service and this again was in gale conditions. At 9 p.m. on the 27th the Duddon schooner HOLY WATH came in to anchor two miles ESE of the harbour entrance. By early morning there was a full-blown ESE'ly gale and at 1.30 a.m. Oscar Corlett (Coast Watcher) and Sgt. Tasker (Isle of Man Volunteers) at the Boatouse saw distress flares from the ship and summoned the Lifeboat Crew. With Coxswain Corkish aboard and Oscar Corlett in charge of shore operations the *Mary Isabella* (2) was quickly launched. Although the tide was well up the slip-way the haul-off warp was used in the on-shore wind. After two and a half hours the Boat returned with the three-man crew of the ketch and was beached. After this rescue, however, the weather quickly moderated and it became possible to bring the HOLY WATH into harbour.

LIFEBOAT DAMAGED

The final "attempted" service of 1915 was a sad one for the second *Mary Isabella* as she sustained enough damage for the Committee to consider it to be the end of her life as a Lifeboat. RNLI Headquarters were asked for a replacement boat. It all happened on Friday, 12th November, after a very fine spell of weather which had lasted over several months.

From Tuesday, the 9th, a large barque had been seen at anchor off Maughold Head. She was the SIGRID of Brevik, Norway, and in ballast from Silloth to Langasund. The weather changed during the early hours of the 12th and the strong SE'ly wind worked around to the East and became a full gale. The barometer dropped steadily and driving rain and huge seas were witnessed on Ramsey Beach. Soon after 9 a.m. Mr. Quine, Principal of the Maughold Lighthouse, sent a message to Ramsey stating that the barque was dragging towards the shore. The Rocket Brigade and the Lifeboat Crew were summoned and it is said that the whole town turned out to witness the start of rescue operations. A detachment of the Shropshire Regiment also assisted. The Rocket Brigade under Lieut. Weales, D.O., left for Maughold and the *Mary Isabella* (2) was launched under Coxswain Corkish. The haul-off warp was used to good advantage but the Boat was filled to the

The *Mary Isabella* (2) on her four horse-power carriage c1900. RNLI Poole

gunwales several times by the huge seas crashing on to the beach. Once clear of the warp, the Lifeboat stood away in a Southerly direction but, owing to the broken water, made little or no headway seawards. She then put about on the other tack but with little more success. The storm, meanwhile, was becoming worse and the seas heavier and attempt after attempt was made to get the Boat clear of the beach. It was all to no avail and the gallant Crew had to accept that the elements had beaten them. The *Mary Isabella* (2) was driven back on to the beach and severely damaged but no members of the Crew were lost.

The authorities then called upon the Douglas Lifeboat to help and it was agreed to attempt to launch her. Meanwhile a further message from Maughold stated that a small boat had left the SIGRID and was being driven Southerly by the storm.

Watchers on Maughold Head kept a keen eye on this event and as the boat approached the rocks the seamen in her pluckily stood it out in tremendous seas, rounded the Head and landed their little craft on Port Mooar beach. Here Mr. R.C. Gill of Baldromma Farm supplied the nine men and Capt. Nielsen with hot tea at his house and then the shipwrecked men were taken to Ramsey and accommodated in the Coronation Restaurant. Their ship became a total wreck within one hour of it stranding and in the conditions it was found impossible to launch the Douglas Lifeboat after all. Mercifully, no lives were lost in this disaster. Ships and lifeboats can be replaced; lives cannot.

The second *Mary Isabella* had a fine record: between 1896 and 1915 she made 48 service launches and saved 161 lives. Up to 1991, no single Ramsey Lifeboat rescued more seafarers from the sea.

CHAPTER 5

Anna Maria Lee 1916 - 1927

16 service launches and 21 lives saved

A BRANCH Committee meeting was held at the Ramsey Courier office on the 14th February, 1916. Among those present were T.H. Midwood, A.E. Chrystal, W. Corkhill, A.J. Evans and A.H. Teare.

It was resolved that:

> "The old (and first) Minutes Book which had been in use from the 20th November 1868 until the 30th December 1915, a period of 47 years, be deposited in Parrs Bank, Ramsey, for safe custody seeing it contains a very interesting and remarkable record of Lifeboat work in this town. It is, in itself, a valuable history of the splendid service rendered by a noble body of gentlemen connected with Ramsey to the Lifeboat Institution, as well as indicating the self-sacrificing work of the various crews of the boats placed in the Ramsey Station."

Another resolution proposed that:

> "The old *Mary Isabella* be sold at a public auction on the 26th February by Messrs. Chrystal Bros. and that the sale be advertised in the (Liverpool) Journal of Commerce and Insular Newspapers."

The boat and its gear later sold for £60. 18. 6d.

The most important resolution of this same meeting was the one concerning the proposed replacement Lifeboat:

> "That in reply to the letter of the 10th January, 1916, the Secretary of the Institution (in London) be informed that the local Committee desire that the new Boat *Anna Maria Lee* be thoroughly examined as suggested in the letter named, especially so after the experience the Committee had with the *Mary Isabella* (1) and further that the local Committee would take no responsibility for any accident that might occur to the Lifeboat consequent upon any conditions which might arise through the boat not having been opened up for examination since her construction in 1897."

Obviously the Crew and Committee were not willing to receive an unsuitable boat or one which would need considerable alteration away from the Station as had happened previously.

Arrival of the *Anna Maria Lee*

The *Anna Maria Lee* arrived on Station within the first few months of 1916 but the Minutes Book makes no mention of the actual date. She was a Boat of the Reserve Fleet and had previously been stationed at Fraserburgh on the East Coast of Scotland. A note in the Minutes Book states that on the 14th April the Area Inspector had requested a costing for the overhaul of the new Boat from a local boat-builder. Apparently he had made a report to the effect that the Boat was in a very unsatisfactory state overall and had unwanted water in the ballast tank. The matter was reported to London. It was not until November that the work was completed at a cost of £139.10s by W. Clucas, a local carpenter. At this time the Inspector had a long conversation with Coxswain Corkish about the overhaul.

Details about the *Anna Maria Lee* seem to be somewhat scarce but it is known that she was built by Rutherford of Birkenhead in 1897. She cost £567 and this was paid for by a legacy from Mrs. Sarah A. Lee. The Boat was a sailing/pulling one with 10 oars and had a length of 37ft. and a beam of 9ft. 3ins.

Fortunately, considering the early state of the replacement Lifeboat, there was only one service in 1916. This was to the brigantine Malpas Belle of Truro on the 25th April. This took place just after a stormy Easter and the morning dawned with a hurricane-force wind and heavy showers. At 5.30 a.m. Coast Watchers E. Kenyon and Capt. J.T. Callow saw a flag of distress hoisted by the Malpas Belle which was at anchor in the Bay. The Crew was summoned and the Lifeboat launched with Coxswain Corkish aboard and Oscar Corlett in charge ashore. The Lifeboat returned after an hour with the brigantine's Master, Capt. Bate, and his crew of five. The ship had been bound from Brest to Preston with pitch and, after a rough passage, came to anchor off Ramsey after her mainsail had carried away. During the night of the 25th/26th she then parted both her anchor cables in the hurricane. However, the ship survived and her crew went out after the storm and brought her safely into her port of refuge. Coxswain Corkish was reported as being satisfied with the launch and the behaviour of the new Boat.

During these First World War years there were important changes within the Lifeboat Committee. In 1915 D. Vondy resigned as Honorary Secretary and Capt. Evans and A.H. Teare were appointed joint Hon. Secretaries and Treasurers. In 1916 High Bailiff Cruickshank, who had been a member of the Committee for

W.S. Basnett collection

The *Anna Maria Lee* under sail.

G.D. Learoyd collection

A Lifeboat Day Appeal from the bows of the *Anna Maria Lee* c1920.
Coxswain H. Corkish.

22 years and Chairman for 16, died. T.H. Midwood was elected Chairman in his place.

At the end of the year J. Garrett was appointed 2nd Coxswain in place of Wm. Martin who resigned because of ill health. Mr. Garrett was selected by the Crew and had 48 services to his credit.

The spring of the following year saw John Crix elected Bowman and John Lord and John Kinnin elected Crew Members.

In July, 1917, Inspector MacLean visited the Station and resolved to go ahead with necessary repairs to the slipway.

On the 16th December the Belfast steamship CASTLEROCK stranded on a sandy beach North of Ramsey. A strong Easterly wind was blowing when the Lifeboat went to her aid or to "Standby" her, as the official records stated. But that is all that is mentioned about the service except a brief sentence later in the month when Capt. Evans informed the Committee that repairs to the Lifeboat were underway after the damage sustained during the CASTLEROCK incident. But perhaps pictures speak louder than words? A well-known photograph which is reproduced here shows the Lifeboat aground and shoreside of the stranded steamship!

HARRY SHARPE HONOURED

Harry Sharpe, Bowman of the *Anna Maria Lee,* made a single-handed rescue late in March, 1918, which earned him a Bronze Medal from the hand of King George V.

He was on passage from Bangor to Ramsey in a yacht, the ARMISTICE, and in the company of a small steamship, the TORBAY. Whilst in mid-channel a gale sprang up and the TORBAY lost her lifeboat and ended up in a sinking condition. Harry, who was in command of the yacht, stripped off his clothing and launched the yacht's small boat to make for the steamship. He had to make three such sorties in order to rescue all her crew as he could only take off one at a time. Shortly after the last man was aboard the yacht the TORBAY foundered. For this deed he was invested with the Sea Gallantry Medal by the Sovereign at Buckingham Palace, upon the recommendation of the President of the Board of Trade.

An entry concerning this incident in the Minutes Book congratulates Mr. Sharpe upon his bravery and award. He continued his Lifeboat Service until his retirement in 1928. At that time he received a Certificate of Service from the Institution recording the fact that he had been Bowman for the previous ten years and a Crew Member for forty years. During this period the Lifeboat saved 315 lives. He died in 1956 at the age of 87.

There were three services during the year of 1918, all of them in the October. At 5.30 p.m. on Saturday, the 5th, following a hurricane on the previous day, a schooner at anchor some two miles NE of the harbour hoisted distress signals. She was the FOREST DEER bound for Cumberland with timber and registered in Dublin. She was 61 nett register tons and built in Newquay, Cornwall, in 1867. A large crowd gathered on the Ramsey shore-line as darkness set in and the Lifeboat's Crew was summoned. It was stormy and low water, and it was not possible to use the normal haul-off warp. The Boat and carriage were taken along the sand to the supplementary haul-off warp at the Queen's Pier. Oscar Corlett was Chief Launcher and Coxswains Corkish and Garrett were aboard the Lifeboat. As weight came on the warp it parted before the Boat was sufficiently far enough into the sea. The warp was made fast a second time. Valuable assistance was given by a Capt. Kinsella of the schooner EMILY BARRATT and Mr. John Lyall who were almost up to their necks in the sea, but luckily it was smooth as the wind was off-shore. The Lifeboat was eventually floated and returned at 8 p.m. with the ship's Capt. Ward and his crew of two. The FOREST DEER survived the night, however, lying to its single anchor.

LOSS OF THE MARIE EDMOND

The final services of the year took place during a busy day on the 7th October. After a bad night of wind, hail, rain, thunder and lightning, a sailing trawler at anchor was seen at daybreak to be flying a distress signal. She was the MARIE EDMOND of Ostend, Belgium. The Lifeboat was launched within 15 minutes of the maroons being fired and returned at 9 a.m. with one sailor from the trawler. He reported that his ship had lost a lot of canvas and that he wished to organise a tow into harbour for her. The other three crewmen remained aboard as they did not wish to leave their ship unmanned. This was just as well, for she soon began to drag her anchor and so they were able to make sail with the remaining canvas and got her under-way.

The storm later increased in violence and a large crowd began to muster on the Promenade to watch proceedings. The Coast Watchers at Ramsey then received a message from the Chief Officer at Port Cranstal that a large Swedish steamer was in difficulties off his Station, some four miles North of the Boathouse. After consultations with the Lifeboat's Crew and all concerned, it was considered a job for a tug. Mr. T.A. Fargher, the local Lloyds' Agent, took up negotiations with a salvage steamer owned by the Ardrossan Salvage Company.

By this time the MARIE EDMOND had let her anchor go, but a long way further seawards, and she was making heavy weather of it. The Lifeboatmen continued to standby ashore and next saw the Swedish ship arrive off the Port, whereupon the salvage tug left the harbour intending to make contact with her.

G.D. Learoyd collection

The ss Castlerock and the *Anna Maria Lee* both aground North of Ramsey, 16th December, 1917.

Shortly after noon distress signals were again hoisted by the Belgian trawler and the Lifeboat was launched at 12.30 p.m. Before she could reach the Marie Edmond the trawler got underway and was making Southwards by the time the rescuers drew alongside her. For a second time it seemed that her crew were refusing to leave their ship as both vessels were seen to disappear together to the South. Eventually the *Anna Maria Lee* re-appeared "having a tough peg to windward" but arrived back with the three Belgians. They had undoubtedly had enough salt water for a day! Their ship was never seen again and the men travelled home some days later.

The Carronpark Service

An unusual Lifeboat episode took place on the 20th March, 1919, which was the next service launch of the *Anna Maria Lee.*

Between 8 and 9 a.m. that day several people walking along the Ramsey Promenade noticed a small rowing boat making for the harbour. There was a strong breeze with sleet and rain showers accompanied by a nasty sea rolling on to the beach. Six men, drenched to the skin and shivering with cold, were taken aboard the fishing vessel Jehovah Jireh, which was in the harbour, by Skipper Fred Price. They were treated to "good fellowship" and turned out to be the Chief Officer and five crewmen of the Greenock steamship Carronpark. Whilst en-route from Maryport in Cumberland to Swansea, light-ship, she had lost her propeller in the vicinity of the Bahama Bank at 9 a.m. on Wednesday, the 19th. Despite flying day-time distress signals and flares by night, no-one had answered the calls for help. Even passing ships had not realised her plight.

The Chief Officer, once ashore, contacted Capt. Evans and Mr. Teare, the Lifeboat Secretaries, and also Mr. Fargher, Lloyds' Agent, and Mr. Kee, the Manager of the Ramsey Steamship Company, who all offered assistance. It was agreed that the weather was too bad for any of the half-deckers to put to sea, so the Lifeboat Crew was called upon. Under Coxswain Corkish the Boat was launched but the haul-off warp parted, sending some of the launchers sprawling. Another rope was then led to the South Pier and, as the tide was making, the Boat floated and cleared the carriage.

During this launch the ss Redstone arrived in the Bay and arrangements were made for her to proceed to the Carronpark which by now had anchored some six miles East of Ramsey. The Redstone was commodore ship of the Ramsey Steamship Company under the command of Capt. John Cowley. She went out to the distressed ship, taking with her the Chief Officer; Mr. F. Brew, the Chairman of the Ramsey Steamship Company; Mr. J.B. Kee, its Manager, and Capt. J.T. Callow, the Deputy Harbour

Master. The REDSTONE also towed out the *Anna Maria Lee* with the remaining five of the CARRONPARK's crew.

After some time the REDSTONE returned to port, followed later by the Lifeboat. It transpired that no suitable towing hawser was available and the CARRONPARK's Master did not feel secure in weighing anchor on a lee shore under the circumstances. Although the Lifeboat had transferred the Chief Officer and crew to their own ship safely, it had been a difficult operation as a strong tide was running and combined with adverse wind and sea, the *Anna Maria Lee* damaged her port-side gunwale whilst getting alongside the REDSTONE. More damage was caused when she got alongside the CARRONPARK and when she returned to Ramsey she was minus her mizzen mast.

The latter ship remained at anchor for some days but her fate was not recorded. She was built in 1912, of 1401 nett register tons and at the time was under charter to the Admiralty.

During the next few months of 1919 the Minutes Book records a series of discussions and letters about the claim the Lifeboat Committee had submitted for the CARRONPARK service. An initial claim for £30 was served on her owners for expenses covering the launch and the estimated cost of repairs to the *Anna Maria Lee*. Obviously this estimate was wildly innacurate as the records show that when Mr. George Kelly, Lloyds' Agent from Douglas, offered £60 in settlement, it was refused. Apparently the repairs cost £92.15.6d. and the Committee then stated that they would accept nothing less. No subsequent mention was made of the affair but no doubt agreement was eventually reached.

COMMITTEE MATTERS

The Annual General Meeting of the Station was held in June and the accounts showed general receipts standing at £216.7.3d. for the year against expenditure of £155.18.1d. The separate Endowment Fund Capital Account stood at £805 which was invested in the Isle of Man Railway and War Loan shares.

At the end of the year a letter was sent to the Lt. Governor, Major General Fry, and also to His Worship the Vicar General for their kindness and interest shown in attending the summer Lifeboat Demonstration. This they regularly did throughout the years.

It was at this time that the RNLI sent out a circular letter to stations in connection with suggestions for awarding Service Badges to Lifeboat Crews. In Ramsey the opinion put forward was for two kinds of badges; one for the number of services performed and a second denoting general association with the Lifeboat Service.

MOTOR LIFEBOAT DISCUSSED

The first "Official" talk of the provision of a motor lifeboat for Ramsey also took place at the very end of 1919. After the First World War the Institution had started replacing the old sailing/pulling boats with motor boats. Although Ramsey was on the list for one, only promises had so far been received. A firm resolution was written down by the Committee which stated:-

> "Resolved that in view of the repeated promises made by the Royal National Lifeboat Institution that a motor lifeboat would be established at Ramsey, and in view of the conspicuous services rendered by the Ramsey Boat, the Committee is of the opinion that the time is now come when the work should be taken in hand and would like an assurance from the Institution that this will be done."

It took another eleven years for this resolution to be acted upon.

No services were recorded for 1920 but the Station battled on, pressing the case for one of the modern lifeboats. During the year Mr. J.H. Slee and other officers of the RNLI Headquarters visited Ramsey to further discuss the matter. Mr. Slee read out a statement which referred to the previous history of the Station and that it was proposed to not only establish a motor lifeboat here, but also to build a new launching station at the seaward end of the Queen's Pier. The total cost was estimated to be some £20,000 for the Boathouse and ramp. This idea made further ammunition for comment and argument and it was some years before the idea was dropped as being unrealistic. In the meantime the Ramsey Crews pressed for a new boat, requesting a Watson non self-righting type motor boat of 45ft. length and 12ft. beam.

During that year arrangements were made for a lorry to draw the Lifeboat up the slip and on to the road in place of horses which were becoming difficult to obtain for the work.

The end of 1921 produced the first service for over two years. On the 30th December, late at night, the Lifeboat was launched to assist the Bristol schooner IANTHE and landed seven seamen.

On the 29th January, 1922, the Area Inspector, Lt. Vaux, was present at a lifeboat exercise and reported that the launch went satisfactorily and that the *Anna Maria Lee* was in good condition. He noticed, however, that new oilskins were required by the crews and said that he would order them forthwith.

At a Committee Meeting on the 7th June, the gathering was informed that a letter had been received from the Institution informing them that a new cabin motor lifeboat had been designed. They wished the Station to consider whether this new boat would be more suitable for Ramsey than the Watson well-deck type for which the crew had shown preference in 1920.

W.S. Basnett collection

Launching the *Anna Maria Lee* : note the Tipping Sand Shoes on the larger carriage wheels.

W.S. Basnett collection

The *Anna Maria Lee* takes to the water.

Capt. Evans, Hon. Secretary, produced the plans of this new design and much discussion took place thereafter.

The Bideford schooner BRACKENHOLM requested assistance in the forenoon of the 8th February and the *Anna Maria Lee* was launched to take off the crew of three.

1923 saw the death of Mrs. Norbury, the widow of the benefactor who had donated substantial sums to the RNLI for two lifeboats and to the Ramsey Branch for the 1890 Boathouse. Mrs. Norbury was equally generous and in 1920 gave another £500 to the Ramsey Station under a Trust Deed, to be used for the upkeep of the Boathouse and the benefit of Crew Members and their families. She also made a £1,000 donation to the Institution which helped in providing a lifeboat named *Norbury* for Anglesey.

FUND RAISING IN MANCHESTER

Early in 1923 the Manchester and Salford RNLI Branch Committee decided to organise a bazaar during the following year, 1924, to celebrate the centenary year of the Institution. It was hoped to raise sufficient money to pay for a new boat for Ramsey. The Minutes of the 27th April, 1923, meeting record that representatives of the Crew and Committee be sent to Manchester in connection with organising the event. £10,000 was needed to fund the new boat for Ramsey, the *City of Manchester*. The four Crew selected were the Coxswain, H. Corkish; Bowman, H. Sharpe; Chief Launcher, O. Corlett; and K. Gawne. The Chairman, T.H. Midwood, represented the Committee and Mrs. Grimble Groves, the Ladies Auxiliary, of which she had been elected Patron.

That year was another quiet one for the Lifeboat with no services. The ever-increasing number of steamships was obviously responsible for the reduction in rescues. During a storm on the 14th January the ss LEERDAM of Guernsey was driven ashore near the Point of Ayre, refloated herself, but later sank off Ramsey whilst under tow by the steamship JADE. During this storm some 42 steam vessels were sheltering in Ramsey Bay, which illustrated convincingly that steam had finally taken over from sail in the fishing fleets.

The bazaar in Manchester was held from the 15th to 17th May, 1924, and £10,000 was raised. Unfortunately a dispute arose over the name to be given to the lifeboat. The Ramsey Committee wished it to be called the *Sir William Hillary* in memory of the Isle of Man founder of the Institution. The Lancashire Committee, however, wanted it named after their two cities. Certainly, Manchester and Salford had raised most of the money, but Ramsey had also made a considerable effort and contribution, and one would have thought that a more "neutral" name would have been acceptable to all parties. However, it was not to be and the boat was sent, in 1925, to Douglas. From records it seems that insufficient discussion was entertained to resolve the disagreement.

ONE SERVICE IN 1924

The only service of the year was on the 10th July in the early evening. This was in answer to a distress signal being flown by the ketch MARIE CELINE of Drogheda. The ship was on passage from Whitehaven to Annalong (County Down) with coal. Whilst off the Point of Ayre she had encountered a strong SW'ly breeze and three of her jibs had carried away. Her Master made for an anchorage close to seaward of the Queen's Pier and because he was short of sail and afraid of dragging his anchor, he requested the Lifeboat. The *Anna Maria Lee* was launched very quickly under Coxswains Corkish and Garrett and the three-man crew was taken off the ketch and landed. The ship was later brought into Ramsey Harbour by ss MANXSONA.

The Institution later held this launch to be "unwarranted" as the weather was fair and there had been no reason for the MARIE CELINE's own boat not to have been used for the disembarkation. Indeed, it stated that a report showed a small boat with two men aboard had previously taken a passenger ashore from the ship!

February, 1925, brought the death of Harry Corkish, Coxswain for 22 years, since 1903. The crew elected John Garrett, 2nd Coxswain, to take over his post. John was the son of Robert Garrett who Coxed the Boat from 1890 to 1903. John Comish now took over as 2nd Cox of the *Anna Maria Lee*.

At the A.G.M. in March it was officially announced that the *City of Manchester* Lifeboat had, without consultations with Ramsey, been sent to Douglas. Even the Press had reported that the new Boat was bound for Ramsey and feelings in the town were bitter. The Institution sent a conciliatory letter and suggested that another lifeboat for Ramsey should be inspected. The Coxswain, Chief Launcher and Secretary therefore went to Scarborough to test a boat with a 35 H.P. engine. Their subsequent report made it quite clear that this boat was unsuitable for Ramsey. It was too light and the engine parts were too difficult to get at should a failure occur at sea. They also stated that she carried too little sail as stand-by propulsion. Mr. Teare, Secretary, also visited Whitby at the same time. This Station was equipped with two sailing/pulling boats similar to the *Anna Maria Lee* and a self-righting motor lifeboat of 40ft. length. Mr. Teare produced a supplementary report and suggested that the course for Ramsey should be:-

> " 1. That the present Lifeboat remain under all existing conditions.

J. Woolnough collection

Ramsey Steamship Co's BEN VARREY and BEN VEG waiting to discharge coal at the West Quay, Ramsey, c.1925.

Ramsey RNLI collection

The *Anna Maria Lee* standing-by the schooner ELIZABETH HYAM off the Ramsey Pier Heads, 1925.

2. That a motor lifeboat of the class of Douglas or Whitby be provided, and if the engineering difficulties prevent her being stationed at Queen's Pier, that she should be housed in Ramsey Harbour and used at all states of the tide possible, as in Whitby, and when not possible, to then use the sailing/pulling boat."

The engineering difficulties at the Queen's Pier referred to recent correspondence between the Institution engineers and the Station. The engineers reported adversely on the erection of a boathouse and launching slipway at the end of the Pier. The main objection was the recovery of the boat in all weathers. This opinion was also held by a number of the Station Staff in Ramsey. The RNLI further proposed that when a new motor boat was available for the Station it would come with a new carriage which would be tractor-drawn. This meant that a boat of only 35ft. length and 8ft 6ins. beam would be suitable for the Boathouse and not the 46ft. one initially promised.

All of the above matters were well-aired again on the 28th October when RNLI officers attended a local Committee Meeting. Suggestions were again brought forward that a Scarborough-type motor boat should be tested at Ramsey, whilst retaining the *Anna Maria Lee*. Certainly the Queen's Pier project was dropped finally in the following year, and perhaps just as well. In the latter half of the twentieth century most seaside resorts have had little money to spare for major repairs to such Victorian structures around the British Isles and Ramsey is no exception. The original Norbury Boathouse survived until 1990 but the pier is not in a good state of repair or in regular use.

Three Services in 1925

The year of 1925 brought three requests for help from the *Anna Maria Lee* and her Crew.

On the 8th February the Falmouth registered ketch Amis Reunis was seen off Ramsey whilst on passage from Killough to Porthmadog with a cargo of potatoes. At 10 a.m. the Coastguard who was keeping a bad weather watch observed the ketch flying a distress signal – the Red Ensign flying inverted from her main rigging. The Lifeboat Authorities were informed but the Lifeboat was not launched until 12.15 p.m. By this time the Amis Reunis was approximately two miles North-East of the harbour. Four of the Lifeboat Crew boarded the ketch and helped to bring her into port. Apparently she had encountered heavy seas during the previous night and had started to leak badly. Her crew had manned the bilge pumps constantly throughout the night but were almost exhausted by daybreak.

The subject of this service was brought up at the next Committee Meeting as it appears that there had been some breakdown in communications and the shore launcher had authorised the launch which was not standard practice.

The schooner Elizabeth Hyam of Chester dropped anchor in Ramsey Bay at 11 a.m. on the 4th April, 1925, only 300 yards South of the pier head. There was a strong gale blowing from the SSE with a very rough sea running. It was soon observed that the ship was dragging her anchor and at 12.35 p.m. she hoisted a red pennant from her after-stay and sounded her fog signal as one of distress. The Lifeboat was immediately summoned and launched but had great difficulty in reaching the schooner in the heavy seas and with the tide on the ebb. The authorities ashore decided to call out the Rocket Brigade who stood-by with their equipment at the end of the North Pier. By the time the *Anna Maria Lee* reached the ship she had drifted 200 yards further North. The crew of four eventually got aboard the Lifeboat and was landed safely. Their ship later ran aground and became a wreck close North-East of the pier head, some 50 yards beyond the low water mark.

A rather similar service was undertaken on the 19th December, the final one of the year. Just before daybreak the Coastguard on duty saw distress flares about a mile East of his Look-out Station close to Ramsey Harbour. The Lifeboat Crew was called and the Boat launched just after 7 a.m. The tide was very low and the seas rough and great difficulty was experienced in getting the Boat into the water. As a precautionary measure the Rocket Brigade was called out and lined the shore equipped with lifelines, belts, a hand lantern and Coastguard lights. The *Anna Maria Lee* took forty minutes to reach the schooner Ben Gullion. The crew of three was taken off and landed ashore at 10 a.m. The ship had been on passage from Garston to Wicklow with coal and anchored off Ramsey for shelter. Her home port was Dumfries.

The Ramsey Committee, ever hopeful of getting a new motor lifeboat for the Branch, were pleased to announce in 1926 that a motor boat costing £10,000 was to be presented to the port by Mr. Wm. Grimble Groves, J.P., (the elder brother of J.G. Groves) and some friends at Windermere. The boat was to be called the *Westmorland*. The Committee expressed their appreciation of this generous gift but requested that the boat be called *Sir William Hillary (presented by the County of Westmorland)*. Once again the name became a stumbling block and the Windermere Committee stuck to their guns and the boat was sent on station to Berwick-on-Tweed instead.

One might well now question "What's in a name?" Surely all parties could understand that what was wanted was a modern, efficient, motor lifeboat to save more lives and to give

Ramsey RNLI collection

The Latvian barquentine AUSTRUMS after grounding West of Rue Point, 1927.

Ramsey RNLI collection

High and dry. The AUSTRUMS became a total loss in 1927.

protection to her dedicated crews? The choice of name should surely have been well down the list of priorities?

Late at night on the 9th October, a Police Constable informed the Coastguard that he had sighted a rocket on the North-West Coast of the Island. The Lifeboat was launched about midnight and sailed around to Jurby Head, a distance of 14 miles. She then searched from Jurby Head back to Rue Point, five miles to the North-East, but nothing was found. The Lifeboat later returned to Ramsey empty-handed.

Some three months later, on the 26th January, 1926, a similar call-out took place somewhat nearer to home. The Coastguard on duty at 3.35 a.m. reported seeing red flares about three miles ExN off the port. The *Anna Maria Lee* was launched, but after a six hour search there was still no trace of a vessel in distress or a wreck and the Crew returned to their Station.

Loss of the Austrums

The final launch on a service for the *Anna Maria Lee* was on the 26th January, 1927. During the forenoon the Lifeboat was called out on a false alarm all the way to the Bahama Bank and back. The Crew had been summoned by the firing of two maroons, in the usual way. The Latvian barquentine Austrums, registered in Riga, was anchored off Ramsey at the time. She was on a passage from Runcorn to San Sebastian with a cargo of pitch. (Obviously sailing North-about from the Mersey). In Riga when two maroons were fired it was a signal for ships to clear an anchorage to avoid damage in adverse conditions. Therefore she weighed anchor and put to sea thinking this was the same procedure and made for the Point of Ayre and Westwards. Rounding the Point she sailed into the teeth of a NW'ly gale and soon put herself on a lee shore. By 3.15 p.m. a message was received in Ramsey from a Mr. Thomas Kneale, of Smeale, that a three-masted vessel was aground West of Rue Point. The Rocket Brigade was assembled, obtained a lorry and left Ramsey at 3.30 p.m., arriving at the scene at 4.45 p.m. Owing to the very high wind – it was a severe gale force 9 to 10 – and sandstorms on the coast, communication by rocket-line was very difficult and it was 6 p.m. before a line was secured to the ship. Thirty minutes later all nine crew members were safely ashore and sent to Ramsey. The Rocket Brigade did not leave the shore until 7.30 p.m., arriving back at their base over four hours after the initial call-out. Meanwhile the Lifeboat had returned to Ramsey from the first service but damaged her bow in gale conditions whilst entering the harbour. She was also told at this point of the Austrums' distress. After hastily inspecting their own damage, the Crew considered the Lifeboat still seaworthy and immediately turned around and put to sea again to try and reach the Latvian ship. Rounding the Point of Ayre, the Crew pulled to within one mile of the ship in the teeth of the storm only to be recalled as the shore rescuers completed their task. The Peel Lifeboat was also called out for this distress. The barquentine became a total loss in a very short time.

G.D. Learoyd collection

The st CEVIC after grounding at Granch, South of Ramsey, 1927.

CHAPTER 6

Matthew Simpson 1927-1931

5 service launches and 10 lives saved

THE sailing/pulling lifeboat *Matthew Simpson* took up station at Ramsey on the 8th February, 1927, to replace the *Anna Maria Lee.* No ceremony of note heralded her arrival, possibly because of the renewed disappointment in not getting a more modern motor boat as promised during the previous years.

The new lifeboat had been built in 1903 by a River Thames builder at Blackwall and came to Ramsey from Berwick-upon-Tweed, whilst listed on the RNLI Reserve Fleet. She was 37ft. in length and had a 9ft. 3ins. beam and pulled ten oars. The displacement of the boat was over 4 tons and she was fitted with two drop keels. The boat was presented to the RNLI by a Mr. Simpson of Lancaster.

Owing to the *Matthew Simpson*'s relatively short period at Ramsey she undertook only five services, two of which were of note and lives saved. The first of these was in the early summer after her arrival on Station, at daybreak on the 26th June, 1927.

The Cevic Stranding

The Fleetwood steam trawler Cevic anchored in Ramsey Bay during the afternoon of the 25th June. The Skipper, Mate, Engineer and Boatswain left the vessel in a small boat to spend the night ashore. A crew member rowed their boat back to the ship and it was tied up astern. During the hours of darkness the boat shipped a lot of water, so a seaman climbed down into her to bail her out. As he did so, the boat broke loose and started to drift away. The remaining trawlermen were soon aware of this, weighed anchor and got under-way to go to the seaman's aid. In doing so, they took the Cevic too close inshore and ran her aground at about 3.20 a.m. It was more than an hour before the Lifeboat Crew was informed of the incident and the *Matthew Simpson* was launched at 5 a.m. All six remaining trawlermen were landed in Ramsey some two hours later but the ship was not saved. To this day part of her rusted hull and engine-block still remain for all to see at low water on the beach near Port Lewaigue. Very soon after this event the Misses Simpson of Lancaster, daughters of the Lifeboat's donor, hearing of the rescue, sent a sum of £10 to the Branch to be shared out amongst the Crew in recognition of their work.

Later in the year Mr. T.H. Midwood died and he was succeeded as Chairman by the Rev. M.W. Harrison. Harry Sharpe, the Bowman, retired after some 40 years' service to the Ramsey Lifeboats. During this time he was awarded the King Edward Long Service Medal and the King Albert Medal for Saving Life at Sea. He was awarded the RNLI Vellum for Long Service the following year. From the Committee's deliberations at the end of the year it is clear that they had not given up hope of a new motor lifeboat arriving in Ramsey and they still talked of the desire to call it *Sir William Hillary.*

On the 23rd August, 1928, the steam vessel Cumberland Coast was on passage Southbound from Glasgow to Manchester. When she was half-way between the Mull of Galloway and the Point of Ayre, a fire was discovered in the main hold in a large consignment of hay, very possibly as a result of spontaneous combustion. This was spotted by the Principal Lighthouse Keeper at the Point of Ayre and he immediately informed the Lifeboat Authorities. The *Matthew Simpson* was launched. The Cumberland Coast then altered course for Ramsey Bay and the ship was beached. With the help of the Harbour Board work-boat Sirdar, which was equipped with a large pump, the fire was extinguished. The Lifeboat stood-by during the emergency and then returned to her Station.

The Rye Lifeboat Disaster

At the end of 1928 the Hon. Secretary reported to the Committee that he had written a letter to the Rye Harbour RNLI Station, Sussex, expressing everyone's grief and sorrow at the loss of their lifeboat and entire crew of 17 during a service on the 28th November. The boat had been out to assist a Latvian vessel in trouble, but was recalled soon after launching as she was not needed after all. Unfortunately the recall signals were not seen and after a long search with bad weather building up she returned to Station. She was capsized by a following sea just short of Rye Harbour and all were drowned. The Government of the Isle of Man, on behalf of all residents, later sent a Manx-stone plaque to Rye to commemorate this disaster.

A. Christian collection

The launch of the *Matthew Simpson,* Lifeboat Day 1927.

G.D. Learoyd collection

The ss CUMBERLAND COAST with her cargo on fire, 1928.

Only in 1927 had lifeboat-to-shore radio communications been adopted by the RNLI, but, of course, were only fitted to the more modern boats.

The Ramsey Committee at this time also discussed with Coxswain John Garrett the advantages of the new kapok-filled life-jackets which had now been in service for a full year. They had replaced the old cork-block ones. Feelings were apparently mixed on the subject, but old habits usually die hard in the Service.

During the year of 1929, Ramsey Lifeboat Station received the Centenary Vellum Award from the RNLI to mark the 100 years since its original foundation in the port.

The first service of 1929 was on the 20th March to the steam trawler FLORENCE BRIERLEY. At 1.35 in the morning the Lifeboat Crew Members were called out together with the Rocket Brigade and were told that the trawler was about one and a half miles South of Maughold Head and required assistance. The *Matthew Simpson* was launched and on reaching the given position found no trace of the distressed ship. Neither did the Life Saving party ashore and so a search was instituted. Two labourers who met this party gave them the information that the trawler had certainly been aground but the crew had carried out their anchor in a small boat and had managed to warp themselves off on the rising tide. The Rocket Brigade stayed on the scene for some further time as conditions were very foggy and they considered they might still be needed. The Lifeboat, meanwhile, returned to her Station.

THE VENUS

On the 31st March, 1929, the Castletown registered schooner VENUS left Douglas for Ardrossan with a cargo of scrap-iron. The following Sunday morning she anchored in Ramsey Bay for shelter. In just over 24 hours conditions worsened and she began to drag her anchor. At 3.30 p.m. on the 1st April, (Easter Monday), a local Coastguard observed her Red Ensign flying inverted from the main-mast. The Crew of the *Matthew Simpson* was called at once and the four-man crew of the VENUS and the ship's cat were successfully landed by 4.45 p.m. Incidentally, the cat jumped out of the Lifeboat at one stage but was recovered again. (Only eight lives left, maybe!) The ship was re-boarded after the gale and continued her passage.

As a sequel to this service the VENUS was in trouble again on the 29th October, 1929. This time she went aground some one and a half miles South of Maughold Head, but the District Officer visited the scene and reported that the crew was in no danger. The ship was later re-floated but only to go aground once more the next morning a half a mile further South on Port Mooar Beach. The crew scrambled safely ashore. This time the vessel became a total loss. Not a lucky ship, it would seem!

It was reported to the Committee on the 29th September, 1930, that Coxswain John Garrett had had to resign owing to continued ill-health. It was noted that during his long service to the Station he had been out on services 65 times. He was voted a £4 gratuity.

NAVAL VESSEL IN TROUBLE

H.M.S. DOON was lying at anchor off Ramsey in the evening of the 18th November, 1930. At 10.45 p.m. the Look-out Man on bad weather watch ashore observed the ship dragging her anchor and immediately got in touch with the vessel to warn her. At 11.05 p.m. the ship got under-way and proceeded North but appeared to be heading for the shore. The Ramsey Look-out Man burnt off two flares immediately to attract the vessel's attention but, as nothing happened, he called out the Rocket Brigade and the Lifeboat Crew. The shore party made for H.M.S. DOON which by this time was ashore one mile North of the port. A signal was made to the Commanding Officer asking if he wished communication to be established with the rocket apparatus and he replied in the affirmative. This was done and the breeches buoy sent out to the ship. As no-one got into it, it was hauled ashore and the District Officer used it to gain access aboard. The Commander then asked the Brigade to "Stand-by" and this they did until 2.45 a.m. the following morning, then returning home. At 9.30 a.m. when in daylight, ss MANXONA towed the stranded vessel off the beach and the ship proceeded South, apparently undamaged.

On the 12th December the Hon. Secretary was able to announce definitely that the arrival of the new motor lifeboat was stemmed for May, 1931.

1931 saw the death of ex-Coxswain John Garrett and Oscar Corlett retired. This latter gentleman had been a Member of the Crew since 1875 and 2nd Coxswain for eleven years, from 1890 to 1901. He then became Chief Launcher until 1931 and thus completed some 56 years of service to the Station.

In the January of 1931 the Committee had a request from a Mr. Jas. Bell, the Isle of Man Steam Packet Co. agent in Ramsey, to use the Norbury "Watch Room" for instructional classes for seamen in respect of handling and launching ship's lifeboats. This request was agreed to, with the proviso that the seamen cleaned up the room after their sessions! For the first time a suggestion was brought forward that a summer caretaker be appointed to the Boathouse for some twelve weeks of the summer months. This was in line with other stations and the duties were to include the general upkeep and cleanliness of the Boathouse: to protect the Boat and property; and to show and explain

Ramsey RNLI collection

The fishing smack HEARTS OF OAK off East Quay, Ramsey, c.1929.

G. Learoyd collection

H.M.S. DOON aground North of Ramsey, 1930.

Fred Henry

A. Christian collection

A normal launch for the *Matthew Simpson*.

W.S. Basnett collection

Launching during an on-shore wind. This time the haul-off warp is made fast to the South Pier-head.

G.D. Learoyd collection

Steam trawler PASAGES ashore at Jurby Head, 3rd December, 1931.

various matters of interest to all visitors. Wages were to be 15/- per week and James Gawne or Harry Sharpe were to be offered the post.

Mr. W. Kennish was appointed the part-time Mechanic of the new Boat and in the April of 1931 he was sent to Cowes, Isle of Wight, for a course of instruction.

Also in April, the Committee and Crew were introduced to the new District RNLI Inspector, Lt. Commander Cousins, R.N., who visited the Island. He expressed general satisfaction with the Station and then, in a "happy" speech, presented a Vellum to Mr. A.H. Teare on behalf of the Institution, in recognition of his 16 years as Hon. Secretary of the Branch. Brigadier General Swabey, District Organising Secretary, was also at this April meeting and informed everyone that the new motor lifeboat for Ramsey was to be the *Lady Harrison* and would, indeed, be on Station within a few weeks.

CHAPTER 7

Lady Harrison 1931-1948

49 service launches and 93 lives saved

BY 1931 the population of the Isle of Man had grown to just over 49,000 and Ramsey still held its own with a 25% share of that number. There were 4,198 residents in the town with double the number in the outlying districts. It remained the Island's second port in importance.

Friday, 12th June, 1931, saw the Station's first motor lifeboat on duty. This was the *Lady Harrison* which cost £3,754 and was the gift of Sir Heath Harrison, Bart., of Liss in Hampshire.

She was a self-righting type of boat with a Weyburn 36 h.p. petrol engine and single screw. Her dimensions were 35ft. 6ins. overall length and 10ft. 8ins. beam. She was built by Saunders Roe Ltd. of East Cowes, Isle of Wight. To supplement her engine power she was fitted with a main-mast and mizzen and accompanying sail outfit and was of timber construction with a solid canopy over the engine sited amidships. Few other details of her seem to have been kept and the Committee Minutes Book only mentions the barest facts.

Earlier in the year ex-Coxswain John Garrett died. He had been succeeded as Cox by J.T. Lord the previous year. In April, 1931, Oscar Corlett, Head Launcher, resigned after 56 years of service in the Crew and shoreside and his post was taken over by William Christian.

Naming Ceremony

The naming ceremony of the new Boat took place on the 16th July and Lady Hill, wife of the Lt. Governor, officiated. It was a fine day with a light NW'ly breeze and considerable ceremony took place with the Lord Bishop, Church Choirs, the Ramsey Town Silver Band and many local dignatories attending.

On the 27th July the old *Matthew Simpson* was towed to her new Station at Llandudno by the steamship Ben Blanche. As the North Wales Branch could not provide a crew for the passage, Coxswain Lord, Bowman J. Christian and E. Starkey, W. Corkish and J. Callow from Ramsey crewed the boat. They had a stormy time and were met and congratulated by District Inspector Cousins.

Apart from local trials and exercises, the *Lady Harrison* was on Station for some five months before her first service call-out. This was on the 3rd December to the Fleetwood trawler Pasages. The Ramsey Courier of the day gave a detailed eye witness account of the events which took place:

"In a severe SSW gale, the Fleetwood steam trawler Pasages ran ashore at Jurby Head (on the NW coast of the Island) at 6 a.m. on Thursday morning, the 3rd December, 1931, and the crew of thirteen subsequently rescued by the Ramsey Rocket Corps. The trawler was returning from the fishing grounds on the NW of Ireland and had a considerable quantity of herring on board. All night she had been badly buffeted by the terrific winds and blinding sleet and rain and she was consequently proceeding cautiously. Just before 6 a.m. it was pitch dark and quite impossible for the Skipper, who had been on the bridge for six hours without a break, to see any land ahead. However the trawler was felt to touch bottom and he immediately ran the engine astern. The trawler would not budge however and the predicament of the crew, grounded as they were, being swept from stem to stern by the wind and spray, and with the ship being buffeted by heavy seas, was such as to strike terror in the hearts of the staunchest. The Skipper decided to send up distress flares and these were seen and the alarm given to District Officer Lace of the Coastguards in Ramsey who ordered the local call-out signal to be fired. As soon as the Corps had assembled the journey was commenced by road to Jurby Beach.

Meanwhile, Peel Rocket Corps and their Lifeboat Secretary had been informed of the grounding of the Pasages and the Corps left the western city to render what aid it could. At Ramsey the Chairman of the Lifeboat Branch the Rev. M.W. Harrison, in the absence of the Secretary Mr. J.B. Kee, who was away on the mainland on business, gave the orders for the motor lifeboat *Lady Harrison* to be launched. She left at about 8.30 a.m. The Peel Lifeboat was also launched and set out in heavy seas on its errand of mercy.

On reaching Jurby the Ramsey Rocket Corps found that the trawler was beached in the shadow of a steep headland just below Jurby Church. In order to reach the beach the men had to trudge with their apparatus over water-logged fields and made an adventurous descent down the headland. To avoid the necessity of having to fire a line to the trawler the Ship's Cook, Norman Platt of Fleetwood, pluckily swam ashore with a line and thus established communication with the Rocket Corps. The life-saving apparatus was then swung up and the remainder of the crew, cold and tired after their

G.D. Learoyd collection

The *Lady Harrison* on her trials, 1931.

W.S. Basnett collection

Crew and some Branch Officers c.1931. Back row L to R: J. Callow, J. Jobson, F. Cottier, A. Martin. Centre: F. Cottier, W. Gawne, D. Clarey, W. Corkish, H. Clarke, W. Kennish (Mechanic), E. Starkey (Asst. Mechanic), W. Crix, W. Christian, R. Christian, E. Corlett (Ch. Launcher), P. Sharpe. Front: J.B. Kee (Hon. Sec.), J. Comish (2nd Cox), Canon M.W. Harrison (Chairman), J. Lord (Coxswain), A.E. Chrystal (Vice-Chairman), D. Christian.

gruelling ordeal, were brought safely ashore by means of the breeches buoy.

In the meantime the Peel and Ramsey Lifeboats were being tossed like corks on the swollen seas but kept manfully at their task until within sight of the trawler when signals were sent up turning them back. The Peel Lifeboat, unable to make the turn for Peel, came on to Ramsey where she put into harbour. The Ramsey Lifeboat came up to the South Beach below the harbour and was hauled ashore. A member of the crew told the "Courier" representative that the *Lady Harrison* which was taking her first service, had behaved splendidly. The crew, he said, were delighted with her.

The trawler Pasages is 125ft 7ins. in length and 23ft 5ins. in breadth and has a gross tonnage of 271. She was built in Toronto in 1917 and has a 62 H.P. steam reciprocating engine. Her owners are the Boston Deep Sea Fishing Co. of Grimsby and she is managed by Mr. B.A. Parks of Fleetwood. She was proceeding to her home port with a cargo of herring. Efforts will be made to refloat her when the wind and weather have subsided.

Ramsey Lifeboat Secretary, J.B. Kee, examined the ship on his return from the mainland and found that she was not badly damaged. He was able to express an opinion that providing she does not sustain any damage through stormy weather, she will probably be refloated between the 7th and 10th of the month. The cargo of fish aboard, valued at £600, has been rendered useless and will probably be dumped overboard. The crew left the Island today (Dec. 4th) and the Skipper will leave tomorrow."

The optimistic predictions did not come true, however. The ship became a total loss and even to this day some remains of her hull can still be seen on the beach a short distance North of Jurby Head.

At the Branch A.G.M. on the 11th December, a week later, a report was read out on the service to the Pasages and the Coxswain's and Crew's very favourable comments on the behaviour of the new Lifeboat and her steaming qualities. It was also announced that Capt. Drewry, the Chief Inspector, and Commander Cousins would inspect the Station on the 21st December. At this meeting it was decided to authorise the Coxswain to employ a Messenger whose task it would be to get in touch with any Crew Members who did not respond to the maroons within a reasonable length of time when a service was imminent.

The 1930s

The 1930s proved a reasonably quiet decade for the Ramsey Station with only two services a year on average. The first was in late 1931, as already stated, to the trawler Pasages and this was followed on 5th January, 1932, to the ss Hawthorn, registered in Liverpool. She was at anchor in Ramsey Bay and at 1.45 p.m. that day her International Code flags "W.O." were sighted flying from a mast. This signalled that a doctor was required. By 1.55 p.m. the *Lady Harrison* was launched with a doctor aboard and made for the ship. It transpired that the ship's 2nd Engineer had fallen in the engine-room and broken some ribs. He was landed and taken to Ramsey Cottage Hospital.

Later in the month a brief note in the Minutes Book records that the new tractor house was completed on the 29th January and the tractor housed therein. A new tractor was soon to be supplied, however, and this was announced at the next Branch Meeting on the 27th June.

Lifeboat Supper

Celebrations of any note were somewhat rare in those years of Depression but the 12th February, 1932, was an exception for the Lifeboat Crew, Committee and helpers. The local Press gave a fulsome account of a Lifeboat Supper which was held in Ramsey.

"The Members of the Crew of the Ramsey Lifeboat were entertained to supper at the Saddle Hotel on Friday night last through the generosity of Mrs. A.E. Groves, President of the Ladies' Committee of the Ramsey Branch. Several members of the Committee were also present and Mr. A.E. Chrystal, Vice-Chairman, presided in the absence of the Chairman the Rev. M.W. Harrison. Mr. J.B. Kee, C.T.C, J.P., Secretary of the Branch, was Master of Ceremonies. About sixty persons sat down to an excellent meal which consisted of hot-pot followed by plum pudding. Mr. J.C. Lees had the tables laid out and the room decorated very nicely for the occasion, the lifeboat colours predominating. A huge lifeboat was suspended over the table and an appropriate touch was lent by the waiters being attired in the familiar "jelly bags". It is some years since a lifeboat supper was last held in Ramsey and the action of Mrs. Groves in reviving this happy event was greatly appreciated. If there are any people in the world who can be relied upon to enter heartily into festivities of this kind – they are the members of the Ramsey Lifeboat Crew and their helpers – and there are none more deserving of such recognition of their services."

The report continues with a detailed account of the speeches and toasts made, with mention of Mr. T.C. Teare, a Committee Member, and Coxswain J.T. Lord. Many old lifeboatmen were present including Capt. Gawne, Oscar and Fred Corlett, Harry Sharpe and Jack Clarey. "Lifeboat" families were especially mentioned in the proceedings with the Kinnins, Gawnes, Martins, Crixs and Corkishes to the fore. District Inspector Dawkins was also present and spoke of the efficiency of the Ramsey Station and made mention of the new motor Lifeboat.

At the June Committee Meeting members were told that Jas. Gawne, the summer caretaker of the Boathouse, was unable to take up this year's duties owing to ill-health. Harry Sharpe was elected in his stead.

The only other call-out of the year was on the 21st December to the steam trawler Velia. At 2 a.m. the *Lady Harrison* was launched in response

THE LIFE-BELT IN USE BY THE CREWS OF THE LIFE-BOATS OF THE NATIONAL LIFE-BOAT INSTITUTION.

The requisite qualities of a life-boatman's life-belt are—

1. Sufficient extra buoyancy to support a man heavily clothed, with his head and shoulders above the water, and to enable him to support another person besides himself.

2. Perfect flexibility, so as to readily conform to the shape of the wearer.

3. A division into two zones, an upper and lower, so that between the two it may be secured tightly round the waist; for in no other manner can it be confined sufficiently close and secure round the body without such pressure over the chest and ribs as to materially affect the free action of the lungs, impede the muscular movement of the chest and arms, and thereby diminish the power of endurance of fatigue, which, in rowing-boats, is a matter of vital importance.

4. Strength, durability, and non-liability to injury

The cork life-belt of the NATIONAL LIFE-BOAT INSTITUTION possesses the first two qualities in a greater degree than any other life-belt, and the third one exclusively. (*Vide* annexed figure.)

From "The Lifeboat", May 1st 1884.

THE LIFE-BELT USED BY THE CREWS OF THE LIFE-BOATS OF THE ROYAL NATIONAL LIFE-BOAT INSTITUTION.

The requisite qualities of a Life-boat man's life-belt are—

1. Sufficient extra buoyancy, 22 lbs., to support a man heavily clothed, with his head and shoulders above the water, or to enable him to support another person besides himself.

2. Perfect flexibility, so as to readily conform to the shape of the wearer.

3. A division into two zones, an upper and lower, so that between the two it may be secured tightly round the waist; for in no other manner can it be confined sufficiently close and secure round the body without such pressure over the chest and ribs as to materially affect the free action of the lungs, impede the muscular movement of the chest and arms, and thereby diminish the power of endurance of fatigue, which, in rowing-boats, is a matter of vital importance.

4. Strength, durability and non-liability to injury.

From "The Lifeboat", May 1st 1907.

RNLI Poole

The No. 3 pattern kapok lifebelt used in the late 1920s.

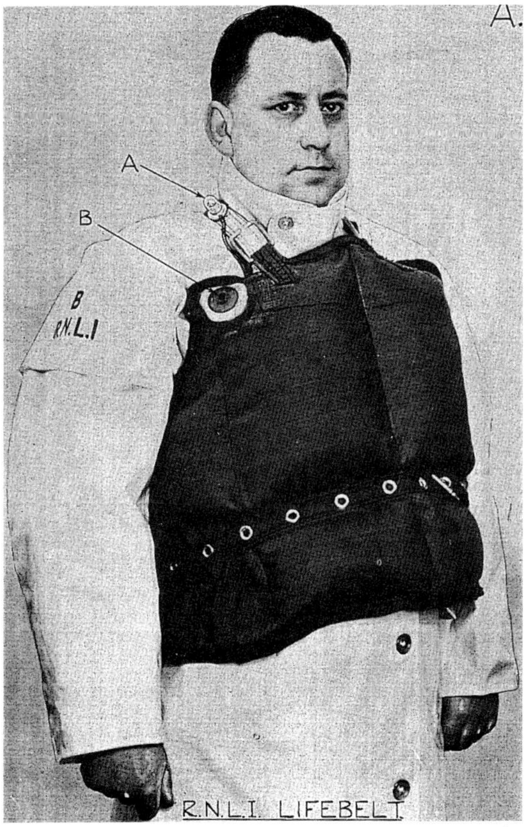

RNLI Poole

RNLI lifebelt of the 1940s and 1950s.

to a telephone call from the Cranstal Coastguard. He reported that a vessel was ashore about half a mile from his Station. However, on reaching the trawler it was found that the only assistance required from the Lifeboat was for her to lay out a sea anchor and this was achieved.

After this launch it was again reported that the tractor had broken down during the operation and the Committee decided to inform RNLI Headquarters of the dissatisfaction with this vital machine.

In 1933, on the 10th March, the Ladies' Guild held a Bridge Drive at the Mitre Hotel in order to raise funds to provide woollen jerseys for the Crew.

Heavy Weather Gear

At this point it should be mentioned that from the very early days the RNLI provided their crews with oilskins, seaboots and lifejackets. The latter varied throughout the years as improvements were made. The early photograph of the crew of *The Two Sisters* in Ramsey in 1887 shows the standard heavy-weather gear of the 1880s and particularly the heavy cork lifejackets. The notes with the sketch give an indication of the qualities of the jacket in those years. From 1906 kapok-filled lifejackets were introduced. Kapok is a type of tree cotton which is very light and buoyant and was obviously a big improvement for the Crews. Even to this day, the British Ministry of Transport require similar kapok-filled lifejackets for British merchant ships. In 1966, however, the RNLI changed over to far more sophisticated air-filled ones which are used today. The heavy-weather clothing has also altered continually with the times and currently the jackets, leggings and crash helmets give the crews a very up-to-date "space age" look and the very greatest protection against the elements. Even though many of the modern lifeboats have adequate cabins and wheelhouses, very many are still virtually open boats like the old *James Ball Ritchie* of Ramsey. Cabins or not, however, much of the seamanship and rescue work is carried out on deck and usually in the fierce weather which has caused the casualty in the first place.

In the year 1934 the death of Mr. J.B. Kee, Hon. Secretary, took place and Messrs. J. Ramsey and W.R. Edwards were appointed Hon. Secretary and Treasurer respectively. The Rev. Edward Paton returned to the Island in that year after an absence of 33 years and rejoined the Committee.

That year also saw the service to the yacht Jubilee. At 15 minutes past midnight on the 6th June the local Police received a telephone message that a small yacht was in distress just off the Queen's Pier, Ramsey. Upon further investigation it was found that the yacht was stranded some one and a half miles South of the

Look-out Point. Her crew of two had already landed. By 1 a.m. the owner decided to return on board with two men for assistance but by 3.20 a.m. they had fired two red flares for further help. The Lifeboat was launched and towed the troubled vessel clear, later mooring her in Ramsey Harbour.

Two days after this service the Committee presented a pipe and pouch to Mr. H. Lace, the District Officer of Coastguards. Mr. Lace was leaving the Island to take up an appointment in Ireland and the gift was in recognition of his good services rendered over the years to the Lifeboat Station.

At the 1934 A.G.M. in December, amongst other items, the Chief Officer of Coastguards (who was also a Committee Member) suggested that one member of the Lifeboat's Crew should be taught to send and receive morse code messages by lamp. Coxswain Lord was asked for his opinion and the answer came that the matter was already in hand with Crew Member J. Callow presently learning just such skills. However, it was decided to take up the Chief Officer's offer, and Callow continued his studies under the direction of this officer.

Services of 1935

The first service of 1935 was on the 10th April to the schooner Edith May of Wexford when her three crewmen were landed. The second one was on the 8th September to another yacht, the Fanstona, registered in Fleetwood. At 1.15 p.m. the Point of Ayre Lighthouse Keeper reported that a small motor yacht was flying the distress signal from her position half a mile North of Cranstal. The *Lady Harrison* was launched and found the yacht disabled with engine trouble. The Lifeboat took the yacht in tow and both arrived back in Ramsey safely at 3.30 p.m.

At a Branch Meeting later in the month the Committee agreed that the Coxswain and his family should live in the Boathouse accommodation rent free. The Chief RNLI Inspector Cousins disagreed with this motion, however. The outcome was not recorded.

In October of that year the *Lady Harrison* and her Crew were launched to go to the aid of the Finnish cargo vessel Esbo of Helsingfors, which went aground on the Selker Rocks near Bootle (Cumbria) during one of the worst gales known in forty years. On the morning of Saturday, 19th October, 1935, word was received in Ramsey that a large steamship was aground off the Cumberland Coast. The authorities requested the launch of the Ramsey Lifeboat and the *Lady Harrison,* under Coxswain Jack Lord, was underway soon after 8.30 a.m. At the time it was blowing a gale from the WSW later to veer NW and increase to hurricane force.

Ramsey Bay was crowded with ships of all sizes. Some of the trawlers, who were equipped with radios by this time, made remarks over the air that the Lifeboatmen must be mad to run offshore in such conditions ... and that they would not like to be with them..... and so on.

Whilst the Ramsey Lifeboat was getting away the Maryport and Barrow lifeboats were also launched to go to the Esbo's aid.

The *Lady Harrison,* after running some 15 miles ENE from Maughold Head in the heavy following seas, decided that to run in on the distress on a dead lee shore would render her useless to offer assistance. The decision was therefore taken to come about and face the storm and head for Laxey, but she was unable to make any headway for some considerable time.

Meanwhile the Barrow and Maryport lifeboats received a severe battering and the Coxswain of the latter had his ribs crushed when a heavy sea hit his boat. The crew of the Esbo eventually managed to get one of the ship's lifeboats to the shore with some Officers' wives who also took a lifeline with them. This was handed to the Bootle Rocket Brigade and they then effected the rescue of the entire ship's crew. The ship was later refloated by a Glasgow salvage firm and sold for scrap. But the cargo ship had the last word, for whilst under tow by two Glasgow tugs on the 28th March, 1936, she sank and was finally lost off the South of Scotland and so in the end cheated the breakers' yard. The Bootle Rocket Brigade and all members of the Lifeboats' Crews, including those of the *Lady Harrison,* were awarded medals and citations by the Finnish Government. A silver and a bronze medal came to Ramsey and a dinner was held in the Crew's honour at the Prince of Wales Hotel at a later date.

The year of 1936 was quiet until the 27th October. At 2.45 p.m. the Lifeboat was launched with a doctor aboard to rendezvous with the London cargo ship Goleta. Four men aboard were treated for food poisoning and an injured man was safely landed in Ramsey for treatment. A second run was made to the ship with medicines and fresh stores.

Then at 7.50 p.m. the same evening a red flare was sighted coming from the schooner Edith May. She was only about 200 yards North of the Queen's Pier and dragging her two anchors. The *Lady Harrison* was launched again and returned within the hour with the ship's crew of three. All these services were conducted in a strong NNW gale with heavy seas.

During the following year of 1937 no services were rendered but the death of Mr. A.E. Chrystal, Committee Vice-Chairman since 1927 and who had served on the Committee since 1914, was noted. Mr. W.L. Corlett succeeded him.

In the January of 1938 a service to the small cargo vessel Nora was recorded in a first-hand account written by our well-known Mr. William

Corlett who was employed on the Ramsey quayside at the time.

"On the 21st January, 1938, the writer of this story had been working in the little BEN VEG (Ramsey Steamship Co.), which was discharging a cargo of fertilizer into railway wagons for the Farmers Club of Douglas. The day was blustery with a SW wind and on the early morning tide the steamship BEACONIA of Whitehaven came into Ramsey Harbour windbound.

However, before the next day dawned, both these ships were to have spent a fearful and eventful night in Ramsey Bay.

A young barmaid from the Saddle Hotel had given up her job and decided to return to her native Whitehaven. With this in mind she asked Captain Shaw of the BEACONIA for a passage home to which he readily agreed. They sailed on the late evening tide that night but anchored out in the Bay, as did the BEN VEG.

At about 8 p.m. both ships left the Bay to make a quick passage to Whitehaven, but by this time the weather was deteriorating quickly. When they reached the Bahama Bank it was blowing a raging gale from the SW and so both ships returned to anchor off Ramsey. By the time they did so the winds were of storm force.

Whilst this was happening various other ships were also seeking shelter, amongst them the little steamship NORA of Liverpool. She was on passage from Liverpool to Palnackie with a cargo of cattle-feed.

At this time I was employed freelance about the quayside and had been working in BEN VEG during the day. I was also doing a bit of hobbling (taking ship's lines when berthing) in my spare time. Needless to say, on this particular night, Robert Carswell and I had teamed up to be on foot in case any of the ships came into the harbour windbound. We eventually berthed the BEACONIA and BEN VEG and also some steam trawlers for which we did not get paid.

About an hour before high water we decided to spell one another and have a bite to eat. As I had the first spell I was somewhat surprised to hear the Lifeboat maroons being sounded shortly after getting my snack. By the time I got to the seafront, the *Lady Harrison* was already under-way. It seems that Robert Carswell had spotted what he thought was a ship on fire and had gone to see Capt. Cleator at the Harbour Master's Office to tell him. The Harbour Master soon confirmed that it was a ship in distress and contacted the Coastguard and then Coxswain Jack Lord, by telephone. The Coastguards were situated at the end of the Queen's Pier but owing to the haze lying over the Bay, they could not see the ship in question. Jack Lord however, who had not gone to bed as he felt uneasy about the stormy night, confirmed sighting the distress and fired off the maroons. Although his action was prompt, it was later found to be unfavourable with the Committee as they had not been consulted.

Once under-way the *Lady Harrison* found the NORA with both anchors down but being driven towards the Whitestone Bank and her Master injured with some of his ribs crushed. Her crew had used all their distress flares and had set a barrel of tar alight to draw attention to their plight. However with the weather conditions prevailing at the time in the Bay, no other vessel could possibly have rendered assistance.

The Lifeboat got alongside safely and put some men aboard then brought the ship into more sheltered waters near the Queen's Pier. The Master was brought ashore for treatment in the Cottage Hospital.

Whilst on their way to the NORA the Lifeboat's Crew passed another steamship, the SNOWCRETE of Glasgow. Her cargo of chippings had shifted causing a heavy list and so once the NORA was in a safer anchorage, the *Lady Harrison* returned to the Scottish ship but found that her crew had got the situation in hand and had righted her.

Although the barmaid from the Saddle Hotel had had more than enough experience of bad weather for one night, she had the pluck to leave again for Whitehaven on the following tide. On finally coming ashore from the Beaconia, she was so sea-sick that she could hardly stand."

Further deaths occurred during the year. The service above was, sadly, the last one for Jack Lord the Coxswain. On the 1st April, his birthday, he was lost in Ramsey Harbour whilst taking out the MANXSONA from the salt berth. His place aboard the *Lady Harrison* was taken by John Comish. Mrs. Groves, the first President of the Ladies' Guild, also died. Her son, Keith Grimble Groves, was elected to the Committee in 1939.

SECOND WORLD WAR

The advent of the Second World War did not see any great increase in the lifeboat services although on several occasions the *Lady Harrison* was called out to search for and rescue aircrews who had come down in the Irish Sea.

The first service during the war was on the 13th September, 1939. The steamship GREYPOINT, registered in Belfast, grounded on the Point of Ayre. She was loaded with general cargo and 300 head of cattle. Both the Ramsey Lifeboat and the local Lifesaving Services proceeded to the location. However, upon reaching there, they found that the ship had refloated herself by lowering her lifeboats and running out kedge anchors despite a fresh NW'ly gale.

Later in the year, on the 10th December, the *Lady Harrison* was launched at 9.30 a.m. to aid the survivors of a bad collision. The SS FIRE KING of Liverpool was on a passage from Glasgow to her home port with a general cargo and had been approaching the Point of Ayre on a fine clear morning. The mail steamer DUKE OF LANCASTER was observed ahead whilst on her passage from Heysham to Belfast, having passed the Point of Ayre. The ships were on a collision course and for some reason the giving-way vessel did not and the larger passenger ship sliced right through the fore-hatch of the FIRE KING. An elderly fireman on the unfortunate cargo ship was badly crushed and he and the

G.D. Learoyd collection

The mail steamship DUKE OF LANCASTER aground near the Point of Ayre, 1939.

rest of the crew quickly abandoned their ship and scrambled up on to the bows of the DUKE OF LANCASTER. The smaller ship sank within minutes.

Meanwhile, the *Lady Harrison* was launched, having been alerted to the accident by Portpatrick Radio Station which had picked up the distress call direct from the mail steamer. The Lifeboat, under John Comish and with a doctor aboard, made for the collision area some six miles NW from the Point of Ayre Lighthouse. Medical supplies were also taken and the *Lady Harrison* escorted the surviving ship back to a safe anchorage in Ramsey Bay. Here the FIRE KING's survivors were taken off the mail steamer and landed in the town. Sadly, the injured fireman died in the Cottage Hospital later in the day. The Lifeboat was then kept busy most of the day taking salvage-men and supplies to the damaged ship and stood by her until salvage tugs arrived to take the DUKE OF LANCASTER away under tow.

Early in the New Year of 1940, January and February saw several more shipping accidents in the Ramsey area, although not all requiring the services of the *Lady Harrison* and her Crew.

The weather was calmer in January but fog took over as the major problem and on the 12th in a light SE'ly wind the MARCHIONESS of Glasgow went aground West of the Point of Ayre. She was refloated the next day and brought into Ramsey Harbour where it was found that she was none the worse for her contact with the shingle shore.

Within a few days the larger Norwegian steamship GRANFOSS grounded near the same place but refloated on the next tide. She was a vessel of over 1000 tons gross and found that she was making water in the way of some sprung rivets. She requested a pilot in order to enter Ramsey Harbour, but Willie Kennish and Ernie Starkey went aboard the ship and advised her Master that as the tides were falling it would be better to carry out repairs in the Bay. These were done in fair weather but it was not to remain calm for very long.

The 16th of the month produced a force 9 NE'ly gale and at 1 p.m. the *Lady Harrison* under Coxswain John Comish was launched into driving snow squalls to go to the aid of three Royal Air Force fast launches. These vessels were anchored in the Bay just off the Queen's Pier. At about the same time Corporal Herbert Kneale of the R.A.F. and a Ramsey man, with two other crew, launched a dinghy from the pier and managed to get out and board one of the launches. This took a lot of good seamanship and some daring but the Corporal came from a well-known seafaring family. The Lifeboat could do no more than stand-by them but the launch got under-way and both boats made back to the harbour and safety and berthed without incident.

LOSS OF THE MERISIA

On the 26th January, in a whole SE gale which turned into a blizzard, the Fleetwood trawler

MERISIA went ashore at Bulgham Bay, some four miles South of Maughold Lighthouse. At 7.30 a.m. a message was received from the Douglas Police that a vessel was in distress two miles North of Laxey. The Ramsey Coxswain was informed and also the District L.S.A. Officer. His team left at 8.10 a.m. but did not reach Bulgham until 9.15 a.m. owing to dense fog. With visibility down to 10 yards, the area of the wreck was located at 10 a.m., some 600 feet below Ballaragh Cliff. A man could be heard calling for a lifeboat, although the trawler was not visible. A rocket was fired from the top of the cliff but with the strong SE gale it blew back. At 11.45 a.m. a second rocket was fired, this time from the bottom of the cliff, but with visibility only 10 yards the results of the firing were not known. By 12.30 p.m. visibility was improving and six feet of mast on top of the funnel were visible. A black object resembling a man was seen on the top of the mast and so a third rocket was fired and the rescue team tried to get a line to the man but it was washed away. A fourth rocket was made ready but by then the seaman had disappeared. At 2.30 p.m. a search was made along the bottom of the cliffs for any bodies but no traces were found. It was 8 p.m. before the would-be rescuers turned for home. It had been impossible to launch the Ramsey Lifeboat and the only one to put to sea was the *Sir Heath Harrison* of Port St. Mary, with Coxswain Kelly. In terrible conditions the Lifeboat came up the East Coast and carried out a search for survivors. There were none. The ship became a total loss.

THE GLENDUN RESCUE

Three weeks later, on the 16th February, the *Lady Harrison* was launched at 1.15 a.m. to go to the aid of the Belfast registered cargo vessel GLENDUN. She had grounded on rocks some two miles SSW from Maughold Head.

An article in the Ramsey Courier of the 1st March, 1940, gave a detailed account of the incident.

"The Belfast steamer GLENDUN which was wrecked on Maughold coast on Friday, 16th February, is lying on the rocks before Mr. Corteen's farm at Ballafayle, and many people have visited the scene during recent days.

Mr. Wm. Brearley of Ballaskeig, who first gave the alarm and went to the assistance of the crew after having word sent to Ramsey for the Lifeboat and Rocket Brigade, has received a letter. It is dated the 22nd February and from Carrickfergus, in which the Captain reports that he has arrived home safely and wishes to thank Mr. Brearley for his kindness to him and members of his crew. He reckons that they would have been a much longer time in their lifeboats had it not been for the help rendered. Capt. Lockhard also says he considers the Ramsey Lifeboat did exceedingly well under the circumstances and wishes to thank the Coxswain and Crew for the prompt attention they gave to the men of the GLENDUN. The people of Ramsey, adds Capt. Lockhard, were very kind and attentive to the crew who all appreciate very much what was one for them.

It will be recalled that when Mr. Brearley, his son and Mr. Fred Davies, got in touch with the distressed vessel, they were able to give directions as to the GLENDUN's position and also a line was got ashore as a means to help the crew land if necessary. What actually happened was that the crew were able to take to their lifeboats and stand-off for the *Lady Harrison* to bring them in to Ramsey. The men lost all their belongings and the cargo of coal on the GLENDUN was also lost."

THE ULSTER QUEEN RESCUE

The month of February in 1940 was to see yet another grounding in the vicinity of Maughold Head; the third, in fact, in only four weeks. On Wednesday the 28th, at 5.15 a.m., the *Lady Harrison* was at sea again and this time to assist a large ship in distress. This was the passenger and mail vessel ULSTER QUEEN with 93 passengers and 53 crew on board. A serious incident, indeed.

The early morning of the 28th was originally calm but with fog, which no doubt initiated the casualty, coupled with the wartime blackout of navigational aids. The ship ran aground on sand and close to rocks between Stack Mooar and Cor Stack at 2.35 a.m. Her distress call was received by Portpatrick Radio and also the Trinity House vessel BEACON and the mail steamship DUKE OF LANCASTER which were both in the vicinity at the time. The alarm was not received in Ramsey until 4.36 a.m., but, in the meantime at 3.20 a.m., the DUKE OF LANCASTER came within two miles of the casualty and anchored. It was the nearest she could get owing to the ground swell and shallow waters.

The Master of the ULSTER QUEEN, Capt. James Arbuckle, decided it prudent to transfer all his passengers to the DUKE OF LANCASTER immediately, as he had received a bad weather forecast. Most of them, of course, were asleep and quite unaware of the predicament they were in. They were awakened and a number of them put into three of the ship's lifeboats and lowered away.

In Ramsey, once the alarm was raised, the Coastguards assembled and set off for Maughold and the *Lady Harrison,* with Coxswain John Comish in command, was launched at 5.15 a.m. There was a freshening SSE wind at the time with a slight sea, rain, and still dense fog. They found the stricken ship without delay and went alongside.

The *Lady Harrison* took off 20 passengers at once and then took in tow two ship's lifeboats, both full of passengers. They made the two mile run to the DUKE OF LANCASTER in company with other motor launches towing lifeboats

G.D. Learoyd collection

The mail vessel ULSTER QUEEN aground near Maughold Head, 1940. Note the wartime degaussing cable around the ship's side.

from the ULSTER QUEEN. These had been sent to the scene from the two other rescue ships. Owing to the swell further out at the anchorage, the *Lady Harrison* was damaged whilst discharging her passengers and Lifeboatman Ernie Starkey had a narrow escape when a block from the lifeboat falls of the larger ship carried away and came down close to him. It was bitterly cold and many of the passengers were women, children and small babies and they were badly affected by sea-sickness. It was not an easy job to get them up on to the mail steamer. Nevertheless, the whole transfer of 93 people was completed in just over one hour in a most efficient manner and with no injuries or loss of life. The DUKE OF LANCASTER thereupon weighed anchor and resumed her passage.

The wind by this time had veered NE and was blowing a whole gale. On making her way back to the distressed ship the *Lady Harrison* came across five more lifeboats and their crews from the ULSTER QUEEN also returning, and she attempted to take them in tow. This had to be abandoned in the circumstances and so their crews, which numbered eight seamen under Second Officer W. Williams, were taken off by the *Lady Harrison* and they then made back for Ramsey where they arrived at 9 a.m. The nine ship's crewmen were taken ashore exhausted and frozen after their ordeal. They were given warm food and shelter.

Later the same afternoon a Liverpool tug attempted to tow the ULSTER QUEEN off the beach at high water. A strong SE gale was blowing and this caused the ship to swing broadside on to the headland. In this position the tug found it impossible to get close enough inshore to exert her full power and so the attempt was abandoned. Assistance in this salvage work was given by the Trinity House ship BEACON which was still at the scene.

The Ramsey Rocket Brigade, under the command of District Officer of Coastguards P. Keohane and Station Officer Crummey, was standing-by throughout. After the unsuccessful refloating attempt they were called upon to take off the remaining 44 of the ULSTER QUEEN's crew soon after 3 p.m. Conditions were severe with the ship broadside on to the weather and taking a terrific pounding. A line from ship to shore had been established earlier in the day and so the breeches buoy was set up and the seamen were brought ashore, one by one. After landing they had to climb up the slippery face of the cliff and the gathered crowds of spectators lent willing hands. The Master was the last to leave his ship. Rope ladders had been left over the ship's side to enable boarding her again at low water. By this time it was 6.20 p.m.

This rescue by breeches buoy was the biggest job ever handled by the Ramsey Rocket Brigade, and all – well, nearly all – were brought to safety. Much regret was felt by everyone that a fine Alsatian dog, belonging to the daughter of the ship's owner, was lost. The breeches buoy was not large enough to accommodate a seaman and the dog as well, so during the evacuation the animal was fastened in alone and sent ashore. Apparently, when it realised it was suspended high above the sea, it took fright and made a wild spring out of the tackle. It fell into the sea and although there were many would-be rescuers it was impossible to reach the dog in the sea running at the time and so he was lost.

On Thursday morning the ship's stewards and galley staff left the Island, but the Master and remaining crew stayed behind to assist with the next refloating attempt and to generally look after the ship. An inspection of the ship was carried out by Commander Smith of Liverpool, representing the London & Liverpool Salvage Association. With him were Mr. Jas. Ramsay, Lloyds' Agent for the Isle of Man and a representative of the owners.

Plans for refloating the vessel were discussed and it was decided not to make another attempt until the tides were more favourable. In the meantime the ship was made somewhat lighter by discharging most of the cargo and other items. Amongst these were the ship's pets, three canaries and a pigeon!

The ULSTER QUEEN eventually refloated herself on Easter Monday, 1940. Her cargo had been discharged into the Ramsey Steamship Co.'s cargo vessels BEN AIN, BEN ELLEN and BEN VOOAR, and they brought it into the port. The famous salvage vessel RANGER of the Liverpool & Glasgow Salvage Association stood-by during the re-floating, together with the SIRDAR. It was found that, had the ship gone aground a few feet further ahead or astern of where she had touched, she would surely have grounded on rocks and never survived to sail again.

The Belfast Steamship Co. owned the motor ship which was built in Belfast in 1929. She had a length of 346 ft. and grossed 3757 tons.

Official records show that the *Lady Harrison* and her Crew were accredited with saving some 60 lives that bleak February morning. Cash rewards given for their efforts amounted to £18.14s.3d.

ROYALIST ON FIRE

During the ULSTER QUEEN episode another ship locally had a bad experience but lived to tell the tale. The London steam trawler ROYALIST was homeward bound from the fishing grounds on the 9th March, 1940, when she caught fire just North of the Isle of Man. The fire started in the forepeak and net store. Her crew beached the ship near the North Pier and the Ramsey Fire Brigade put a hose aboard and extinguished the fire. The salvage vessel RANGER was still off Maughold Head attending the ULSTER QUEEN when she was called to the ROYALIST. The fire was under control by the time she arrived but, nevertheless, she remained to pump the trawler out. The ROYALIST was refloated the next morning and sailed for Fleetwood.

The final call-out of the year for the Lifeboat was on the 9th November. The motor vessel PRINCESS IRENE of Groningen ran aground at 6 a.m. in a Southerly gale, right abeam of the Point of Ayre Lighthouse. She was on charter to John Kelly of Belfast and loaded with coal from Garston to Belfast.

The alarm was raised and both the *Lady Harrison* and the Coastguards were called to the scene, but the ship was high and dry by the time they got there and their services were not required. After discharging a certain amount of cargo, her crew were able to lay out kedge anchors and she was later safely refloated and brought into Ramsey Harbour.

Problems on the Ramsey Coast for the following year of 1941 commenced with the wrecking of H.M. Yacht SELENE on the 25th January. Whilst entering Ramsey Harbour in the company of H.M. Yacht NINA, she struck the North Pier in a force 6 SE wind. As she drifted disabled around it, the crew abandoned ship by climbing up on to the wooden jetty and they were then able to make the yacht fast. The Coastguards stood-by with lifelines in case they were needed as there was a heavy sea running. During the night, however, the SELENE broke loose and drifted ashore on the North Beach where she became a total loss. The Naval authorities took charge and mounted a guard but apparently this did not prevent her from being looted. She was later sold to Mr. Herbie Nelson and broken up for scrap.

Lifeboat Day for 1941 was arranged for 19th August. At a previous Committee Meeting it was agreed to invite Service Officers stationed locally and to include the Commandant of the Ramsey Mooragh Prisoner-of-War Camp.

On the 7th September, the Portpatrick Coastguard received a message from a lookout at the Isle of Whithorn (near Burrow Head, Wigtownshire) to the effect that an unknown vessel appeared to be sinking in a position some 181 degrees and 12 miles from Whithorn. The Ramsey Lifeboat was requested and she was launched at 12.33 p.m. A search of the area took place in the company of an RAF speedboat and an aircraft. Nothing was ever found and the craft returned to their bases at 5.40 p.m.

The lack of engine power of the *Lady Harrison* was highlighted in an episode off Ramsey on the 31st January, 1941, and resulted in further requests for a faster and more powerful boat.

On that day, the mv GOLDFINCH of London arrived in Ramsey with a general cargo from her home port. Just South of Maughold Head she had sighted the mv SATURNUS of Dezful (Holland) apparently steaming very slowly with a barrage-balloon aloft.

It was not all that it seemed for, shortly afterwards, this ship came ashore at Port Mooar in the light NE'ly wind. When the RAF duty launch went to investigate her Commanding Officer found no crew aboard! The ship had been abandoned.

It soon came to light that she was a barrage-balloon ship originally stationed in the River Mersey. During a heavy German air raid she had been the subject of a near miss and her crew had abandoned ship. She then broke from her moorings and drifted North, eventually to the Isle of Man. The Douglas Lifeboat put an RN Lieutenant aboard with some ratings and then towed the ship back to Douglas.

Coxswain Comish of the *Lady Harrison* decided not to launch the Ramsey Boat as there was no danger to life and his Boat did not have enough power to successfully tow a vessel of some 250 tons.

At the very end of October a Committee Meeting was held and it was announced that Lifeboat Mechanic Thomas Arthur Corlett was being called-up for war service. Mr. S. Lindsay, on the other hand, was being discharged from the Navy and so he would take his place.

STRATHAIRLIE RESCUE

The next successful service for the *Lady Harrison* and her Crew was on the 20th November, to the steam trawler STRATHAIRLIE registered in Aberdeen. At 5.40 a.m. the Auxiliary Coastguard at Dog Mills, just North of Ramsey, reported seeing red and white rockets off Shellag Point. At 6.10 a.m. the District Coastguard Officer requested the Station Officer to go to the LSA Office and order the Team out and to collect their gear. At 6.38 the Lifeboat Hon. Secretary and the Coxswain were informed that the vessel was probably drifting ashore and that a launch was advised. This was done, but for some reason the *Lady Harrison* was delayed on the slip for a considerable time. The two Coastguard Officers then proceeded to the scene in a police car and found the ship ashore and burning flares. The line-throwing equipment was transported across a field, down a steep cliff and the first line was shot at 7.10 a.m. A force 6 inshore wind was blowing at the time and caused it to fall short. By 7.40 a.m. the full Coastguard Team arrived with all the lifesaving equipment, having had to carry it by hand some two miles along the beach. At 8 a.m. a second rocket was fired but this also fell short. Fifteen minutes later the third rocket took the initial line right across the ship and the crew were able to start to haul in the heavier lines.

Rescue was also at hand from the sea by this time as the *Lady Harrison* approached from windward. The crew of the STRATHAIRLIE therefore abandoned setting up the breeches buoy rig in favour of a Lifeboat rescue, but it was a long and difficult task for the Lifeboatmen. Coxswain John Comish took the Lifeboat alongside the stricken trawler thirteen times by the end of the rescue, taking one crew member off at a time. Crowds watched from the shore with bated breath, expecting that at each run the *Lady Harrison* would be smashed against the hull of the trawler and wrecked. It did not happen and John Comish was later awarded the RNLI Bronze Medal for his superb seamanship and the successful service.

1942 was a quieter year and the only busy day was the 14th September. At 4.27 in the afternoon the Ramsey Harbour Master informed the Coastguards that the locally registered fishing vessel CARIBOU was overdue and requested a search. The Lifeboat Crew was also assembled and soon after 4.30 p.m. the *Lady Harrison* was launched. Half-an-hour later the RAF Base at

G.D. Learoyd collection

Steam trawler STRATHAIRLIE ashore North of Dog Mills, 1941.

Jurby was asked to provide an air search and they replied that this would be done as soon as an aircraft became available. At 7.45 p.m. the Lifeboat returned with the CARIBOU in tow. She had been found drifting off the Point of Ayre.

In 1943 there were three unsuccessful call-outs for the Lifeboat but in late March there was an interesting incident which took place at Ramsey and which did involve some members of the Crew of the *Lady Harrison* but not the Lifeboat herself.

SALVAGING THE NOLISEMENT

On the 23rd, the Cardiff registered cargo ship NOLISEMENT came into Ramsey Bay under tow from the Dutch tug SEINE. Whilst outward bound from the UK to the Middle East with a cargo of military equipment, the ship struck rocks off the South of the Isle of Man. She was badly damaged and made water fast. As it was considered that Ramsey had the only safe beach for grounding, the NOLISEMENT was brought Northwards. There was a strong NE wind at the time and the Dutch tug Skipper decided to get the ship on to the North Beach, above the harbour entrance. The local fishing boat ATLANTIS, Skipper Frank Cottier, took out Willy Kennish and Ernie Starkey to act as pilots and also Salvage Officials from the Liverpool & Glasgow Salvage Association. After consultations all round, the local pilots advised that the beach just South of the Queen's Pier had an excellent sandy bottom with no obstructions and was the most suitable area. The beaching was successfully carried out. The Admiralty salvage tug FIRST then arrived with powerful pumps and she also took out gear obtained in Ramsey. A cement box was fitted in way of the NOLISEMENT's damaged hull and after a number of days an attempt was made to tow the ship across to Liverpool. After only reaching a few miles off Maughold Head the ship started to make water again and was quickly towed back to Ramsey. She was beached for a second time at low water, some one and a half cables ENE from the Queen's Pier. At the next high water she was brought higher up the beach, very near the Pier. Once again she was pumped out. After working around the clock, the vessel was eventually towed away to Liverpool on the 5th April.

The NOLISEMENT was built in 1928 at Howdon-on-Tyne and was owned by the Nolisement Shipping Co. of Cardiff. She was 5084 gross tons and 412ft. long.

On the 28th May, 1943, arrangements for the annual Lifeboat Day were agreed upon and the date was set for the 14th August. It was decided to ask the Lt. Governor of the Island, Earl Granville, to be the Chief Guest and to ask him to make the annual Appeal for funds. Other guests to be invited were Group Captain Williamson of the RAF Station, Jurby; Group Captain Marson, RAF Station Andreas, and Major H.O. Daniel, Officer Commanding Mooragh Camp. Presumably the event took place as planned but no further note of it was made in the Station Minutes Book.

The 29th December, 1943, saw the only call-out of the year. This was to the motor vessel CAIRNGORN. Just before 1 o'clock that morning the Lighthouse Keeper at the Point of Ayre reported to the District Coastguard Officer that a ship was ashore near the Point. At 1.51 a.m. the *Lady Harrison* was afloat and she was followed by the Coastguard Rescue Team taking their equipment by road to the area. Soon after 3 o'clock everyone was informed that the crew of the CAIRNGORN was not in any danger and would remain aboard to refloat the ship at the next high water. The Rescue Services returned to base and the ship cleared the beach at 12.12p.m. under her own power.

The final entry in the second volume of the Station Minutes Book (1916-1944) deals with the A.G.M. of that year and about writing to the RNLI on the subject of a more modern lifeboat for Ramsey. Committee Chairman Canon M.W. Harrison presided at the meeting. He was aided by Vice-Chairman W.L. Corlett and Hon. Secretaries and Treasurers J. Ramsey and W.R. Edwards.

John Comish continued as Coxswain; Stanley Lindsay as Mechanic; F.L. Ball as 2nd Coxswain and W. Crix as Bowman.

REQUEST FOR A FASTER LIFEBOAT

In the December of 1944 a letter was written by the Branch to the Institution Headquarters requesting that a larger and faster lifeboat equipped with a radio telephone be sent to Ramsey. Such a boat would also be more suitable for rescuing aircraft crews. The letter pointed out that 50% of maritime casualties around the Isle of Man had come within the Ramsey Station area and also a large proportion of aircraft casualties. A boat capable of 15 knots, and similar to the present Dover lifeboat, would meet the local present-day needs. It was also recommended that a slipway be built at the end of the Queen's Pier so that the lifeboat could be launched directly into the sea. This same recommendation had been made in 1926 when the Institution decided that it was not practicable. The Inspector of the N.W. District came to the Island in April, 1945, and discussed this proposal very fully with the Committee. He stated that it would be very costly to make a slipway on the Pier and that he had doubts about launching the boat at low tide and that it would also be difficult to get back in bad weather. That view has persisted to the present day and the lifeboat remains a carriage-launched one. Even up to the end of 1990 that elusive 15 knots had still not been attained as the *James*

G.D. Learoyd collection

ss Little Orme aground near the Point of Ayre, 1936.

Ball Ritchie, on station for the past 20 years, remained an eight knot boat. In 1991, however, her new Mersey Class replacement has – at last – doubled that speed.

Apart from the visit to the Station by District Inspector Capt. Innes and a special Committee Meeting on the 23rd April to hear his views, no other items of interest were recorded for the year of 1945. There were no lifeboat services.

On the 3rd February, 1946, at 2.45 a.m. HMS Jan Van Gelder reported that she had run down and sunk the Dutch motor vessel Rian. At 3.20 a.m. the *Lady Harrison* was launched and together with an RAF rescue launch proceeded to the scene. At 6.30 a.m. the Lifeboat returned with six survivors from the Dutch vessel who had been picked up by the Jan Van Gelder.

At 5.05 p.m. on the 10th September the same year, word was received in Ramsey that the local fishing vessel Majestic was overdue. In view of the bad weather prevailing, the Hon. Secretary was informed of the matter and asked to have the Lifeboat Crew ready on stand-by. At 5.27 p.m. the Majestic was sighted some two miles NE of the Queen's Pier, but she was soon lost to sight in heavy rain. At 6.12 p.m. the *Lady Harrison* was launched and it was 9 p.m. before she returned and safely landed the fishing vessel's crew of four at the Pier. The Lifeboat had been unable to take the other ship in tow and so had anchored her off the port for the night.

Last Service of 1945

The last service of the year was on the 12th October. At 2 o'clock in the afternoon a message was received in Ramsey from Mr. Lace of Glen Mona. He reported that a vessel one mile East of Maughold Head was continuously sounding her siren. The Lifeboat Crew was alerted and by 2.50 p.m. the *Lady Harrison* was launched. She found the vessel only half a mile off the shore, North East of the Carrick. It turned out to be "Mob 7" belonging to the Royal Army Service Corps. Her Captain stated that the ship's feed to the boilers had failed and so he had lost power. The Lifeboat stood-by her until repairs were effected, when she proceeded to Douglas. The *Lady Harrison* returned to her Station at 9.35 p.m.

During 1946 there were many changes in both the Lifeboat Crew and the Branch Committee. Coxswain John Comish retired and Ernest Starkey took his place. Fred Ball was elected 2nd Coxswain and W.F. Cottier, Bowman. Chairman Canon Harrison and Vice-Chairman W.L. Corlett both died. Canon Harrison had been on the Committee for 36 years, 20 as Chairman. Mr Corlett had served for 40 years which included three as Secretary and nine as Vice-Chairman. The Rev. Halford Young, who had been on the Committee since 1930, was elected Chairman and K.G. Groves, Vice-Chairman. Major Groves was later to be the author of the first history of the Ramsey Lifeboat Station, 1829-1968, dealing mainly with Committee and Crew matters.

At a Committee Meeting on the 18th June, 1946, Major Groves, Vice-Chairman, intimated that he and his wife wished to present a sum of money to the RNLI in memory of their son, Sgt. Met/Air Observer Louis G. Groves, who lost his life on returning from a sortie on 10th September, 1945. Major Groves stated that he wanted to give £100 to the RNLI; £100 to the Ramsey

Branch Endowment Fund; and also, if the RNLI would equip the Ramsey Lifeboat with radio-telephony, he would donate a further £100 towards the cost of its installation. Canon Harrison, on behalf of the local Branch, expressed grateful thanks to Major Groves for his intended gifts.

At another Committee Meeting on the 18th September numerous subjects were aired. Although the tractor was now "officially" in good order, it was still difficult to start-up on occasions. The Institution Tractor Inspector said, however, that the stock of petrol at the station was "no good" and should be replaced immediately.

The subject of Coxswain's houses was next discussed. Mr. Comish had retired and should vacate the Boathouse flat to make way for Mr. Starkey and family. Getting alternative accommodation was difficult and the flat was too small for the Starkey family, especially with one son invalided out of the Services. The Institution was to be made aware of the problem and suggestions were to be put to them in order to resolve the matter.

Note was made of a launch of the Lifeboat a few days before, on the 12th September. An RAF Rescue Launch went to the aid of a boat in distress after the maroons had been fired summoning the crew of the *Lady Harrison*. It was agreed to request the RAF officials to liaise with the Lifeboat Station and let their intentions be known.

The suggestion that a second and subsidiary lifeboat for Ramsey should be supplied and stationed at the Queen's Pier also came up again. The matter was to be put to RNLI Headquarters in a letter.

The meeting noted the deaths of Canon Harrison and Oscar Corlett and paid fitting tribute to their services to the Branch.

The one and only service in 1947 was to the aid of the motor fishing vessel Capella and a member of her crew. At 3.45 a.m. on 14th August red flares were observed some two miles ENE from the Queen's Pier. The Lifeboat was launched and at 4.25 a.m. reached the distress. It was found that the vessel had engine trouble and was stopped. One of her crew of two had been caught in the ship's capstan and was severely injured. A doctor and ambulance were summoned to the Queen's Pier where the seaman was shortly landed and taken to the Cottage Hospital. The *Lady Harrison* then returned to the scene and towed the Capella into harbour.

Loss of the Teazel

On the 6th January, 1948, the *Lady Harrison* had a lucky escape.

At 5.25 a.m. information was received from the Coastguards and the Port St. Mary Lifeboat Mechanic that they had intercepted a MAYDAY signal, via Seaforth Radio, from the mv Teazel. She was apparently in distress some six miles East of the Point of Ayre with a heavy list. The Ramsey Lifeboat was launched at 6.50 p.m., in badly deteriorating weather. The wind was soon SE force 8-10 with visibility down to half a mile. The salvage tug Salveda was dispatched from Campbeltown, Kintyre, to assist in the distress. At about 8 p.m. word was received that the *Lady Harrison* had been blown ashore some 500 yards West of the Point of Ayre Lighthouse. The wind was force 9-10. Douglas and Peel Lifeboats were informed and asked to launch and both were at sea within two minutes of each other within the hour.

At daylight on the 7th some ten aircraft took off from Aldergrove to join the search. By noon that day the Salveda reported that she had found nothing and was returning to Campbeltown. The Douglas Lifeboat also returned to her Station. At 12.10 p.m., however, the ss Dromain picked up two bodies from a raft, some seven miles West of the Point of Ayre. She landed them in Northern Ireland and they were later identified as crew members of the Teazel. By 2 o'clock in the afternoon the Peel Lifeboat returned home, having found nothing, but the RAF continued an air search until darkness.

Meanwhile on shore a Coastguard patrol was instituted, stretching from the Point of Ayre to Jurby, on the NW coast. A 16ft. ship's lifeboat was found at Jurby Point. It contained two burnt-out distress flares and it was confirmed that it had belonged to the Teazel.

The RAF maintained their search on the third day, but nothing else was ever found. It is understood that eight men from the cargo ship perished that storm-ridden night. The *Lady Harrison* survived to tell the tale and was not seriously damaged. Coxswain Ernest Starkey was washed over her side at one point but was hastily hauled aboard again by 2nd Cox Ball, who later received a letter of thanks from the Institution.

A month later the Lifeboat attended the Swedish steamship Noreg of Gothenburg on the 5th February. This was at midday when she was called upon to take out stores to the ship and return her Master who had come ashore by a local boat to purchase them. Adverse weather prevented him getting back to his ship the same way.

At 7.20 a.m. on the 27th July a watchman reported a vessel aground one mile East of Rue Point and making an SOS signal on her siren. This was the steam trawler Northness of Hull. The *Lady Harrison* was launched at 8.05 a.m. and the Coastguard Team also proceeded to the grounding. They found the ship ashore with a heavy list to port. The Lifeboat arrived at 9.55 a.m. and helped to lay out a kedge anchor.

There was a five knot flood tide at the time and so the Coastguards stood-by until noon. The trawler was refloated at 2.10 p.m. with the aid of the Lifeboat.

Six weeks later, at 7.35 p.m. on the 8th September, word was received that the yacht SEAMEW was overdue at Douglas, having left Ramsey at 4 p.m. Enquiries were made but there were no sightings of the yacht reported and so a watch was set at the Queen's Pier, Ramsey, and another at Douglas Head. The Ramsey Lifeboat was launched at 9.30 p.m. and returned one and a half hours later with the SEAMEW in tow. The crew of two reported that they had had engine trouble whilst East of Maughold Head.

Only four days later, on the 12th at 3.10 p.m., a radio message was received from Portpatrick that the tug WARRIOR was making for Ramsey with an injured man on board. It was requested that the Lifeboat should stand-by her and for transport to be arranged to take the man to hospital. An ambulance was therefore arranged and at 3.55 p.m. the *Lady Harrison* was launched with a doctor aboard. On examining the injury, however, the doctor deemed it unnecessary to land the man by boat as the tug was due to berth in Barrow within an hour and a half. The Lifeboat returned at 4.30 p.m.

This was to be the final service for this gallant Lifeboat at Ramsey.

In later years the *Lady Harrison* was used by the Welsh National Trust for work with the bird sanctuaries on Grasholme and Ramsey Islands off St. Brides Bay, Pembrokeshire.

The following list gives added services of the *Lady Harrison* during her 17 years at Ramsey. No lives were saved during these missions and therefore were not included on the Boathouse Service Boards. They do, however, show the amount of time the Lifeboat and her Crews spent at sea on false alarms or looking for missing aircraft, especially during the war years.

1936 Nov. 11 6.50-10.30 p.m. Attended beached ss LITTLE ORME at the Point of Ayre. Five crew taken off by Coastguards and breeches buoy.

1937 Jul. 21 3.30 p.m. - 2.15 a.m. 22nd. Searched for missing aircraft GAEIJ. 11 hours at sea in a severe gale. Nothing found.

1939 Mar. 11 3.45 - 10.30 p.m. Called to dinghy with two crew in trouble off Laxey. Nothing found as dinghy had beached herself off Groudle.

Oct. 26 3.15 p.m. Called to drifter B84 in distress off Maughold, but vessel managed to reach Douglas. Lifeboat moored overnight as wind NNE x 7.

1940 Jul. 29 3.00 - 10.30 a.m. Searched for missing aircraft off Burrow Head. Nothing found during a two-hour search.

Nov. 9 8.15 - 10.30 a.m. Launched to assist mv PRINCESS IRENE aground at the Point of Ayre. Services not required.

1941 Apr. 17 5.40 - 8.30 p.m. Launched to assist mv CARITA in trouble five miles South of Ramsey. Vl. already under tow on reaching her.

Sep. 7 12.30 - 5.15 p.m. Launched to aid vessel reportedly sinking NE from the Point of Ayre. Nothing found.

1942 Mar. 2 4.15 - 6.45 p.m. Searched for missing aircraft off the Point of Ayre. Returned when aircraft found crashed on Jurby Beach.

Mar: 27 5.00 - 9.35 p.m. Searched for missing aircraft towards Douglas.

1943 Mar. 6 0.15 - 8.30 a.m. Searched for missing aircraft between Point of Ayre and Jurby Head. Nothing found.

Jun. 24 9.30 p.m. - 0.30 a.m. 25th. Launched to aid distressed fishing vessel off Laxey. Ship berthed and so services not required.

1944 Jun. 29 2.00 - 5.30 a.m. Called out for red flares seen East of Ramsey. Nothing found after a two-hour search.

Dec. 7 8.15 - 9.15 a.m. Crew on Stand-by for ss GLENMAROON hit by an aircraft and on fire. A destroyer picked up crew. Ship sank.

1945 May 14 3.30 - 6.30 p.m. Launched to assist one man in RAF dinghy off Cranstal. On reaching distress RAF Rescue Launch took up tow.

1948 Jun. 11 12.30 - 1.45 a.m. Making for an aircraft reported ditched off St. Bees Head. Returned when advised alarm false.

CHAPTER 8

Thomas Corbett 1948-1970

72 service launches and 18 lives saved
(incl. two relief boats)

ON 24th September, 1948, the *Thomas Corbett* arrived on station at Ramsey. She was a gift from the Thomas Corbett Charity of London and cost £9,581. This was the first Lifeboat at Ramsey which was all motor-powered with no auxiliary sails. She had two collapsible masts, nevertheless, but these were to support the radio aerial as she was fitted with the long sought-after radio-telephone.

The Boat was a Liverpool-type vessel, 35ft in length and of the normal timber construction with a wooden canopy over the engine well. This also afforded the Crew just a little protection from the weather, but not much! She had the usual decking forward and in the stern sheets, with side benches running alongside the engine casing. The boat was twin screw and non-self-righting with two petrol engines of a standard RNLI design. She was certainly finished to a high standard and there were a vast amount of brass finishings, all of which looked fine when gleaming in the sunlight. Perhaps not such a brave sight for the Mechanic when it needed cleaning after a service or an exercise!

The First Service

A month later came her first call-out on the 21st October. This was at 7.00 a.m. in answer to a report that the Point of Ayre Lighthouse Keeper had seen a light resembling a torch being flashed wildly in his direction from a position some six miles NExN from the Queen's Pier. A two-hour search was undertaken without anything being found.

The Crew Members named in this first service were Coxswain E. Starkey, 2nd Cox F. Bull, Bowman F. Cottier, Mechanic S. Lindsay, 2nd Mechanic A. Cottier and Crewmen W. Cottier, W. Gawne and J. Callow.

On the 6th December, 1948, the *Thomas Corbett* was called for her second service. At 8.07 p.m. a watchman reported that a vessel was believed to be aground just East of the harbour entrance. This proved to be correct when the Coastguard Station Officer found the ship in the beam of his searchlight, only 100 yards off the port. At 9.07 p.m. the Lifeboat Authorities were informed and within 20 minutes the *Thomas Corbett* was afloat. The full L.S.A. Team also turned out and their first rocket was fired to the ship at 10.22 p.m. The vessel was the ss Saxton of Middlesbrough. A wire from the ship was secured to the harbour wall, but the crew refused to leave their vessel. As the wind increased, the wire parted and the ship was taken further from the harbour entrance, pounding heavily. A second line from her was secured but the crew still remained aboard. The Lifeboat stood-by until 5.27 a.m. on the 7th but there were no casualties and the ship was refloated and towed into harbour at 4.42 that afternoon by the fishing vessel Irene.

In 1949 four services were recorded with the first of these taking place on the 4th March to the Ramsey fishing vessel Capella.

At 10.15 in the evening a watchman reported seeing a red light off Shellag Point, three miles North of Ramsey. The Coastguard Station Officer was called to the Harbour Lookout and he made it out to be flames close inshore. The Lifeboat was requested to launch and the L.S.A. Team assembled and proceeded to Shellag, finding the Capella ashore some five miles from the port. A rocket was fired from the shore and the line passed over the ship but no signals were received from the fishing boat and the whip line was not hauled out. A second rocket was therefore fired but this proved to be very erratic and only made 100 yards before hitting the sea and carrying on at right angles to the line of fire. The rocket line parted. The *Thomas Corbett* thereupon decided to risk the shallow water and heavy sea which was running on-shore from the strong SSE wind and got alongside the boat. Her crew of two jumped aboard together with the ship's cat and they were safely returned to Ramsey. There were no casualties but upon inspection the next morning the Capella was found to be completely wrecked.

Naming Ceremony Arranged

At a Committee Meeting a month later, on the 8th April, it was agreed to ask Lady Bromet, wife of the Lt. Governor, Air Vice-Marshal Sir Geoffrey R. Bromet, to name the new Lifeboat. Sir Geoffrey was also one of the Deputy-Chairmen of the RNLI Management Committee. The Lord Bishop was to be asked to take the Service of

J.J. Cottier collection

The *Thomas Corbett* on her arrival in Ramsey, 1948. Recognised in this photograph: E. Corlett (Ch. Launcher), J. Callow, R. Christian, W. Cottier and Abby Cottier.

Dedication and the date of 14th July was set for the ceremony.

At 9.15 a.m. on the 29th June information was received in Ramsey from Ronaldsway Airport in the South of the Island that a "Sea Hornet" aircraft had come down in the sea one mile WSW of the village of Kirk Michael on the West Coast. Both Peel and Ramsey Lifeboats were launched accompanied by five Peel fishing boats. RAF Aldergrove dispatched a "Sea Otter" and this aircraft located and picked up the pilot of the crashed aeroplane. All boats were recalled with the *Thomas Corbett* arriving back at 2 p.m.

The 24th August saw the *Thomas Corbett* at sea again for another search. At 4.30 p.m. Ramsey Harbour Master reported that the motor fishing vessel INYATI had picked up a man clinging to an upturned boat at 3 p.m. The small boat LARUS had capsized two hours before this and a second man from the boat had attempted to swim ashore to raise the alarm. The Lifeboat searched until 7.25 p.m. in company with other fishing vessels and with shore assistance from the Police and Coastguards but no-one was found.

The following year of 1950 saw further Crew changes in the Lifeboat. Fred Ball, who had been Assistant Coxswain for 12 years, retired. He had been a Member of the Crew for a total of 25 years. Frank Cottier, Bowman for five years and a Crew Member for 26 years, also retired. They were both awarded Long Service Certificates which were presented to them at a Committee Meeting on the 28th April. William F. Cottier was then elected Second Coxswain and F.W. Kinnin, Bowman.

The year saw three services, the first of these on the 17th February to the motor tanker BEN HENSHAW registered in London. At 9.45 a.m. the ship was one and a half miles East of Ramsey's Queen's Pier and hoisted a signal requesting a doctor. The *Thomas Corbett* was launched with a doctor and returned to the harbour at 11.05 a.m. with the news that the previous Master of the ship, who was travelling as a passenger, had been found dead in his cabin. The necessary arrangements were made and the Lifeboat brought the body ashore at 2 p.m.

The next service, on the 24th February, was an abortive one to the vessel SAINT ORAN. At 1.38 p.m. this ship was seen in Ramsey Bay flying a signal requesting a doctor. This was answered immediately by the Lifeboat with a doctor on board. Upon arrival alongside the ship, however, the Coxswain was informed by the Master that he had been flying the wrong signal by mistake and they only required provisions! Unfortunately the Returns of Service Report doesn't mention the reply Mr. Starkey gave the Master!

Mid-summer brought a sad incident with it. On the 24th July at 8.35 p.m. word was received that a boy had fallen over the cliffs at Maughold Head and was too badly injured to be hauled back up the cliff face. The Ramsey Lifeboat was launched with a doctor and nurse aboard and towing a small dinghy. The Coastguard L.S.A. Team also proceeded by land to the base of the 400ft. cliffs. The doctor and nurse were landed from the dinghy on to a small rocky beach near the incident and the boy given immediate aid before being transferred to the *Thomas Corbett* and then to hospital. He later died from his injuries.

It was nearly nine months before the next call-out. This was during the evening of the 22nd May, 1951. At 5.17 p.m. a Coastguard Officer on duty observed what looked like a ship on fire about six miles NE of Ramsey. She turned out to be the Belfast registered motor fishing vessel BRIGHTER HOPE for at 6 p.m. an R/T message was received from her asking for immediate assistance. The Lifeboat was launched but in the meantime the drifter BOY TOMMY had taken off the five seamen from the BRIGHTER HOPE and commenced towing the distressed ship. On arrival at the incident Coxswain Starkey transferred to the BOY TOMMY in order to pilot the two ships to a suitable beach for grounding. He sent the *Thomas Corbett* back to the Queen's Pier to tell the Coastguards to inform the Fire Brigade of their intentions. On returning to the burning ship the Lifeboat Crew found her beached on the North Promenade and they got as close to her as possible before firing a line ashore. A fire hose was attached to this line and hauled back out to the Lifeboat. It was about half a mile long and thus it was some considerable time before the Lifeboat Crew started fighting the fire. It was to be of no avail and the BRIGHTER HOPE was completely gutted. The Lifeboat did not return to her Station until after midnight.

LACK OF FUNDS

The Minutes Book for 1951 shows that funds were stagnating for the local RNLI Station and efforts to generate contributions were doubled. At a meeting on the 29th June permission was received from the Steam Packet Company for subscription boxes for the Ramsey Station to be placed aboard the Ardrossan and Belfast packet boats which called in at the port. Two hundred and twenty-six circular letters were also sent out seeking more funds but only £7.2s.6d. resulted. A further 410 names of possible subscribers were given to the Ladies' Guild. Press articles about the forthcoming A.G.M. on the 23rd November were also issued in an attempt to generate more interest in the Station's activities.

The day of the 10th July, 1951, was spent at sea by the *Thomas Corbett* in yet another aircraft search. At 9.29 a.m. Ronaldsway Airport reported a "Rapide" twin-engined passenger aircraft overdue on a flight from Blackpool to the Isle of Man. Only a pilot was aboard. She was last contacted at 7.29 a.m. about 10 miles SExS from Maughold Head. The *Thomas Corbett* was launched at 10.03 a.m. and searched until 8 p.m. when she returned with a section of an aircraft which was identified as an escape hatch. No sign of the pilot was ever found and the search was eventually called off at 10.00 p.m.

At the very end of the year Coxswain Ernest Starkey announced his retirement and in 1952 W.F. Cottier replaced him with F.W. Kinnin as Second Cox and Ivor Crowe as Bowman.

1952

Early in 1952, on the 31st January, a Committee Meeting was held in the Boathouse and attended by the North-West District Inspector of Lifeboats, Commander L.F.L. Hill, R.D., R.N.R. At the time the Rev. H.W. Young was Chairman with Secretaries J. Ramsay and W.R. Edwards. Also present at this meeting were Committee Members W. Cunningham, B. Pardoe, G. Crellin and R. Kneale. Commander Hill explained that the reason for his visit was to discuss with all concerned the tenancy of the Norbury Boathouse accommodation following the retirement of Coxswain Starkey. The new Coxswain, W.F. Cottier, had his own house which understandably he did not wish to leave and Second Cox Kinnin was in a similar position. It was hoped that some arrangement could be made about using the accommodation provided by offering it to the new Bowman, Ivor Crowe, who was soon to be married.

The first lifeboat service of the year was a short one to the motor fishing vessel NABRO of Dublin. On the 16th March, at 3.35 in the afternoon, the NABRO was seen flying a distress signal off Ramsey. The *Thomas Corbett* was launched and found the ship had engine trouble. She was towed into the outer harbour initially and then, when there was sufficient water at midnight, the Lifeboat towed her into the inner harbour. Regrettably Head Launcher E. Corlett fractured his left elbow in two places during the launch and spent several days recovering in hospital.

On the 28th October the ss SECOND of Belfast was off the Queen's Pier at Ramsey soon after noon. She signalled that she had an injured man aboard who required medical attention. The Lifeboat was launched, took the seaman off and, after hospital treatment, returned him to his ship.

The next day saw another launch of the Lifeboat at 5.15 p.m. This was in answer to information passed to the Coastguards that some kind of distress flare had been sighted from a yacht some four miles SSE of Maughold Head. On completing a thorough search of the area nothing untoward was found. Only the fishing vessel TOMMY was in the vicinity and her Skipper reported seeing nothing unusual during the whole afternoon's fishing.

The next call-out was on Thursday, the 20th November. Soon after 11 p.m. Mr. Ramsay, Manager of the Ramsey Steamship Co., reported

J.J. Cottier collection

Lifeboat Day, August 1952. Lt. Governor Sir Ambrose Flux Dundas inspecting the crew of the *Thomas Corbett*. L to R: W. Cottier, Coxswain; W. Kinnin, 2nd Cox; I. Crowe, Bowman; J. Callow; A. Cottier, Asst. Mechanic; S. Lindsay, Mechanic. "Abby" Cottier later lost his life in the Ramsey Bay Disaster of 1956.

that his ss BEN JEE was aground one mile South of the Point of Ayre. The Ramsey L.S.A. Team and the Lifeboat Crew were called out and proceeded to the casualty. The *Thomas Corbett* arrived at the scene at 00.15 a.m. 21st. and found the ship lying broadside on to the shore in a SE gale with heavy seas. A line had been floated ashore from the ship and the L.S.A. Team had made it fast. As seas were breaking right over the ship and she was pounding heavily on the beach it was imperative to get her seven crewmen off. This was done successfully by the shore Rescue Team within thirty minutes. The Lifeboat then returned to Ramsey. The ship was later refloated and towed into port, but eventually sold for scrap.

A local "Courier" newspaper reporter wrote up the BEN JEE incident and it could well have been a story from the previous century. Little seemed to have changed.

"A dramatic and spectacular rescue was carried out about midnight last night by the Ramsey L.S.A. Team and seven men were taken ashore by breeches buoy from the Ramsey Steamship Company's vessel BEN JEE which had run aground near the Point of Ayre in a strong inshore wind.

Crowds of people watched the Ramsey Lifeboat being launched in tempestuous seas. It was a never-to-be-forgotten experience to first of all see the Lifeboat launched into huge breakers rolling in on the beach and later to watch the spray-drenched men of the Rocket Brigade working their apparatus in the glare of lamps so that the crew from the ship could be relayed ashore in the breeches buoy.

The angry sea threw mountainous waves over the BEN JEE as she swung broadside on to the beach only a few yards from the bank of gravel from which the Rocket Brigade operated. At times the spray, whipped into a fury by the force of the inshore wind, cascaded over the rescuers and rescued and hid them from the spectators standing on the brows overlooking the scene.

The job of getting the men ashore went on expeditiously and altogether it was a smart rescue for which the Rocket Brigade men deserve top marks.

The first chapter in this thrilling series of episodes occurred when the BEN JEE sailing light from Carrickfergus, Northern Ireland, to Garston, met with a South East wind which reached gale force at times. The steamer had left at 3.30 in the afternoon after discharging a cargo of salt and difficulty was experienced in getting round the Point of Ayre. The Master, Stanley Morrison of 34, Parliament Street, Ramsey, told the "Courier" reporter that the incoming tide and inshore wind combined to drive him on to the beach and the steamer went ashore at 10.15 p.m.

The Lifeboat was launched at 11.30 p.m. A crowd of about 100 people had been drawn to the Promenade by the firing of the three maroons and the spectators watched spellbound as the *Thomas Corbett,* in the charge of Coxswain W.F. Cottier, was thrown high on the crest of a wave and then a moment or two later the light almost disappeared from view as the surging sea caused the craft to dip down again. The Lifeboat did not get back until 2 a.m.

It was an eerie and exciting scene at the Point of Ayre where the rescue was effected. At intervals the Lighthouse siren was sounded and from the Lighthouse itself a brilliant red light was showing. The Rocket Brigade lamps illuminated the beach and the red and black hull of the steamship with the lettering BEN JEE glistening like fresh paint as every now and then the waves pounded over her and gave her a gigantic showerbath.

Members of her crew riding over the breakers in the breeches buoy were sometimes caught in one of these sheets of water and cold and wet they were rushed into Ramsey and dried themselves before the Police Station fire. They were also given a cup of tea and were well looked after and were later accommodated in the Prince of Wales Hotel.

True to tradition, the Captain was the last to leave his ship which should not come to much harm on that beach unless the weather worsens....."

Note. During the ss BEN JEE rescue and indeed, throughout the book, mention is made of the Rescue Services being called out by the maroons. These are rocket signals which have been fired throughout the years from a location close to the Boathouse to summon the required Service – one rocket to summon the Coastguard and Marine Rescue Team, two rockets to summon the Lifeboat Crew and three rockets to signify that both Services are required to report to their bases. In modern times Members of both Services carry radio "bleepers" in addition.

The final service of 1952 was to offer assistance to the Fleetwood trawler PATRICIA HAGUE, on the 12th December. At 4.35 p.m. information was received that this trawler was in distress some three miles NWxW from the Point of Ayre. Her boiler was losing water rapidly and she was unable to draw the fires for steam. The *Thomas Corbett* was launched and reached the trawler at 6.15 p.m. She lay alongside her until the trawler NORTH NESS was able to take the PATRICIA HAGUE in tow. The Lifeboat then accompanied both vessels during their passage to Douglas and it was 7.30 a.m. on the 13th before she arrived back on Station.

The next rescue of note took place on Saturday, 17th April, 1954, and involved Coxswain W.F.

G.D. Learoyd collection

Ramsey Steamship Co's ss BEN JEE after her grounding near the Point of Ayre, 1952.

Cottier – but without his Lifeboat this time! At 3.00 p.m. a message was sent to him that a small boat had capsized about a quarter of a mile from the harbour entrance. As the *Thomas Corbett* was off-station undergoing a survey, Mr. Cottier, his brother A. Cottier and 2nd Coxswain W. Kinnin, commandeered a small rowing boat which was lying in the upper harbour. They immediately put to sea and found a small upturned boat with a sail and two men clinging to it. One, the boat's owner Dr. Taylor, was pulled into the rescue boat without difficulty but retrieving the second man was much more difficult due to his condition. The rescued men were brought back into harbour and taken care of by the Police who were on hand. The rescuers then returned to the dinghy, righted it, baled it out and towed it back into a safe berth. There is no doubt that Coxswain Cottier's prompt action saved the lives of these two men as they would not have survived much longer in the water and there was no other shipping around at the time.

On the 22nd July a search was undertaken for a missing aircraft. The Coastguards requested a launch because an "Oxford" trainer aircraft was believed to have ditched some 10 miles East of Maughold Head. The *Thomas Corbett* was away soon after 5 p.m. in a Southerly gale with heavy seas. She searched the area indicated until told to return to Ramsey at 11.45 p.m. After refuelling during the night, at 5.30 a.m. on the 23rd she was instructed to "Stand-by" at the Queen's Pier, which she did all day. However the emergency was called off early in the evening and the Lifeboat rehoused. No mention was made of the final fate of the aircraft and crew.

After this service strong efforts were made to get the Boat's batteries replaced. They were the original 1948 ones and in a bad state. The searchlight was inoperable and the radio's strength of signal very much reduced.

At 3.30 p.m. on the 19th September the Douglas registered yacht FULMAR was seen by the Coastguards to be making heavy weather of a moderate SSW wind off the Point of Ayre. Soon after 5 p.m. a trawler reported finding wreckage of a yacht in a similar position but with no sign of its occupants. The *Thomas Corbett* was launched at 5.15 p.m. and on reaching the area found two trawlers also searching. By 8.30 p.m. the Lifeboat had found nothing and so returned to Station.

A later report stated that the crew of the yacht had been taken aboard a trawler and landed in Fleetwood.

In 1955 two more fruitless searches were made and then on the 29th December two services were undertaken on the same day. During the forenoon Dr. Bridgewood was taken out to the steam trawler RED LANCER to give medical attention to two crewmen. Then, in the evening at 7.30, the Lifeboat was launched again to land a sick man for hospital from the Fleetwood trawler RED DRAGON. The weather was squally with a strong Westerly wind all day.

During the year the Queen paid a visit to Ramsey in August and some of the Lifeboat's Crew were invited to the Town Hall for the occasion.

THE RAMSEY BAY TRAGEDY

The spring of 1956 brought a tragic accident to Ramsey and the Boat's Crew. On Thursday morning, 8th March, the Ramsey Police were informed of a body floating in the sea off the Hydro (now the Grand Island Hotel). The *Thomas Corbett* was about to be launched when the news came that four other bodies had also been recovered. Among these were Albert Cottier, the Lifeboat's Assistant Motor Mechanic and the Coxswain's brother; Eric J. Lyall, who had been out in the Lifeboat on a number of occasions and Arnold Brew who frequently acted as one of the launchers. The others were crew members of the Fleetwood trawler FLEETWOOD LADY which had anchored in Ramsey Bay overnight and still missing was the ship's Skipper Reginald Wright. It appeared that the crew members were being returned to their ship during the late evening of the 7th in a small local rowing boat when it capsized unknown to anyone on shore. Once the tragedy unfolded in the morning a search was immediately initiated for the missing Skipper by the Lifeboat and an Air Sea Rescue Launch and this lasted all day, but to no avail.

Minds were cast back to another tragic disaster on this same North Shore in 1905 when 11 lives were lost aboard the tug CONQUEROR when she grounded there.

The "Ramsey Courier and Northern Advertiser" of Friday, 9th March, 1956, gave the following account of this latest tragic event.

> "The chain of incidents which culminated in disaster began when the Fleetwood trawler FLEETWOOD LADY came into the Bay on Wednesday, 7th March. Robert Slapp of Fleetwood, Mate of the trawler (belonging to the Boston Deep Sea Fishing Co. of Fleetwood) states that the trawler left Fleetwood on Wednesday for the fishing grounds and anchored during the afternoon in Ramsey Bay. She carried a crew of 15. At about 4 p.m., seven members of the crew put of for the shore in the ship's boat. This was primarily to allow three Manx members of the crew, the two Lyall brothers and Allan Bradford, to visit relatives in Ramsey.
>
> At about 7 p.m. four of the crew members returned to the trawler leaving Bradford, Eric Lyall and the Skipper Reginald Wright to return later.
>
> Mr. Ernest Starkey of Ramsey, owner of the boat concerned in the tragedy, and father-in-law of Arnold Brew, states that he put his boat down the harbour on Wednesday night to take the Skipper and two members of the crew back to the trawler

in the Bay. It was understood that they were to go back about 10.30 to 11.00 p.m., and actually the party left the harbour at 10.30 p.m.

For most people in the town the first intimation that anything was amiss was the firing of the maroons summoning the Crew of the Lifeboat *Thomas Corbett* at about 8 a.m. on Thursday 8th. A little earlier the Police had been notified by Mr. Ian Cannon, grocer's assistant, of the fact that what appeared to be a body floating on the water had been seen just beyond the Hydro.

Just as the Lifeboatmen were preparing to go to sea came the sad news that four more bodies had been discovered on the beach. Coxswain W. Cottier, of Mona Street, did not know as he mustered his men that among the four was his own brother "Abby" Cottier, Asst. Mechanic of the Lifeboat. Abby was one of the most popular figures on the Ramsey quayside and ever since they were lads he and his brother have been fishing and operating their own boat the GOWAN HILL.

An anxious group of people assembled at the Lifeboat slipway just before 9 a.m. – there was no raging storm to give the launch the background we usually associate with rescues – but when it was whispered around that it was believed a small boat with several men in it were missing from the previous night, there seemed to be a hushed stillness amongst the onlookers as the significance of that news was realised.

Dr. Bridgwood, who has newly joined the Crew as M.O., sped to the front in his car and clambered aboard and the *Thomas Corbett* was away by 8.30 a.m. The search was made along the Mooragh but only some bottom-boards from the dinghy were found. The Coastguards searched the shore and and RAF Air Sea Rescue Launch was dispatched from Peel to assist the search in Ramsey Bay.

The identity of the four bodies was established when they were brought to the mortuary. Two of these had been found by the Hydro and two near Dog Mills. First identified were Eric Lyall Snr. and his son Eric James Lyall followed by Albert Cottier and Allan Bradford. Later and again at Dog Mills, the body of Arnold Brew was washed up. There was no sign of Skipper Reginald Wright.

Following the discovery of the bodies, the 13 ft. rowing boat which had carried the six men the previous night, was washed up at Vollan Beach. It was minus its oars but did not seem to be badly damaged or give any indication as to how the men met their fate.

The full story of how the tragedy happened will probably remain a mystery."

Two other services took place during the year: one on the 25th August to the motor fishing boat DREADNOUGHT which was disabled with engine trouble and towed back into harbour; the other one on the 2nd October was a medical call to the trawler BOSTON VALIANT for a doctor to examine the ship's cook for possible appendicitis.

The following year of 1957 was one of numerous services of varying nature. On the 28th January the *Thomas Corbett* took stores out into Ramsey Bay to the ss BARON RAMSAY of Ardrossan. She had been weather-bound whilst waiting to berth in Workington.

On the 29th May the Lifeboat was at sea again after the possible sighting of a parachute in the sea off the Dhoon Glen, two miles North of Laxey. The search took nearly three hours but nothing was found.

LONG SERVICE

The 16th June saw a long service to the motor fishing vessel PYGMALION owned by a Fleetwood company. The Lifeboat was at sea by 4.15 p.m. after a call stating that the vessel required a tow. She was picked up some four miles North of the Bahama Bank Buoy at 5.50 p.m. and found to have a rope around her propeller. She was towed to Ramsey Bay and tied-up to a buoy there at 8.40 p.m. but the Lifeboat had to stand-by her until there was sufficient water in the harbour to berth her. The *Thomas Corbett* did not return to her Station until 1.15 a.m. on the 17th.

Lifeboat Day in 1957 was on the 14th August. As bad luck would have it, a call was received at 5.45 p.m. from the Coastguards that a small boat had capsized just North of the harbour. Coxswain Cottier telephoned Bowman Crowe and suggested using Mr. Crowe's own motor boat for the rescue. This was readily agreed to and Mr. Crowe also obtained the services of his two brothers and all four men proceeded to the dinghy. They found one man clinging to the hull and got him into their launch. The dinghy was then righted, mast stepped and they towed it back into port.

Nine days later another small yacht, the ZULU, was suspected of being in difficulties in a SSE gale off Laxey. The *Thomas Corbett* was launched and escorted her safely into Ramsey.

The final rescue of 1957 was another one made without a Lifeboat launch. In the forenoon of the 5th September Coxswain Cottier was informed of a capsized dinghy in the Bay off the Boathouse. In port he found the mfv MASTER FRANK alongside with a crew aboard. The Skipper immediately agreed to give assistance and, taking the Coxswain and two other volunteers from the quayside, he put to sea. The casualty was found to be the dinghy MANX MAID crewed by four RAF Cadets who were clinging on to her hull. Only two of them had lifejackets. The sea was rough with a fresh Westerly wind. The boat and crew were brought safely into harbour.

In 1958 the first service that saw the *Thomas Corbett* at sea was preceded by a very sad event. At 10.20 p.m. on the 10th May word was received that two red flares had been seen off Maughold Head. A launch was decided upon immediately and as the Crew were donning their oilskins, Mr. E.B. Kinnin, a regular Crew Member, collapsed and died whilst putting on his heavy-weather gear.

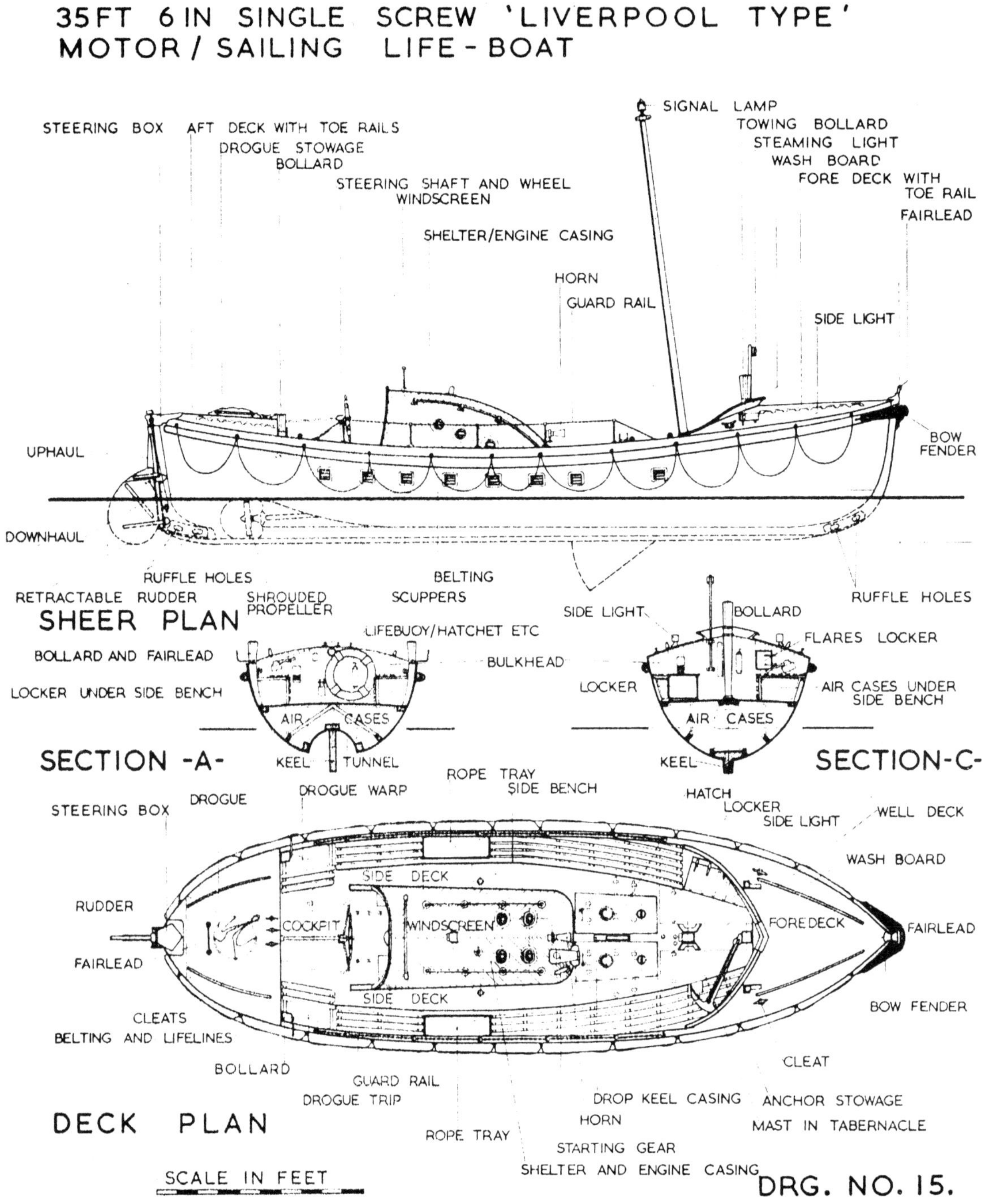

RNLI Poole

The Lifeboat was launched and, after sighting more flares, got alongside the mfv Sea Lion soon after midnight. She had been immobilised with engine trouble. As there was a fresh NE'ly wind and the tide was at five hours ebb, Coxswain Cottier decided it prudent to tow the vessel to Douglas. They arrived there at 2.25 a.m. on the 11th and it was 5.30 that morning before the *Thomas Corbett* berthed back in Ramsey Harbour.

The next call-out on the 23rd July was to four youths in a rubber dinghy which was quickly drifting offshore in a fresh NW'ly wind. The Lifeboat launch was cancelled, however, when the mfv Manx Maid, which had been anchored in the Bay, got under-way and took the dinghy in tow.

The final launch of the year was on the 10th November at 7.15 p.m. in a SE'ly gale and very rough seas. This was in answer to a distress call from the trawler Lord Plender which had grounded on the North end of the Whitestone Bank.

However, 45 minutes after being launched, the *Thomas Corbett* was recalled as the trawler had refloated herself and was continuing her passage to the fishing grounds.

1958 not only saw the death of E.B. Kinnin, but also the death of the Chairman, the Rev. Halford Young. He had served on the Committee

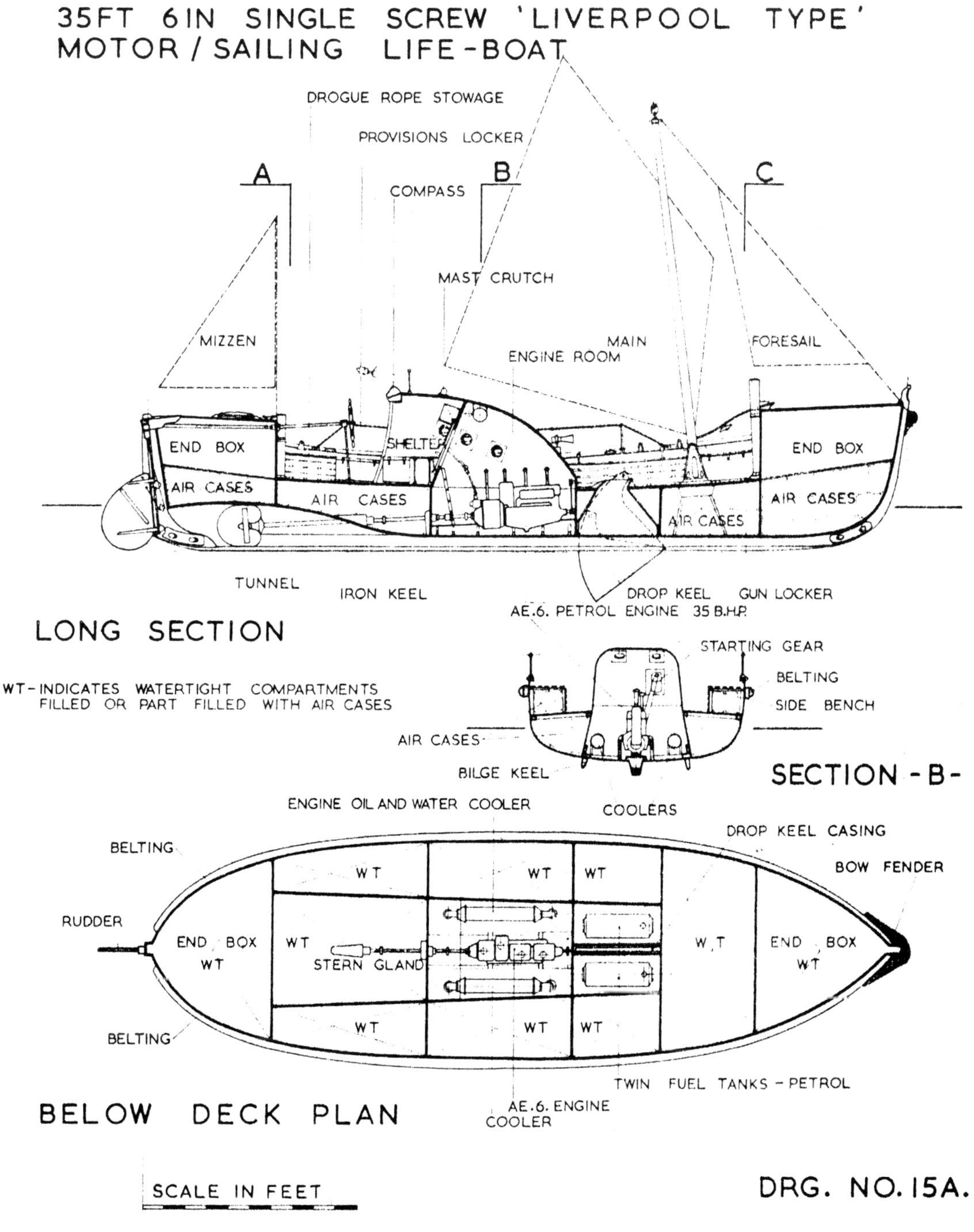

RNLI Poole

for 28 years and as Chairman for a further twelve. The Vice-Chairman, Keith Grimble Groves, succeeded him.

Another long-serving Committee Member, Canon Edward Paton, also died. He had joined the Branch on the death of his father, the Rev. George Paton, in 1900. Although he had to resign again shortly afterwards because of a London appointment, he returned to the Committee in 1935. Thus his span of service to the Branch covered some 58 years.

At the 1958 A.G.M. of the Branch Committee on the 28th November, the question was raised for the last time about stationing the Lifeboat at the seaward end of the Queen's Pier. The old arguments arose but were finally put to rest and it was generally accepted as an impracticable idea.

In 1959 only two call-outs were recorded.

The first was for an air and sea search for a jet fighter reported ditched 10 miles NExN of the Point of Ayre on the 1st October. The *Thomas Corbett* was at sea from 12.00 noon until darkness at 9 p.m., but nothing was found. After this service the Crew reported that the two-band UHF radio was inoperable after only a short time in use and that the R/T set was also unsatisfactory.

The second was on the 30th December to the motor trawler WYRE MAJESTIC. At 9.48 p.m. it was reported that she had struck bottom on the Mull of Galloway and although she had refloated herself she was heading for Ramsey but making water fast. The Lifeboat was launched at 10 p.m. but an hour later was recalled as the fishing vessel stated that her condition had stabilised. A stand-by watch was maintained all night at the Lifeboat House but at 6.30 a.m. the trawler was seen off Maughold Head making a course for Fleetwood.

February, 1961, saw the last service of the *Thomas Corbett* before she went to Beaumaris, Anglesey, for a survey and repairs. This service took place on the 20th February at 2.17 p.m. when the Boat put to sea. An RAF Avro Anson aircraft was overdue at Jurby Airbase and a search was requested in an area between Maughold Head and the Point of Ayre, 10 miles offshore. Less than an hour later, however, her recall was ordered as it had been ascertained that the aircraft had crashed on the North Barrule mountainside, South-West of Ramsey. Six lives were lost.

The following month saw the departure of the *Thomas Corbett* from Ramsey to undertake her first big overhaul in Beaumaris, Anglesey. On the 26th March a Reserve Lifeboat took over the Station soon after noon and the Ramsey Boat left to spend the night in Port St. Mary and thence across the Irish Sea to Beaumaris.

The passage is well documented because her own Mechanic, Thomas Arthur Corlett, went with the *Thomas Corbett* and the Relief Crew led by Coxswain Hill. Tom kept his own private log of events and even now, at the age of 87, he remembers the episode with singular clarity. They left Ramsey at 2.20 p.m. and on the passage South saw the disabled yacht DOLORES being towed Northwards by the ss COLEBROOK. Further South they had trouble themselves when a collar slipped on the rudder stock and rendered the steering unserviceable. A steering oar was used in conjunction with varying the engine rpm to complete the last few miles into Port St. Mary.

On Tuesday the 27th the day's passage to North Wales commenced at 8.15 a.m. in a NNW wind which varied from force 4 to 7. The two engines ran well at 2800 rpm, but again the collar on the stock slipped. This time it was repaired quickly and held good for the rest of the passage. Beaumaris was made by 4.45 p.m., having taken over eight hours. 26 gallons of petrol were consumed. The Boat was moored for the night and then slipped the next day at the shipyard of Morris and Levitt. The Supply Crew returned to their bases and Tom returned to the Island via Chester and Liverpool. It was to be an unexpected four months before he returned to take the Lifeboat on trials again.

THE *Frank and William Oates*

In the meantime the Reserve Lifeboat, No. 795, the *Frank and William Oates*, carried on the rescue work at Ramsey. Her first assignment was to tow in the auxiliary yacht DOLORES on the 26th March, 1961. This craft had left Rhyl, North Wales, the previous evening bound for Ramsey and was overdue. She was crewed by two RAF officers stationed at the local Jurby Base. Then the British cargo vessel COLEBROOK reported that she had the "Delores" safely in tow and would like to be relieved of her charge off Maughold Head. So the *Frank and William Oates* was launched at 6.35 p.m. and returned at 9.15 p.m. with the yacht which had been dismasted.

Later in the spring of 1961, on the 5th May, the Lifeboat was requested to launch and tow a dinghy to the foot of Maughold Head to retrieve an injured boy who had fallen down the cliffs whilst collecting seagulls' eggs. He was picked up and returned to the town where a waiting ambulance took him to hospital where he recovered. The report on this incident recorded further problems with the R/T set and the fact that it was three hours before the Lifeboat could be rehoused due to tractor troubles.

It is interesting to note the names of the Crew at the beginning of the 1960s and also the fifteen Launchers who were still required to get the Boat into and out of the water. Those mentioned for the above service were:- Crew: W. Cottier (Coxswain); W. Kinnin (2nd Cox); D. Walker (Bowman); T. Corlett (Motor Mechanic); I. Crowe (Asst. Mechanic); L. Martin; B. Kinnin; F. Kinnin. Launchers: J. McCormick; J. Crowe; W. Graham; A. McCormick; E. Fisher; W. Corkish; E. Corlett Jnr; D. Leadbeater; J. Kennish; E. Starkey; T. Graham; O. Hardman; E. Corlett; E. Callister and J. Kneale.

The "Courier" newshawks were on the spot again and reported the local cliffs incident in more detail:

> "Ramsey's Reserve Lifeboat, the *Frank and William Oates* carried out her second service since coming to the Station six weeks previously when on Friday evening an injured boy was taken from the beach at Maughold and landed at the Stone Pier.
>
> The boy, Patrick Simpson, aged 10 years, of 6, Queen's Pier Road, Ramsey, had gone to the headland with three other boys to look for seagulls' eggs and slipped. He was, at the time, about 5.45 p.m., on a grass slope 150 feet above the beach and he rolled down and then fell off the edge of the cliff, this last drop being about 50 feet. Fortunately his fall was cushioned by a bed of seaweed covering the rocks or he would almost certainly have been killed.
>
> Patrick, or "Paddy", as he is known, was accompanied by Roger McCormick (10), Vincent Lyall (12) and David Thompson (9), all of Ramsey.....
>
> Two years ago Paddy was rescued from drowning in Ramsey Harbour!"

The point where the accident happened is a cove just North of Maughold Lighthouse and the exact spot where a boy lost his life whilst bird-nesting two years earlier. Regrettably, this incident was not to be the last accident of its kind to take place in the area.

At a Committee Meeting on the 14th July it was stated that, despite great efforts, it had been impossible to recruit an attendant for the Boathouse. It was agreed that Chairman Groves and Secretary Edwards should prevail upon the Mechanic, T. Corlett, to keep the doors of the Boathouse open during the summer whilst he was on duty tending the boat.

On the 25th July, Mechanic Corlett arrived back in Beaumaris as the overhaul of the *Thomas Corbett* was complete. He was met by RNLI District Inspector McMillan and Mr. Maskell, the Hull and Carriage Inspector. The Lifeboat was not a pretty sight. She had been open to the weather for much of her overhaul and her brass-work was heavily tarnished and sticky paint was everywhere. There was trouble with her wiring circuits and on trials the following day the propeller shaft ran hot. There were oil pressure troubles and the starboard dynamo cut-out twelve times. The control rod was stiff and the same radio transmitter was still weak. Some six and a half hours were spent on passage from Puffin Island through the Menai Straits and Swellies Channel towards Caernarvon and back whilst adjustments and repairs were made.

On Friday the 28th a Delivery Crew under Coxswain Syd Hill, together with Tom Corlett, made the return passage to Port St. Mary with the Lifeboat.

> "We were away to the shipyard early on the 28th (from overnight digs) and I put my suitcase and bag of food down when we got there and within four minutes some ..... Welshman pinched the cakes! We refuelled the Boat and started the engines but the port one was very sulky to start and stopped several times – seemed to be starved of fuel. Slipped moorings at 9.25 a.m. – unable to get my oilskins out of the lifeboat shed as it was locked and that department had not turned up for work. Typical!"

The weather for the run was wind NWx5 with spray and a lumpy sea. The starboard engine struggled to hold 2900 rpm and it burnt 24 gallons of fuel. The port engine ran better and consumed only 16 gallons. Port St. Mary was made by 6.15 p.m. and the Boat was moored and the Crew stayed ashore overnight.

The final leg was commenced at 9.15 on the morning of the 29th in fine weather with an offshore breeze. The port engine was sulky again and three plugs were changed but they appeared dry and it made no difference to the engine. Ramsey was made in good time, running before a spring tide.

Back in Service

So the *Thomas Corbett* duly arrived back from her survey and her first service was on the 28th August, 1961, to the RAF Launch No. 1653. This vessel was reported to be in trouble off Jurby Head and the Peel Lifeboat had already been launched to go to her aid. The Air Force craft was on a training exercise with 15 U.K. Air Training Corps Cadets aboard. They were stationed at the Jurby Base. It was then that RAF Jurby requested the Ramsey Lifeboat to launch and when the Lifeboat got near the vessel after rounding the Point of Ayre, it was found that she had suffered a broken windscreen. She was taking in water which the crew could not pump overboard due to a broken pipe on their bilge pump. She was escorted safely back to port.

On the 1st September the Lifeboat Crew was alerted to a possible distress in the making, but which fate decreed should not happen. With four bars of chocolate and two flasks of tea, two Instructors from the Ullswater Outward Bound School crossed from St. Bees to Ramsey in canoes. They were Ian Smeaton (31) and John Elliot (28) and they took 14 hours to make the crossing. On arrival in Ramsey they were welcomed by Mr. A.H. Martin, J.P., Chairman of the Town Commissioners. Their 18ft. canoes were covered with tin-foil to assist radar detection and in case they got into a distress situation.

Later in the year, on the 28th November, the Everard coastal tanker mv AUSPICITY was in collision with a trawler off the Point of Ayre. This was during a passage from Greenock to Bromborough in the River Mersey. She suffered severe damage to her port-side hull plating, some of it below the waterline. After the Hon. Secretary had spoken on the radio to the Master of the tanker, the Lifeboat was launched to stand-by the damaged ship until she berthed in Ramsey. The *Thomas Corbett* left the Boathouse at 10.20 a.m. and found the distressed ship listing badly but making her way South. Once in the Bay the Lifeboat took the Master of the AUSPICITY ashore to arrange repairs and then returned him to his ship and stood-by until 2.30 p.m. when the ship safely berthed. Her repairs were undertaken by the local shipyard, Booth W. Kelly Ltd.

On the 28th March, 1962, James Ramsay died. He had been joint Secretary and Treasurer with W.R. Edwards since 1934 – the long period of 28 years. They had both been presented with binoculars by the Institution after serving as joint Secretaries for 25 years. James Ramsay had been Assistant Secretary of the Whitehaven Branch before he came to the Island and had over 40 years' service in the RNLI.

An obituary in the local Press gave a brief insight into his accomplishments:

A. Christian collection

Thomas Corbett off Granch, SE of Ramsey, c.1961.

G.D. Learoyd collection

Making fast the recovery chains in the 1960s.

"The Maritime community – indeed the town of Ramsey – was shocked this week to learn of the sudden death of Mr. James Ramsay at the age of 60. He came to Ramsey in 1928 to assist the late Mr. J.B. Kee in the management of the Ramsey Steamship Company, and his drive and ability – his concern too for the welfare of the crews – stamped him as a man in a thousand. The mantle of the late Mr. Kee, who was a man of brains and energy, fell on to Jim Ramsay easily and he strove through the years of the Depression to keep the Company going and then steered the ship into better waters financially. It must have given him great satisfaction when last November he went away with Mr. Billy Kneale of Messrs. Booth W. Kelly Ltd., the Engineering Superintendent, to place an order for a new motor vessel to be built for the firm.

Jim Ramsay came here from Whitehaven – the port which has many associations with Ramsey – and was of course in constant touch with his home town in his business activities and he was well known there and also on Merseyside on account of his membership of the Shipowners' Association."

Boathouse Repairs

During the spring of 1962 extensive repairs were carried out on the Norbury Boathouse and Committee Meetings were held in the Town Hall in the meantime. The Boathouse was over 70 years old and extensive dry-rot had been found in much of the building. A specialist on the subject came over from Edinburgh and big repairs were undertaken to the living accommodation and the first floor Committee Room. Partition walls were taken down and considerable renovations were included in the work which took most of the year.

On the 12th June a meeting of representatives of all Lifeboat Committees on the Island, including the Ladies' Guilds, was held at the Sefton Hotel, Douglas. Major J.G. Disley, District Organising Secretary, presided and the following officials were present:- From Ramsey Mr. W.R. Edwards and Miss R Shaw; from Douglas Capt. Robertson and Mrs. Kissack; from Port Erin Mr. and Mrs. L.J. Kewley; from Castletown Lady Qualtrough; from Port St. Mary Mr. W.R. Bridson; from Laxey Capt. Skinns and Mrs. Landless; and from Peel Mr. A. Hill and Mrs. Cove.

The meeting was called to discuss the possibility of holding a function to commemorate the founder of the Lifeboat Institution, Sir William Hillary. It was agreed to hold a Dinner in Douglas, probably on the 20th November, 1962. It was also agreed that two tickets be allotted to each member of the Branches and Ladies' Guilds, with the price of the tickets not to exceed 25/- each. Dress to be optional.

It was further suggested that the following be invited as guests: The Lt. Governor and Lady Garvey, the A.D.C. and Lady, the Mayor and Mayoress of Douglas, District Officer McGarrie and Mrs. McGarrie, the Coxswain of each Lifeboat and wife and one other member of the Crew and wife, together with representatives of the Press. It was put forward that the principal guests from London might be the Chairman of the Institution, Earl Howe, and the Secretary, Mr. S. Whorlow. A Sub-committee was appointed to make the necessary arrangements and report back to the General Committee at a later date.

Lifeboat Day 1962

The annual Lifeboat Day for 1962 was held on Tuesday the 31st July. It was a pleasant July morning and large crowds, mostly holidaymakers and children, were on the seafront to watch the proceedings. A band from the Worcestershire Army Cadet Force marched through the town prior to the launch and they also provided the Guard of Honour for Group Captain A.P. Dart, D.S.O., D.F.C.

The guests aboard the Lifeboat with the Group Captain included Colonel J.D. Ricketts, D.S.O., Major Alexander from the Worcestershire A.C.F., the Chairman of Ramsey Commissioners Mrs. D.M. Quayle, J.P., and the Town Clerk Mr. W.E. Faragher, M.B.E. They were welcomed by Major J.D. Disley, the North West Organising Secretary for the RNLI, and Group Captain Dart, Commanding Officer of RAF Jurby was introduced by Major Keith Groves, J.P., Chairman of the Ramsey Branch, who took the opportunity of thanking all those who worked on behalf of the Station.

In his address Group Captain Dart said that he was grateful for the opportunity to express not only his own admiration for the men of the Lifeboat Service and their proud record of over 80,000 lives saved, but also of repaying in a very small way the very real debt of gratitude which his own Service owed to the Lifeboatmen:

> "In fact, during the Second World War in 1940 the Lifeboat Service was called out on the greatest number of occasions in its history. This was the year of the Battle of Britain when pilots of Fighter Command struggled against the whole weight of the Luftwaffe. Many pilots shot down owed their lives to the Lifeboat crews. Since then and in peacetime, we in the Royal Air Force, have been proud to have developed close links with the RNLI. When one of our aircraft is forced down into the sea, we know that alongside our own rescue organisation the Lifeboat Service will be playing its own vital role in the rescue of the crew."

Group Captain Dart went on to mention the founding of the Institution here on the Island by Sir William Hillary nearly 140 years ago and the fact that Ramsey had had nine lifeboats since the Station opened and a total of 524 lives were recorded as having been saved. This record of service compared very well with that of any other station in the country. In his appeal for continuing funds, Group Captain Dart stated that the *Thomas Corbett* had cost £35,000 and that it was only one of many provided around the UK coasts by public subscriptions.

The following month, on the 4th August, the Formby Coastguards (Lancashire) requested the *Thomas Corbett* to launch to identify a yacht five miles East of Ramsey. Apparently the yacht PLAYMATE of Lytham, which was on passage from her home port to Port St. Mary, was overdue. The Lifeboat was at sea within 15 minutes of the request, at 3.50 p.m., and happily ascertained that the PLAYMATE was indeed off Ramsey and that all was well on board.

The Lifeboat was rehoused at 6 p.m. after this incident but it was taken out of service until 2 a.m. the following Sunday morning as a result of damage to the tractor. Tractor Driver J. Kneale's report stated:-

"Near-side steering stopped working when rehousing the Lifeboat. The matter was reported by telephone by the Tractor Driver to the District Engineer, Mr. D. McMillan, at Bangor, who gave instructions for the tractor T41 to be stripped. A broken eye on the near-side steering band was discovered and this was removed, welded and refitted by the Tractor Driver and Maintenance Engineer and the Lifeboat was placed on service again at 2 a.m. Sunday, August 8th."

In 1963 only one service took place and this was on the 30th July. Just after 7 p.m. a message was received from the Ramsey Police that a boy was missing. He had been with his parents on the shore at Ballakinnag, Andreas, (near Rue Point) and had disappeared. The Police had searched without success. After consultations between the Hon. Secretary and the Coastguards it was decided to launch the *Thomas Corbett* and this was done at 7.26 p.m. The Lifeboat searched an area four miles West of the Point of Ayre until darkness set in. She was joined by an Air Sea Rescue Launch from Peel. It was midnight before the Lifeboat returned to Ramsey but no trace was found of the missing boy. Constant radio communication between the Lifeboat and Police and Coastguards had been maintained and Secretary W.R. Edwards also joined the Crew at sea. Sadly, ten days later, the body of the boy was washed up on the shore at the Point of Ayre.

During the following year, 1964, a new tractor was supplied to Ramsey. It also turned out to be one of the busiest years for a long time for the Lifeboat Crews of the port.

PASSAGE TO COWES

On Sunday, the 2nd February, 1964, the Reserve Lifeboat from Llandudno, No. 792 the *Annie Rowland Isabella Forest*, arrived on station to relieve the *Thomas Corbett* which left the following day for a big refit at Cowes, Isle of Wight. The main purpose was to take out the original twin petrol engines and replace them with two modern diesels to increase fuel efficiency and ease maintenance and overhauls. The alterations were expected to take three to four months.

Once again a long sea passage for the Lifeboat was to be undertaken. Usually such occurrences go unnoticed and books on the RNLI mention only important services and gallant rescues and, perhaps only rarely the more mundane events. All lifeboats undergo regular periodic surveys and sometimes major overhauls and these are carried out by well-known boat-builders, often many miles away from the home station of the boats. The RNLI have special crews who take on this work, but the boat's own Mechanic is usually spared from his base to make the delivery. This was, indeed, the case again with the *Thomas Corbett*. For the second time in three years Thomas Arthur Corlett accompanied the Boat on a long passage and again he kept his own diary of events. The notes are concise, even terse, but give a clear picture of yet another side of the Lifeboatman's work.

"We launched the Lifeboat at 4.10 p.m. and were in the harbour (at Ramsey) in 15 minutes. The Llandudno Reserve Boat arrived at 5.00 p.m. and we helped the Crew to switch over and Coxswain Harding hopes to leave Ramsey at 11.00 a.m. tomorrow.

3rd February (1964). Left Ramsey at 11.05 a.m. bound for Port St. Mary. Bright sun and clear sky. Cold, wind WNW x 3-4. Maughold Head abeam 11.25. Called Anglesey Radio to tell them that we were on passage to Pt. St. Mary. Cornaa abeam 12 noon, Douglas Head Lighthouse abeam 1.30 p.m., wind increased to force 5, some fair lumps of water running in the race at Langness – fell into some "hollows" with hefty thumps and bumps. The old engines doing 2950 rpm port and 2700 rpm starboard, instead of the 3200 which is their normal speed. Arrived at Port St. Mary at 3.25 p.m. and refuelled with 18 gallons of petrol (four gallons per hour) and stayed the night there.

4th February. Left Port St. Mary at 9.05 a.m. Lot of bother starting, the port scrapheap difficult and the starboard one not much better. We set up the canvas dodger as soon as possible. Wind Westerly, 7-8 and right on our beam all the way to Holyhead. The Boat behaved magnificently but for all that she set her gear swimming when an odd one broke aboard and filled her up. Cups, kettle and personal gear having fun and frolics in the scuppers! Just like standing in the Sulby River for eight hours! Both engines screaming their hearts out to keep us going at six knots. Arrived Holyhead at 5.00 p.m. and got a nice meal at 7.00 p.m., the first bite since breakfast at 7.00 a.m. The slimming course has started! The Cox hopes to make Fishguard on the next hop, a distance of 84 miles, in 12 hours.

5th February. Port scrapheap only got compression on one cylinder. Took an hour to get it running. Left Holyhead at 8.00 a.m., wind NNE x 4. Both engines on 2800 rpm. Saw the Whistling Sand Buoy before making Bardsey Island which was abeam at 1.30 p.m., wind lighter and sea lumpy, clear bright sky all day. The Island was higher than I expected and its houses larger. Sun setting in cloudy sky at 5.10 p.m. as we set on across Cardigan Bay. 6.20 p.m. the Coxswain drew attention to a Sputnik travelling North and in 10 minutes it had gone. 7.40, another Sputnik going NNW and yet another at 8.05 p.m. Arrived Fishguard at 9.15 p.m. having used 35 gallons fuel. Topped up the tanks and an extra 12 gallons in cans stowed on deck. Slept at Fishguard. 7/- for lodgings and £1.00 for stores.

6th February (Thursday). Left Fishguard at 2.15 p.m. in calm seas and bright sunshine. Both engines hard to start. Fitted new packing to both water pumps as they were leaking badly on the last run. 2.58 p.m. Strumble Head abeam. NNW cat's paws – calm sea. 4.38 St. David's Head abeam and at 4.50 p.m. going through Ramsey Jack Sound, which is rather narrow. Seals in the water, islands interesting, sun setting low over a glassy sea, keen frosty air, coast rocky and forbidding with only a few houses miles apart. Saw St. David's Lifeboat Station well hidden in a rocky inlet. Had short R/T greetings with them each way. Two more Sputniks seen tonight. A long, weary, wet, cold night with a quartering wind and sea as we crossed the Bristol Channel. Managed a brew of tea and a bite to eat. A splendid crew and I like them all.

7th February. Before dawn we eased down and the Coxswain got us into Padstow at 7.15 a.m. Damn good navigator the Coxswain, Roy Harding. Went aboard the Padstow Lifeboat (a 50-footer moored afloat), got warm and had a drink of tea aboard her. Later refuelled with 40 gallons and got a huge breakfast - cost 5/6d. and stores at 6/6d. Quite a pretty place, Padstow. The Hon. Secretary is like Charlie Craine (a Ballaugh man and a bank manager). An old steam yacht in the harbour.

Around the Corner

Away again at 9.55 a.m. Frosty and cold last night but now bright sun. 10.55 Trevose Head abeam. Starboard engine only doing 2400 rpm and port 2700. Fitted a new set of plugs but no improvement. Cape Horn abeam (Land's End) at 5.20 p.m. Turning cold again tonight; sea slight. Arrived Newlyn (Cornwall) at 7.15 p.m. Used 33 gallons fuel. Saw Longships Lightship and Wolfe Rock Lighthouse a way off. Perished with cold on this bloody raft. Lodgings 18/6d, very poor bed and bedding.

8th February. Left Newlyn at 7.40 a.m. The starboard scrapheap now the worst and very hard to start. Once at sea it was coaxed into life up to 1000 rpm and the port only doing 2500 rpm. Eventually starboard ran at 1900 and the port at 2550. The dynamo won't work on the starboard engine as the revs are too low.

10.30 a.m., the Lizard abeam and at 2 p.m. saw the Lizard Lifeboat Station. Clear bright sun and wind NE x 2, almost calm. Arrived Plymouth at 7.10 p.m. 40 gallons of fuel aboard. Supper 4/- and a super super bedroom at the YMCA for 17/6d. Saw Eddystone Lighthouse 11 miles out to sea. The Plymouth Lifeboat Mechanic was a bright cheerful man like my friend Tom Holt. Saw practically nothing of Plymouth but it looks an interesting place.

The Final Leg

9th February (Sunday). A most comfortable night at YMCA. 10.30 a.m. left Plymouth. Both the scrapheaps were very difficult to start. Wind NNW x 2 with a smooth sea. 1.35 p.m. Salcombe abeam. 2.30 p.m. Start Point Lighthouse abeam which depends entirely upon rain for its water. Bright sun and clouds. Wind NNW x 3-4. Port engine 1900 rpm., starboard 1950 rpm – she is gradually dropping off. Too slow for dynamos to charge. Portland Bill 7 miles off. It has taken nine hours to do five miles. Dark, lumpy and cold. Faltering engines and batteries running down. The best is only just good enough for the RNLI!

10th February (Monday). After a long, cold night dodging French trawlers and keeping an eye on the Shambles Lightvessel, we arrived in the Solent doing 4 knots with a fluffy, woolly-sounding exhaust and a useless R/T set. Handed over boat to Groves and Gutteridge at East Cowes at 9.25 a.m. (her builders). This was 22 hours and 55 minutes from Plymouth.

They won't get me on another run of this kind!! Full marks to all the crew and she was a grand sea boat.

Coming home, bus arrived for ferry to Portsmouth, train to London, taxi to Euston Station, train to Liverpool, taxi to Exchange Station, train to Formby where I went to see an Uncle and Aunt. Stayed with them the night and turned in at 10 p.m. - 48 hours since turning in at Plymouth! After a very comfortable night and a good rest I felt much better and greatly enjoyed the day. Came home on the I.O.M. steamer.

The *Thomas Corbett* returned to Ramsey on the 30th October with her new diesel engines and Jimmy Kneale has already taken over as her Mechanic."

This account tells of just one of the many passages regularly carried out as "routine" work. It took place in 1964 and even in this year of 1991 there are still numerous older lifeboats on station that remain "open" boats. It is one thing to make a long six-day passage in the relative comfort of a warm cabin with twin engines giving you a comfortable speed of 16 to 18 knots but quite another to cover the miles open to the elements and at only seven knots or less.

One associates the call of duty of the lifeboatmen to assist ships and their seamen when in distress, but the call of their duties often go beyond that, as such accounts prove to us.

In the meantime the first service for the Relief Lifeboat, the *Annie Rowland Isabella Forest,* came two months after she had taken up station at Ramsey, on the 3rd April, 1964. At 2.20 a.m. the Hon. Secretary was contacted by the Coastguards who informed him of a report that they had received that a loud explosion and a cloud of black smoke had been observed (at night?) about three to four miles offshore between the Point of Ayre and Rue Point. The Lifeboat was launched at 3 a.m. and proceeded

W.S. Basnett collection

One of the regular carriage overhauls. The tractor is a Case, USA, model and adapted by the RNLI.

to search the area in question. At 5.30 she was joined in the search by a Shackleton aircraft from Northern Ireland. Nothing was found and the Lifeboat returned to Ramsey at 9.45 a.m.

Three more services in May, 1964, followed in quick succession.

At 12.17 a.m. on the 18th the Coastguards passed on a message from the Maughold Lighthouse Keeper that a red flare had been sighted on the Northern tip of Port Mooar Bay, just South of the Lighthouse. The Lifeboat was in the water by 12.40 a.m. in a moderate SE'ly wind and sea and reached the distress by 1.10 a.m. The Lifeboatmen found the yacht WYNDRUSH aground and wedged in between rocks. However, her crew of two, both from Liverpool, had managed to get ashore by themselves and were brought into Ramsey by car.

YET ANOTHER CLIFF FALL

The following day, the 19th, an anticipatory message was received at 3.23 p.m. to the effect that a 15-year-old boy had fallen over the cliff edge on to rocks below at the Dhoon, between Maughold and Laxey. Just after 4 p.m. a definite request for the Lifeboat plus a small dinghy was made and Reserve Boat No. 792 was at sea 20 minutes later. Dr. Jones of Ramsey accompanied the Crew. The boy, Keith Prosser of Birmingham, was attended at the scene of the accident by Dr. Paton of Ramsey and Dr. Cussons of Laxey. He had suffered a severe scalp wound and bruising to the back and arms. He was duly picked up by the dinghy crew, transferred to the Lifeboat in a calm sea, and soon landed at Laxey where a waiting Police van took him to the Ramsey Cottage Hospital.

The 26th May, 1964, saw yet another call-out for the *Annie Rowland Isabella Forrest.* During a hazy night with a light ENE'ly breeze, the Coastguards advised an immediate launch at 10.15 p.m. after they had seen red flares six miles ExN from Ramsey. The Lifeboat was in the water within 15 minutes. In the meantime the mfv LORRAINE of Whitehaven had found three men adrift in a rubber dinghy. They were all suffering from burns, one of them very badly. They were the unfortunate crew of the Fleetwood motor fishing vessel PYGMALION which had sunk immediately after an explosion. The LORRAINE brought the injured men directly into Ramsey and they were taken to hospital in the town. The Lifeboat returned to her Station.

The PYGMALION had, seven years earlier, been under tow from the *Thomas Corbett* after she had been disabled with a rope around her propeller shaft off the Bahama Bank. An unlucky vessel, indeed.

The next call-out happened during the evening of the 24th August, 1964, in answer to a message relayed by the Coastguards. Mr. Foster of Port-e-Vullen had spotted a rowing boat, with an outboard motor, towing an ex-RAF inflatable dinghy. The craft were being blown down on to the cliffs just inshore of the Stack at about 8.25 p.m. The Lifeboat was launched at 8.50 p.m. and reached the scene in about 15 minutes. In the meantime Dr. Corlett (now the RNLI Ramsey Branch Chairman) and his 12-year-old son, who lived nearby, launched their outboard-engined boat PUTT PUTT from Port-e-Vullen and got a line to the other craft. By getting the two men in the inflatable boat to join the other two in the larger boat and cutting the inflatable free, it was possible to edge the two boats out to clear the Stack and then obtain a lee from it to hold position until the Lifeboat arrived. The *Annie Rowland Isabella Forrest* took the towline from the PUTT PUTT, embarked the four men and returned them with their boats to Ramsey Harbour.

Another holiday escapade took place on the 8th September and resulted in the Reserve Lifeboat being launched at 5.15 p.m. A small boat with no motor had left Laxey at 11 a.m. with a family of four aboard and by 4.30 p.m. was considered overdue. A later message indicated that the boat had been beached at Bulgham Bay. The husband scaled the 150ft. cliffs to raise the alarm, leaving his wife and two children on the beach. When he returned with Coastguards and Police he found that the Lifeboat, with a small dinghy in tow, had gone very close inshore and picked up his family safely. They were returned to the Queen's Pier at Ramsey and, after hot drinks, taken back to Laxey by the Coastguards They were visitors from Lytham St. Annes. The Lifeboat was housed at 9.30 p.m.

At 4.36 p.m. on the 22nd October next, information from the Coastguards indicated that the mfv WANDEROBO WARRIOR of Castletown had run out of fuel some two to three miles off the Point of Ayre Lighthouse. The mfv ZULU WARRIOR had already left Ramsey in order to take the ship in tow but failed to get alongside the distressed vessel. The wind was NW and force 6 to 7. The Lifeboat was launched at 5.20 p.m., arrived at the scene at 6.45 p.m. and towed the disabled ship back to port, berthing her at 9.15 p.m.

FINANCIAL MATTERS

The third Minutes Book of the Branch Committee takes the history of the Ramsey Station up to the 10th July, 1964. An historical note at the end of the book made by the Chairman, Major Keith Grimble Groves, covers financial matters which give some insight into the funds available to the Branch in 1959.

"There are three bank accounts at the Westminster Bank, Ramsey, in the names of the Chairman K.G. Groves and the Joint Secretaries W.R. Edwards and J. Ramsay.

The RNLI Ramsey Branch Bank Account:

There is no record of the date when this account was first opened but there was probably an account at Dumbell's Bank in the middle of the last century. This account at the Westminster dates from June, 1900, and this is the date when the Westminster took over the accounts of Dumbell's Bank. The account contains all the receipts and payments relating to the working of the Branch including all the receipts and payments to and from the RNLI Headquarters.

The Ramsey Branch Endowment Account:

In 1904 a legacy of £100 was left to the Branch by Mrs. Elizabeth Cowle of Andreas and this formed the start of the Endowment Account. In 1913 there is a record that this account was in the names of Frederick Evans and Albert Hugh Teare who were joint Secretaries and Treasurers. They were succeeded by J.B. Kee and A.E. Chrystal and later the name of the current Chairman the Rev. M.W. Harrison was added. Since that date the account has been in the names of the Chairman and Joint Secretaries. In June, 1917, the sum of £100 from the account was invested in the I.O.M. Railway 4% Debenture Stock. The investment was increased from time to time and the holding in 1959 had grown to £500.

On the 1st September, 1926, £100 3% War Loan was purchased and a year later a further sum of £210 was invested in the same stock. This may have been a legacy of £200 of the original 5% War Loan. In 1948 the Chairman donated £100 in memory of his son and this was invested in a further £100 of 3% War Loan which was bought at £104. The total holding in 1959 is £410. This latter donation was expressly made for the purposes of the Branch, as the Committee might see fit. The Chairman at the same time donated a further £100 to the RNLI which was remitted to Headquarters.

The Elizabeth Norbury Trust Account:

On the 2nd December, 1920, Mrs. Elizabeth Norbury of The Carrick, Port Lewaigue, settled a sum of £500 in trust for the following purposes:- The upkeep and maintenance of the Norbury Lifeboat House, Ramsey, and for the benefit of Members, past, present and future, of the crew of the Ramsey Branch and the wives, widows and relatives or dependents of the crew.

The fund and accumulations of interest have been invested. In recent years an annual payment has been made to the Endowment Fund to assist in making the Christmas distribution and other gratuities to the crew. Assistance has also been given to retired members of the crew and their relatives.

The Ladies' Guild:

The Ladies' Guild have their own banking account out of which they make donations to the Branch or for other suitable purposes."

At a Committee Meeting on the 13th March, 1964, a letter from the RNLI Headquarters was read out to the assembled members. It intimated that the Management Committee of the RNLI had decided to confer the exceptional award of the Gold Badge to the Hon. Secretary, Mr. W.R. Edwards. This was in recognition of his very long service, 30 years as Secretary and a total of

J. Kneale collection

Ready for the fray! One of the many services to the "pirate" radio ship RADIO CAROLINE stationed in Ramsey Bay in the mid 1960s.

34 years on the Committee. The award was to be presented to Mr. Edwards by Princess Marina, Duchess of Kent, at a ceremony at Central Hall, Westminster, on Sunday, 7th April, at 3 p.m.

At the same time the Silver Badge was awarded to Mr. E. Corlett in recognition of his service of 26 years as Treasurer of the Peel Branch. He had, during the year, been transferred from Peel by the Westminster Bank to become their Branch Manager at Ramsey. He was thereupon elected to the Ramsey Committee.

At the Branch A.G.M. on the 4th December the Chairman congratulated Coastguard District Officer, Mr. D.T. McGarrie, for his recent award. This was the Queen's Commendation for rescuing a girl on the cliffs at Howstrake, near Douglas, on the 25th May.

A.C. Teare Retires

Also at this meeting, Mr. A.C. Teare, C.P., Vice-Chairman, announced his retirement. He had held this position for the past six years and had served a total of 36 years on the Committee. He moved that his successor should be Major-General Sir Henry Sugden, K.B.E., C.B., D.S.O., M.H.K., who had now come home to the Island after distinguished military service. The motion was carried.

Earlier in the year yet another distinguished officer had been elected to the Committee. This was Air Marshal Sir Paterson Fraser, K.B.E., C.B., A.F.C., M.A., C.Eng., F.R.AeS., (Rtd.), who still serves on the Committee in 1991.

At the very end of October, 1964, the *Thomas Corbett* returned to Ramsey after her refit. Her first task was on the 9th November at 2.31 in the afternoon. Word was received that the mfv CHILDREN'S FRIEND of Fleetwood had broken down with engine trouble, some two miles South of the Point of Ayre. She requested a tow from the Lifeboat and this was complied with. The weather was rough with poor visibility in a SE'ly wind when the Boat was launched at 2.40 p.m. By 4.55 p.m. she was back again with the fishing vessel safely in tow.

Radio Caroline Services

On Boxing Day, 1964, a message was received at 2.24 p.m. that a seaman on the "pirate" radio-ship RADIO CAROLINE had received a deep wound in his right hand and needed medical attention. This ship was permanently anchored, at the time, in Ramsey Bay. The *Thomas Corbett* was launched at 2.45 p.m. and the man brought ashore and taken to the Cottage Hospital for stitches to be inserted. He remained ashore for the night.

A similar call for help from RADIO CAROLINE occurred again almost exactly a month later, at 11.25 a.m. on the 27th January, 1965. This time it was a sailor who was bleeding excessively from the mouth after dental treatment. As the tide was at four hours' ebb and the ship's own tender could not leave the harbour for another five hours, the Lifeboat was launched to bring the man ashore for hospital treatment.

Some quiet months followed but then, on the 22nd July, the *Thomas Corbett* was on service again. At 2.15 p.m. the Boat was launched in answer to information that an RAF "Lightning" aircraft was down in the sea some 19 miles ExN from Ramsey Harbour. On arrival at that position the local Lifeboat joined the Workington Lifeboat and the smaller inshore Lifeboat from Barrow. They all searched for wreckage until a helicopter found and rescued the two aircrew who were taken direct to Workington Hospital. Dr. Paton had accompanied the *Thomas Corbett* and her Crew and they all returned to port by 8.30 p.m. Fortunately the weather had been good throughout, with a light NW'ly wind and smooth sea.

Two weeks later, on the 4th August at 8.56 p.m., an anticipatory message was received that a small yacht was in trouble two miles NE of Ramsey. There was a SW'ly gale at the time with squally conditions and poor visibility. A short time later another message from the Coastguards stated that the yacht was making very heavy weather in the conditions and was now only 70 yards or so from the beach. The Lifeboat was launched at 9.22 p.m. and soon had the boat and her crew of three in tow and brought them into harbour. The managers of Isle of Alanis Hotel offered them dry clothes and a meal and then accommodation for the night as their guests, which was much appreciated. The yachtsmen had been en route from Beaumaris to Douglas for 15 hours, but had been blown off course by the gale.

The next service was an abortive one and took place later in the month on the 27th August. The Lifeboat was launched at 3.50 a.m. after word was received that the Fleetwood trawler Loch Lein was aground at the Point of Ayre. On arriving at the Lighthouse the *Thomas Corbett* found the boat high and dry and that five of her crew had scrambled ashore by themselves but leaving two still aboard to tend the fishing vessel. The Lifeboat returned to port. The weather was fine with a light wind and smooth sea.

On the 1st October the Radio Caroline was in trouble again; this time with hull damage. She called for her own tender at 11.15 p.m. but the *Thomas Corbett*'s Crew Members were assembled as a precautionary measure for an hour and a half. They were, however, not needed.

The last call-out of the year was yet again to the Radio Caroline. (It would have been a quiet year without her!) On the 22nd December at 2.42 a.m. the *Thomas Corbett* took Dr. Paton out to the ship's Master. He had been bitten by a dog and had to have eight stitches to sew up his hand. The Lifeboat returned at 5.34.

At the Branch A.G.M. at the year-end Mr. B.T. Swales announced his retirement as Hon. Treasurer. He had officially held the post for 15 years although he had been involved "unofficially" with the work even longer. Mr. W.J. Corlett took his place.

At this meeting a question was asked as to whether there was any official liaison between the Lifeboat Service and the local Fire Service in the event of a fire at sea. The Hon. Secretary promised to look into the matter and report back in due course.

1966

The first notable event of 1966 for the Station was on the the 11th February. That day the Chairman of the Institution, Captain The Honourable V.M. Wyndham-Quinn, R.N., inspected the Branch and reported that he was greatly impressed with what he saw and that the Ramsey Station was one of the best-kept that he had visited. He also complimented the Committee on their fine Committee Room in the Norbury Boathouse.

At the first Committee Meeting of the year on the 6th May not only was reference made to the above visit but also to yet another award to a member of the Branch. This time Mrs. G.J. Teare, J.P., had been honoured with a Silver Badge by the Institution for outstanding services to the Ladies' Lifeboat Guild over a period of 40 years. A lunch at the Grand Island Hotel was organised for the ceremony and was held on the 8th June.

The year of 1966 began as the old one had ended for the Lifeboat Crews. At 11.00 p.m. on the 22nd March the Ramsey Coastguards intercepted a message, on 2182 Kcs, that a crew member of Radio Caroline had badly gashed a hand and a doctor was required immediately. The *Thomas Corbett* was launched at 11.16 p.m. with Dr. Paton on board once more. First Aid was rendered and then the injured man was brought ashore and he had to have a finger amputated at the Ramsey Cottage Hospital.

On the 2nd August the motor fishing vessel Master Frank was due into Ramsey at 3 p.m. However, at 5.41 the local Coastguard Station warned the Lifeboat Service that the fishing vessel had been sighted seven miles ENE off the port and was apparently flying a large flag which could be taken as a distress signal. Soon afterwards the *Thomas Corbett* was requested to launch and she was in the water by 6.14 p.m. The weather was good with a moderate ENE'ly wind. Soon after 7 p.m. the Lifeboat got alongside the Master Frank and it was found that she had sheared a crankshaft and required a tow. Yes, the "large flag" had indeed been one of distress – in fact it was a mattress from one of their bunks! (Probably the Engineer's!) The Lifeboat and tow anchored off the Queen's Pier at 8.25 p.m. but had to wait until 9.53 p.m. when there was sufficient water in the harbour to berth. The fishing vessel had a crew of five.

G.D. Learoyd collection

Thomas Corbett returning from an exercise, in the early 1960s.
Shown in this photograph, Wm. Cottier (Cox), Wm. Kinnin (2nd Cox), T.A. Corlett (Mechanic), W. Buttell, I. Gawne, I. Crowe.

Twenty days later in the month, on the 22nd, the Ramsey Coastguards spotted an SOS signal being flashed by a morse lamp from the harbour entrance. This was from the yacht COTICK which had grounded. The Lifeboat was launched at 11.45 p.m. and was alongside the yacht in 15 minutes. A line was put aboard the small boat and she was towed to the Queen's Pier for an hour to await water in the harbour to enable berthing. The COTICK had a crew of three and was on passage from Gavin in Scotland to London. Her outboard engine had failed off Ramsey.

The Crew of the *Thomas Corbett* listed for this service were Coxswain W.F. Cottier, 2nd Coxswain F.W. Kinnin, Mechanic J.H. Kneale, Asst. Mechanic I. Crowe, Bowman D. Walker and Crewmen A. Garrett, G. Crowe and P. Turner.

The last call-out of 1966 was during the evening of the 5th November. At 5.28 p.m. the Coastguards informed the Hon. Secretary that they had observed red parachute flares between six and eight miles out to sea, ExN from Ramsey. It was decided to launch the Lifeboat at 6 p.m., using the haul-off warp. Twenty minutes later, whilst in the look-out tower, the Hon. Secretary saw another red flare and shortly afterwards the Keeper at Maughold Lighthouse reported that he had seen what appeared to be a white light about one mile North of the Bahama Bank. The Crew of the *Thomas Corbett* searched the area for four hours in near gale conditions and very rough seas but nothing at all was found. They were recalled and returned to Station at 10.45 p.m. Later a message was received by the Ramsey Coastguards from Whitehaven that it was thought that several red parachute flares had been sent up from the Cumberland Coast. As is often the case, the culprits were never found.

During the year of 1966, Mr. W.R. Edwards' long service to the Branch was further recognised when he received the M.B.E., the citation stating that it was for services to the RNLI. Only a few years previously his sister, Miss Edwards, received the M.B.E. for her work in organising the Cancer Appeal and also in connection with her work for many other charities.

At the Branch A.G.M. and final Committee Meeting of the year Mr. J.K. Green, Member, brought the attention of those present to the very low wages being paid to the Boathouse Attendant. This was £2 per week plus 5% commission on the souvenirs sold from the Boathouse. It was decided to refer the matter to the Committee of the Endowment Fund to see if they could supplement the wage by a grant of £1 per week. The Hon. Treasurer further suggested that the Attendant should be paid a lump sum of £15 for his summer's work in addition to the wages he had already been paid.

1967

The first service of 1967 was on the 30th April at 4.05 in the afternoon. There was a force 8 NW'ly gale at the time and the Hon. Secretary received word that the fibreglass catamaran BOBBIE was making distress signals in a position three to four miles ESE from Ramsey Harbour. The Lifeboat reached the yacht within 25 minutes but on arrival found that the mfv PEEP OF DAWN had taken off the four crew of the BOBBIE and was attempting to take the boat in tow. The first line parted, however, but the *Thomas Corbett* got a second line aboard and towed the vessel into port.

On the 30th July information was received in Ramsey at 3 p.m. that the cabin cruiser GAMECOCK had left Barrow-in-Furness at 9 a.m. the previous morning bound for Douglas but had still not arrived. The *Thomas Corbett* was launched and proceeded to search an area from Laxey Bay to the Bahama Bank Buoy to the North. It was 9.15 p.m. before it was learned that the Barrow Lifeboat had found the GAMECOCK and her crew of four off the South Cumberland Coast. The Ramsey Lifeboat was recalled and was rehoused at 10.55 p.m.

DEATH OF W.R. EDWARDS

On the 1st June, 1967, the sudden death occurred of Mr. W.R. Edwards, M.B.E., the Hon. Secretary, so soon after receiving his public award for services to the RNLI. Later in the year the Institution posthumously awarded him a Vellum with a citation which read: "The Committee of Management of the RNLI has resolved that the thanks of the Institution be accorded posthumously to William Reginald Edwards in acknowledgement of his valuable services as Honorary Secretary for 33 years from 1934 to 1967." Mr. Edwards was succeeded by Mr. B.T. Swales who had already served as Treasurer from 1950 to 1965.

On the 11th July of that year Chairman Major Groves and Miss F. Weldon, representing the Ladies' Guild, attended Princess Marina's reception at Kensington House, London, to celebrate Her Royal Highness's 25 years' association with the RNLI.

The pirate radio ship RADIO CAROLINE was back in the news again on the 4th September, 1967. A local Press report painted the picture of events:

> "The action of two RADIO CAROLINE disc jockeys who broadcast their intention to swim ashore for a bet whilst gale warnings were in force was described here today by a Lifeboat Official as "utterly irresponsible and thoughtless".
>
> Ramsey Lifeboat was at sea for two and a half hours in a force eight gale last night after Mr. Ronan O'Rahilly, founder of the Radio Caroline Organisation, had telephoned Coastguards and the Lifeboat Station from London asking them to prevent the two men from making the attempt.
>
> Mr. O'Rahilly agreed to pay for the full cost of the launch – it will be at least £50 – and the Lifeboat was sent out with a seven-man crew to deliver an urgent message to the pirate radio ship ordering the disc jockeys to call the stunt off.
>
> Today, Mr. Bernard Swales, the RNLI's Hon. Secretary at Ramsey, said that he was genuinely worried and wanted this stunt stopped at all costs. Since there was the possibility of the men already being in the sea with their lives at risk, the Lifeboat obviously had to be launched. It is always better to have a false alarm rather than be too late, he added.
>
> Mr. William Cottier, Lifeboat Coxswain, said that his Crew was not very pleased at the job. When he had checked that there was no-one in the water, he boarded the ship and handed the message over. The Captain of the CAROLINE apologised for the trouble that had been caused.
>
> Today RADIO CAROLINE went off the air for four minutes, and again later for three minutes, whilst disc jockeys were reporting that the ship was in the worst gale experienced for two and a half years."

1968 began with a muster for the Crew at 11.30 p.m. on the 12th January. The London registered mv YARVIC reported having steering-gear trouble off Maughold Head. However the vessel later managed to make Ramsey Harbour safely under her own power.

Nearly a month later, on the 4th February, the local Coastguards advised that the Swedish motor vessel IRENE of Helsingborg was storm-bound off the Cumberland Coast with a dead seaman on board. She was unable to dock at Workington because of the conditions and intended to cross over to Ramsey Bay and seek shelter. This was soon after 12.00 noon. By 5 p.m. the IRENE was four miles East of Ramsey and requesting medical assistance and the Police. The *Thomas Corbett* was launched at once with Dr. R.B. Jones and Constable M. McHarrie aboard. The weather had moderated from SW storm force 10 earlier to W'ly force 6 to 7 when the Lifeboat took to the water. She returned at 7.15 p.m. with the body. After a post-mortem it was revealed that the death had been from natural causes.

The 19th May saw the *Thomas Corbett* at sea again at 9.40 a.m., a Sunday. This was in answer to distress flares from the local motor fishing vessel LADY ELEANOR. She was completely immobilised with a failed engine East of the Point of Ayre. Sensibly, she had moored herself to the Whitestone Bank Buoy, where the Lifeboat found her, in good weather, at 10.20 a.m. A tow was undertaken as far as Ramsey Bay where they both awaited sufficient water to berth at 3 p.m.

A LIFEBOAT DAY TO FORGET

Lifeboat Day that year was on the 7th August. Once the Annual Appeal for funds had been made it was arranged for the Lifeboat to carry out an exercise off the Queen's Promenade.

J. Kneale collection

The tractor submerged, Lifeboat Day, 1968.

W.S. Basnett

G.D. Learoyd collection

The problem continues, Lifeboat Day, 1968.

The *Thomas Corbett* was to go to the aid of a fishing vessel on fire in the Bay. An injured seaman on the vessel was to require medical attention. Doctor Paton from Ramsey was aboard the Lifeboat and a helicopter was flying overhead in order to facilitate the transfers required.

The unexpected always happens and when arrangements go astray it is often when there is an unwanted audience! In this case, however, the audience had been especially gathered and so there were numerous cameras on the scene to record events.

As the tractor was slipping the Lifeboat at the launch its gears jammed in "ahead" and, instead of reversing back up the slip-way at the crucial moment, it continued its way down and followed the Lifeboat into the sea! The driver was soon washed overboard from his controls. It took a considerable amount of effort to free the *Thomas Corbett* from her carriage and not before one propeller shaft became fouled. The proposed exercise was abandoned and instead of the "injured casualty" aboard the fishing vessel getting medical attention from the doctor, the doctor himself was brought ashore by the helicopter! Some time later, when the Lifeboat was eventually made fast in the harbour, a bystander who had been watching events asked Mechanic J. Kneale: "Does it usually take this long to launch the lifeboat?" His reply was not officially recorded.

The Zineh in Trouble

The 14th September next was a bad day for Mr. G. Brown of Bacup, Lancashire. At 8.25 a.m. he was reported to be drifting ashore in his yacht Zineh, between the harbour and the Queen's Pier. After consultation with the Coastguards it was decided to assemble the Lifeboat Crew and launch but before this could be achieved the yacht went aground. Her crew of three scrambled ashore through the surf from their own inflatable dinghy. The weather was fresh with the wind ENE, force 5 - 6.

Mr. Brown, the vessel's owner, together with help from Coxswain Cottier, Capt. H. Kinley, the Harbour Master, and Coastguard Officers, laid out two anchors, one from the yacht's bow and the other from her stern to keep the boat from falling down on to the Queen's Pier. After consultation Mr. Brown said that he would remain ashore and see how the yacht behaved when the tide made. By noon he was seen to be back aboard again. The Coastguards had put out two lines to the Zineh to maintain contact but she received a considerable hammering and again Mr. Brown abandoned his vessel and came ashore. The yacht floated on the tide and the anchors appeared to be holding, but the wind started to freshen. Yet again the owner decided to board his vessel and he did this by swarming down one of the ropes made fast to the Pier. By this time, 2.45 p.m., the Hon. Secretary decided it was time to launch as Mr. Brown's position was becoming more and more dangerous. The haul-off warp was used and the *Thomas Corbett* was water-borne by 3.10 p.m. It was an excellent launch under difficult conditions. As the Lifeboat approached the Zineh Mr. Brown cut his moorings, started up his engine and made a safe berth in the harbour, escorted by the Lifeboat.

Under the "Remarks" column in the official Returns of Service Book the Hon. Sec. magnanimously recorded:

> "Whatever the reason originally for the Zineh's troubles, Mr. Brown's enthusiasm in saving his yacht must be warmly commended. He refused to be beaten."

Two abortive services took place in December, 1968, to round off the year's work. The first, on the 14th, was a four-hour search for a man overboard from the British trawler Robert Hewett. This was undertaken three miles NW from the Point of Ayre in conjunction with a Shackleton aircraft. No-one was ever found. The second one on the 19th December was in answer to a call that a ship was aground West of the Point of Ayre, at Rue Point. The Lifeboat was at sea from 10.15 p.m. until being recalled at 11.45 p.m. Nothing was found but it was presumed that the coastal tanker Helmsman of London was the vessel thought to be in trouble, as she was the only one in the vicinity at the time. The original information came from the British trawler Spes Melior which reported that she had seen a ship ashore in the position indicated. The weather was foul with a S'ly force 8 gale, heavy rain, rough seas and poor visibility. Launching into heavy seas breaking on the beach had been achieved by an excellent turn-out of Crew and many helpers.

At the first Committee Meeting of 1968 on the 10th January the Chairman announced that a signed photograph of H.R.H. Princess Marina, President of the RNLI, had been received from London. It was agreed to hang the photograph in pride of place in the Norbury Boathouse Committee Room.

During the year several mentions are made in the Minutes Book about the completion and publication of the first booklet on the Ramsey Lifeboats by the Chairman, Major Keith Grimble Groves. It was entitled: "The Story of the Ramsey Lifeboat Station established 1829 and the founding of the RNLI by Sir William Hillary in 1824". It dealt mainly with the workings of the Branch from the Committee's point of view and was undertaken at the Chairman's own expense.

1969 was the last year of services for the stalwart *Thomas Corbett* at Ramsey. In all, 20

W. S. Basnett

G.D. Learoyd collection

Changing of the guard in 1970.
The *James Ball Ritchie* takes over from the *Thomas Corbett*.

years were covered by this Lifeboat and she undertook 60 service launches and saved some 13 lives during this time. Another nine services with 10 lives saved were undertaken by relief boats in the period.

Her first call-out was to the mfv VERBENA on the 18th May. Although this fishing vessel did not ask for assistance, HM Coastguards reported at 7.30 a.m. that the ship was in Ramsey Bay and making water fast. Her Skipper, M. Birch, was intending to beach her. Nevertheless, the Hon. Secretary decided to launch the Lifeboat with a pump on board. This was done at 8.10 a.m. in squally conditions and with a fresh NNE'ly wind. The pump was put aboard the VERBENA whilst aground and the boat was pumped dry. To prevent her being driven further up the beach the *Thomas Corbett* held her in position during this operation and then refloated her. The fishing vessel's insurers promised to make a donation to the Ramsey Branch for the valuable services rendered.

The second service of the year was to the yacht OURSINE on the 18th July. Just before 8.00 p.m. the Coastguards alerted the Hon. Secretary to the fact that they had received a "PAN" message direct from this yacht which was moored to a buoy just inside the Queen's Pier. At the time the weather was squally with a SSW wind of force 7 - 8. The situation was closely watched whilst the Coastguards managed to get a line to the yacht from the Pier. They were, however, unable to haul the boat any closer. The decision was then taken to launch the Lifeboat and she was waterborne by 9.20 p.m. The OURSINE was re-moored to a larger buoy and the owner, Mr. John Gould, taken off and brought safely ashore.

THEFT AT DOUGLAS

The 4th October brought an abortive search for a dinghy late in the evening. At 7 p.m. the Coastguards informed the local Lifeboat Service that the crew of the mv SELBY had observed a white fibre-glass dinghy afloat, unmanned, and in a position bearing 253° x 7 miles from Maughold Head. They had seen her oars in position, clothing on the thwarts and fishing tackle lying on the bottom-boards. After reporting the finding, however, the ship resumed her normal passage. The *Thomas Corbett* was launched immediately at 7.15 p.m. and in good weather with a light Southerly breeze. The area was searched using parachute flares and the searchlight but after an hour no sign of life was found.

In the meantime the Douglas Police informed the local authorities that a motor launch moored in the outer harbour at Douglas had been stolen and found beached some distance South of the port. A small fibre-glass dinghy had also been stolen from the harbour and apparently used to board the larger launch. It was now considered that this had been cast adrift and was the one found by the mv SELBY. The Lifeboat was thereupon recalled.

The Hon. Secretary commented in the Service Book:

> "I cannot recall any occasion when a British ship has observed and reported anything of this nature and then did not stand-by or appear to give any assistance whatsoever."

The final service listed for the *Thomas Corbett* was on the 10th December, 1969. At 4.13 p.m. the Hon. Secretary was informed by the Coastguards that two skin-divers were missing in Ramsey Bay. Within 12 minutes the Lifeboat was at sea and proceeded ENE from the harbour. The fishing vessels HEATHER BELLE and NEW VENTURE were also in this vicinity and at 5.05 p.m. this latter ship made it known that she had found the two divers safe and well. The *Thomas Corbett* went alongside the NEW VENTURE to check on the information and offer a passage ashore for the two men, but they declined.

The Crew Members listed on this last service were Coxswain W.F. Cottier, 2nd Cox F.F. Kinnin, Mechanic V.G. Crosthwaite, Bowman D. Walker and Crewmen P. Turner and A. Garrett. A note is added that J. Kneale, the regular Mechanic, was in Littlehampton taking over Lifeboat No. 995, the new *James Ball Ritchie.*

In actual fact the *Thomas Corbett* did not leave the Ramsey Station until February, 1970, when the new Lifeboat arrived. The old Boat left for Milford Haven in the first instance and was later stationed in Ireland. It was not until 1982 that she was finally withdrawn from service with the RNLI.

B.P. Grenfell

The *James Ball Ritchie* returns to her Station, late 1980s.

B.P. Grenfell

The *James Ball Ritchie* in Ramsey Harbour, late 1980s.

CHAPTER 9

James Ball Ritchie 1970-1991
incl. Reserve lifeboats
157 service launches and 78 lives saved

RNLB O.N. 995 was the next Lifeboat on the Ramsey Station and she faithfully served the area for 21 years. She was "born" in the boat building yard of William Osborne Ltd., in Littlehampton, Sussex, during 1969. Richard Oakley was the designer from whom the class obtained its name. Oakley served his apprenticeship in the Isle of Wight boatyards and then spent most of his working life with the RNLI. He became eventually their Naval Architect and his first "Oakley" Lifeboat was put into service at Scarborough in 1958. Twenty-six of this design were built during the next decade and a half.

Very early in December, 1969, Jimmy Kneale, the Station Mechanic, left Ramsey for three weeks in Littlehampton. Here the engine and equipment of the new Boat were put under stringent tests and preliminary sea trials were undertaken. Acceptance Trials under the scrutiny of RNLI Officials then followed, but were broken off for Christmas holidays when Jimmy returned home.

Early in the New Year the Ramsey Delivery Crew set off from the Island for Sussex. Willie Cottier, Coxswain, headed the team which included Jimmy Kneale, Donald Walker and Isaac Gawne. Further exhaustive trials and training were carried out until the Lifeboat was handed over to the RNLI. The long passage to her new home commenced on Saturday, 12th February, 1970.

The "Motor Boat and Yachting" journal of the 3rd April, 1970, gave an interesting and detailed account of 48 hours of the Lifeboat's eight-day passage Northwards. Two of the journal's staff, reporter Alex McMullen and photographer Eric Coltham, accompanied her for this part of the journey:

"Whistle for the wind and, by Jove, you get it -- or something like that. We had expressed hopes, I must confess, for something more than a light breeze for our two days on board RNLB *James Ball Ritchie*, so I hope the crew will forgive us for the full gale and more we encountered off the Pembrokeshire Coast.

We joined the Boat at Newlyn, Cornwall, for two of her eight one-day hops from Littlehampton, where she was built, to her new Station at Ramsey, Isle of Man.

A lifeboat on delivery is skippered by the Inspector of the area in which the boat is to be stationed. The Inspector of Area No. 2 which takes in Southern Scotland, part of North-West England and the Isle of Man is Lt. Commander Peter Gladwin, an ex-Merchant Navy man who has been an Inspector of Lifeboats for seven years; one year in Area No. 2. Also on board were Stan Brett, RNLI District Engineer North West and some of the Lifeboat's permanent crew: Coxswain Willie Cottier, together with Mechanic and Radio Operator Jimmy Kneale, Bowman Donald Walker and Isaac Gawne.

We left Newlyn soon after 9 a.m. for the 60-odd miles to Padstow, estimated to take about seven-and-a-half hours; it seems that whatever the conditions you can plug on at near maximum speed (8 knots for a 37-ft Oakley). They'd had a rough time around the Lizard the evening before and though the wind seemed decidedly light now the 6.40 a.m. forecast had hinted at worse to come. Lifeboats on passage don't by any means go whatever the weather. They will stay put in harbour for days rather than waste time punching into a gale, a quite frequent occurrence as deliveries (and passages for other purposes such as overhauls or new engines) are made at all times of the year. Jimmy called up the Coastguards on vhf to tell them of our departure and of our eta at Padstow. Throughout the trip we listened in to the distress frequencies on vhf and on the medium frequency coastal radio. A lifeboat is a lifeboat whether it be in its boathouse or on a passage and we could at any time have been called to a vessel in distress. Deciphering the crackling messages that every now and then burst forth from the lifeboat's radio must be an art. I couldn't make head nor tail of most of it but Jimmy seemed to have no difficulty. He says he used to "practice" by simply listening into crackling radio messages.

As we approached Land's End we were pushing into an increasingly lumpy sea, the result of the tidal race met off almost any headland and of a gradually increasing wind. For a while I felt very sick, but I was cured, rather surprisingly, by eating a cheese sandwich.

A 37ft Oakley has no cabin, only a shelter, just forward of the steering position, room enough for two on either side sitting on box seats. Dodgers can be put up on either side of the cockpit and we also had a sheet of canvas draped over the canopy (itself an innovation) on the windward side. Comparatively cosy but all this would have had to come down during a tricky rescue operation. However exposed the boat may seem she is so

1 Manx Press Pictures

E. Coltham 2 Motor Boat & Yachting

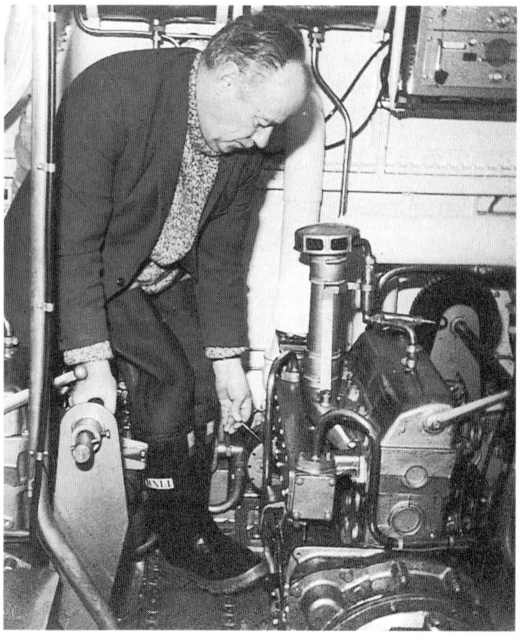

E. Coltham 3 Motor Boat & Yachting

1. Coxwain Willie Cottier, B.E.M. - Crew Member 1941-49, 2nd Coxswain 1950-51 and Coxswain 1952-73.

2. Ramsey Station Mechanic & Radio Operator Jimmy Kneale, B.E.M., 23 years the Station Mechanic and a total of 39 years serving the Ramsey RNLI Branch.

3. RNLI NW District Engineer Stan Brett checking the oil in one of the 52 bhp Parsons diesels.

E. Coltham Motor Boat & Yachting

The *"James Ball Richie"* coming in to bunker at Newlyn, Cornwall, whilst on passage from Littlehampton to Ramsey, February, 1970. L. to R: Coxswain Willie Cottier, Crewman Issac Gawne, Mechanic Jimmy Kneale, Bowman Donald Walker, Lt. Cdr. Peter Gladwin, Reporter Alex McMullen.

stable that even in the conditions we met the next day very little water came into the cockpit (and what did disappeared almost immediately down the ample drain holes); the main source of any soaking is from rain and flying spray. The forward well is used mainly for storage and would take rescuees if necessary, though the constant up and down movement in any sort of sea makes it pretty uncomfortable.

We moored just inside the outer harbour at Padstow, took on 30 gallons of fuel, and were driven off in the local lifeboat station's Land-Rover to our respective hotels. Supper, a quick drink and an early night to get our full quota of sleep before breakfasting at 6.15 a.m. and getting away at 7 the next morning.

The forecast was for Westerly winds becoming South-Westerly, force 5 or 6 possibly increasing to 7 or 8. Night turned into day as we left the Cornish Coast behind us, with no dramatic dawn for Eric's cameras to revel in. Jimmy brewed us some tea in the forward well by holding a kettle on a small portable gas stove for nearly half-an-hour.

The 97 miles from Padstow to Fishguard would take about 12-13 hours – seven of them out of sight of land as we crossed the Bristol Channel. A midday gale warning screamed out from the radio and, as we approached the Welsh Coast, sure enough the wave tops started blowing off and long white streaks of foam appeared in the troughs. With the sea coming at us from the quarter the boat was still remarkably dry. A few times we had to hang on tight as an extra large wave caught the boat, but now (and later with the waves dead astern) she showed no tendency to broach.

Throughout all this (bar a few minutes after he

37 FT. OAKLEY TYPE LIFEBOAT

(SELF-RIGHTING)

LENGTH	37′-0″
BEAM	11′-6″
DRAFT	3′-4″

POWERED BY TWIN FORD MODEL 592 E DIESEL ENGINES, MARINIZED BY THE PARSONS ENGINEERING COMPANY L^TD.

1. STEERING GEAR BOX.
2. DROGUE.
3. NON-SKID DECK COVERING.
4. EMERGENCY TILLER.
5. AIR CASES.
6. DROGUE CABLE TRAY.
7. LINE THROWING GUN LOCKER.
8. COXSWAIN'S PLATFORM.
9. COMPASS BINNACLE.
10. HATCH TO BATTERIES.
11. FIRE EXTINGUISHER.
12. RADIO TELEPHONE.
13. ENGINE CONTROLS.
14. ECHO SOUNDER.
15. BREECHES BUOY.
16. ENGINE EXHAUST SILENCER.

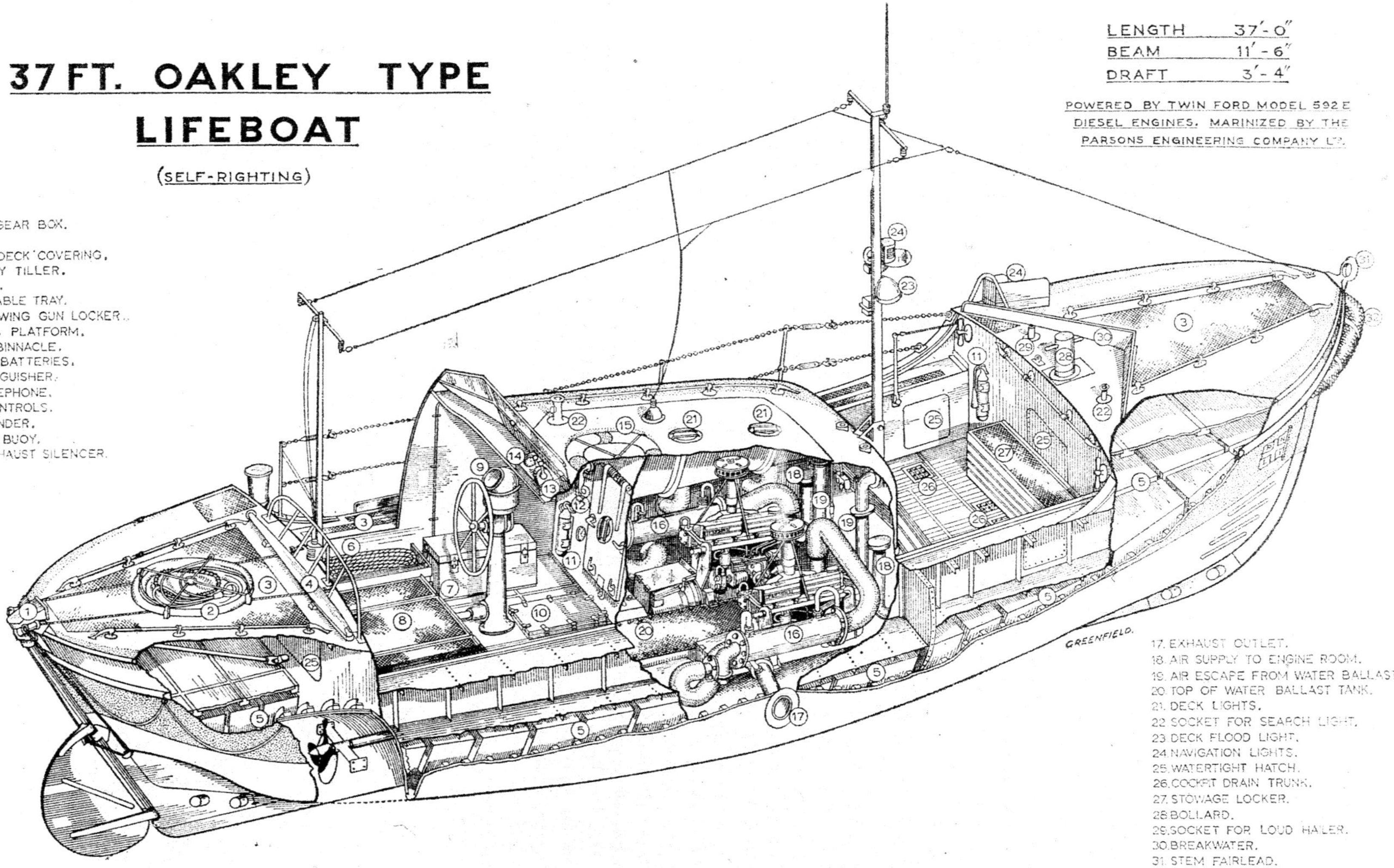

17. EXHAUST OUTLET.
18. AIR SUPPLY TO ENGINE ROOM.
19. AIR ESCAPE FROM WATER BALLAST TANK
20. TOP OF WATER BALLAST TANK.
21. DECK LIGHTS.
22. SOCKET FOR SEARCH LIGHT.
23. DECK FLOOD LIGHT.
24. NAVIGATION LIGHTS.
25. WATERTIGHT HATCH.
26. COCKPIT DRAIN TRUNK.
27. STOWAGE LOCKER.
28. BOLLARD.
29. SOCKET FOR LOUD HAILER.
30. BREAKWATER.
31. STEM FAIRLEAD.
32. BOW PUDDING.

came out of the shelter looking distinctly white) Eric kept clicking away, his pictures turning out as sharp as if taken at a 500th on dry land and on a calm day.

We saw dimly in the distance a giant tanker, obviously making for Milford Haven – if it wasn't for the tricky entrance we might have gone in ourselves – although it was probably safer to go on as long as we passed through Ramsey Sound (not to be confused with the Lifeboat's destination) before dark. The only concession we made to the weather was to pass outside Skomer Island instead of through the narrow Jack Sound.

The wind, now definitely a good force 8, was impairing visibility considerably and we didn't see the high cliffs of Ramsey Island until only a mile or so off. Here, too, as we approached shallower water, the waves were at their most threatening and, I would estimate, were topping just about 20ft. The drogue was prepared for throwing over but stayed on deck.

We'd passed Skomer at about slack water but now the tide, as calculated, had turned to help us through the Sound. An eerie place it seemed, lifeless in the grey mist with water frothing around the many jagged rocks. It was much calmer of course inside the Sound but a peculiar little tide race stretched right across, about half-way through, sending spumes of white water vertically into the air.

Darkness fell as we rushed head-long, wind and mountainous waves behind us, into the safety of Fishguard Harbour."

The Boat

RNLB *James Ball Ritchie* was the 24th of her type to go into service. This class of boat had the unusual distinction of being not only self-righting but also more stable than the slightly smaller non-self-righting Liverpool Class lifeboats which the *James Ball Ritchie* and most other Oakleys replaced.

The secret of the Oakley's self-righting action was in the water ballast tanks. If the boat was to capsize the ballast in the bottom tanks emptied into a tank on the port side above them (or rather below them when the boat was upside down) and this movement of water, which took about six seconds, gave the boat a self-righting moment, clockwise looking stern to bow. Large drain-holes in the cockpit and forward well disposed of any water remaining after righting. She was therefore a very safe and seaworthy vessel. Her hull was divided into 11 watertight compartments with approximately 183 wooden air cases as well as 32 blocks made from polyvinylchloride.

Good stability was effected by keeping the centre of gravity well down; the water ballast tanks helped do this and air tanks along both sides lent a powerful righting moment to any heel. Propellers were situated further forward than was conventional to ensure continuous immersion when the boat was pitching.

Construction was of double-diagonal mahogany. Dimensions were: overall length 37ft., beam 11ft. 6in., draft 3ft. 3in., weight (with crew, gear and water ballast) 12 tons. Power was provided by two Parsons Porbeagle Mk 2 diesels (marinized Ford industrial engines) developing 52 bhp each at 2000 rpm, each engine fitted with 2:1 reduction gear. Maximum speed was eight knots and with a fuel capacity of 88 gallons, range at maximum speed was 180 miles. At cruising speed – seven knots – the range was nearly doubled.

The two three-bladed propellers were positioned in "tunnels" for protection and for ease of access (through hatches) when fouled; a special multi-edged tool, looking rather like some mediaeval weapon, was carried for this purpose. Steering was by wheel through rods to a rudder hung on the sternpost. A tiller could be fitted in the case of a breakdown in the steering linkage. The rudder was lifted when the boat came out of the water.

There was no fully covered accommodation aboard a 37ft. Oakley; the only enclosed spaces were the engine room and lockers. There was room for four to sit under the shelter forward of the steering wheel and one of these was the mechanic/radio operator. Normal crew on the boat was seven.

Navigational equipment consisted of the Sestrel compass on a binnacle just forward of the wheel and a DF set. There were three radio transmitter-receivers. A "Curlew" coastal radio with medium frequency range was used for passing messages to Coastguards and for listening in for distress signals on 2182 kcs. The vhf set, which had a range of about 20 miles, was also used for calling up Coastguards and for listening on Channel 16, a distress frequency. Vhf was used for communication with helicopters and aircraft during rescue operations. The two distress frequencies were kept open whenever the boat was afloat.

Other equipment included a line-throwing gun, breeches buoy, searchlight, signalling lamp, flares and a first-aid kit. There was usually at least one qualified first-aid man aboard. Probably the most important piece of equipment was the drogue, used to steady the boat in a nasty following sea; the Ramsey boats used one frequently, especially when approaching the beach after a service or exercise.

James Ball Ritchie was launched and recovered off the beach at Ramsey. Two-and-a-half tons heavier than the boat she replaced, a larger tractor was supplied to get her in and out of the water on the carriage. A 37ft. Oakley lifeboat was the largest that could operate off a beach at that time.

Back at Home

In Ramsey arrangements for the naming ceremony of the new Boat got underway at a

W. S. Basnett

The *"James Ball Richie"* on her arrival at Ramsey for the first time on the 21st February, 1970.

W. S. Basnett

The *"James Ball Ritchie"* on her arrival at Ramsey on the 21st February, 1970, showing Coxswain W. Cottier (bobble hat only!), Mechanic J. Kneale, M. McCormick, E. Collister, I. Gawne, A. Garrett, D. Walker.

Branch Committee Meeting on the 30th October, 1969. This was held in the offices of the Ramsey Gas Light Company as alterations were being made to the lintel of the main door of the Boathouse to accommodate the new arrival. Major K.G. Groves chaired the meeting and those present included Mr. B.T. Swales, Hon. Secretary, Mr. W.J. Corlett, Hon. Treasurer, Sir Paterson Fraser, Capt. Hovenden, District Officer McGarrie (H.M.C.G.), Police Inspector Lowey, Messrs. P.G. May, D. Robinson, T.Q. Gaffikin, E. Corlett, C. Kinrade, C.C. Craine, Mrs. W.A. Callister and Miss Weldon. Also present were Commander Gladwin, RNLI Inspector of No.2 District, Major J.D. Disley, North West District Organising Secretary, and Mr. Brett, District Engineer, who attended in order to help organise the forthcoming event, because naming ceremonies are RNLI Headquarters events which are carried out to a standard procedure. It is the occasion when the new Lifeboat is officially handed over to the care of the Station. The date was set for the 9th July, the following year.

Earlier in 1969 the Isle of Man Daily Times had explained how the cost of the new Lifeboat was to be covered, some £38,500.

"Last year when Mr. J.B. Ritchie, former Chairman of the Heron and Brearley Group of Companies, learned that Ramsey was due to have its lifeboat renewed in 1970 he decided to make a gift of a new lifeboat to the RNLI for use in Ramsey.

Even during his final illness, prior to his death in December, Mr. Ritchie continued negotiations, with the help of his wife, with the National Secretary.

Now it has been announced that the new lifeboat, equipped with the very latest aids, will be delivered early in 1970 to Ramsey and it will be named *James Ball Ritchie*. Mrs. Ritchie says, "This is my husband's gift. I have only completed the arrangements he made in accordance with his wishes."

The late Mr. Ritchie loved the sea and in the last years of his life owned two magnificent yachts; the SILVER SAL was replaced by the GOLDEN LAL only months before his death. These yachts gave him much pleasure and fulfilled his ambition which he could only implement after he retired from business. He was always a generous supporter of the RNLI and, with so many other charities, his gifts were almost always anonymous.

It was Mr. Ritchie's intention to have the boat named after his wife, Ann. But his widow has made the only alteration to his wishes, insisting that the boat be called *James Ball Ritchie*."

The *James Ball Ritchie* arrived on Sunday, 21st February, 1970. She was met by Mrs. Ritchie, together with the Chairman of the Commissioners, Mr. H.G. Plumb, the Town Clerk, Mr. G.C. Swales, and Lifeboat Officials. Farewells were then soon said to the *Thomas Corbett* which left for Milford Haven. Frequent exercises took place during the following weeks to familiarise the crew with their new charge.

A modern tractor was also supplied by the RNLI to coincide with the arrival of the Lifeboat. This was a Case tracked vehicle with a Leyland engine and of the type much favoured by the Institution for the carriage-launched lifeboats.

The first call for a service came some weeks later on the 24th May. This was to the yacht RHIAN. She had been on passage from Mostyn in North Wales to Ramsey for over 24 hours. Her owner/crew later stated that with the SW wind, force 4 - 6, he was unable to make any further headway to the port. He made his predicament known by setting off red distress flares which were immediately seen by the Coastguards. The *James Ball Ritchie* was launched at 4.05 p.m. and towed the yacht into port. It was all done in just over an hour.

Another call-out occurred only a week later to the capsized sailing dinghy SOLAN GOOSE, but by the time the Lifeboat reached the boat help was in hand from the yacht FERN.

The naming ceremony duly took place as arranged on Thursday, 9th July, 1970. An article in the Isle of Man Courier of the following day painted a picture of the scene.

"Ramsey's new £38,500 lifeboat, the *James Ball Ritchie*, was named by the donor yesterday afternoon at a ceremony attended by a large crowd of people on the sea front.

The donor, Mrs. Ann Ritchie, who prior to the ceremony was introduced to the Officials, Crew and Helpers was presented, as she ascended the platform, with a lovely bouquet of flowers. The presentation was made by six-years-old Julie Kneale, daughter of the RNLI Mechanic at Ramsey, Mr. Jimmy Kneale.

There were two unplanned items in the programme. Major Keith Groves, J.P., Chairman of the Branch, was unable to attend through illness and Sir Henry Sugden, M.H.K., Vice-Chairman, deputised.

As Capt. N. Dixon, R.N., Secretary of the RNLI, began his speech accepting the boat from Mrs. Ritchie, something triggered off the bottle of champagne which prematurely splashed down on to the side of the Lifeboat.

In a very short time, without fuss, another bottle was produced and two members of the Crew had it back in position, carefully wrapped with red, white and blue ribbon, in time for the moment later in the proceedings when Mrs. Ritchie pressed a button to release the bottle and again "christen" the Boat in traditional fashion.

Mrs. Ritchie, in naming the Boat after her husband – *James Ball Ritchie* – said "This was my husband's last wish. It is his gift and I am gratified that I have carried out what he intended to do."

Mr. Bernard T. Swales, Hon. Secretary of the Branch, accepted the Lifeboat on behalf of the Station and Mrs. Stuart Callister, Chairman of the Ladies' Lifeboat Guild, in proposing a vote of thanks, revealed that Mrs. Ritchie, who took such a keen personal interest in the Branch, had consented to be President of the Guild.

The Dedication Service was performed by the Lord Bishop, assisted by the Rev. Francis Wood and the Rev. E.J. Le Poidevin (Methodist)."

Further services to yachts were undertaken within two days of each other on the 30th August and the 1st September. The first was to the VARUNA which was lying anchored off the port in deteriorating weather with engine failure. The *James Ball Ritchie* towed her to a safe berth in the harbour and then returned to the Bay and escorted two other craft to safe moorings. The owner of the VARUNA made a donation to the RNLI.

At 5.10 p.m. on the 1st September the trawler WYRE VICTORY reported to the Coastguards that there was a small yacht in difficulties near Ballacash (Ballakesh) Bank. The trawler had been unable to offer assistance owing to the shoal waters. The *James Ball Ritchie* was launched at 5.23 p.m. and arrived at the casualty at 6.10 p.m. Engine trouble was the problem once again and the crew of two informed their rescuers that they were really on passage from Laxey to Douglas! A tow took them to safety in Ramsey. The wind was WSW, force 5.

The last call-out of 1970 was on the 5th October when the Lifeboat was launched at 9.55 p.m. This was to tow the disabled mfv ELLAN VANNIN into port. She had fouled a net with her propeller whilst in a position some two miles SE from Maughold Head. The weather was moderate with a WSW force 5 wind. A gratuity was paid to the Lifeboat Crew.

At the Branch A.G.M. on the 18th December the usual Annual Report was made. This included reference to the excellent fund-raising by the Ladies' Guild which contributed over £600 to the local funds as well as to the special effort for the Fraserburgh Disaster Fund. (This port lost its lifeboat and all but one crew member on the 21st January – the second such capsize in 18 years). Mention was also made of the retirement of 2nd Coxswain F.W. Kinnin who had served the Station for over 30 years. It was noted, at the same time, that a member of the Kinnin family had been in the Ramsey Lifeboat for over 100 years – a truly magnificent record. Mr. Donald Walker was welcomed as his successor.

The meeting concluded with notification that the Ramsey and Peel District Round Table had offered an inshore rescue boat for the Station. RNLI Headquarters had stated that it was not their intention to establish an IRB at present but the Committee urged that a letter be sent to HQ to reverse their decision. They did not.

1971

1971 proved a successful year for the Lifeboat and five services were undertaken and 11 lives saved. The first of these took place when the *James Ball Ritchie* was launched at 9.35 a.m. on the 22nd January. The small coaster mv RAYLIGHT had engine failure off the Point of Ayre whilst on a passage from Troon to Douglas. On arrival at the crippled vessel Coxswain Bill Cottier found that the mfv GIRL MARGARET was already in attendance and arranging the tow. Another fishing vessel, the SPES MELIOR, had also been despatched from Ramsey to assist. As the wind began to increase, the ship was towed to Peel and the *James Ball Ritchie* accompanied them as far as Orrisdale Head, some six miles North of their destination. It was 3 p.m. before the Lifeboat was back at her Station.

At 9.10 p.m. on the 26th May the Coastguards sighted three red rockets off Maughold Head. The Lifeboat was waterborne within 25 minutes and soon found the power boat CARINA making faltering way and steering with a paddle. She had a fractured rudder and had been taking part in the Blackpool to Snaefell Race. Her two occupants were very cold and the Coxswain ordered rum to be administered! They were landed at the Queen's Pier and the *James Ball Ritchie* towed their craft into the harbour.

Two days later the Lifeboat was at sea again in answer to a "MAYDAY" call. An air search was also organised as the yacht PARULA was overdue at Workington. The *James Ball Ritchie* was recalled, however, when contact was made with the boat. She was not in any trouble and had not made the "MAYDAY" call. Her owner appreciated the concern, nevertheless, and made a donation to the RNLI as a "Thank You".

LEVITATION TRI RESCUE

The 3rd June saw the *James Ball Ritchie* out again for another yacht rescue. The Returns of Service Book entry gave the details concisely and stated that H.M. Coastguard had telephoned Hon. Secretary at 8.50 p.m. advising that a yacht had been sighted off Maughold Head firing a flare. Hon. Sec. asked the Coastguards to fire maroons and contact the Coxswain W.F. Cottier and Mechanic J. Kneale.

In view of the weather conditions, a strong ENE wind and rough sea on the beach, the *James Ball Ritchie* was launched with the haul-off warp and was off the beach at 9.05 p.m. and proceeded towards Maughold Head. Shortly before 10 p.m. the trimaran LEVITATION TRI was reached, one mile South of Maughold Head. Two men were already in an inflatable dinghy, tied astern of the trimaran, with all their gear. They were taken aboard the Lifeboat, together with the dinghy. The trimaran was taken in tow with the owner/skipper remaining aboard.

The Coxswain advised Anglesey Radio that in view of the weather conditions he intended to tow the trimaran to Douglas Harbour. The yacht was difficult to manoeuvre in the following wind and off Clay Head the tow rope parted, but contact was made again and the *James Ball Ritchie* arrived in Douglas safely at 11.55 p.m.

In the meantime Hon. Secretary had arranged with the Hon. Secretary Douglas, to provide hot drinks etc. for the Lifeboat Crew and survivors.

Coxswain Cottier decided not to return to Ramsey that morning in darkness, but to wait until daylight when water was clear of the slipway to recover the Lifeboat.

The *James Ball Ritchie* sailed for Ramsey at 9.00 a.m. 4th June and was housed by midday. An excellent recovery was made considering the conditions on the beach at Ramsey, a strong NE wind and a rough sea.

A few days later the local Press commented on the use of the haul-off warp in these more modern times.

> "In the recent Ramsey Lifeboat rescue the haul-off warp had to be brought into use to aid the Lifeboat to be safely launched as the sea running at the water's edge was treacherous. It is about five years since this method has had to be used in launching but it is a very valuable aid to safety and I am told is a precaution against the Lifeboat being swung broadside by the waves.
>
> The cable is attached to a fastening embedded somewhere about the low water mark and is always available when required. The operation involves bringing the rope up from the beach and then it is swung at right angles and is drawn along the promenade by the tractor. The other end is held by a member of the Crew and at a signal from the Coxswain it is cast off the Boat."

In later years this warp was dismantled as it fell into disuse with the Lifeboat having more engine power at its disposal. It also helped to reduce the Station's maintenance costs, because the warps had to be regularly renewed.

Six Lives Saved

Six lives were saved on the next service which was the last one for 1971. At 3.40 a.m. on the 10th August the Coastguards informed Capt. H. Kinley, Branch Deputy Launching Authority, that they had picked up a "MAYDAY" distress call on 2182 khz from the mfv Starbank which was aground on rocks South of Maughold Head. The *James Ball Ritchie* was waterborne at 4.10 a.m. and reached the casualty 40 minutes later. The Lifeboatmen found four crewmen and two passengers from the fishing vessel aboard a raft. They were rescued but one man collapsed and he was treated for shock by Lifeboat Crewman A. Garrett. A doctor and ambulance were therefore requested by the Coxswain to meet the Lifeboat and the survivors were landed at 5.30 a.m. The hospitalised survivor recovered after 24 hours.

On the 3rd May of that year, a Committee Meeting was held in the Norbury Boathouse. Reference was made to the death of Mr. A.C. Teare, C.P., who had been a Committee Member for some 43 years and Vice-Chairman for eight.

Commander Hill, Lt. Commander Rowe and Mr. Brett from the RNLI also attended in order to explain the decision of HQ to decline the gift of an inshore lifeboat (IRB) for the Branch. The cost of maintenance and depreciation, estimated at about £100 per month, could not be justified when checked against the Service Records for the Station for occasions when such a craft would be used instead of the *James Ball Ritchie*. The RNLI policy was to place such craft at stations where they were a definite necessity.

At the following Branch Meeting on the 7th July Chairman Groves announced that in the Queen's Birthday Honours List the B.E.M. had been awarded to Coxswain W.F. Cottier and the M.B.E. to H.M.C.G. District Officer McGarrie, a Committee Member. They were both congratulated by all present.

The final meeting of the year was the A.G.M. on the 17th December. Apart from reporting on the year's events, mention was made of the inspection of the Station by Rear Admiral Sir Edmund Irving K.B.E., C.B. This had proved successful and he had been very impressed with the great keenness and efficiency shown. Sir Edmund was an RNLI Vice-President, Chairman of the Executive and Boat Committee and a member of the Search and Rescue Committee and of the Technical Consultative Committee.

Numerous changes in the Committee took place. Major K.G. Groves retired as Chairman and was elected Vice-President. Sir Henry Sugden was elected in his stead and W.J. Corlett as Vice-Chairman. Other Officers continued in their posts; B.T. Swales, Hon. Secretary; T.E. Tregellis, Hon. Treasurer, and Dr. J.G. Paton, Hon. Medical Adviser. Squadron Leader J. Sands was welcomed to the Committee; he was destined to become the Station's Administrative Officer.

1972

1972 was a reasonably busy one for the Lifeboatmen and two lives were saved from seven services.

The first of these was on the 25th January to the mfv Lustre. She had lost her rudder some four miles East of Ramsey, in the forenoon. The *James Ball Ritchie* initially towed her to the Queen's Pier in order to await the tide. Weather conditions were good. A donation to the RNLI was promised.

On the 27th March the weather was very far from good with a force 8 - 9 SW'ly gale, very rough seas and, at times, torrential rain. Soon after midnight 26th/27th the Ramsey Authorities were advised that the Douglas lifeboat had been launched to search for the missing catamaran Sea Kitten, based in that port. The weather was deteriorating badly and it was decided to launch the Ramsey Lifeboat at 3.15 a.m. and for her to search to the South of a line from Ramsey to the Bahama Bank Buoy. Conditions were very bad with heavy seas but the new Lifeboat behaved well. At 8.00 a.m. a

W. S. Basnett

The *James Ball Richie* returning to Ramsey after a 12 hour service to the catamaran SEA KITTEN, 27th March, 1972, when two yachtsmen were saved after being adrift for 14 hours.

Shackleton aircraft joined the search and within 36 minutes had found the casualty and passed her position on to the *James Ball Ritchie*. The two crewmen aboard the SEA KITTEN wanted to remain with their vessel when the Lifeboat arrived but Coxswain Cottier persuaded them to board his Boat as it was too risky to leave them. A tow was undertaken for a while but the catamaran obviously became waterlogged and had to be let go. Only after doing so did it become known that an Alsatian dog had been left aboard SEA KITTEN but, under the circumstances and most reluctantly, the Coxswain felt that another rescue attempt was quite impossible.

The Lifeboat disembarked the survivors at Ramsey and they were taken into the care of the Civil Defence Commission. It was 3.00 p.m. before the Lifeboat was rehoused.

The Hon. Secretary commented on this rescue that this was a particularly arduous service and the greatest credit must reflect on Coxswain Cottier and his Crew Members for the excellent turn-out in appalling conditions and for the rescue of the two men who had been drifting for 13/14 hours in such severe conditions. The Service again reinforces the fact that in these search operations the use of spotting aircraft is invaluable. The Coxswain reported that he was within one mile of the casualty before it was actually sighted owing to the turbulent conditions.

CLIFF INCIDENTS

On the 21st May a sad incident took place in the vicinity of the cliffs at Maughold Head. The Hon. Secretary was informed at 4.30 p.m. that the Coastguard Rescue Party and the Police and Fire Brigade were all attending a small boy who had fallen over the cliffs. Well knowing the problems with such rescues, the *James Ball Ritchie* was launched under Acting Coxswain Donald Walker, taking a small dinghy. Unfortunately the boy died whilst on a stretcher and so it was deemed wise to take the body back up the cliff-side. The Lifeboat was not needed and returned to her station.

The following day at much the same time the Coastguards were out again to another boy in similar difficulties, some four miles South of Maughold Head. This time the youngster was rescued uninjured.

Two services to sailing dinghies were carried out in June. On the 3rd a dinghy with three occupants overturned in the Bay some three miles from Ramsey. They were picked up by a nearby yacht but the Lifeboat was launched meanwhile and the Crew attempted to right the small boat. As the mast was still stepped and the sail waterlogged they were unsuccessful and so towed the craft into port on her side. The weather was sunny but with a fresh SW'ly wind, force 4 - 5.

In the late evening of the 21st the Coastguards alerted Lifeboatman P.I. Crowe to the fact that a small motor boat was in difficulties near Maughold Head. As he had his own motor boat, he put to sea to give assistance. On reaching the scene he found that the crew of the small boat had scrambled ashore and were ascending the cliffs. As darkness was approaching the *James Ball Ritchie* was launched, under 2nd Coxswain Walker, but was not needed as the Coastguards made contact with the climbers and gave the required help. The Crew received a gift.

The 24th July saw the Lifeboat out again at 5.10 p.m. This was in response to a request for medical assistance for the Chief Engineer of the trawler WYRE DEFENCE. He had sustained injuries falling down a ladder. Dr. Paton was taken out and the patient landed for hospital treatment.

The Crewmen listed for this service were: Coxswain W. Cottier, B.E.M., 2nd Cox D. Walker, Mechanic J. Kneale, Asst. Mechanic A. Garrett, Bowman J. Corkish, L. Gawne and R. Crowe. The Tractormen were W. Callister and E. Collister and Launchers M. McCormick, E. Fisher, K. Crowe, J. Shimmin, T. McKnight, K. Perry, F. Walker, R. Kinrade, E. Kinnin, R. Wilkinson, G. Leeming, R. Corlett and G. Kaighen.

A search took place during the next call-out. This was at 1.35 p.m. on the 5th August when the *James Ball Ritchie* was in the water ten minutes after the maroons were fired. The crew of the Fleetwood trawler LUNEDA had informed the Authorities that they had a man overboard in the Ramsey Bay area. The Lifeboat was joined in the search by the passenger ferries DUKE OF ARGYLL, DUKE OF LANCASTER and the TYNWALD and two trawlers. No sign of the missing seaman was found and the Lifeboat was rehoused shortly before 7 p.m.

The usual Branch Committee Meetings were held during 1972. On Lifeboat Day, 26th July, a presentation was made to Mr. J.E. Corlett who had retired as Head Launcher some months earlier. Tribute was paid to his ability and conscientious work at the Station for over 50 years. Mr. M. McCormick was appointed Head Launcher in his place.

The A.G.M. for the year was held the following January, 1973. The Committee was informed that Coxswain W. Cottier, B.E.M., had reached the age of retirement and that 2nd Coxswain D. Walker had been elected Coxswain in his place. Unfortunately, later in the year, a new RNLI requirement for the post required him to take an eyesight test of which he failed the colour perception element. It caused disappointment all round. Lawrence Gawne took the position in the autumn.

1973

The first service of 1973 did not take place until the 30th June. The Lifeboat was at sea for two and a half hours and escorted the yachts AMETUSTUS and APHELION into harbour. There was a force 7 Southerly wind and the AMETUSTUS had been making heavy weather of the conditions very close inshore.

The yacht ESCAPE had most welcome assistance from the *James Ball Ritchie* and her Crew on the 20th September during a five hour service. She had been on a passage from Glasson Dock, Lancashire, to Peel and ended up at anchor some 14 miles SE of Maughold Head in a fresh NNW wind. On reaching this position Acting Coxswain Gawne found the single crewman of the ESCAPE in an exhausted condition. Lifeboatmen T. Clarke and K. Crowe were put aboard the yacht and attempted to weigh anchor but it appeared fouled, so the cable was cut. A safe tow back to Ramsey was carried out.

Coxswain L.W. Gawne carried out his first "official" service in charge on the 27th October. The mfv FIONA had reported engine failure off the Point of Ayre at 00.20 a.m. and the Lifeboat was away at 00.43 a.m. The Coastguards used their mobile tracking station to direct the *James Ball Ritchie* to the distressed ship and a tow line was in place by 2 a.m. As tidal conditions were not favourable for berthing at Ramsey, it was agreed to proceed to Peel where the two vessels berthed at 5.15 a.m. After hot coffee and soup for the rescuers they commenced the passage back and were on station again at 9.45 a.m. The weather had been fair with a choppy sea and a SE wind, force 4 - 5.

At a March Committee Meeting a report was made on the proposed arrangements for the all-Island celebrations in 1974 to mark the 150th anniversary of the RNLI. During the coming year a church service was to be held at St. George's, Douglas, and a Ball at the Majestic Hotel for the combined branches.

An "Isle of Man Examiner" of September, 1972, carried a report on the Ramsey Lifeboatmen and the change of Coxswain.

> "Lifeboatmen keep up family traditions. During the past year or two the ranks of the Ramsey Lifeboat Crew have taken a new look with several new members filling vacancies and the average age at present is much lower than previously.
>
> In most cases the Lifeboatmen are "sons of the sea" and are worthily maintaining the family tradition going back many years.
>
> I was chatting to some of the Crew last weekend when they held an exercise and the Boat *James Ball Ritchie* taken out to sea.
>
> On the previous night the Crew had recommended unanimously that Lawrence Gawne should be Coxswain. It was very fitting because Lawrence's father Isaac, was a Lifeboatman before him and his grandfather, Willie Gawne, is the last survivor of the Crew of the days of sail before motor power was installed. The other survivor of those days was Freddie Ball who died just recently.
>
> To return to the question of appointment of

D. Reed

The Royal Visit of the 2nd August, 1972.
HRH The Duke of Edinburgh in Ramsey talking to Coxswain W. Cottier, 2nd Coxswain D. Walker, W. Gawne. R. Crowe and Mechanic J. Kneale.

Coxswain. The procedure is that the Crew make their choice and this has to be confirmed by the Committee in consultation with the Institution. As Lawrence has passed his medical and eyesight test, tonight's meeting is the last hurdle. He is in his early 30s and is married.

Lawrence has been deep sea sailing and also been with the Isle of Man Steam Packet Company and now he has a shore job. He joined the Crew four years ago and the RNLI will arrange a special training course for him.

Lawrence finds himself selected by his colleagues to succeed Donald Walker who was expected to take over from his father-in-law, Willie Cottier. But Donald failed his eyesight test in colour, a bitter disappointment for him and the Crew who recognised his fine qualities. Willie, too, relinquished his post because of this new eyesight test but in any event he neared the age limit of 60.

Lawrence told me that he is looking forward to his new responsibility and is happy to have the confidence of the entire Crew. He says that Freddie Kinnin, who as his name suggests belongs to a family connected with the sea for many generations in the port of Ramsey and is the son of a Lifeboatman, is being proposed as 2nd Coxswain and this should be a good choice.

Among the new boys who have joined the Crew are Kevin Crowe, Raymond Kinrade of Jurby who now lives in the town and Terry Clarke, son of Harry Clarke, a well-known Lifeboatman in his day.

Other Lifeboatmen of the younger school include Ron Crowe, son of a lighthouse-keeper, Paul Turner, son-in-law of Willie Cottier and Keith Parry. There is also George Leeming of Ballaugh, a power boat enthusiast. Mechanic is Jimmy Kneale with Arthur Garrett as 2nd Mechanic and it will be remembered that Maurice McCormick this winter succeeded veteran Eddie Corlett as Chief Launcher.

Among those who have retired are Jack Corkish, son of Harry Corkish, Coxswain for 22 years from 1903 also Willie Kinnin who was 2nd Cox and Richard Wilkinson. But among the men who have retired there remains a tradition of service and they take a keen interest in the Station and would give a helping hand if needed."

"Note. In 1991, Ronnie Christian of Tower Street, Ramsey, is the oldest surviving member of the crew of the last sailing lifeboat, the *Anna Maria Lee*. He is now aged 83 and joined that lifeboat when he was 16, in 1924. He saw service in four Ramsey lifeboats before retiring at 67. His RNLI Long Service Vellum, dated 1975, states that he served as a Crew Member for 51 years and during that time 154 lives were saved."

1974

1974 was a busy year for the *James Ball*

D. Reed

The Royal Visit of the 2nd August, 1972.
HRH The Princess Anne with Mrs. F. Stephenson, wife of the Chairman of the Ramsey Commissioners, Coxswain W. Cottier, J. Corkish, 2nd Coxswain D. Walker and W. Gawne. The Police Inspector of the Special Constabulary to th left of the photograph is Mr. W. J. Corlett, Ramsey RNLI Committee Vice-Chairman at the time and later Chairman, 1977-81 and Vice President 1982-87.

Ritchie and her Crew. Eight services were undertaken together with 20 other launches for exercises and special occasions. One life was saved.

At 1.00 a.m. on the 2nd February the local Coastguards were informed that the Ramsey Steamship Company coaster mv BEN VEG had engine failure and was anchored 10 miles SE of the Mull of Galloway. As the forecast was for deteriorating weather with winds SW force 6 - 10, it was decided to send the Lifeboat to stand-by the vessel until a tow could be arranged. The *James Ball Ritchie* was waterborne by 1.30 a.m. but it took her nearly four hours to reach the ship in rough seas. A tug arrived from Northern Ireland at about 8 a.m. and very soon afterwards the BEN VEG was under tow to Belfast. The Lifeboat returned to Ramsey and was on station again at 11.10 a.m. The vessel's owners made a donation to the Ramsey Branch. Crew Members for this service included Coxswain L. Gawne, Mechanic J. Kneale, Asst. Mechanic A. Garrett, I. Gawne, R. Crowe, K. Perry and C. Gaines.

On the 21st February a "Man Overboard" alarm was raised by the Fleetwood trawler WYRE CONQUEROR. The *James Ball Ritchie* was at sea within 15 minutes at 7.00 p.m. and soon covered the three miles North East to the search area. Two small motor fishing vessels and the launch FAIR TIME also joined the search. At 8.35 p.m. the Skipper of the WYRE CONQUEROR indicated that he had sighted something in the water and one of his crewmen jumped over the side in an effort at rescue. Nothing was found and the Lifeboat picked up the fisherman and returned him to his ship. At 9.59 p.m. the trawler reported that the missing man had been found wedged in behind his bunk! The Lifeboat returned to Ramsey.

Within minutes of the Hon. Secretary getting home the Coastguards were on the telephone again. This time it was the launch FAIR TIME that was in trouble with a rope around her propeller. The Lifeboatmen and helpers were put on stand-by until 1.15 a.m. (22nd) but fortunately the mfv PEEP OF DAWN gave the required assistance and towed the launch to the Queen's Pier.

The British sail training ship MALCOLM MILLER contacted the Coastguards in Ramsey on the 6th May whilst on a passage from Portsmouth to Preston. She wished to land a sick trainee. As the weather was only moderate with a fresh SE force 5 wind it was deemed unsuitable to send out a small launch and the *James Ball Ritchie* was launched at 5.12 p.m. to undertake the task. An ambulance took the boy to hospital once he was landed and it transpired that he suffered from epilepsy. The Hon. Secretary personally transferred him to Douglas later in the evening into the care of the Society of St. Vincent de Paul who looked after him and arranged his return to the Midlands.

At 3.00 p.m. on the 2nd August red flares were seen in a South Easterly direction from Maughold Head. The Lifeboat was at sea within 15 minutes and found the speedboat BAJO with engine failure. She had no anchor and in the Westerly off-shore wind was drifting away from the land. Her two occupants were pleased to be towed to Ramsey and were berthed within the hour.

More red flares were sighted two days later at 10.19 p.m. off Jurby Head on the NW Coast. Coxswain Gawne agreed to launch the Lifeboat and she was away by 10.38 p.m. Thirty-five minutes later, however, the service was called off as the Peel lifeboat reached the casualty first. Once again it was a motor boat with engine failure.

A short service took place on the 15th September when the Coastguards informed the Hon. Secretary that one of their members was out sailing single-handed in his yacht TRIDENT OF MANN. He was taking part in a local race but as he had a vhf set and had not made contact since 9.00 a.m., concern for his safety was arising. The Lifeboat was launched but found the yacht within 20 minutes. All was well on board.

In mid-afternoon six days later, on the 21st, the Point of Ayre Lighthouse Keeper informed the Coastguards that two soldiers had launched an inflatable dinghy from the beach at the Point and were in trouble with engine failure. The weather was dull with a strong SW'ly wind, force 6 - 7. *James Ball Ritchie* was launched at 3.51 p.m. with the intention of towing the dinghy back to port. Mr. D. Midwood, however, had been fishing nearby from his motor launch JULIE DAWN and heard details of the Lifeboat launch over the vhf radio. He also proceeded to the casualty and in rough seas located the soldiers, got them aboard his launch and took on the tow. He kept in touch with the Lifeboat which escorted them both back to calmer waters off the port. After this incident Coxswain Gawne made it known officially that he considered Mr. Midwood's rescue to be quite courageous under the circumstances and that he had shown a high degree of good seamanship.

The last service before the *James Ball Ritchie* left Ramsey for a survey took place on the 1st November at 8.00 p.m. Assistance was given to the motor fishing vessel HARRIET. The Lifeboat was at sea for three and a half hours and escorted the ship to port. She was single handed and making water at the time. The HARRIET was engined but had originally been a sailing vessel and was of timber construction and elderly.

RNLB VINCENT NESFIELD

During Sunday afternoon on the 17th November the Reserve Lifeboat O.N. 994 *Vincent Nesfield* arrived to take up her duties. The following morning the *James Ball Ritchie* left for Beaumaris with her passage crew. She was to undergo her first special survey and the resultant necessary repairs and did not return to her Station until the late spring of 1975.

Celebrations of the 150th anniversary of the founding of the RNLI by Sir William Hillary were carried out throughout the RNLI world in 1974 and Her Majesty the Queen held a Garden Party in the grounds of Buckingham Palace during July. An allocation of 15 invitations was issued to the Ramsey Branch to include three Crewmen and their wives, two Shore Helpers and seven Branch Officials. Lots were drawn and the following attended: Mrs. A. Ritchie, Mr. and Mrs. B. Swales, Mr. and Mrs. T. Tregellis, Coxswain L. Gawne, Mechanic J. Kneale and Crew Members I. Gawne and K. Crowe, all with their wives.

The Manx Star of the 9th March covered the event in the following article:

"Isle of Man Lifeboatmen at Buckingham Palace. As maroons go off from every Lifeboat Station in Britain this morning to celebrate the beginning of the 150th year of the RNLI, there comes the news that a party of more than 50 Manx Lifeboatmen, their Wives, Branch Committee Members and Ladies' Guild Delegates, will be entertained at a Garden Party at Buckingham Palace on the 16th July.

They will join Lifeboat Crews from all over Britain to meet the Queen, but will certainly receive special attention because they come from the Island in which Sir William Hillary, who lived at Fort Anne in Douglas, founded the RNLI a century-and-a-half-ago.

Celebrations in the Island start today (4th March) with the issue of commemorative stamps by the Manx Post Office and the firing of maroons from all the Stations. A Ball is to be held at the Majestic Hotel on Thursday night and next Sunday there will be a special Thanksgiving Service at St. George's Church in Douglas."

Locally, the "Ramsey Courier" newspaper carried the following report of the events:

"For the first time all the Island's Branches of the RNLI joined together in the organisation of a dinner dance to celebrate the founding of the RNLI here on the Island 150 years ago by Sir William Hillary.

Branches throughout the United Kingdom are celebrating this important anniversary. The Institution now operates some 200 Lifeboats of which the Island is proud to have six operational boats in Manx waters.

Over 400 people attended the Majestic Hotel in

Onchan, in the presence of the Lt. Governor Sir John Paul and Lady Paul, the Mayor and Mayoress of Douglas, Councillor and Mrs. Ernest Ackary and many other distinguished guests. The guest speakers were Colin and Rosie Swale who shared the microphone to give a most interesting and entertaining talk on their round-the-world voyage which took three years."

The stamp issue mentioned consisted of a set of four. The 3p stamp depicted a portrait of Sir Wm. Hillary and the 3 ½p one reproduced the oil painting in the Manx Museum which illustrates Sir William's most famous rescue from the wreck of the steamship St. George on St. Mary's Isle in 1830. The 8p stamp showed the Lifeboat *Manchester and Salford* leaving Douglas harbour during her period on station between 1868 and 1887. To the left of the picture was the old pierhead and to the right could be seen the Tower of Refuge. The last stamp, with a face value of 10p, showed the latest addition to the Manx fleet, (in 1974)the *Osman Gabriel* which is stationed at Port Erin. The designer of the stamps was local artist Mr. J.H. Nicholson R.I., who undertook all artwork for the Postal Authority at that time.

The sale of the "First Day Covers" of the above stamps made a substantial profit for the Ramsey Branch. Coxswain Lawrence Gawne autographed each cover sold locally, thereby greatly enhancing their value. A donation of £150 was also made to the Branch by the Douglas High School for Boys in connection with their own sales of the covers.

At the end of October, 1974, Mr. J.M. Bubb, MNI, Inspector of Lifeboats, NW Division, inspected the Station for the first time in that capacity. He also drew attention to the Station's entitlement to appoint a Station Administrative Officer and at this time Squadron Leader John Sands was confirmed in the post.

During the year some structural problems arose with the roof of the Norbury Boathouse. As the Coxswain's flat was no longer in use (times had changed and the space was unsuitable for family accommodation), it was decided to dispense with the top floor completely before the re-roofing was undertaken. This left the Boathouse with the first floor Committee Room and kitchen area and a large shallow loft above it for storage space. The old tractor house alongside the building was put into use as a store and later in the 1980's was fitted out as a modern Crew Room.

The year was rounded off by the first service of the *Vincent Nesfield* when she was launched at 3.30 p.m. on the 19th December. An elderly lady had fallen down a cliff some distance South of the Station. Although the Coastguard Rescue Team was at the scene, the Lifeboat was sent as a precaution. She was not needed, however, and the rescue was effected from the shore. The injured lady was hospitalised.

1975

During the first four months of 1975, the Reserve Lifeboat undertook four services and then the *James Ball Ritchie* returned to make a further five to the end of the year.

The first service of the year was a long one to the mfv Random Harvest. She sent out a "MAYDAY" distress call when her engine failed at 11.30 a.m. on the 7th February. At the time she was off the Point of Ayre bound for Ireland from Ramsey. The *Vincent Nesfield* was launched within 12 minutes of the call. There was a moderate sea with a fresh E'ly wind, force 4 - 5. As no other vessels were in the vicinity the Lifeboat made haste to the casualty which was drifting on to the shore. A tow was undertaken and in view of the weather and tide, Peel was chosen as the port of refuge. Arrival was made at 3.20 p.m. and after a meal the Crew of the *Vincent Nesfield* made a course for home, arriving at 7.00 p.m.

A similar call-out took place three weeks later on the 1st March. The motor fishing vessel Pern also had engine failure fourmiles WSW from the Point of Ayre. No other vessels were available to help at the time and so the Lifeboat was launched at 12.53 p.m. in fair conditions. This time a tow by the *Vincent Nesfield* was not needed as another fishing vessel took on the task and made for Peel. The Lifeboat was back on station at 7.00 p.m. A note was made by Coxswain Gawne in the Records of his appreciation of the help given by the Coastguard Mobile Patrol Vehicle and also of the help from the Radar Operators from the RAF Air Weapons Range at Jurby.

The last service of that spell of duty for the Reserve Lifeboat was at 4.37 p.m. on the 9th April. The trawler Wyre Victory came into Ramsey Bay en route from Fleetwood to the Icelandic fishing grounds. She had an injured man aboard. Doctor Paton and Police Constable Kneen were taken out by the *Vincent Nesfield* and the seaman transferred and landed for hospital attention.

The *James Ball Ritchie* returned from Bangor after her first major survey in the late spring but it was not until the 26th July at 11.23 p.m. that she was called out on a service. A Police Officer had observed a red flare exploding some five miles East of Laxey. Lawrence Gawne took the Lifeboat out on a search of the area and fired two parachute flares, but after two hours found nothing and was recalled. It later became known that the yacht Greyling had taken the Wensly Ann, a small cabin cruiser, in tow at about 10.50 p.m. The latter had had an engine breakdown and although both boats realised that the Lifeboat was on hand, they were unable to communicate. The weather was good.

B. Ramsey

Committee Officers and the Crew, c1976. Back: G. Evison, W. Callister, E. Collister, T. Clarke, A. Garrett Snr, M. McCormick, D. Walker, R. Crowe, T. McKnight, A. Faragher, G. Kaighen, Hon. Station Administrative Officer Sqn. Ldr. J. Sands Middle: Capt. A. S. Carine, Hon. Treasurer T. E. Tregellis, J. Kinnin, J. Shimmin, K. Crowe, 2nd Coxswain F. Kinnin, Coxswain L. Gawne, Mechanic J. Kneale, Asst. Mechanic A. Garrett Jnr., C. Gaines, R. Kinrade, Master Peter Faragher, D. Kaighen, Harbour Master Capt. H. Kinley, R. Gaines. Front: Hon. Medical Adviser Dr. J. G. Paton, Vice-Chairman W. J. Corlett, President Major K. G. Groves, Ladies' Guild President Mrs. A. A. Ritchie, Chairman Major General Sir Henry Sugden, Ladies' Guild Chairman Mrs. I. Teare, Hon. Branch Secretary B. T. Swales

More disabled vessels called for lifeboat assistance in August and early September. On the 6th August the Peel registered fishing vessel REGINA MARIS fouled her propeller with a net in Ramsey Bay. She could only make very slow progress and, with the wind freshening to S'ly force 6, the Lifeboat was launched at 7.52 p.m. and escorted the vessel safely into port.

During the afternoon of the 30th August the Coastguards on watch advised the Hon. Secretary that the auxiliary yacht DUKE OF ATHOLL was being severely buffeted by rough seas whilst she lay moored to buoys outside the harbour entrance. She was awaiting the tide to berth and had a crew of two. Radio contact had been established. Soon the yacht slipped her lines and attempted to "dodge" the seas. The wind was NE force 5 - 6 so it was decided to launch the *James Ball Ritchie* at 3.13 p.m. as a precautionary measure. Coxswain Gawne suggested that the yacht should proceed seawards until there was sufficient water to enter harbour; he also handed over two lifejackets to the occupants. All went well and the Lifeboat was back on station at 5 p.m. The RNLI received a donation and the Crew a bottle of rum for their efforts.

At 5.15 p.m. on the 9th September the small launch WINIFRED called for immediate assistance as she had had an engine failure off the Point of Ayre. The Lifeboat was launched 10 minutes later and reached her at 6.12 p.m. A tow back to Ramsey was effected in rough seas and the launch was moored to buoys at 7.40 p.m. The owner was a local Sulby man and he had a crew of two with him.

The last call-out of the year on the 27th September turned out to be a fruitless night-time search. In the late evening the Coastguards confirmed that two parties had observed red flares in the sky NW of the Isle of Man. The Record of Services gave an account of what followed and stated when confirmation of flares by a second party had been received it was decided to launch and the *James Ball Ritchie* was waterborne at 9.45 p.m. There had been very severe weather during the day with winds backing from SE to NE and a consequent very heavy swell on the beach, although at the time of launching the wind had backed to the NW and there was a slight moderation. As it was virtually low water the *James Ball Ritchie* was launched without the haul-off warp and succeeded in entering the water without mishap. It was a difficult launch and credit must be given to both Coxswain and Crew and to the two Tractor Operators for a very efficient job. *James Ball Ritchie* proceeded to the indicated position and searched. Assistance was received from the passenger vessel ULSTER PRINCE on passage from Belfast to Liverpool and the ro-ro ship BISON on passage from Belfast to Fleetwood. When these vessels and the Lifeboat had given negative reports the Hon. Secretary recalled the Ramsey Lifeboat which was safely rehoused at 3.30 a.m. There had been no indication of any person in distress; visibility was exceptionally good on this occasion.

With the new appointment of an Administrative Officer, liaison meetings between the Hon. Secretary, Hon. Treasurer, Administrative Officer, Coxswain and Mechanic were held monthly during the year. The A.G.M. for 1975 was held on the 7th January, 1976. A resumé of the year was read out and included an acknowledgment and appreciation of the Ladies' Guild for raising £1269 for Branch funds which included the special efforts made throughout 1974 for the 150th anniversary year. The Rt. Rev. Vernon S. Nicholls, Lord Bishop of Sodor and Mann, was thanked for making the Annual Flag Day Appeal on the 6th August and collections that day made £542, another record.

The new appointment of a Branch Press Officer was also made at this meeting and Mr. Podmore was unanimously elected. This was done at the Institution's suggestion that good Press reports would undoubtedly enhance the fund-raising activities.

Mr. P.J. May, Committee Member, voiced the disappointment generally felt at the veto by the UK Department of Trade and Industry placed on equipping the Coastguard trailer with radar provided by a local firm, Bevan Radio. This had proved very successful on several occasions and had illustrated how relatively inexpensive equipment on the Island could provide cover for a comparatively long coastline. Coastguard District Officer Richardson explained the constraints imposed upon him and the reasons for them and pointed out that the first priority now should be for the *James Ball Ritchie* herself to be equipped with a radar set. Mrs. Ritchie pointed out the Boathouse could cause headroom problem with such equipment and its mast. It was resolved to request the NW Division Inspector to discuss the matter with the Branch.

The attention of the meeting was also drawn to a letter from the Institution commenting on statements on Britain's Maritime Search and Rescue Services made by Mr. S. Clinton Davis, M.P., Parliamentary Under Secretary for Shipping. In this he had outlined recent developments by the Institution such as the introduction of more fast off-shore and in-shore boats; the improved helicopter coverage provided by the Ministry of Defence and the new developments in the organisation and duties of H.M. Coastguard. The statement also stressed the importance of the different units involved in Search and Rescue maintaining their own identity and responsibilities as no single organisation could provide the whole spectrum of Search and Rescue facilities which were available. The Institution warmly welcomed this statement which in no way altered the responsibilities or authority of the RNLI, but which stood to improve the co-operation between the various Services.

But changing governments adopt changing policies as future years were to show.

The A.G.M. concluded with Chairman Major General Sir Henry Sugden presenting to Mrs. Ritchie, President of the Ladies' Guild and donor of the *James Ball Ritchie*, a photograph taken in the previous summer of the Crew, Committee and Officials and signed by the Crew.

1976

1976 was a somewhat quieter year for the Lifeboatmen and five services were undertaken. The *James Ball Ritchie* was also at sea on 12 other occasions for exercises and routine inspections.

The first service of the year was for escort duty and was somewhat unusual. At 10.00 a.m. on Sunday, 4th January, H.M. Coastguards advised that the mv IVY of Limassol, Cyprus, a ship of about 2000 tons deadweight, was anchored in Douglas Bay with only the Master and Chief Engineer on board. The crew was ashore, having been taken off the Douglas Lifeboat the previous day in a very severe W'ly gale. Negotiations proceeded all day with various officials and the crewmen but they refused to rejoin their ship. It was then deemed advisable for the IVY to leave Douglas and proceed to Ramsey Bay where there was more shelter available. Accordingly the Douglas Lifeboat escorted the ship to Laxey Bay where the Ramsey Lifeboat took over the duty. It was understood that mv IVY had shifted her cargo in the recent storm and had a list of approximately eight degrees. The *James Ball Ritchie* returned to the Boathouse at 7.00 p.m.

At 5.10 p.m. on the 20th May the Ramsey Coastguards informed the Hon. Secretary that red flares had been sighted off Laxey. Very shortly afterwards a farmstead owner near Laxey reported sighting more flares and so the Lifeboat was launched. It was a fine evening and the Coxswain proceeded SE and at 6.40 p.m. found the small motor boat GLEN ROY with a fouled propeller. She had crew of two. The *James Ball Ritchie* towed her to Laxey.

A flare observed North of the Point of Ayre was reported to the Ramsey Authorities at 12.45 p.m. on the 18th July. The *James Ball Ritchie* was in the water at 12.55 p.m. and proceeded to the position given. This was later amended and at 1.45 p.m. Coxswain Gawne and the Crew sighted another red flare and they replied using one of their own parachute flares. The casualty turned out to be the motor launch ESTHER ANNE with six people aboard. They had left Ramsey earlier in the day on a fishing trip and the engine had failed. As there were no other suitable vessels in the vicinity the Lifeboat towed the boat back to Ramsey. The weather was overcast with a slight sea and a SSE wind, force 4 - 5.

The 22nd August saw more yachts with problems in Ramsey Bay. The Lifeboat was launched at 3.00 a.m. after red flares had been sighted North of the port. By the time help arrived by sea one yacht had grounded and the Coastguards assisted the sole occupant ashore. During the service it was reported to the Coxswain that two yachts had sailed from Ravenglass, Cumberland, to Ramsey and one was unaccounted for. This one was soon found anchored off Ramsey by the *James Ball Ritchie* and, as the weather was on-shore and moderate, Coxswain Gawne deemed it wise to stand-by her until dawn. In the meantime the owner of the beached yacht returned to his boat but was unable to float her single-handed on the incoming tide. The Lifeboatmen, aware of the situation, thereupon passed him a line, towed him clear and escorted both yachts into a safe berth.

THE ROBERT CHARLES SERVICE

At 3.50 a.m. on the 23rd November the Coastguards telephoned Hon. Secretary Swales to say there was concern about the mfv ROBERT CHARLES which had sailed from Peel the previous evening for Ramsey. Only the Skipper was aboard her and had informed the Coastguards that his ship was making water but could not give much idea of his position. It was decided to launch the *James Ball Ritchie* and she was away by 4.30 a.m. She headed for the Point of Ayre and to search the NW promontory of the Island. The Hon. Secretary remained at the Coastguard Headquarters, which were very near the Boathouse in Ramsey, throughout the service. This was the normal procedure. After a time he decided to ask the Donaghadee lifeboat to assist. The Irish Sea ferry ULSTER QUEEN joined the search and the ROBERT CHARLES was located approximately 11 miles East of the South Rock Light Vessel on the Northern Irish Coast. The ULSTER QUEEN stood-by until the Donaghadee lifeboat arrived and took the fishing vessel in tow. It was intended that the *James Ball Ritchie* would take the tow and make for the nearest port of Peel. However the Northern Irish Coxswain indicated that he was not too happy about his fuel situation and that he would prefer to effect the tow and thus call at Peel and bunker there before proceeding back to his own Station. This was done and the Ramsey Lifeboat returned and was back on station at 11.30 a.m.

On the 12th February, 1976, Mr. Bubb, the RNLI NW District Inspector, attended a special Committee Meeting to discuss fully the Institution's policy on radar and, in particular, the fitting of shipborne radars to operational lifeboats. The RNLI tended to favour only such units and all boats under construction were to have sets fitted as standard. At that time one Oakley Class boat was being fitted with a system for trials. There were many problems to overcome, such as the power supply, internal fitments, the effect on the boat's self-righting capabilities and, not least of all, the problem highlighted by Mrs. Ritchie in connection with the height of Boathouse doors for the carriage-launched boats. Members at the meeting were assured that the Institution was very well aware of the wish for the *James Ball Ritchie* to be fitted with a suitable set and if trials were successful no doubt the request would be looked upon favourably. He expected that it would be at least another year before definite decisions were taken. Mr. Bubb made a particularly valid point concerning the radar scanner's limited height above sea level. He explained that the radar's value would be mainly for navigational purposes and its capabilities for searching would be limited. The range was likely to be only five miles.

The A.G.M. was held on the 21st January, 1977. It was noted that earlier in 1976 2nd Coxswain F.H. Kinnin had resigned on medical grounds and that Mr. J. Kinnin had taken his place.

Mrs. Ritchie, President of the Ladies' Guild, was welcomed to Ramsey as a resident. She had previously lived nearer to Douglas.

His Honour Deemster A.C. Luft was thanked for making the Annual Flag Day Appeal on the 28th July. This produced the sum of £664.

Once again the Ladies' Guild was thanked for all their efforts and their social fund-raising functions which had realised £1300 during the year.

1977

1977 was a very busy year after a relatively quiet one. Twelve services were rendered and eight lives saved. Three yachts were brought to safety. Exercises for the year numbered eight.

The 12th April saw the Lifeboat called to the motor launch SOLVA disabled with engine failure off the Point of Ayre. She had been on a passage from North Wales to Glasson Dock when it happened and the two occupants contacted Ramsey Coastguards. The Lifeboat was launched at 10.25 p.m. and towed the SOLVA back to Ramsey but had to stand-off to await the tide and it was 6.00 a.m. on the 13th before *James Ball Ritchie* was rehoused.

Red flares at 9.45 p.m. on the 5th May signalled that a serious incident had occurred some 14 miles NE of Ramsey. The mfv NIELS JOHN had sunk whilst fishing half-way between the Isle of Man and the Cumbrian Coast. Her three survivors had taken to their liferaft. The *James Ball Ritchie* was launched at 10 p.m. and made for the distress area and several other vessels were also soon on the scene, including the mfv FRED WOOD, mv BEN VEG and mv SILLOTH. The FRED WOOD picked up the three survivors and landed them at Kirkcudbright in Southern Scotland. The Ramsey Lifeboat returned within an hour of launching.

At 2.27 p.m. on the 11th June the Lifeboat was launched to assist a small motor boat which had missed the tide to enter the port. The sea was rough with a NE force 7 onshore wind. Coxswain Gawne showed considerable skill in getting the *James Ball Ritchie* off the beach at five hours ebb and the Lifeboat stood-by the boat until she was able to berth at 6.30 p.m.

The Isle of Man Yacht Race was held on the 5th June and bad weather conditions caused problems for several craft. The *James Ball Ritchie* was launched at 3.15 p.m. originally to go to the aid of the yacht FREJOY which was dismasted some three miles East of the Station. Soon after launching the Lifeboat was directed to a skin diver in difficulties. He was picked up at 3.20 p.m. and taken into the harbour with all speed, landed and hospitalised. He was detained for treatment. The Lifeboat stood-by for the remainder of the afternoon as the wind increased to NW force 6 - 7. Soon the Coastguards asked for assistance for the launch JULIE DAWN which had fouled the Queen's Pier. This was followed by the dismasting of the yacht KAY DEE CEE off Maughold Head. She was escorted into Ramsey. The FREJOY, in the meantime, was escorted into harbour by the sail training ship FRANCIS DRAKE. The diver offered a gratuity to the Crew. A remark made in the Service Book by the Hon. Secretary after these events stressed the fact that as far as the Yacht Race was concerned, although there were several incidents, there was no loss of life or personal injury.

The Service Boards in the Boathouse next list the 11th June for a launch to escort the motor yacht SAZA BARI into port after she missed the tide. Apparently it was a difficult launch at low water and in rough weather but no other details seem to have been recorded.

During a town fete on the afternoon of the 25th June the *James Ball Ritchie* was being displayed on her carriage in Ramsey Market Square. At 4.40 p.m. the Coastguards saw a small vessel in the Bay showing a distress flag and Coxswain Gawne was contacted. Not less than 20 children were, at that time, enjoying themselves clambering all around the Lifeboat. Suddenly they found themselves being hastily ejected from all angles; there were legs and arms everywhere but the Lifeboat was waterborne 12 minutes later, nevertheless! The casualty turned out to be the converted lifeboat SHARRON with engine failure. She was towed into port.

A week later on the 2nd July, in the forenoon, Coxswain Gawne and Mechanic Kneale were working in the Boathouse and also watching the small auxiliary yacht NEMESIS at anchor in the Bay and unable to start her engine. She was dragging her anchor and drifting North in a Southerly force 8 gale. The Coxswain was unable to contact the Hon. Secretary or the Deputy Launching Authority and so decided to get the Lifeboat away to assist before anything disastrous happened. The *James Ball Ritchie* was afloat at 12.04 p.m. and towed the yacht with her crew of three into the harbour within 36 minutes. However, it was not until 3.05 p.m. that the Lifeboat could be housed. Coxswain Gawne was later complimented on his skill in bringing the yacht into a safe berth under such conditions. A donation as a "Thank You" was made to the Crew.

On the 15th July the sailing dinghy ALI BABA with a crew of two capsized one mile SE of the Boathouse. Within 10 minutes the Lifeboat was under-way and very soon picked up a man and his wife from the water. Their dinghy was towed astern and in towards the beach. A letter of thanks was later received for this rescue and a donation made to the RNLI.

At 1.15 a.m. on the 27th July the Coastguards received a request for immediate lifeboat assistance from the mfv M.D.B. She was nine miles WxN from the Point of Ayre and making water fast. The *James Ball Ritchie* was launched at 1.36 a.m. and reached the casualty at 2.45 a.m. The fishing vessel was making way very slowly at about two knots and the Lifeboat escorted her to the Queen's Pier. The weather was fine and clear with a NW'ly wind force 5. It was 4.30 a.m. by the time the Lifeboat was back on station.

Severe gale conditions were encountered for the next service on the 24th August. The Coastguards advised the Lifeboat Authorities at 4.26 p.m. that the trimaran KYLIE was drifting in heavy seas off the Bahama Bank. She was on passage from Port St. Mary to Glasson Dock in Lancashire. The Lifeboat was launched at 4.37

B. Ramsey

The Crew c1976.

Back: W. Callister, K. Crowe, J. Shimmin, A. Garrett, C. Gaines Middle: D. Walker, M. McCormick, E. Collister, G. Evison, R. Crowe, R. Kinrade, Hon. Branch Secretary B. T. Swales
Front: 2nd Coxswain F. Kinnin, Coxswain L. Gawne, Mechanic J. Kneale

p.m. and took 65 minutes to reach the casualty. Coxswain Gawne decided to tow the yacht back to Ramsey despite the conditions in the SE'ly gale, force 9. Both boats made it safely back to port at 7.30 p.m., but it was another two hours before the weather and tide were right to rehouse the *James Ball Ritchie.* The Deputy Launching Authority, Capt. Carine, noted in the Service Book that it was an excellent launch and recovery in gale-force onshore conditions and with a heavy surf.

THE DINAH MIGHT TRAGEDY

At about 8.50 p.m. on the 17th September Hon. Secretary B.T. Swales heard a single maroon explode, summoning the Rocket Brigade. (Coastguard Marine Rescue, officially). He telephoned their office to learn that a man was missing from an inflatable dinghy belonging to the yacht DINAH MIGHT. A quick decision was made to launch the Lifeboat as a back-up and James Kinnin, on his first service as Acting Coxswain, had the *James Ball Ritchie* in the water by 9.14 p.m. There was a rough sea on the beach with a NE wind, force 4 - 5, and it was almost low water. The Coastguards stationed their Mobile Patrol Unit at the end of the Queen's Pier and kept constant vhf radio contact with the Lifeboat and fired parachute flares to assist in the search. The casualty was found at 9.20 p.m. It was later understood that three people from the yacht had intended to land at the Pier from the dinghy but had suffered a puncture from the barnacle-encrusted steelwork. Deflation had taken place and all the occupants took to the water. One managed to scale the Pier and raise the alarm but another was caught by the tide. He was found by the Lifeboat off the Beach Hotel and Lifeboatman Charles Gaines went over the side of the *James Ball Ritchie* to assist in getting him into the Lifeboat, which proved a very difficult task. All speed was then made for the beach where a doctor and ambulance awaited their return. The doctor, however, had to pronounce that no life had been saved on this occasion. At the inquest which was attended by Acting Coxswain J. Kinnin, it was stated that the cause of death was a heart attack.

The Ramsey registered motor fishing vessel ROYSTAN VENTURE called for help at 6.20 p.m. on the 9th November. She was some six miles East of the Station and immobilized with a net around her propeller. Thirteen minutes later the *James Ball Ritchie* was away to assist and towed her back to port. The service took three hours in total. Conditions were rough with the wind in the SW, force 6.

At a Branch Committee Meeting on the 19th May, 1977, tribute was paid to the late Chairman, Sir Henry Sugden, who had died a little earlier in the year. He had returned to the Island upon his retirement from a distinguished Army career and became Vice-Chairman in 1965. He was elected Chairman in 1971. President Major K.G. Groves assumed the chair and proposed that Mr. W.J. Corlett be elected Chairman and this was carried. Mr. P.J. May was elected Vice-Chairman. At this meeting Dr. E.C.B. Corlett and Capt. R.C. Watkin were welcomed on to the Committee.

Mention was made by the Hon. Secretary that the Institution had informed him that it was their intention to fit the *James Ball Ritchie* with radar during her next special survey. He also stated that Mrs. C. Gaines, wife of the Crew Member, had voluntarily taken over the duties of providing refreshments for the Crew after services. It was agreed to present her with a small gift on Lifeboat Day in recognition of her initiative and support to the Branch.

The A.G.M. for 1977 was held a few days into the New Year. The deaths of Mr. J.K. Green and Mr. E. Corlett were noted. Members were informed that the Institution H.Q. had advised that they wished to present Mr. B.T. Swales, Hon. Secretary, with a pair of inscribed binoculars in recognition of his individual services to the RNLI. In turn, Mr. Swales read out his annual report which covered the very numerous services. He especially commended Crewman Charles Gaines for his efforts to save a visiting yachtsman from the water; commented upon the skill and seamanship of Coxswain Lawrence Gawne, the appointments of James Kinnin as 2nd Cox, Ronnie Crowe as Asst. Mechanic and the retirements of Fred Kinnin and Arthur Garrett. Jimmy Kneale, Motor Mechanic, was thanked for his continued and devoted service to the Station.

1978

1978 was not so hectic a year for the Lifeboatmen and the *James Ball Ritchie.* She was launched for three services and some of the Crew undertook a further one in a Reserve Lifeboat. Ten exercises were carried out.

On the 23rd January the Reserve Lifeboat O.N. 890 *Thomas Forehead and Mary Rowse* was in Ramsey whilst on a passage through the Irish Sea to Scotland. Staff Coxswain Tom Beattie was in charge. The diving tender DUTCH, which was a converted ship's lifeboat, suffered a fouled propeller some 14 miles East of Maughold Head. The weather was deteriorating and it was overcast with rain in a SW wind, force 6, with accompanying rough sea. The Shaw Savill vessel CAIRN LEADER initially took the DUTCH in tow but when the line parted the tow was taken up by H.M.S. SOBERTON which was on fishery protection duties in the area. She brought the casualty to calmer waters in Ramsey Bay but was unable to berth her. The Ramsey Coxswain, Mechanic and five other Crew

W. S. Basnett — J. Kneale collection

Service by the Barnett Class RNLB O.N. 890 *Thomas Forehead & Mary Rowse* to the diving tender DUTCH, 23rd January ,1978.

W. S. Basnett — J. Kneale collection

Riding the swell entering Ramsey Harbour, 23rd January, 1978, RNLB *Thomas Forehead & Mary Rowse* and the tender DUTCH.

Members boarded the Reserve Lifeboat and together with her own crew, put to sea at 10.24 a.m. to bring the tender in. The DUTCH, with her crew of three, was berthed in an hour. This service provided an unusual but good opportunity for the Crew to experience work in a RNLI "Barnett" Class of lifeboat.

The passenger ferry ULSTER PRINCE, whilst on passage from Belfast to Liverpool on the 25th March, contacted the Coastguards at 10.25 p.m. She had a sick passenger aboard who required landing for medical attention. The *James Ball Ritchie* was away at 11.45 p.m. after a rendezvous position in Ramsey Bay had been agreed. Doctor Cowley accompanied the Crew and supervised the lowering of the patient into the Lifeboat by Neil Robertson stretcher. The weather was fine but there was a choppy sea in the W'ly force 6 wind and the Lifeboat sustained slight damage to some stanchions from the rubbing strake of the ferry. The patient was landed at 1.00 a.m., 26th.

The 2nd August was Lifeboat Day and the *James Ball Ritchie* had been out in the Bay taking passengers for trips. At 3.08 p.m. she had returned to the beach prior to rehousing when a request was received from the Coastguards to assist a sick man on Dhoon Beach, four miles to the South. An ambulance had failed to get near him. The Lifeboat was relaunched at 3.15 p.m. and reached the Dhoon 40 minutes later. Second Coxswain Jim Kinnin and Crewman Kevin Crowe launched the small inflatable dinghy carried by the *James Ball Ritchie* and went ashore to pick up the sick man and get him to the Lifeboat. The patient was put ashore in Ramsey for hospitalisation at 4.50 p.m.

At 11.30 a.m. on the 13th September Mechanic Jimmy Kneale took charge of the Lifeboat in the absence of the Coxswains. He had received a call from the Coastguards asking for a capsized canoeist to be picked up quickly near the harbour entrance. Just as the Lifeboat was at the water's edge, word was received that the mfv BOY JAMES, who had heard the radio exchanges about the incident, had left the harbour and picked up the young man. He was landed for hospital treatment but discharged by nightfall. This was to be the last call-out of the year.

Only one full Committee Meeting was held in 1978 and this was on the 4th October. Apart from the normal business, plans began to evolve for the 1979 celebrations for the 150th anniversary of the Ramsey Station. It was noted that as the whole Island was to celebrate its Millennium the same year, care would have to be taken so that events did not clash.

Another Committee Meeting dealing with 1978 was held on the 31st January, 1979. In addition to the normal attendance, the new RNLI NW District Inspector, Lt. Cdr. G. Cooper, and District Organising Secretary, Mr. D.M. Jones, were also present. Members were advised that the Honorary Medical Adviser, Dr. Paton, had resigned and Dr. J.K. Brownsdon was elected in his stead.

In connection with the celebrations it was made known that the RNLI were to make a presentation to the Branch of a Vellum commemorating the 150th year. It was agreed that the forthcoming Service of Re-dedication would be a suitable time to accept the Vellum. A discussion on arrangements and the guest list followed. The District Inspector also announced that the Duke of Atholl would be in attendance on Lifeboat Day, 1979.

The A.G.M. for 1978 was not held until the 25th May, 1979. Tributes were paid to the Branch's President, Major K.G. Groves, and Committee Members Mr. C.C. Craine, Mr. R.C. Teare and Mr. C. Kinrade, all of whom had died in recent months. It was reported that Mr. Roy Corkill had been appointed Assistant Tractor Driver, replacing Ernest Collister who had reached retirement age. Capt. Hugh Kinley and District Officer Tom Richardson had to leave the Committee owing to transfers from Ramsey and Vice-Chairman P.J. May also had to resign as he was leaving for the UK. Mrs. A.A. Ritchie was elected President of the Branch after the death of Major K.G. Groves. The haul-off warp had been withdrawn on the authority of Headquarters. This would help to reduce the running costs on the Station. Capt. Watkin suggested that the Manx Sailing and Cruising Club be invited to elect a member to the Lifeboat Committee and also that a letter of congratulations be sent to the Humber Station Committee on the unique award to their Coxswain of the Gold, Silver and Bronze Medals for gallantry in the preceding year.

1979

Four services were carried out during 1979 by the *James Ball Ritchie* and in addition one call-out for a fruitless search. Two more services were undertaken by the Reserve Lifeboat *Vincent Nesfield*. Ten other launches covered the standard exercises and special occasions.

Just before midnight on the 27/28th June a drama concerning yachtsmen unfolded in Ramsey Bay. The Returns of Service Book records the events of that night. At 11.50 p.m. 27th June, 1979, H.M. Coastguard telephoned the Hon. Secretary advising that a dinghy was missing with two persons on board. Apparently the yacht SEEKABOUT was anchored in Ramsey Bay and at a later time the yacht SIBELIUS with two people on board anchored nearby sometime during the 27th. A young man and his companion from the SIBELIUS went aboard the SEEKABOUT for dinner. The wind was fresh – strong at times– a local effect in Ramsey Bay. It was observed that the SIBELIUS had drifted away from her close proximity to the SEEKABOUT, ESE of the Ramsey Lifeboat Station. The Skipper of the SIBELIUS, together with a crew member of the SEEKABOUT, launched their dinghy to look for the SIBELIUS. The engine of the dinghy failed and the Skipper decided to swim back to the SEEKABOUT. Neither men had lifejackets and it was dark. In the meantime those aboard the SEEKABOUT heard the dinghy engine stop and decided to start and move towards the dinghy. In the darkness contact was lost. The SEEKABOUT radioed H.M. Coastguards for assistance and they asked Hon. Sec. to launch. The *James Ball Ritchie* was waterborne at 00.20, 28th, and commenced to search an area Eastwards of the Station. The SEEKABOUT joined in the search. 2nd Coxswain J. Kinnin, who had returned to town and heard that the Lifeboat had been launched, went out immediately in his own power boat to search the area. The Coastguards had personnel searching the beach and piers. On launching, the *James Ball Ritchie* fired a parachute flare and from its light the SEEKABOUT soon picked up the dinghy with one man aboard. Eventually the SIBELIUS was also located and the Lifeboat Crew searched her in case there were any survivors aboard. The SEEKABOUT took the SIBELIUS in tow and berthed safely in Ramsey harbour. In the meantime the Lifeboat continued the search using flares and searchlight, but to no avail. The search was continued until dawn and was eventually called off. The *James Ball Ritchie* returned to her Station at 05.36 a.m., 28th. The Skipper's young companion was very distressed and the whole sad affair high-lighted so many errors of judgement. First of all, two men entered a dinghy in darkness without lights to search for a small unlit yacht – neither was equipped with a lifejacket. Then the Skipper of the SIBELIUS left the safety of the inflatable dinghy and attempted to swim, after shedding all his clothing. He would have been perfectly safe had he remained in the dinghy.

At 1.38 a.m. on the 29th July the *James Ball Ritchie* was launched to proceed to Rue Point, some 3 miles SW from the Point of Ayre, where the Belfast fishing vessel FISHER LAD was reported aground. In fact the vessel had refloated herself by the time the Lifeboat reached her and so was escorted back to Ramsey Harbour.

On the 1st September the Coastguards had a yacht in the Bay under observation. The seas were rough from a SSW wind, force 7, and the yacht had a split mainsail. She was under power from an auxiliary engine. Coxswain Gawne and Mechanic Kneale were asked to stand-by and soon the yacht asked for help. The *James Ball Ritchie* was launched at 6.28 p.m. and took the TRZYGROSZE in tow and berthed her in the harbour at 6.52 p.m.

A LONG SEARCH

A futile all-night search took place on the 10th September. At 11.40 p.m., 9th, the Coastguards informed D.L.A. Capt. Carine that red flares had been reported some 12 miles North of the Point of Ayre. The Lifeboat was away at 11.55 p.m. and it took two hours to reach the search area. The weather was fine with a moderate sea in the NW'ly wind, force 4. Nearly three and a half hours were spent searching but nothing untoward was found. The *James Ball Ritchie* was back on station at 5.17 a.m. (10th). Only then was it found that her port fuel tank was leaking. RNLI Headquarters at Poole were informed and the Lifeboat taken out of service. A replacement tank arrived on the 12th, however, was fitted immediately and the Lifeboat was back on service again at 8.00 p.m. that day.

The last service of the year, and also one of the fastest launches for the *James Ball Ritchie*, took place at 3.53 p.m. on the 28th October. The Lighthouse Keeper at the Point of Ayre informed the Coastguards that three men in a launch off the Whitestone Bank Buoy were waving to attract attention. The Coastguards contacted the ro-ro ferry MELBOURNE UNION which confirmed the position of the launch but was unable to help owing to shoal waters. The maroons were fired at 3.47 p.m. for the Lifeboat Crew and the *James Ball Ritchie* took to the water six minutes later at 3.53 p.m. The casualty turned out to be the Peel motor launch THACKERY with a crew of three. They had suffered engine failure and so were towed back to Ramsey.

Early in November, 1979, the *James Ball Ritchie* left for Beaumaris and her second special survey. She was replaced, as usual, by the Reserve Boat O.N. 994 *Vincent Nesfield*. The first service for this Lifeboat came very soon on the 4th November at 12.45 p.m. when she was launched with Doctor J. Brownsdon on board. A request for medical assistance had been received from the large stern trawler IDENA. She was, at the time, some 12 miles NW from the Point of Ayre where the state of the sea was very rough in a SW force 6 wind. It was agreed to rendezvous in Ramsey Bay where the Doctor could board her safely. Upon doing so he was called to examine the ship's Skipper and had to pronounce life extinct. He had died in his bunk. The trawler proceeded to her home port of Fleetwood and the Lifeboat returned to Ramsey.

Another medical call-out came on the 11th November when the small mfv BOY ANTHONY requested medical assistance. At first Doctor Brownsdon spoke to the Skipper on the vhf radio but it was then decided to launch the *Vincent Nesfield* in order that he could examine the patient. The Lifeboat was away at 11.10 a.m. and reached the vessel at 12.25 p.m. It was advised that the fishing vessel should bring the patient into Ramsey herself, which she did, and the seaman was taken to hospital and detained. The Lifeboat returned at 2.00 p.m.

1979 was somewhat of a watershed for the Ramsey Station. The 150th anniversary ceremonies were held in the form of a Church Service at the Norbury Boathouse on Sunday, the 17th June. The Bishop of Sodor and Mann, the Rt. Rev. V. Nicholls, conducted the service assisted by the Vicar of the Parish, the Rev. J.F. Foster, and the Rev. Father F. Wood. His Excellency the Lt. Governor, Sir John Paul, presented the Vellum on behalf of the RNLI and Hon. Secretary B.T. Swales accepted. Also present were Vice-Admiral Sir Arthur Hezlet, an RNLI Vice-President and member of the Committee of Management, and Lt. Cdr. G.R. Cooper, NW Divisional Inspector. All the Crew and Committee attended together with many dignitaries from around the Island and Ramsey in particular. All Crew Members and shoreside personnel were given suitably inscribed tankards to mark the occasion.

Later, on Lifeboat Day, the 20th July, the Duke of Atholl, Chairman of the RNLI Committee of Management, made the Annual Appeal and the Ladies' Guild collected a record of £882 on the day. During the whole year their fund-raising produced £2800 for the Branch - yet another record!

In his annual report later in the year the Hon. Secretary laid out some RNLI facts and figures for 1979 covering the whole of the UK. Offshore lifeboats were launched over 1000 times and saved 368 lives. In-shore lifeboats were out on 1400 occasions and saved 575 lives. Annual expenditure for the RNLI as a whole had reached £6 million plus capital expenditure of £2 million. In 1972 these figures had been £2 million and £750,000 respectively.

The Gawnes

The Isle of Man Press reported on the above proceedings and the "Examiner", in June, 1979, carried a more personal article on the Gawne family:

> "It is appropriate this week when we are about to celebrate the 150th anniversary of the establishment of the Ramsey Lifeboat Station to call attention to the remarkable record of the Gawne family whose service spans the best part of a century.
>
> The present Coxswain is Lawrence Gawne and his great-grandfather, William Isaac (known as "Kenna" Gawne), joined the Ramsey Lifeboat in the early 1890s. He died at the age of 51.
>
> Lawrence's grandfather, also William Isaac and known as Willie Gawne, is 88 years of age and he resides with his daughter and son-in-law, Mr. and Mrs. Jim Knight, in Ballure Glen.
>
> Willie was in the Ramsey Lifeboat Crew with the late Jack Lord, Coxswain. They were awarded special medals in 1937 by the Finnish Government for going to the aid of the Finnish steamer Esbo of Helsingfors off the Cumberland Coast in what were described as the worst gales known for 40 years.
>
> Willie's son Issac followed in the family tradition and served in the Boat as member of the Crew during the time Bill Cottier was Coxswain.
>
> And in more recent years Issac's son Lawrence joined the Crew and was made Coxswain of the *James Ball Ritchie* last year, a very popular appointment.
>
> Several families in Ramsey can claim long family tradition in connection with the Lifeboat, an outstanding instance being the Kinnin family. There was a William Kinnin in the Crew of 1868 and today Jimmy Kinnin is 2nd Coxswain."
>
> Another Press article covered the sale of new Isle of Man postage stamps:
>
> "The Coxswain of the Ramsey Lifeboat, Lawrence Gawne, completed on Friday morning his signing of the first 2000 first day covers. As the 150th anniversary of the Ramsey Lifeboat coincides with the Millennium of Tynwald, the cover bears four Millennium stamps to the design of Manx artist John Nicholson.
>
> In addition, it was announced at the weekend, that a further special issue of 1000 similar covers is being made, except that they bear one lifeboat stamp with the cancelled hand stamp. These stamps are now out of circulation. The covers will be similarly signed by the Coxswain and will contain the same inset as in the Millennium envelope. These will all be sold at £1.00 each and it is expected there will be a brisk demand."

1980

The *Vincent Nesfield* carried on the lifeboat work into the spring of 1980 and undertook three services. The *James Ball Ritchie* then returned to her duties and completed 11 more services. Two vessels and two lives were saved in 1980.

A long search started off the year on the 14th February when the *Vincent Nesfield* was launched at 6.31 a.m. in answer to a request from the Coastguards. The 32ft mfv Triton was making a delivery passage from Rhyl, North Wales, to Maryport in Cumbria. She was due to make an overnight stop at Douglas, eta 6.00 p.m. on the 13th, but had failed to do so. Radio contact was made with the vessel by the Ramsey Coastguards but she was unsure of her position although she reported having seen red and white navigational lights on the 14th. These lights were assumed to be the Point of Ayre Lighthouse and so the Lifeboat was directed to make for a position one mile North of the Point. Vhf transmission signal strengths picked up by Coastguard Mobile Units on the Mull of Galloway, Burrow Head and the Cumbrian Coast were compared and the *Vincent Nesfield* was then directed to an area more to the North East. The search was called off when H.M.S. Orkney found the fishing vessel and her crew of three with engine failure. She was towed to Kirkcudbright by the Navy. The Lifeboat

B. P. Grenfell

Looking towards East Quay, Ramsey, 1989, showing the Ramsey Steamship Co's BEN VANE and BEN AIN and Mezeron's COLBY RIVER.

B. P. Grenfell

The *James Ball Ritchie,* Lifeboat Day, 1986.

returned to Ramsey at 2.33 p.m. The weather was very poor throughout this service with heavy rain, sleet and a strong force 7 SE'ly wind.

Another vessel unsure of her position called for assistance on the 10th March. This was the yacht ECLIPSE, bound to Glasson Dock from Troon. The weather was deteriorating with an increasing SE'ly force 7 wind and rough seas. The Lifeboat was launched at 6.00 a.m. with 2nd Cox Jim Kinnin in charge and the ECLIPSE was found quickly and escorted into Ramsey.

At 3.15 a.m. on the 7th May the Coastguards informed the Hon. Secretary that at daybreak a search would be mounted for the small fishing vessel OSPREY in the Solway Firth. The vessel was overdue in her home port of Maryport. Accordingly the *Vincent Nesfield* was waterborne at 4.53 a.m. with Jim Kinnin at the wheel again. The search was made by all area lifeboats, inshore lifeboats, a helicopter and numerous fishing vessels. Sea Conditions were moderate with an ENE wind, force 3-4, good visibility and overcast skies. It was a long and arduous sixteen-hour search to no avail. The vessel was never found and it was 8.20 p.m. before the Lifeboat reached Ramsey again. The Crew list read: Acting Cox J. Kinnin, Acting 2nd Cox K. Crowe, Acting Mechanic R. Crowe, Assistant Mechanic C. Gaines and D. Martin, R. Stanfield and R. Gaines.

The Shore Team comprised: Head Launcher T. McKnight, Shore Attendant B. Faragher, Tractor Driver R. Corkill, Assistant Tractor Driver G.W. Callister and R. Christian, K. Christian, R. Wilkinson, B. Corlett, C. Quirk, D. Kaighen, I. Gawne, E. Collister, W. Callister and M. Pate.

The small motor fishing vessel DAYBREAK was saved from the rocks at 9.00 a.m. on the 10th May. This was the first service for the *James Ball Ritchie* back from her long special survey and complete with her new radar set. The Coastguards alerted the Lifeboat Authorities at 8.05 a.m. and the Lifeboat was launched 12 minutes later with Coxswain Gawne in charge. The DAYBREAK had a rope around her propeller and by the time the Lifeboat reached her she was but 15 yards off the rocks South of Maughold Head. A tow was put in hand immediately and the vessel was brought safely into Ramsey harbour at 10.30 a.m.

Four days later on the 14th May the Skipper of the mfv JACOB JOHANNES of Castletown informed the Coastguards that he might need assistance as his ship had an ingress of water. At 2.00 a.m. the Lifeboat was launched and made a rendezvous with the casualty 35 minutes later. She was escorted back to Ramsey and the Lifeboat stood-by her until 4.15 a.m. when the Skipper advised he had the leak under control.

A seriously ill seaman from the Castletown mfv RADIANCE was assisted by the *James Ball Ritchie* on the 31st May. This vessel asked for medical help at 4.32 a.m. from a position East of the Bahama Bank. The *James Ball Ritchie* was away at 4.52 a.m. and escorted the RADIANCE back to Ramsey Bay where the patient could be safely transferred. The Lifeboat then berthed where an ambulance was waiting to take the seaman to hospital. He was detained.

On the 20th July at 3.38 p.m. the *James Ball Ritchie* had just been recovered after being out on a radar exercise. The Coastguards warned that two yachts were in trouble to the West of the Island. The Lifeboat was back in the water at 3.45 p.m. It transpired that the yachts WINDSTRIKE and ANGUILLA had been returning in company to Northern Ireland after a holiday visit to the Isle of Man. The wind was Northerly and moderate. The forestay of the WINDSTRIKE carried away and then her mast fractured. She was taken in tow by the ANGUILLA which soon suffered a split mainsail. The tow was cast off. The ANGUILLA further suffered an engine fault and had to make for land under the jib. The Port Erin lifeboat was alerted and launched and she found and assisted the drifting WINDSTRIKE. The *James Ball Ritchie* was not required and was rehoused at 5.30 p.m.

The small mfv EVENING TIDE, whilst on a passage from Preston to Ullapool via Ramsey, suffered a sheared propeller shaft just before midnight, 24/25th July. She was some four miles West of the Point of Ayre. The Lifeboat Authorities were advised of the fact by the Coastguards but at first did not respond. The coaster SOLWAY FISHER went to give assistance but in doing so struck the casualty damaging her bow, mast and steering gear. The *James Ball Ritchie* was launched at 11.58 p.m. on learning of the damage and reached the EVENING TIDE at 1.17 a.m. and relieved the SOLWAY FISHER which had been standing-by. A tow was made up and the fishing vessel brought to Ramsey by the Lifeboat. Once the tide was right, the ship was berthed at 6.10 a.m. Coxswain Gawne reported that the casualty was observed on the radar screen at a distance of two miles.

At 11.30 p.m. on the 29th July the Coastguards advised that the commercial fishing vessel SAPPHIRE with a crew of three, was anchored about one mile North of Laxey Head with her propeller fouled by nets. Coxswain Gawne and Mechanic Kneale were alerted and proceeded to the Coastguard Station where they learned that, in fact, the SAPPHIRE was anchored only two cables from rocks in Bulgham Bay. The full Lifeboat Crew was immediately called and the *James Ball Ritchie* was away by 00.10 a.m., 30th, reaching the endangered craft an hour later. The sky was overcast and there was light rain in the SE'ly wind, force 5 - 6. The seas were rough. A tow was undertaken immediately and both

Fotoflite

Sea Breezes collection

The Norwegian liner VISTAFJORD. On the 9th December, 1980, in Ramsey Bay, she was the subject of a service by the *James Ball Ritchie* to land the Managing Director of British Leyland.

vessels returned to Ramsey safely at 2.20 a.m. Later the owner of SAPPHIRE recorded his appreciation and made a donation to the RNLI.

Yet another midnight call-out took place on the 17/18th August. The Coastguards had received a "MAYDAY" call from the yacht PANDORA stating that she was sinking fast some 10 miles West of the Point of Ayre. The *James Ball Ritchie* was in the water at five minutes past midnight and reached the search area two hours later. A full search was being co-ordinated and H.M.S. STUBBINGTON, mv ULSTER QUEEN, mfv FLEETWOOD LADY, container vessel LUNE BRIDGE and a helicopter from R.A.F. Valley, Anglesey, all took part with the Lifeboat. Nothing was found and the search was aborted at 7.20 a.m. Later there were strong indications that the call had been a hoax.

VISTAFJORD SERVICE

During September of 1980, British Leyland were launching, in the Isle of Man, their new "Metro" small car to the Automobile World and the Press. They had chartered the Norwegian liner VISTAFJORD for their guests. The weather was bad on the 12th of the month and the large ship was anchored in Ramsey Bay, sheltering from a SWxS force 8 gale. At 8.20 a.m. that day the Coastguards informed the Hon. Secretary that they had learned that Mr. Ray Horrock, Managing Director of British Leyland, who was aboard VISTAFJORD , was very urgently required to attend a Board Meeting of his Company in London. Weatherwise it was impossible to launch a ship's lifeboat, nor was it possible to send out a launch from the harbour. It was agreed to let the *James Ball Ritchie* undertake the task. It was very difficult to get the Lifeboat alongside the ship in the conditions but once achieved Mr. Horrock was "plucked" off her with great speed and landed ashore for a flight to the capital. No injury or damage was sustained in this service. A donation was made to the RNLI for this assistance. This incident did, in fact, give the Lifeboat Crew a chance of experiencing the problems of getting alongside a high sided ship in adverse conditions. It was rare for such a chance to arise. The Crew included Coxswain L. Gawne, 2nd Cox J. Kinnin, Mechanic J. Kneale, Assistant Mechanic R. Crowe, R. Stanfield and D. Martin.

A valuable service was rendered during the dark early hours of 23rd September. At 3.00 a.m. the Ayr fishing vessel FREEDOM reported that she was aground three miles North of the Lifeboat Station. The *James Ball Ritchie* was away within 20 minutes but on reaching the stranded ship found that she was more or less high and dry with the tide still ebbing. The Lifeboat stood-by and then on the flood accepted a tow-rope from the fishing vessel and pulled her off the beach. By this time the wind had freshened considerably and was up to force 6 from the SE and there was a rough sea on this very exposed coast. Fortunately the FREEDOM got under-way with her own power and the Lifeboat escorted her to Ramsey harbour and was rehoused at 9.55 a.m. The vessel's owner expressed his appreciation for a very good service.

Yet another five-and-a-half hour night-time service ended in a fruitless search. This took place at 9.25 p.m. on the 8th November and was the last call-out of the year. The launch was in answer to the sighting of a red flare out to the East of the Station. The area was searched from 10.20 p.m. until nearly 2 a.m., 9th, with seven parachute flares being fired to illuminate the darkness. The weather was grim with overcast skies, rain and a rough sea in the NE'ly wind force 6 - 7. Nothing was found and the Lifeboat was rehoused later that morning at 3.40 a.m.

A Committee Meeting was held on the 21st May and arrangements were put in hand for Lifeboat Day and the Annual Appeal which was set for Saturday, 26th July.

On the 26th September a further meeting was held and discussions took place to organise a prominent Speaker for the 1981 Lifeboat Day. His Excellency the Lt. Governor, Rear Admiral Sir Nigel Cecil, had been invited but it was thought that he might be off the Island at the time. An approach to Rear-Admiral W.J. Graham, Director General of the RNLI (and former Captain of H.M.S. "ARK ROYAL") was therefore put forward and accepted by him at a later date.

The A.G.M. for 1980 was held on the 20th February, 1981. Mr. Swales, Hon. Secretary, drew attention to the large number of services for the year and calculated that the Crew had spent over 64 hours at sea in the 12 months. He gave an example of what involvement meant for the Crew and of their constant reliability; in a recent service which took five-and-a-half hours the Boat returned to the beach at 2.50 a.m., was rehoused, washed down, refuelled and ready for service again at 3.40 a.m.

1981

1981 saw the Lifeboat out on seven services and a similar number of exercises were held. Four lives and two craft were saved.

The first was on the 3rd March in the search for a small fishing vessel with one man aboard which was overdue at Workington. The Liverpool Coastguards organised a search and it was agreed to launch the *James Ball Ritchie* at 6.15 a.m. to cover the Ramsey Bay area. This was done with very rough sea conditions on the beach. There was an ENE'ly wind, force 7, with overcast skies. The launch went well, however, and the Boat behaved well. A helicopter found the casualty at 7.10 a.m. and the Lifeboat returned to station at 8.12 a.m.

At 3.54 a.m. on the 27th May the Coastguards telephoned the Hon. Secretary to inform him that the Douglas based tug SALISBURY had reported a "man overboard". She was on passage from Glasson Dock to Ramsey and was towing a barge. The missing crewman was, in fact, the Skipper. The Lifeboat was in the water by 4.17 a.m. and reached the search area two hours later. No-one was found by 10.05 a.m. and the search was called off. The *James Ball Ritchie* then commenced the two hour run back to her Station.

A surf-boarder with problems caused the next call-out for the Crew. On the 5th June at 3.30 p.m. the Coastguards were alerted to the fact that a man on a surf board was unsuccessfully attempting to paddle back to the shore against an offshore breeze. The Coastguards were unable to raise by radio any boats in the harbour or two yachts out in the Bay. The Lifeboat was launched at 3.44 p.m. and got the local man ashore within 14 minutes. He was taken home by the Coastguards in an exhausted state.

Eight days later the *James Ball Ritchie* was afloat again to assist pleasure craft. At 4.20 a.m. on the 13th June red flares were seen by the Coastguard Officers on duty, to the East of the Station. The Lifeboat was launched at 4.39 a.m. and found the auxiliary "Atlantic 28" type craft SHAULA unable to make any headway in a force 8 Southerly gale. When Coxswain Gawne got the Lifeboat within hailing distance of the yacht he learned that she also had a fouled propeller. A tow was organised and both boats made for sheltered waters and to await the tide at Ramsey. The SHAULA was berthed at 6.00 a.m. but as there were two other yachts sheltering in the Bay, it was decided to keep the *James Ball Ritchie* afloat for a little time longer. She was later rehoused at 8.15 a.m.

A few days after this incident the Hon. Secretary received a letter of thanks from the owner of the yacht SHAULA which showed a considerable depth of appreciation for the RNLI and its crews.

> "Dear Sir, Re Rescue incident Ramsey Bay a.m. Sat. 13th inst.
>
> Writing on behalf of all hands I take pleasure in conveying our heartfelt appreciation towards the Ramsey Lifeboat Station and in particular the Coxswain and Crewmen who so unselfishly came to our assistance and escorted us to the safety of the shore Saturday last.
>
> The unpredictable ways of the seas have, and always will, continue to confound and surprise those who accept its challenge . . . and so it was, that we three and cautious boatmen who having in respect of many unfavourable weather forecasts delayed our outwards passage from Merseyside for 12 tides – finally sailed reliant upon "expert" weather advice for Ramsey Bay – only to be "caught out" at the very entrance of the harbour and safety.
>
> In this modern life in which people compete daily against each other with often hardly a thought for his neighbour's feelings or needs, our experiences

D. Reed

The University of North Wales (Bangor) research vessel PRINCE MADOG at Booth Kelly's Shipyard, Ramsey, in the 1980s. In 1968 she was the last ship to be built at the yard.

in the safe and surely dedicated hands of the brave men of Ramsey will remain in our minds for all time.

Long live the RNLI. We hold that surely the example set by its unsparing duty towards its fellow beings should be a living lesson to us all. Yours again in deep appreciation....and etc."

The powered pleasure craft MAKAIRA, registered in Maryport, suffered engine failure at 12.53 p.m. on the 31st August. She reported this to the Coastguards and gave her position off the Bahama Bank Buoy. The Lifeboat Crew was alerted and the *James Ball Ritchie* was launched at 1.07 p.m. with Mechanic Jim Kneale as Acting Coxswain. The Casualty was not reached for some two hours, however, as her actual position was off the King William Bank Buoy. The boat was towed to the Queen's Pier until there was sufficient water in the harbour to berth. The Lifeboat was not rehoused until 6.15 p.m. Peel lifeboat Crewman J. Connelly joined the Ramsey men for this service.

At 8.09 p.m. on the 18th September the *James Ball Ritchie* was at sea again in answer to a request for help from the fishing vessel ARCTIC SWAN. Apparently she was subject to leaks and as the main engine had stopped and could not be restarted, her pumps were also out of action. The Lifeboat reached her in a position some three miles East from Maughold Head and towed her to Ramsey. It was 1.25 a.m. on the 19th before the Lifeboat was rehoused.

On the 3rd November at about 5.40 a.m. the Ramsey Steamship Company cargo vessel BEN AIN anchored in Ramsey Bay with machinery trouble. During the day the weather freshened to a full SW'ly gale, force 9. At 8.33 p.m. the Lifeboat Crew was called out to launch as the BEN AIN was seen to drag her anchor. The mfv EASTER MORN also left the harbour on the ebb tide to assist if required. Subsequently the tug SALISBURY arrived from Douglas to effect the tow into port and this was achieved as the weather moderated at 2.00 a.m. (4th). The *James Ball Ritchie* remained on hand in the Bay until the vessel berthed. Her owners settled the cost of the Lifeboat launch.

The Branch A.G.M. was held on the 18th December in the Norbury Boathouse. Apart from the usual business, reference was made to the past annual Flag Day and of the guests who attended: the Lt. Governor Rear Admiral Sir Nigel Cecil and Lady Cecil; Rear Admiral W.J. Graham, Director and Secretary of the RNLI, and Mrs. Graham; Captain J.B. Leworthy, a member of the Committee of Management, and Mrs. Leworthy.

The Crew List for 1981 contained the following names: Coxswain L. Gawne, 2nd Cox J. Kinnin, Mechanic J. Kneale, Asst. Mechanic R. Crowe, Emergency Mechanic G. Evison and Crewmen K. Crowe, T. Clarke, W. Gaines, R. Stanfield, R. Gaines, C. Callister, D. Kaighen Jr., D. Martin, K. Christian, C. Clarke. Shore staff: Head Launcher T. McKnight, Tractor Driver G. Callister, Tractor Driver Helper R. Corkill and Lightman C. Faragher.

The last meeting of the year was held four days later on the 22nd December. Much attention was given to organising events to raise money for the official RNLI Penlee Disaster Fund in the wake of the loss of that lifeboat and all her Crew off the Cornish Coast. The Rev. Cox of St. Paul's offered the proceeds of a church collection and the Ladies' Guild initially proposed a coffee morning with added attractions. It was also agreed to liaise with other branches on the Island to co-ordinate fund-raising for this special appeal.

During the year a dinghy donated by Mrs. D. Dobbs was sold for £350 in aid of Branch funds. This had been overhauled and put in good order by the Crew and Shore Helpers.

1982

During 1982 the *James Ball Ritchie* was launched for five services and 11 exercises were carried out.

The first of these was in the late afternoon of the 5th January. The local mfv ASHLEIGH M had been under observation by the Coastguards all afternoon. She was hove-to in the Bay and awaiting the tide to berth. There was a full force 8 NE'ly gale with rough seas at the time and the Skipper was in constant radio contact with his observers. At 4.15 p.m. it was decided to launch the Lifeboat to assist the fishing vessel and the *James Ball Ritchie* was alongside her by 4.30 p.m. At first storm oil was spread around the vessel to stop the waves breaking but had little effect in the conditions. Then the Lifeboat demonstrated the best approach in which to enter harbour and, after returning to the ship and offering moral support, escorted her into a safe berth. The Lifeboat had to remain in harbour herself overnight and was "off station" for four hours during the low water period.

At 6.18 a.m. on the 28th March the Coastguards informed the Lifeboat Authorities that the mfv CADNO was disabled some 15 miles East of Ramsey with a fouled propeller. The *James Ball Ritchie* was away at 6.50 a.m. and it took just under two hours to cover the distance to the casualty. The weather was calm but foggy. A tow was undertaken and the CADNO safely berthed at 11.00 a.m. She had a crew of three and was registered in Inverness.

Yet another tow took place during the next service on the 4th July. The Lifeboat was already on the slipway undergoing radar trials when word was received that a small yacht, some two miles NE of the Station, was firing red flares. The *James Ball Ritchie* was waterborne at 11.00 a.m. She found the Ramsey based JOHN DOD, with four people aboard, suffering from rudder problems. It did not take long to tow her back and she was berthed at 11.55 a.m.

The 7th July was a bright summer's day with a fresh NW'ly breeze. During the afternoon the Coastguards noticed a person in a wet-suit lying aboard a sail surf-board with the sail folded away. It appeared that he was attempting to paddle in towards the Queen's Pier, but making only limited progress in the offshore wind. Concern grew and, as there were no other boats or yachts in the vicinity, the Lifeboat Secretary and Crew were alerted. The *James Ball Ritchie* was launched at 3.07 p.m. with Mechanic Jim Kneale as Acting Coxswain. On reaching the surf-board he found the intrepid sailor to be an elderly lady who assured him that in no way was she in any danger or in the need of a lifeboat. Jim, equally adamant, assured her that he had launched to come and rescue her and rescue her he would! She was landed safely in the harbour. Subsequently the Hon. Secretary was informed by the lady that at no time did she feel in any danger and that she had had two lines of sight and was certainly not drifting out to sea! As the story of this "rescue" began to circulate it came to light that this was not the first time that this surf-boarder had caught the attention of the RNLI. Other times had been off the South of the Island, so possibly she thought that her name wouldn't be known in "the far North"!

The year was rounded off with a medical service on the 23rd November. The large bulk carrier SPERANZA from Panama was anchored in Ramsey Bay awaiting orders. At 2.48 a.m. the ship informed the Coastguards that they had a sick seaman who required assistance. The *James Ball Ritchie* was launched at 3.15 a.m. with Doctor Brownsdon aboard. The weather was poor out in the Bay with very heavy rain and a SW wind, force 4 - 5. The Doctor decided to get the patient ashore and he was landed for hospital observation.

THE 1982 A.G.M.

The A.G.M. for 1982 was held on the 14th January, 1983. Reference was made to the £503 raised earlier in 1982 for the Penlee Disaster Fund and the subsequent £956 raised at a later date which was forwarded to the RNLI Fund for Pensions and Widows. According to Press reports £5000 was raised Island-wide following the Disaster Appeal. During the year Mr. W.J. Corlett resigned as Branch Chairman and Mr. S.C. Callister took his place. Mr. G.W. Callister, Tractor Driver, also resigned after many years of

D. Reed

In heavy weather gear c1982.
L. to R: Asst. Tractor Driver P. Kennish, T. McKnight, Mechanic J. Kneale, Asst. Mechanic R. Crowe, 2nd Coxswain J. Kinnin, D. Martin, Coxswain L. Gawne, K. Christian, K. Crowe, R. Stanfield, C. Gaines.

loyal service. Lifeboat Mechanic Jim Kneale was presented with the Institution's Long Service Award by Mrs. A. Ritchie on Lifeboat Day.

The Branch Committee at the time of this A.G.M. included: President Mrs. A.A. Ritchie, Vice-President Mr. W.J. Corlett, Chairman Mr. S.C. Callister, Vice-Chairman Mr. G.C. Swales, Hon. Secretary Mr. B.T. Swales, Hon. Treasurer Mr. T.E. Tregellis, Hon. Administrative Officer Sqn. Ldr. J. Sands, Hon. Auditor Mr. R.C. Gell, Hon. Medical Adviser Dr. J.K. Brownsdon and Hon. Optician Mr. R.B. Corlett. The General Committee had an additional 24 men and three lady Members.

The Ladies' Guild Officers were: President Mrs. A.A. Ritchie, Vice-President Mrs. V.S. Nicholls, Chairman Mrs. B.M. Green, Hon. Secretary Mrs. E. Corlett and Hon. Treasurer Mrs. J. Sands. There were 53 further Members in the Committee.

1983

The *James Ball Ritchie* was launched for eight services in 1983 and accredited with saving five lives and one dinghy.

At 4.15 a.m. on the 4th May the Lifeboat, under Coxswain Gawne, was launched to take the Doctor to the Coe Metcalfe cargo ship FIRETHORN. She was on passage from Northern Ireland to the River Mersey and reported an injured man aboard. A rendezvous was arranged in Ramsey Bay and the seaman was taken off for hospital treatment. The weather was good and the Lifeboat was rehoused at 5.40 a.m.

It was just over a month later on the 7th June when the powered pleasure craft SARAHEY of Glasson Dock, with a crew of three on board, suffered engine failure 11 miles SE of Maughold Head. The Coastguards were unable to raise any other vessels in the vicinity by radio and so the *James Ball Ritchie* was launched at 10.40 a.m. The weather was fine with a light SE'ly wind. A fixed wing aircraft on fishery patrol joined in the service and spotted the casualty. It flew over the SARAHEY until the Lifeboat reached her at 11.55 a.m. A tow to Ramsey was undertaken. The owner made a "Thank You" contribution to RNLI funds.

One of the speediest launches on record took place on the 2nd August. At 7.23 p.m. the Coastguards informed the Hon. Secretary by telephone that a dinghy had capsized just East of the Queen's Pier and that its crew of two was in the water. The maroons were fired one minute later and the *James Ball Ritchie* was herself in the water at 7.28 p.m. The men were rescued and the dinghy towed back to the beach. The whole operation was completed within 30 minutes in fair weather with a SSW'ly wind, force 3. One survivor was detained in hospital.

Four days later, on the 6th August, another tow was completed. The powered pleasure craft SUSIE JANE, with six people on board, had engine failure five miles NNE of the Station. The Lifeboat was launched at 3.12 p.m. and the boat brought back to port. The weather was very good.

The next proposed launch had to be aborted on the 8th August. The Lifeboat was about to launch at 11.00 p.m. in answer to cries for help which had been heard in the Bay. One of four securing chains did not release at the correct time during the launch and the Lifeboat had to be moved back on to the carriage. Two bolts had detached from the swing arm on the port chain. However the casualty reached the shore safely in the meantime and no further action was needed.

A prompt service on the 14th August saved the lives of three fishermen. At 4.50 p.m. the Coastguards contacted the Lifeboat Deputy Launching Authority, Capt. Mike Brew, to inform him that the commercial fishing vessel LEMBAS was making water in a position East of the Point of Ayre. The *James Ball Ritchie* was launched at 5.03 p.m. and made her way North East. Vhf radio contact was then made with a helicopter which had been diverted from Jurby Air Base and this aircraft found the casualty and remained on hand until she was sighted from the Lifeboat. As Coxswain Gawne was speaking to the crew of the LEMBAS whilst drawing alongside, the fishing vessel took another sea aboard and began to sink. Her crew jumped into their liferaft which was made fast to the bow of the ship and frantically tried to let go the painter. They succeeded with but one minute to spare before the LEMBAS sank completely. The weather at the scene was fine but with a rough sea and force 5 S'ly wind. The survivors were landed in Ramsey at 7.18 p.m. The fishing vessel had belonged to Peel.

The 13th September saw another fishing vessel in trouble. At 5.50 p.m. the Ramsey Coastguards sent their Mobile Tracking Unit to investigate red flares seen from the NW Coast of the Island. Shortly afterwards the Unit reported seeing more red flares being fired from a vessel and requested the Lifeboat to launch. This she did at 6.12 p.m. In the meantime the Peel lifeboat was also launched and at 6.30 p.m. found the mfv CUSHEN drifting with engine failure. She was taken to Peel with her crew of two. The *James Ball Ritchie* was recalled and was back on station at 8.00 p.m.

A fishing vessel with a crew of two suffered machinery and pump trouble at 4.40 p.m. on the 29th September. This was the BOY BRYN whilst she was on passage from Douglas to Glasgow. The *James Ball Ritchie* was requested to launch and, as the casualty's position was not definite, Coxswain Gawne set on a North Easterly course to intercept the course of the Kirkcudbright lifeboat which was also searching. At 6.07 p.m. the Ramsey Lifeboat was recalled when the ship was found and her tow to Kirkcudbright commenced. The weather was overcast with poor visibility and a SE force 4 wind.

Yet another fishing vessel service took place on the 16th November. The Peel registered mfv SUSTAIN radioed at 11.26 a.m. to the Coastguards that she was sinking. The *James Ball Ritchie* was in the water at 11.33 a.m. – a very speedy launch – and made up for a position six miles North of the Point of Ayre. A fixed wing fishery patrol aircraft was in contact with the distressed ship and confirmed this position. A container vessel also offered assistance but was released by the Coastguards. At 12.46 p.m. the *James Ball Ritchie* was recalled. The SUSTAIN had sunk and three survivors had been picked up by mfv STILL WATERS. The Lifeboat was rehoused at 2.40 p.m.

One of the regular Branch Committee Meetings was held on the 22nd April, 1983. The usual annual Lifeboat Day arrangements were put in hand for the 20th August. The Ladies' Guild announced that they had several suggestions for speakers for the day which included Miss Ivy Benson, Miss Isle of Man, "Flashman", Sir Basil Parkes and Mrs. Daphne Murray (Quite a variety!)

On a point raised by Capt. Watkin, a discussion took place on the level of co-operation between the Branch and the Ramsey Coastguards. (Or Ramsey Marine Rescue Sub-Centre – MRSC, as it was now officially designated). It was agreed that the two Services worked together very well and that it was most fortunate that the Rescue Centre was only yards away from the Boathouse.

Members at the meeting agreed to send a message of congratulations to the Oban RNLI Station on the occasion of the naming ceremony of their new Brede Class Lifeboat to be called ANN RITCHIE. Mrs. Ritchie was to be the guest of honour on the day as the donor of the boat. The Duke of Atholl, as Chairman of the Committee of Management of the RNLI, was also to be present.

The A.G.M. for the year was held on the 1st February, 1984.

1984

1984 produced seven services and 11 exercises for the Ramsey Lifeboat and her Crew. Three lives were saved and one boat.

D. Reed

The *James Ball Ritchie* in the early 1980's.
L. to R: 2nd Coxwain J. Kinnin, Coxwain L. Gawne, C. Gaines, K. Crowe, D. Martin, and K. Christian

The first service was very well into the year and took place on the 2nd July. The Coastguards informed Hon. Secretary Swales at 9.20 a.m. that a local young rod fisherman was missing since the previous day and requested a search to the South of Ramsey. The *James Ball Ritchie* was away at 9.35 a.m. As the Branch's inflatable dinghy was under service in the UK, Acting Coxswain Jim Kinnin arranged for his own boat to be taken to Cornaa Beach and the Lifeboat took it in tow from there. The young man was sighted at 11.20 a.m. and the dinghy used to recover him from the beach. He was seriously injured, having fallen 60ft down the cliff on to rocks at Bulgham Bay and remained there for some 18 hours. The Coxswain took him to Laxey Beach where he was taken ashore to a waiting ambulance and thence to Noble's Hospital, Douglas. He suffered multiple fractures of the pelvis but made a satisfactory recovery. On returning from Laxey to Ramsey the Coxswain's dinghy was used again at Bulgham Bay to pick up four members of the Coastguard who had been unable to scale the cliffs after the rescue. The Hon. Secretary in his report on the incident made a special mention of the first class all-round assistance given by the Crew during this service. It became known later that the young man had purposely hidden his motor cycle from view at the top of the cliffs and this is why the Coastguards failed to locate him from the shore. He also wore his crash helmet on descending to the shore and no doubt this helped him to avoid severe head injuries. He did, in fact, attempt to attract the attention of a fishing boat close inshore during the evening, but was unsuccessful.

Three weeks later on the 22nd July the Coastguards requested a launch as red flares had been sighted East of Maughold Head. Within six minutes the Lifeboat was in the water and found the casualty three miles ESE of the headland. She was the powered cabin cruiser LU-AN with two persons aboard. The weather was good and a tow to Ramsey was put in hand.

At 11.42 p.m. on the 13th August the two-man crew of the auxiliary yacht PISCES asked the Coastguards for assistance. They had mechanical problems and their batteries were very low after being becalmed in fog after 16 hours at sea. The *James Ball Ritchie* was in the water one minute after midnight and reached the casualty in 65 minutes with the help of mv PUMA and the Lifeboat's radar. The yachtsmen were very tired and so two Lifeboatmen boarded the craft to assist them and after a tow back in calm conditions they were safely berthed in Ramsey at 2.30 a.m.

The Lifeboat Authorities were advised by the Coastguards at 5.44 p.m. on the 15th August that they had received a request for help from the auxiliary yacht KINTAIL, registered in Fleetwood. There were two adults and two children aboard and as they had started their engine it had "blown up". One child was suffering from the effects of fumes but otherwise there were no injuries. Initially the response was to find other craft in the vicinity to give assistance but to no avail. No boats could leave the harbour until the next flood tide, so the Lifeboat was launched at 6.25 p.m. It took an hour to reach the casualty as she had drifted nearly to Laxey Bay on the ebb. A tow line was quickly established and the yacht was safely moored to a visitor's mooring buoy in Ramsey Bay at 8.45 p.m. When the KINTAIL'S crew landed it was apparent that they had been badly shocked by the explosion.

The next incident followed three days later but in the end did not involve a launch for the Lifeboat. It concerned the two occupants of the rowing boat ACME. At 2.10 a.m. on the 18th August the Coastguards were informed by the crew of a yacht moored in the Bay that they had heard shouts for help from two men in the water. Another yacht, the TERN, went to investigate. It was requested that the Lifeboat Crew be put on 10 minute's notice and this was done. At 2.16 a.m. no follow-up report came from the TERN and the Lifeboat Crew assembly signal was made. Ten minutes later word was received that the two men had been picked up and so the launch was cancelled. One survivor required hospital attention. Luckily the weather was fine with only a slight breeze.

On the 23rd August the *James Ball Ritchie* was waterborne at 11.40 a.m. after the cabin cruiser REIGHT CHAMPION had suffered engine failure and was out of control. She had a crew of two and was in a position two miles SE of the Station. The call for help was cancelled, however, before the Lifeboat reached that position. The engine had been restarted and the craft continued her passage to Ramsey. A donation was made to the RNLI for the call-out.

A small dinghy found abandoned on Ramsey Beach late on the 16th November caused the next stand-by for the Lifeboat Crew. A lady walking her dog reported her find to the Police at 10.00 p.m. and the Coastguards commenced a search. The Crew assembled at 10.30 p.m. but were stood down soon after midnight as nothing further was found. It was presumed that the dinghy had drifted in from the UK as nothing had been reported missing locally.

The events of 1984 were reviewed at the Branch A.G.M. which was held on the 8th February, 1985. Mr. B.T. Swales, Hon. Secretary, resigned on the 31st July after holding the post for 17 years. Prior to that he had been the Treasurer for a further 15 years. He was presented with an Illuminated Address by the RNLI Management Committee and elected Chairman of the Ramsey Branch. Dr. E.C.B. Corlett was elected his Vice-Chairman. Capt. Michael Brew was welcomed to his first A.G.M. as the new Honorary Secretary together with Mr. James Kinnin who was now Coxswain. Note was made of the threatened down-grading of the Ramsey Marine Rescue Sub-Centre. It was not welcomed but Capt. Brew stated that it should make little difference to the operation of the Station providing that the Snaefell direction-finding facility and the call-out service were retained.

1985

The *James Ball Ritchie* was launched for nine services during 1985 and the large total of 15 other occasions for exercises, inspections and special events.

For the first time at the Station, radio "pagers" were used to call-out the Crew for the first service of 1985. They proved effective. At 8.34 p.m. on the 31st March the Coastguards informed the Hon. Secretary that a yacht with a dead engine had attempted to sail into the harbour but with the SSW wind up to force 6 - 7, she had not been successful. She had then anchored nearby but was not holding and the craft was dragging. No other vessels were available from the harbour so *James Ball Ritchie* launched at 9.54 p.m. and had a tow line aboard in ten minutes. The yacht was the BLUE SILK from Carrickfergus, Northern Ireland, and she had a crew of three. She was safely berthed at 10.35 p.m.

Another yacht from Northern Ireland required help on the 25th May. At 5.54 p.m. the SECRET WATERS, from Donaghadee, was dismasted off the Whitestone Bank Buoy in a Southerly gale, force 6 - 8. The *James Ball Ritchie* was launched at 6.02 p.m. and reached her in 27 minutes. The yacht was making very slow progress towards Ramsey with her auxiliary outboard engine and the Skipper thought that he would make it if the Lifeboat acted as escort. This was agreed but, briefly, the *James Ball Ritchie* left to check another yacht nearby in case assistance was needed. It was not. At 6.55 p.m. the SECRET WATERS was taken in tow as she was making almost no headway. She was safely berthed in Ramsey some 45 minutes later.

The 26th May was the day for the Round the Island Yacht Race. Initially the *James Ball Ritchie* was launched to go to the aid of the catamaran POW WOW which was dismasted in the Northern part of Ramsey Bay. She was not participating in the race and streamed a sea anchor at first to prevent tide and wind putting her on a lee shore. The sea state was rough with a S'ly force 6 - 7 wind. The Lifeboat launched at 4.20 p.m. and escorted POW WOW to port under her auxiliary engine. As this task was completed the racing yachts began to appear from the South and were encountering frequent heavy gusts of wind. The Lifeboat proceeded to Maughold Head to offer any assistance required and was eventually rehoused at 8.01 p.m.

D. Reed

The Crew, Launchers and Helpers c1984.
Top: 2nd Coxswain J. Kinnin, K. Christian, Mechanic J. Kneale, Coxswain L. Gawne, Asst. Mechanic R. Crowe, R. Stanfield, A. Christian, K. Crowe Bottom: Asst. Tractor Driver J. Martin, T. McVicar, D. Kaighen, T. McKnight, K. Holland, D. Gawne, M. Brew, A. Clague, C. Gaines, T. Gaines, M. Quine, Tractor Driver R. Corkill, I. Gawne, E. Collister.

At 8.00 p.m. on the 6th June the wife of the owner of the cabin cruiser TOMMY B, based in Ramsey, alerted the Coastguards to the fact that her husband was overdue. The Rescue Centre instituted a search from the shore and the Isle of Man ferry LADY OF MANN was contacted and asked to investigate a craft seen due East of Ramsey. The ferry was on passage from Douglas to Belfast. At 8.33 p.m. the LADY OF MANN confirmed that the Tommy B had engine failure and the *James Ball Ritchie* was launched at 8.41 p.m. The casualty was towed to the harbour entrance where shore helpers took over and the Lifeboat was rehoused at 10.45 p.m.

For the next service the Reserve Lifeboat O.N. 942 *J.G. Graves of Sheffield* was on station at Ramsey. The *James Ball Ritchie* was in the Ramsey Shipyard being fitted with a semi-permanent wheelhouse. The cabin cruiser MAIMIE of Glasson Dock had machinery failure at 11.06 p.m. on the 24th July. The craft was fogbound East of Maughold Head and had no definite position except that her Skipper could hear the Lighthouse fog signal. The Reserve Lifeboat was in the water at 11.20 p.m. and Coxswain Kinnin made for Maughold Head. Shortly before 1.00 a.m. the Lifeboat Crew could occasionally hear the MAIMIE on her vhf radio and continued on course 100°T as the vhf D/F was giving the same bearing as a radar echo. At 1.55 a.m. the Lifeboat found the casualty and commenced a tow. It was 4.45 a.m. before the MAIMIE was berthed in Ramsey.

Three children in difficulty caused the next call-out for the Crew of the *James Ball Ritchie* on the 22nd August. From 9.25 that morning the Coastguards had been trying to get nearby craft off Laxey harbour to give assistance to the young sailors in an open motor boat whose engine had failed. No success had been achieved at 10.04 a.m. so a Lifeboat launch was requested. The *James Ball Ritchie* was away eight minutes later but after a flare was fired by the Coastguards the mfv USEFUL and a lobster boat responded and made for the casualty. The USEFUL took the dinghy in tow at 10.20 a.m. and the Lifeboat was recalled.

The 31st October dawned with overcast skies, squalls and a force 7 ENE'ly wind. The Belfast trawler WELCOME was heading for Ramsey from a position 12 miles West of the Point of Ayre. She was making water and her bilge pump was out of action. The Coastguards were aware of her predicament but the Skipper did not request assistance. At 6.51 a.m. the Honorary Secretary was informed of the incident and passed it on to the Coxswain and Mechanic. At 7.31 a.m. it was decided to launch as a precaution. Conditions on the beach were bad with rough onshore seas and a heavy surf. The *James Ball Ritchie* was launched at 7.45 a.m. and had a very rough passage to the Point of Ayre to make the rendezvous. Coxswain Kinnin offered advice to the trawler about the best course to steer to avoid the worst seas and both craft made the harbour entrance safely at 9.20 a.m. They had to await the tide until 10.18 a.m. before berthing. The Lifeboat was rehoused at 11.00 a.m. and it was found that she had suffered some damage during the launch. The edge of the tunnel to the port propeller was badly chipped and the outer skin above this was chipped and scored.

THE MV SULBY RIVER EPISODE

The motor coaster SULBY RIVER was owned by the Ramsey based Mezeron Ltd. and engaged on the general cargo trade around the Irish Sea to the Isle of Man. She was of 200 tons dwt and carried a crew of three.

At 7.00 p.m. on Friday, 22nd November, she left Glasson Dock for an overnight passage to Ramsey, eta 7.00 a.m. 23rd. Her cargo consisted of palletised animal foodstuffs, fertilizers and agricultural trailers. The vessel passed the Lune Deep Buoy at 9.36 p.m. and at about 3.00 a.m., 23rd, the Master, Capt. Ken Horsley, handed over the bridge watch to Mate Neil Crawley. The weather was moderate with a NNE'ly wind, force 4 - 5.

At 4.20 a.m. the Master was called back to the bridge as the ship was taking a starboard list. A few minutes later he informed the Ramsey Coastguards of the problem on vhf Channel 67. No cause for the list could be ascertained but it was presumed that a shift of cargo had taken place. At 4.32 a.m. the list was increasing and the Coastguards requested the Lifeboat Crew to assemble. The *James Ball Ritchie* was launched at 4.56 a.m. under Coxswain Kinnin and she was alongside the SULBY RIVER 20 minutes later. The ship was still making way towards Ramsey but the list had increased to about 20 degrees. At 5.23 a.m. the Master asked the Coxswain to take off the ship's Engineer, Brian Shepherd, and the Lifeboat was manoeuvred along the port side of the ship. This was the lee side but very difficult to negotiate with the heavy list of the vessel; however, on the second pass of the Lifeboat, the Engineer managed to jump into the forward well of the *James Ball Ritchie*.

The Lifeboat remained close alongside the stricken ship but Capt. Horsley warned that she might capsize at any time. Owing to insufficient water in the harbour at the time, it was decided to ground the ship close South of the harbour entrance where the beach gently shelved and was made up of unobstructed sand. Leading lights ashore were set up for the ship to aim for; the Mate was at her helm. The *James Ball Ritchie* relayed navigational information continually during the last mile and at 6.07 a.m. the vessel touched bottom with the engine still turning slow ahead. She moved slowly up the beach. At 7.10 a.m. water began to enter the ship's accommodation vents and the Master requested that the Mate be taken off by the Lifeboat. Again the lee side was used but the manoeuvre was even more difficult this time as the port side was facing the shore and the water there very shallow. Seas were breaking right over the ship. A second run down the side proved successful and the Mate was taken off; both survivors were then quickly landed on to the quayside. The *James Ball Ritchie* returned and at 7.44 a.m. the Master agreed to leave the ship. Due to the very severe list by this time, Capt. Horsley had to slide down the ship's side into the water and was picked up immediately. The three crewmen suffered exposure and shock but there were no injuries. One Lifeboatman was somewhat bruised when the Engineer landed on him after jumping from the ship's side. The Lifeboat was rehoused at 9.35 a.m.

A fracture in the shell plating of the SULBY RIVER was found to be the cause of water ingress into the hold. It was possibly pierced by the tow bar of a piece of machinery. It took some two week's work to right the ship and get her into harbour. The work was undertaken by Capt. Stephen Carter and his Laxey Towing Company, based in Douglas. The ship was not put back into Mezeron service and was eventually sold to new owners in the UK. The Lifeboat Crew listed for this rescue included: Coxswain J. Kinnin, 2nd Cox D. Martin, Asst. Mechanic R. Crowe, and Crewmen R. Stanfield, G. Evison, A. Christian, A. Clague and K. Christian. The Shore Personnel were: Head Launcher B. Faragher, Signalman A. Corlett, Tractor Driver J. Martin and Asst. Tractor Driver P. Faragher.

The last call-out of the year came at the very end, on the 30th December. At 2.35 p.m. the Hon. Secretary was made aware that the Master of the passenger ferry SAINT COLUM I had requested a lifeboat from Ramsey to land a passenger who had collapsed into a coma. A rendezvous in the Bay was arranged for 3.30 p.m. and the *James Ball Ritchie* was made ready on the slip and, once the Honorary Medical Adviser had boarded, was launched at 3.35 p.m. In the meantime, however, the patient made a recovery aboard the ferry and the Master decided not to land him after all. The Lifeboat was recalled and rehoused at 4.40 p.m.

At the A.G.M. on the 19th December, 1985, the Committee was notified of senior Crew changes which had taken place during the year. Coxswain Lawrence Gawne had retired through ill-health and tribute was paid to him for his loyal service both as Coxswain and as a Crew

D. Reed

The Sulby River rescue, 23rd November, 1985.
The *James Ball Ritchie* makes her first pass around the grounded vessel in Ramsey Bay at 5.15 a.m. before taking off the crew.

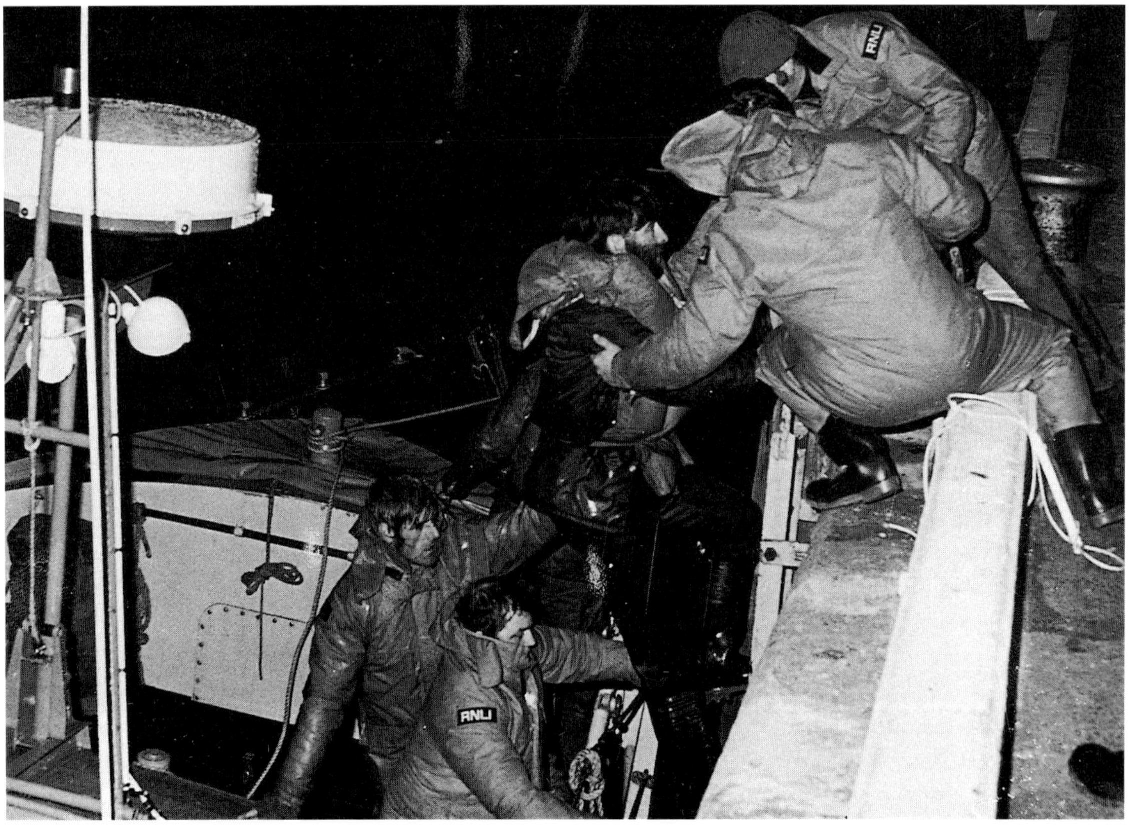

R. Stanfield collection

The Sulby River rescue, 23rd November, 1985. Capt. K. Horsley being helped ashore by Crew Members of the *James Ball Ritchie*.

W. S. Basnett

The SULBY RIVER takes a pounding at High Water, November 1985.

D. Reed

The Laxey Towing Company tug SALISBURY prepares to tow the righted SULBY RIVER into Ramsey harbour, November, 1985.

Member. Second Cox James Kinnin had been elected Coxswain and Crewman Douglas Martin as Second Cox. Several senior Officers of the Branch died in 1985. They included Mr. B.T. Swales, Chairman and former Hon. Secretary; Mr. S.C. Callister, Vice-President and formerly Branch Chairman; Capt. A.S. Carine, a Committee Member and Deputy Launching Authority and Mrs. L. Stidwill, Chairman of the Ladies' Guild and formerly their Hon. Secretary. Dr. E.C.B. Corlett was elected Chairman, Major Jack Kissack Vice-Chairman and Mr. A.B. Dailey Hon. Treasurer. The existing Members of the Committee were re-elected en-bloc, as was customary. Mention was made that the *James Ball Ritchie* had been fitted with a more weatherproof wheelhouse and a vhf D/F set had been added to her navigational equipment. Capt. M. Brew, Hon. Secretary, put forward reasons for creating an Executive Committee to consist of the Branch's Officers, the Coxswain and two Members from the Ladies' Guild Committee. This suggestion was approved and put into operation immediately with meetings arranged three times a year in between the A.G.Ms. and to report to the full Committee at similarly spaced meetings.

1986

The Lifeboat Crew was very active in 1986 with 11 services and eight exercises. Twenty-three people were saved with five of their craft.

The first call-out was at 2.12 p.m. on the 16th March. A floating body had been seen off Port Mooar and as no other vessels were available the *James Ball Ritchie* was launched to recover it. However, the Coastguards completed the task from the shore but the Lifeboat searched the area for anything else untoward. Nothing was found.

Very severe weather four days later on the 20th March accompanied the next launch. The Fleetwood owned trawler DAWN WATERS was believed to have sunk in a SW'ly gale force 8 - 10 and the Douglas lifeboat and other vessels were searching for five possible survivors. At 11.25 a.m. the Ramsey Lifeboat was asked to assist and the *James Ball Ritchie* was away at 11.55 a.m. The search area off the Island's East Coast was reached in an hour and the search pattern was being co-ordinated by the Commander of an S.A.R. helicopter at the scene. At 2.26 p.m. the search was officially abandoned and the *James Ball Ritchie* returned and was rehoused at 5.15 p.m. The Douglas lifeboat picked up one body but four fishermen were never found.

More severe weather was waiting for the *James Ball Ritchie* on her next service. At 12.01 p.m. on the 10th April the Coastguards informed the Hon. Secretary that the powered cabin cruiser MAID OF THE MIST had engine failure off the Island's North West Coast. The mv BISON had replied to the Coastguard's "PAN" call and she located the pleasure craft with her radar. The Lifeboat was launched into a NE wind, force 6 - 7, at 12.17 p.m. and battled her way up to the Point of Ayre. Weather conditions became even more severe rounding the Point with high seas and a 10ft swell. The casualty was reached at 1.50 p.m. and the mv BISON was dismissed from the scene. The tide at Ramsey was low water by this time, so Coxswain Kinnin decided to tow MAID OF THE MIST to Peel breakwater which they reached at 4.10 p.m., after the tow line had parted once. The *James Ball Ritchie* left Peel at 5.30 p.m. and it was 9.00 p.m. before the Lifeboat was rehoused and on station again at Ramsey.

YACHT RACE RESCUES

The "Round the Island Yacht Race" for 1986 took place on the 25th May and ended in severe weather conditions with SSW gales up to force 10. This service for the Ramsey Lifeboat Crewmen earned them not only the thanks of many yachtsmen but official recognition from the RNLI in the form of a Vellum marking the exceptional rescues in heavy weather.

At 10.20 p.m. on the 25th the Hon. Secretary was informed that owing to gale conditions in Ramsey Bay several yachts in the race were in difficulties and were unable to make the harbour. The *James Ball Ritchie* was launched at 10.48 p.m. into a SSW force 8 gale with rough seas. By 5.10 a.m. on the 26th fourteen yachtsmen and three of their craft had been brought to safety. Several donations were received by the RNLI from the rescued crews.

The Crew of the *James Ball Ritchie* on this memorable night included: Coxswain J. Kinnin, 2nd Cox D. Martin, Asst. Motor Mechanic R. Crowe, and K. Crowe, G. Evison, A. Christian, K. Holland and A. Gaines. The Shore Team was: Head Launcher B. Faragher, Signalman B. Corlett, Tractor Driver J. Martin and Asst. Tractor Driver P. Faragher.

On the 30th May the "Gazette" newspaper gave a full account of the night's drama:

> "It was a night Lifeboatmen will remember. Repeated rescues...dramas...and danger.
>
> It happened on Sunday when yachts in the Round the Island Race organised by Ramsey's Manx Sailing and Cruising Club were hit by a severe storm.
>
> What happened in the next four to five hours was a classic tale of lifeboat heroism. It all began at 10.48 p.m. when the Ramsey Lifeboat was called out to go to the assistance of a yacht in difficulties in Ramsey Bay.
>
> The AIRY FAIRY had crossed the finishing line by Ramsey harbour mouth when it found it could not make any way in due to the strong winds and rough sea conditions. The Lifeboat quickly found the yacht, passed two tow ropes (the first one

parted) and took her into harbour where, in its shelter, she started her engines and found her own berth. The Lifeboat was now requested to proceed on a four-mile plug to the Whitestone Bank where another yacht, the BILLY WHIZZ, was similarly unable to make any way towards Ramsey. Her engines had given up and with the wind being South West, estimated at force 9, the seas running really high, she had battened down and conditions now made it impossible for her to sail.

By a combination of vhf D/F on the Lifeboat and the Coastguards she was quickly found at 00.27 a.m. (26th), not quite at Whitestone Buoy but about half a mile off shore. Her final position was pinpointed with the BILLY WHIZZ burning a flare for the Lifeboat to spot and home in on.

Passing a tow was made difficult in the high seas, estimated by those present at 20ft. Manoeuvering from upwind and with skilled use of the engines, Coxswain Kinnin closed with the yacht. As the line was about to be thrown a larger wave picked up the yacht and hurled it at the Lifeboat, causing the yacht to strike with her bows and narrowly missing the Crew stationed there. Ignoring the threat, 2nd Cox Douglas Martin passed the tow line which was rapidly made fast by the yacht's crew. The tow back was slow and very rough, the Lifeboat making for Ramsey directly into the driving seas and spray. Once in the harbour the BILLY WHIZZ's ropes were passed to waiting shore crew whilst instructions for a third casualty were being passed by the Hon. Secretary from the quayside and from the busy Coastguards via radio. This yacht's name was BROADAXE and her position was some four-and-a-half miles North East of Ramsey.

Once again the wet Lifeboat Crew proceeded to sea and the *James Ball Ritchie* headed out towards the helpless yacht. Her engines had failed whilst she was close to land but the strong spring tide, currents and high winds had carried her out to sea. Progress towards the BROADAXE was rapid with the Lifeboat running before the seas and wind. Radio contact with the yacht enabled the vhf D/F to be fully utilized and when the yacht was requested to fire a flare with the Lifeboat less than a mile away in the darkness, it appeared almost directly in front of the Lifeboat.

Once located, the Lifeboat slowed and the erratic confusion of the sea became apparent. The Lifeboat was well out of Ramsey Bay and must have been close to the Bahama Bank where tidal currents run strong to the Point of Ayre. Radar confirmed that the Lifeboat was some eight miles from the Point of Ayre and 10 miles from Maughold - giving a distance out from Ramsey of nine miles - well past the Bahama Bank.

At 2.40 a.m. a line was passed at the second attempt, made fast by the crews, and for the third time the *James Ball Ritchie* set course for distant Ramsey. But the line parted within minutes and the whole process had to be repeated to re-establish the tow.

This line seemed to hold but due to the conditions and fearing the line parting again, the Coxswain proceeded to Ramsey at slow speed. Initially the radar operator reported that the Lifeboat was making no ground towards Ramsey, the speed being only enough to hold both vessels into the wind and weather and to just stem the tide. Gradually speed was edged up as the tow line held and the homeward passage began.

A SECOND LIFEBOAT LAUNCHED

Meanwhile, another yacht had indicated her problems to the Ramsey Coastguards. Much earlier that night the RONALDSWAY had failed to enter Ramsey harbour when her engines seized. Advised to anchor, she was forced down on the coastline, her anchor still out. Whilst the Ramsey Lifeboat was towing the BROADAXE, the RONALDSWAY was nearing the Point of Ayre. This situation was alleviated by the Coastguards who requested the Port St. Mary lifeboat to launch - a fast Arun Class - and proceed North to assist.

Dawn broke at about four in the morning and to the Lifeboatmen of Ramsey and their tow, harbour and shelter were still some four miles off. During the night other yachts in and around Ramsey Bay had shared the onslaught of the weather. One had been seen to be nearly capsized at the harbour mouth and another, later in the same place, had had her mast literally bent double by the force of the wind on her bare pole. This yacht was aptly named the DEVASTATION.

At dawn an improvement in the weather was noticed with the wind dropping and breaking seas calming slightly. Speed was increased and finally at full speed Ramsey Lifeboat and tow reached harbour with just enough water left to moor the casualty safely with the other yachts.

As the *James Ball Ritchie* headed back for the beach, the Port St. Mary Lifeboat could be seen crossing the Bay. Her name, *The Gough Ritchie*, shows her to be Ramsey's sister boat and this is probably the only time these two Lifeboats have been on service in the same area on the same day. Ramsey's Lifeboat was rehoused and ready for service at 6.20 a.m. whilst the Port St. Mary boat still hunted down the RONALDSWAY, which was eventually found five miles North of the Point of Ayre and towed to Douglas.

All crews returned safe and well and no injuries were reported."

The auxiliary yacht ROSIE DAY of Glasson Dock called for assistance at 6.42 p.m. on the 5th June. Her owner had two children with him and the craft had suffered engine failure. He was also unable to make headway under sail. The *James Ball Ritchie* was waterborne at 7.03 p.m. and headed towards Maughold Head. The position of the casualty was uncertain but she had a good vhf set and Coxswain Kinnin was able to get a fix from the Lifeboat's vhf D/F and home in on the yacht. She was found at 8.50 p.m. and towed back to Ramsey.

A dinghy capsize caused the next service on the 29th June. This was spotted by the Coastguards at 7.22 p.m. and one person could be seen in the water but unable to right his craft. It was thought that a second person was also in the sea, possibly under the dinghy. This information was relayed to the Deputy Launching Authority and he agreed to authorise a launch. The Lifeboat was away at 7.35 p.m. and reached

R. Stanfield collection

Heading into a North Easterly. The *James Ball Ritchie* in late 1985 after being fitted with a semi-permanent wheelhouse.

the casualty in five minutes. It was then ascertained that only one person was involved and with the help of Lifeboatmen, the dinghy was righted and towed in to the beach with the owner.

At 8.02 a.m. on the 18th August, Capt. Brew received a report that the Hull mfv NORDBORG was four miles West of the Point of Ayre and heading for Ramsey but making water with the level over the propeller shaft. Her pumps were not containing the inflow. The *James Ball Ritchie* was launched at 8.17 a.m. and reached the casualty at 8.53 a.m. In the meantime the nearby mfv FIONA THOMPSON had been advising NORDBORG how to navigate around the Point of Ayre safely to avoid the banks. Once alongside the NORDBORG the Lifeboat Coxswain was informed that the water level was falling and the pumps coping. She was escorted to port.

An aborted service took place next on the 18th August. The trawler ESTHER ELIZABETH was fishing one mile East of Laxey Harbour. A crew member had been trapped by a winch and was badly injured. As the vessel had her gear down she could not make for port and requested assistance. This was offered by the *James Ball Ritchie* with a doctor aboard. She was in the water at 12.03 p.m. but less than 20 minutes later was recalled as the fishing vessel had lifted her gear and made Laxey. An ambulance took the injured man away.

A long search involving three of the Island's lifeboats took place on the 6th and 7th September. This was for the Ravenglass registered cabin cruiser ARGOS with two people aboard. Early on Saturday afternoon, the 6th, Capt. Brew and Coxswain Kinnin attended the Coastguard Office and listened in to radio traffic connected with a search underway off Douglas for a missing yacht. At 2.22 p.m. the Ramsey Lifeboat was asked to assist and was launched at 2.30 p.m. Once off Maughold Head, at 2.55 p.m., the Lifeboat was asked to make for Clay Head and search about one mile offshore and inside the other vessels already on the scene. This included both the Douglas and Port St. Mary lifeboats and the coastal tanker SHELL DIRECTOR. At 7.30 p.m., and with nothing found, the oil tanker proceeded on her passage and left the lifeboats to form a line abreast search starting off Langness and heading North. At 7.45 p.m. the *James Ball Ritchie* picked up a floating cabin door from a small vessel. A box search was completed by 9.05 p.m. and, as darkness was upon the searchers, operations were called off for the night. The Ramsey Lifeboat was rehoused at 00/15 (7th). At 6.10 a.m. the Lifeboats were at sea again and at 9.05 a.m. the *James Ball Ritchie* arrived at a new datum point off Douglas and took up another box search with the other craft. Nothing was found and at 1.15 p.m. the search was called off. The Ramsey Boat was rehoused and ready for duty again at 4.15 p.m. 2nd Coxswain D. Martin took charge of this second day operation.

Eleven days later, on the 18th September, the Lifeboat was called out at 12.20 p.m. to proceed to Cornaa. With the help of the dinghy, a floating body was recovered by the crew of the *James Ball Ritchie* and returned to Ramsey.

The Belfast ferry ST. COLUM I made local news when she requested assistance from the Ramsey Lifeboat once again. This occasion was on the 7th November at 3.26 p.m. when she informed the Coastguards that she had a passenger aboard with a suspected heart condition and requested that the patient be landed for hospitalisation. The *James Ball Ritchie* was launched at 3.42 p.m. in a very fresh SW force 6 wind. Half-an-hour later a rendezvous was made South East of the harbour and the patient was lowered down the side of the ST. COLUM I in a ship's lifeboat. The transfer into the Ramsey Lifeboat was made safely and the passenger was landed at 4.40 p.m. to a waiting ambulance.

LIFEBOAT FOR REPAIRS

A very significant occurance took place on the 26th November when the *James Ball Ritchie* was inspected by a RNLI team headed by Commander George Cooper, Deputy Chief of Operations. In line with findings on other Oakley Class lifeboats, it was found that a rapid deterioration in parts of the hull was taking place and the Boat was immediately taken out of service. Coxswain James Kinnin and a Ramsey Crew delivered the Lifeboat to Workington on the 29th November for her overland haulage to Eyemouth, Berwickshire, for major repairs.

Due to the sudden withdrawal of three Oakleys in the space of a few days there was no relief boat of the same type immediately available. Ramsey therefore remained off station until the 6th December when the 47ft Watson Class HERBERT LEIGH O.N. 900 arrived from Penlee. Coxswain Kinnin and Crew sailed the Boat up from Cornwall and had the distinction of doing so in the oldest lifeboat in service with the RNLI. As the HERBERT LEIGH was unable to sit on the Oakley carriage she was moored in the harbour and was thus on call for only 12 to 14 hours per day, as the tides permitted. However, she conducted no services whilst on station and was replaced by the usual Oakley relief lifeboat *Vincent Nesfield* on the 11th March, 1987.

1986 was an active year for the Branch Committee. At their meeting on the 3rd March, Mr. K.M. Vlasto, Inspector of Lifeboats, West Division, was welcomed to the meeting. Amongst other matters, Chairman Dr. E.C.B. Corlett explained the aim of creating a small library of films and videos for in-house work and charity showing. It currently consisted of: Video of 1984 Lifeboat Day (Chairman); Video of the visit of HRH Princess Alexandra (Hon. Secretary); Video of the *James Ball Ritchie* being lifted out at the shipyard (Alan Christian); Film of the Bicentenary voyage of the STAR OF INDIA (RTC John Donelly). Mrs. Barbara Green was elected Press Liaison Officer to cover aspects not dealt with by Mr. Kim Holland, Crew Member. Mr. Holland was congratulated by the Chairman for obtaining an Open University Honours Degree. Notice was given of the forthcoming Isle of Man Lifeboat Conference to be held in Douglas on the 5th March. The occasion was being organised by Mr. D. Jones, RNLI North-West Regional Organising Secretary, Manchester, and would be chaired by Mr. Donald Redford, Chairman of the Institution's Search and Rescue Committee. The Lt. Governor and Mrs. New were to attend amongst other dignitaries. On the 6th June a reception was held at the Villa Marina in Douglas for the Island's lifeboat people to meet the Institution's President, HRH the Duke of Kent. Lifeboat Day was held on the 2nd August and the Annual Appeal was made by the Lt. Governor, Major General Lawrence New. The event raised £1550 for the RNLI.

At the A.G.M. on the 18th December Inspector Vlasto reported officially on the condition of the *James Ball Ritchie*. The fleet of Oakley Class lifeboats had been found to be deteriorating prematurely. There were places in the boats where steel, aluminium and brass were used together. The resultant electrolysis caused the softening of adjacent wooden structures. The *James Ball Ritchie* was already 18 months overdue for a major overhaul and because of her condition it would be many months before her refurbishment would be completed. It was expected that a relief Oakley Class boat would be available for Ramsey in February, 1987, but in the meantime the Watson type HERBERT LEIGH would fill the gap.

The Chairman paid tribute to Mr. Tregellis for his past services as Hon. Treasurer and asked him to accept a framed painting by Mr. J. Codrington showing a launch of the *James Ball Ritchie* from the beach.

During the year the Crew completed the conversion of the former tractor shed into a suitable Crew Room and the Chairman congratulated Coxswain Kinnin on all the hours of labour that had been expended. It seemed that HQ would not approve of any collected monies being used for the project. However, most of the materials were being donated by local firms and individuals. It was also mentioned that it was hoped to refurbish the Committee

B. P. Grenfell

Lifeboat Day, 2nd August, 1986.
The Annual Appeal for funds being delivered by the Lt. Governor, Major General Laurence New (now Sir Laurence). To his left is the Committee Vice-Chairman Major J. Kissack and on the right Chairman Dr. E.C..B. Corlett and Mr. L. Clague, Chairman of the Ramsey Commissioners.

Room at a later stage. Lifeboat Inspector Vlasto cautioned against doing anything too ambitious which might impinge on the Institution's responsibility for the maintenance of the structure. He advised that a full maintenance survey of the building was due in 1987. In fact a brand new Norbury Boathouse was very much nearer than envisaged at the time.

1987

During 1987 seven services were undertaken; six by the relief lifeboat *Vincent Nesfield* and one by the *James Ball Ritchie*. Nine exercises were carried out and these were shared between the two relief boats *Herbert Leigh* and *Vincent Nesfield* and the *James Ball Ritchie* upon her return. The *Vincent Nesfield* saved two people and one boat.

At 3.09 p.m. on the 28th March the Skipper of the trawler Janmar contacted the Ramsey Coastguards informing them that he had a seaman aboard who had badly gashed his hand and that he wished to land him for medical attention. Capt. Brew, as Hon. Secretary and Duty Harbour Master on watch, informed the ship that she would be unable to berth owing to the state of the tide. It was agreed that the *Vincent Nesfield* should rendezvous with the Janmar in the Bay and bring the casualty ashore. This was done in a very fast time and the seaman was in an ambulance in exactly one hour. The Lifeboat was rehoused at 4.40 p.m.

Much of the summer passed uneventfully on the coast until the 15th August. Soon after noon that day the locally based cabin cruiser Sea Follie reported that she had a fouled propeller in a position half-a-mile offshore at Rue Point. Twenty minutes later she reported that efforts to clear away an offending rope had been unsuccessful and that she was anchoring to await assistance. The *Vincent Nesfield* was launched at 12.30 p.m. in fair weather and reached the casualty at 1.18 p.m. By this time the cruiser was dragging rapidly towards the Point of Ayre. A tow line was quickly made fast and both boats arrived back in port at 2.15 p.m.

The wind was a fresh NE'ly force 6 with rough seas at 10.13 p.m. on the 23rd August. At that time the Coastguards informed the Hon. Secretary that the local auxiliary yacht Freedom of Mann was approaching the harbour under jury rig. Her steering gear had failed. It was deemed wise for the Lifeboat to stand-by the yacht and the *Vincent Nesfield* was waterborne at 10.26 p.m. The craft made her berth under her own power without mishap and the Lifeboat was rehoused at 11.15 p.m.

Eight days later the *Vincent Nesfield* was on service again and launched at 1.23 p.m. into rough seas and a SSE wind, force 6. This was in answer to difficulties being experienced by the crew of the yacht MOCHRUM SCART of Ramsey. The craft was North West of the Point of Ayre with machinery failure. Her two-man crew was very tired and seasick and unable to sail the yacht. It was 2.46 p.m. before the Lifeboat reached the casualty; Coxswain Kinnin had some difficulty in finding her owing to radio problems aboard the MOCHRUM SCART. It was necessary to transfer two Lifeboatmen to the yacht to effect a tow and to lower her sails which were still set. This was easier said than done in the prevailing conditions as the vessel was blowing around violently. H.M.S. LEEDS CASTLE was nearby and assisted in giving a lee for this operation and at 3.34 p.m. the tow to Ramsey was commenced. The yacht was safely berthed at 4.45 p.m. and the Lifeboat was rehoused at 5.25 p.m. A donation was received by the RNLI for this rescue.

At 9.16 p.m. on the 1st September a member of the public reported seeing a red flare approximately eight miles East of Laxey harbour. The *Vincent Nesfield* was launched at 9.30 p.m. and reached the datum position at 10.21 p.m. A white flare was then fired but no response observed. Some white lights were seen some three miles distant and these were investigated but after firing more flares and using the searchlight, no casualty was found. The Lifeboat returned to Ramsey and was beached at 1.50 a.m. (2nd). Liverpool Coastguards later remarked that there had been meteorite activity over Merseyside during the night.

Faint radio signals caused an unnecessary call-out for the Crew of the *Vincent Nesfield* 18 hours later on the 3rd September. At 12.24 p.m. Capt. Brew was attending the Coastguard Centre when very faint transmissions from the Douglas fishing vessel AMANDA JANE were received. She was requesting assistance and it appeared that her position was near the Whitestone Bank Buoy. The Ramsey Lifeboat was launched at 12.44 p.m. and set a course for the Buoy. Meanwhile the fishery patrol aircraft WATCHDOG 91 sighted a vessel considered to be the casualty three miles North of Peel. This was nowhere near the original position thought to have been indicated. At 12.46 p.m. the Peel Lifeboat was paged and at 1.06 p.m. drew alongside the AMANDA JANE North of Peel. The *Vincent Nesfield* was recalled to Ramsey. It later transpired that the radio signal had given the position off "White Strand" and this had been mistakenly heard as "Whitestone" owing to the weak strength. The *Vincent Nesfield* was rehoused at 2.15 p.m.

A LONG SERVICE

A five-hour service took place next on the 16th October when the *Vincent Nesfield* acted as an escort to a large cargo vessel in trouble. The ro-ro mv SPHEROID, managed by a Douglas based company, reported at 4.20 p.m. to the local Coastguards that she had suffered an engine-room fire and that one of her two engines was out of commission. She was some six miles South of the Mull of Galloway in a strong WSW'ly gale and was unable to navigate fully. Although her sister ship SAGA MOON was standing-by, the Master of the casualty was very concerned about his limitations in being able to avoid land under the prevailing conditions and so he requested additional assistance. The *Vincent Nesfield* was launched at 4.38 p.m. in good conditions off Ramsey. It took the Lifeboatmen two hours to reach the SPHEROID because once they rounded the Point of Ayre they began to feel the full effect of the force 7 gale and the 12ft to 15ft waves. Upon arrival at the rendezvous position it was found that the engine-room fire aboard the SPHEROID had been extinguished and her second engine restarted under reduced power. Course was then set to get the ship to the East of the Island and into the lee, bearing in mind the forecast was for the wind to increase to SWxS force 11. It was 9.55 p.m. by the time the Lifeboat saw the cargo vessel safely anchored in Ramsey Bay. The Lifeboat Crew had had an extremely uncomfortable time North of the Island with very heavy rolling from the beam swell and were very pleased to get their craft rehoused at 10.15 p.m. The Ronaldsway Meterological Office forecast for local waters overnight was for the wind to decrease to force 4 and back to the SW. The Bay was a safe anchorage.

The last service for the Reserve Boat during her seven month tour of duty at Ramsey took place on the 25th October. The locally based cabin cruiser ELMAR, with a crew of four, had machinery failure off the Point of Ayre. At 2.10 p.m. the Lifeboat was in the water and under the guidance of 2nd Cox D. Martin. The wind was SSW force 5 and the tide was ebbing and this combination was taking the casualty away from the land. The Auxiliary Coastguard Patrol had proceeded to the Point by road and had the ELMAR in sight. Her position was relayed to the *Vincent Nesfield.* The 2nd Cox issued instructions to the ELMAR by radio for the required preparations to be made for the tow and once the vessels met up at 2.55 p.m. a line was quickly passed and the towing commenced. Progress into the wind and against the ebb tide was slow and it was 4.30 p.m. by the time the boats were off the harbour entrance. Insufficient water was available to berth and the 2nd Cox decided to remain at anchor with the ELMAR until she was safely berthed at 9.45 p.m. The Lifeboat was rehoused at 10.40 p.m.

B. P. Grenfell

Lifeboat Day, 2nd August, 1986.
Recovering the *James Ball Ritchie* in a fresh Easterly wind.

On the 29th October, 1987, the *James Ball Ritchie* returned to her home base after very extensive hull rebuilding. She made the journey from Eyemouth to Workington overland and then Coxswain Kinnin and Crew sailed her to Ramsey. The *Vincent Nesfield* was delivered to her next assignment at Pwllheli by 2nd Cox D. Martin and his Crew. The Pwllheli lifeboat was also an Oakley suffering from deterioration and was due for delivery to a boatyard for similar major repairs.

The final call-out of the year took place during the evening of the 29th November. An experienced yachtsman reported sighting a red flare in the area of Rue Point off the Island's North Coast. As this area was frequented by weekend anglers, the report was taken seriously and the *James Ball Ritchie* was launched at 6.07 p.m. The Lifeboat searched for some two and three-quarter hours between the Point of Ayre and Rue Point and she was joined by the Peel inshore lifeboat, but nothing was found. The Ramsey Boat was beached for recovery at 10.35 p.m. The weather had been good.

The new-style Executive Committee and General Committee meetings which began in 1986 continued throughout 1987. The Executive meetings were held at the very end of February, May and August with full Meetings following one week later each time. This worked well and gave the Executive Officers of the Branch time to prepare an agreed agenda for the full meetings.

At the full meeting on the 6th March the Committee agreed to go ahead with the proposed new Station History and the author was asked to commence work and report back in one year. Originally it was proposed only to update the 1968 History written and produced by the then Chairman, Major Keith Grimble Groves, but a fuller version covering the actual lifeboat services was finally decided upon.

The Ladies' Guild agreed to arrange the purchase of an embossed Book of Honour which would contain entries of benefactors and donors of funds to the Branch. This would be displayed with the Visitors' Book in a suitable display case.

On Saturday the 5th September His Excellency the Lt. Governor, Major-General Laurence New, accompanied by Mrs. New and their daughter, visited the Boathouse and presented Coxswain James Kinnin with the "Thanks of the Institution" inscribed on Vellum and Certificates to Members of his Crew. These related to those who had been aboard the *James Ball Ritchie* when, on the occasion of the 1985 Round the Island Race, they had been responsible for saving the lives of 14 crew members of three of the competing yachts in difficulty in storm conditions in Ramsey Bay. At the same time Mr. T.E. Tregellis, who had recently retired as the Branch's Honorary Treasurer, was presented by the Lt. Governor with the Institution's Silver Badge in recognition of his individual service to the RNLI and the Ramsey Branch in particular. A celebration of these events, in the form of a Ball, was held at the Grand Island Hotel, Ramsey, the same evening.

PRESS REPORT

The Manx Independent newspaper covered the Award Ceremony and reported:

"The Coxswain and seven members of the Ramsey Lifeboat who went to the rescue of three yachts who found themselves in trouble at the end of the 1986 Round the Island Yacht Race, have received the formal "Thanks of the Committee of Management of the RNLI."

On Saturday morning the Cox, Mr. Jimmy Kinnin, was presented with the "Thanks of the RNLI" on Vellum by the Lt. Governor, Major-General Laurence New. His Excellency also presented the Crew of the Ramsey Boat with Vellum Service Certificates - 2nd Cox Douglas Martin, Acting Mechanic Ronald Crowe, Emergency Mechanic Gerald Evison and Crew Members Kevin Crowe, Alan Christian, Kim Holland and Anthony Gaines. His Excellency and Mrs. New were introduced to all the Ramsey Crew Members by the Chairman, Dr. Ewan Corlett.

Also at the Lifeboat Station to meet His Excellency were Ramsey Member of the House of Keys, Mr. Allan Bell, the Chairman of the Ramsey Commissioners Mr. John Kaighen, Town Clerk, Mr. David Evans, the Chairman of the Ladies' Lifeboat Guild, Mrs. Pat Dearden, the Administrative Officer, Sqn. Ldr. John Sands, Hon. Secretary, Capt. Mike Brew, Treasurer, Mr. Brian Dailey, Hon. Medical Adviser, Dr. John Brownsdon, members of the Lifeboat Executive Committee and Mr. Jimmy Kneale, the Lifeboat Mechanic, who only recently was awarded the B.E.M. which he received from his Excellency".

The article then goes on to describe the rescue in detail and concluded:

"The Crew were, at the time, sent a letter by Rear Admiral W.J. Graham, RNLI Director, conveying thanks to them for their efforts in such adverse weather. Ramsey RNLI Chairman, Dr. Ewan Corlett, described these as "very noteworthy rescues" and said that by kindly undertaking to present these awards that morning His Excellency had illustrated his very keen interest in the Institution.

His Excellency also made a special presentation to the former Ramsey RNLI Treasurer, Mr. Tom Tregellis. Mr. Tregellis was Treasurer of the Branch for 17 years. "A long time," said Dr. Corlett, "and involved a lot of effort and we are very grateful to him." Mr. Tregellis was presented with the Silver Badge of the RNLI.

After the presentations, His Excellency said that he and his wife and daughter were honoured to be there to make the presentations. He said: "We watch all that happens within the Lifeboat Service with very great interest, concern and appreciation."

The Annual General Meeting of the Ramsey Branch was held on the 3rd December for the year 1987. Much of the business discussed was contained in a Press report in the Manx Independent of the 24th December:

"It has been revealed that there will be major changes at the Ramsey Lifeboat Station in the not too distant future. Details of these changes are expected to be announced by the RNLI shortly.

The Institution is developing new faster boats by continually reappraising the requirements for rescue services and deciding on the allocation of all boats within the fleet. It seeks to make the most effective use of the boats and the most effective application of its funds, which are all donated by the public throughout the British Isles, whether they live inland or by the coast.

Ramsey RNLI has a proud history and has rescued over 600 lives since the establishment of the Station in 1829 and because of its position and the particular pattern of sea traffic in adjacent waters, will continue to play a very prominent part in providing rescue services in the North Irish Sea.

The importance of the Ramsey Station is accentuated because of tidal and other limitations which restrict the operation of some lifeboat stations on adjacent coasts - Cumbria, Solway Firth and the South Coast of Scotland. Station Administrative Officer, Sqn. Ldr. John Sands, told the Manx Independent this week that it seems very probably that in the not too distant future there will be major changes at the Ramsey Station.

If these follow the general pattern of similar improvements in equipment on other stations throughout Britain, it is going to present a challenge to the public and obviously particularly to the people of Ramsey and adjoining districts in helping to finance this. Sqn. Ldr. Sands says that the RNLI have every confidence that Ramsey will move forward in this continuing replacement of equipment and the introduction of new boats.

The Ramsey Branch of the RNLI held their A.G.M. earlier this month when a special presentation was made to retiring Motor Mechanic at Ramsey, Mr. Jimmy Kneale. He retires on his birthday, Christmas Day.

Jimmy has served the Station for 38 years and the presentation took the form of a mounted clock and barometer with an inscribed plate expressing the "Sincere thanks of the Branch for 38 years devoted service to the Station." Jimmy has given tremendous service to the Station at sea and in maintaining the boats and the equipment in the Boathouse. He has also been very helpful in the Committee Room and, in fact, whenever and wherever there has

B. P. Grenfell

Lifeboat Day, 2nd August, 1986.
Swinging the Lifeboat after recovery. The Lt. Governor and his family aboard after a trip around the Bay.

been lifeboat activity of any sort afloat or onshore, whether at meetings or fund raising activities.
Replacing Jimmy as Mechanic is Mr. Jimmy Martin who has been connected with the Ramsey Branch of the RNLI for some years, latterly as Tractor Driver. Mr. Mark Matthews takes over from him as Tractor Driver."

The Crew List for December, 1987, included:

Coxswain J. Kinnin, 2nd Cox D. Martin, Station Mechanic J. Martin, Asst. Mechanic R. Crowe, and Crewmen K. Crowe, G. Evison, R. Stanfield, K. Christian, A. Christian, Alistair Clague, K. Holland, A. Gaines, Alan Clague and J. Clague.

Shoreside: Head Launcher A. Faragher, Tractor Driver M. Matthews, Tractor Driver's Asst. P. Faragher and Lightman K. Airey.

Station Officers: President Mrs. A.A. Ritchie, Vice-President Mr. E. Corlett, Chairman Dr. E.C.B. Corlett, Vice-Chairman Major J. Kissack, Hon. Secretary Capt. M. Brew, Hon. Treasurer Mr. A.B. Dailey, Station Administrative Officer and Deputy Launching Authority Sqn. Ldr. J. Sands, Deputy Launching Authority Capt. N. Luck, Hon. Chaplain Fr. L. Lynch, Hon. Auditor Mr. S. Moorhouse, Hon. Medical Adviser Dr. J. Brownsdon, Hon. Optician Mr. R. Corlett.

Committee Members: Rev. Sir Paterson Fraser, HMCG Controller J. Appleton, Police Inspector J. Cook, Messrs. P. Cannan, J. Colman, B. Corlett, L. Clague, D. Cranshaw, N. Hendy, J.Mellor, M. Pugh, J. Stanton, P. Wilson, G. Swales, T. Tregellis and Capts. R. Watkin and W. Seybold.

Ladies' Guild Officers and Members of the Branch Committee: Chairman Mrs. J. Sands, Hon. Secretary Mrs. E. Corlett, Hon. Treasurer Mrs. M. Pugh, Souvenirs Mrs. P. Wilson.

1988

Six services were carried out by the *James Ball Ritchie* in 1988. Four people were saved with two of their craft.

The first service of the year was not until the 18th April when the Grimsby trawler St. Britwin went aground at the Point of Ayre at 4.26 in the morning. The Lifeboat was in the water at 4.45 a.m. and reached the casualty 40 minutes later. The fishing vessel was well aground but not making any water. As the tide was ebbing swiftly it was not possible to tow the vessel off at the time and Coxswain Kinnin advised her Skipper to run out a kedge anchor in view of the forecast of a Southerly force 5 wind. As no further help could be given by the *James Ball Ritchie* until the following tide, the Lifeboat returned to her Station. At 9.44 a.m. she was back in the water again and returned to the Point of Ayre. Mfv CONMORAN was also standing-by to assist but as she had a 10ft draft the Lifeboat passed a tow line from the ST. BRITWIN to the CONMORAN. This operation took some 25 minutes as the tide was running very strongly parallel to the beach and it was difficult to run the line without putting too much strain on it and risk it parting. At 11.00 a.m. the connection was made and with the CONMORAN'S engine steaming ahead and that of the ST. BRITWIN going astern, the stranded ship eased herself off the beach in 15 minute's time. The Lifeboat returned the tow line and then escorted the ST. BRITWIN to the safety of Ramsey harbour. The *James Ball Ritchie* was rehoused at 1.04 p.m.

The above service is the subject of the cover photograph of this book.

A hoax call brought the Lifeboatmen out on the 23rd April. The Coastguards informed Capt. Brew that they had received a report from a young boy to the effect that his friend had fallen into the sea from the Queen's Pier. All were suspicious of the call but a launch was agreed to "just in case!" The Lifeboat was in the water at 10.17 a.m. and searched around the Pier and half-a-mile down wind but nothing was found. When the Coastguards attempted to trace the telephone call it was found to come from a local call box but not in the area given by the caller. The Lifeboat was recalled. Two days later the culprit admitted to his prank.

On the 8th August at 9.30 a.m. the Hon. Secretary was advised that the sail training ship FRANCIS DRAKE was off Maughold Head and unable to use her auxiliary engine. She had a crew of 18 and 14 of these were inexperienced cadets. The sea state was moderate in a force 4 SE'ly wind and it was one-and-a-half hours after high water at Ramsey. The ship wished to berth in Ramsey to effect repairs and bearing in mind the make-up of her crew, it was agreed to launch the *James Ball Ritchie* at 10.10 a.m. Due to the limited time left to berth on the tide, the Lifeboat took the FRANCIS DRAKE in tow at 10.27 a.m. and berthed her half-an-hour later. At the outset of this service the local Coastguard aerial became faulty and most of the Lifeboat Crew did not receive the paging signals. Two hand-held signal rockets were fired to summon the Lifeboatmen and it was later decided to always use such signals as a back-up system.

Two days later, on the 10th August, two services were carried out from one launching. The replica Viking Longship THE ARTHUR GUINNESS, with a 15 man crew, had left Ramsey earlier in the day bound for Northern Ireland. At 3.57 p.m. she reported rudder problems from a position West of the Point of Ayre. The *James Ball Ritchie* was launched at 4.10 p.m. and made a Northerly course for the Point. Half-an-hour later the Viking ship reported that the rudder had completely fractured and that they were proceeding back to Ramsey using a steering oar. The casualty was reached at 5.10 p.m. but as the jury rig was effective the Lifeboat only acted as escort until some two miles North of the port. She then left the ARTHUR GUINNESS and proceeded to the small yacht HO. This craft had an auxiliary engine but had anchored close off the beach at Cranstal as she could make no headway against the head seas and ebb tide. The wind was Southerly, force 6. The *James Ball Ritchie* fired a rocket-line across the yacht at 5.40 p.m. to facilitate a tow line being connected and soon headway was being made towards port. On reaching the harbour entrance the mfv JACKIE G offered to tow the craft into a berth when the tide made and this was completed at 7.20 p.m. In the meantime the Lifeboat returned to stand-by the ARTHUR GUINNESS and escorted her to a berth at 7.00 p.m.

Officer cadets of the Edinburgh and Heriot-Watt University required Lifeboat assistance on the 6th October. The sea state close offshore was calm but the wind was WSW force 6 in the Bay. At 11.15 a.m. Capt. Brew attended the Coastguard Centre and was informed that 10 members of the University OTC had been wind-surfing opposite the Boathouse during the morning. As the wind increased the leader of the group called them all in and their own rescue boat went to assist the last wind-surfer out who was in difficulties. Then the boat's outboard engine failed about a quarter-of-a-mile offshore . Both casualties were being rapidly blown out to sea. The Lifeboatmen were paged and the *James Ball Ritchie* was in the water at 11.39 a.m. The windsurfer was picked up within minutes as he had managed to paddle close in and the Lifeboat then took the boat and four occupants in tow at 11.50 a.m. The Lifeboat was back on station at 12.50 p.m.

J. KNEALE PRESENTATION

In the spring of 1988 a further presentation was made to Mr. Jimmy Kneale, the recently retired Station Mechanic. The Manx Independent covered the proceedings:

> "Crews from Douglas and Moelfre, Anglesey, joined the Ramsey Lifeboat Crew on Saturday evening for a farewell presentation to Ramsey Mechanic, Mr. Jimmy Kneale, B.E.M. Jimmy, who has been with the RNLI Ramsey Branch for 38 years, retired officially on his birthday, Christmas Day, 1987, and has already been presented with a farewell gift by the Ramsey Administrative Committee. He was

B. P. Grenfell

The *James Ball Ritchie* towing in the Ocean Youth Club schooner FRANCIS DRAKE after engine failure, 8th August, 1988.

B. P. Grenfell

Safe arrival. Berthing the FRANCIS DRAKE in Ramsey on the 8th August, 1988.

awarded the B.E.M. in the Queen's Birthday Honours List in May, last year, something of which his colleagues at the Ramsey Station are justifiably proud.

It was a moving moment for Jimmy on Saturday evening at the Britannia Hotel, when the farewell present from the Crew to him was revealed. They had arranged for a model of the original *James Ball Ritchie* to be made by one of the Lifeboat Launchers, Colin Jones. This beautiful exact replica of the *James Ball Ritchie* as she was before the recent work was carried out on her, was made from the actual timber of the Ramsey Boat which was retrieved when extensive repair work was carried out at Eyemouth last year. Cox Jimmy Kinnin and Members of the Crew decided as long ago as Christmas, 1986, that this would be their farewell gift to Jimmy Kneale and they approached Colin Jones, who is a marine electrician with Bevan Ltd. of Ramsey, to see if he would make the model for them. Colin, who has been making model boats for some time, was delighted to have the honour and says that it has taken 12 months of "tender loving care" to make this replica. The model is three quarters of an inch to the foot and is 25 inches long and exact in every detail to the original *James Ball Ritchie*. It was presented to Jimmy in a glass case, made by Jimmy Kinnin and Dougie Martin, with three inscribed plaques kindly donated and inscribed by Mr. John Stanton, who is a member of the Ramsey Lifeboat Committee.

The first plaque lists the members of the crew, the second all the launchers, and the centre one commemorates the occasion and bears the inscription: 'Presented to motor mechanic James Kneale, B.E.M., from the crew and launchers of the Ramsey RNLI in recognition of his 38 years of dedicated service to the Ramsey Lifeboat Station 1949-1987. This model was made by Colin Jones from the timbers of the original *James Ball Ritchie*'.

Previously Mr. Kneale had been presented with a certificate of long service by District Inspector, Mr. Michael Vlasto, who was in Ramsey for this special occasion. Mr. Vlasto thanked Jimmy for the many years of service he had given to the RNLI. He also thanked the Ramsey Lifeboat Crew for their hospitality that evening to himself and the other visiting Lifeboatmen. The Moelfre Lifeboatmen were on crew training and were delighted that their visit to Ramsey coincided with this special occasion.

Mr. Vlasto went on to say that during the time Jimmy Kneale had been with the Ramsey Lifeboat, 38 years, 85 lives had been saved. 'The award of the B.E.M. comes to very few people,' he said, 'and this, with the Institution's Long Service Badge, makes up a very distinguished lifeboat career.' "

During the year the third Isle of Man RNLI Conference was held. This took place in Douglas on the 9th March. Many members of all five branches attended and addresses were made by several RNLI Officers from the UK, including Mr. David Jones, Lt. Commander Brian Miles, Mr. R. Darbyshire, Mr. M. Vlasto, Mr. E. Wake-Walker and Mr. I. Wallington. Many topics were discussed with an open forum for questions and answers and a film was shown. Awards were presented to several Branch Officers. The event took up much of the day. The following day an RNLI delegation inspected the Ramsey Station, together with all other Island Stations. Ramsey Branch Officers were officially informed of the changes due to take place within the next three years and these included a new boathouse, tractor and lifeboat.

On the 6th April, as part of an extensive trials, a prototype Mersey Fast Carriage Boat (FCB) O.N.1125, of aluminium construction, visited Ramsey. Many Crew and Committee Members took the opportunity to go aboard and were very impressed with the new style, equipment and accommodation. A very different boat to the *James Ball Ritchie*! She had twice the speed – to say the very least!

In early April it was announced that HM Coastguard Service was to be withdrawn from the Isle of Man before the 31st March, 1989. Responsibility for Search and Rescue around the Island was then to be transferred to Liverpool, using the existing aerial site on Snaefell mountain for radio contact. A local coast-watching organisation to replace the Coastguard Auxiliary Service (the mobile units) would be set up and run by the Manx Government. The RNLI was assured that the new system would be as good, if not better, than the old service. All seafarers earnestly hoped that such optimism would prove correct.

2nd Cox D.K. Martin resigned on the 30th June and he and his family emigrated to Australia. He was thanked for his 11 loyal years of service to the Branch and wished well for the future. Mr. R. Stanfield was elected to replace him.

Mr. J. Kinnin, Coxswain, attended a one week training course at RNLI HQ in Poole during the year. Several other Crew Members attended courses at the Fleetwood Nautical College. This was part of the on-going commitment by the RNLI to ensure the highest standards of crew training and competency and also to make the transition to the faster and more sophisticated type of lifeboats, now replacing the older models, as smooth as possible.

All these matters were set out at the December A.G.M. and once again the Ladies' Guild was congratulated on raising another record sum of £10,543 during the year for the Station.

1989

Nine services were carried out in 1989, resulting in at least two lives being saved.

The first service of 1989 took place on the 28th February in conjunction with the Liverpool Coastguard Centre (MRSC). At 12.27 p.m. the small cargo vessel POLARLIGHT, registered in Ramsey, broadcast a general "MAYDAY" radio signal for assistance. She had a cargo of bagged cement and was in a position some seven miles North of Ramsey. Four minutes later the UK

R. Oram — Manx Independent

Station Mechanic Jimmy Kneale with his wife Hilda in January, 1988, being presented with a model of the RNLB *James Ball Ritchie* on the occasion of his retirement after 32 years of lifeboat service.

Coastguards paged the Ramsey Lifeboat Crew but for some reason none of the 16 receivers on the Island accepted the signal. On a second attempt, at 12.41 p.m., all Crew Members were successfully alerted and the *James Ball Ritchie* was in the water at 12.54 p.m. Just as the Boat launched the POLARLIGHT sank and her crew of four took to their liferaft. Fortunately the Isle of Man Fishery Protection Vessel ENBARR was on patrol in the area and had also received the distress signal. She picked up the survivors at 1.05 p.m. and landed them in Ramsey. The Lifeboat returned to her Station. The weather was squally with a Westerly gale, force 7 - 9, at the casualty position.

At 2.45 a.m. on the 21st May the Liverpool Coastguards alerted the Hon. Secretary to the fact that the small cabin cruiser SANS PEUR was two miles East of Ramsey with machinery failure and a small engine-room fire. The Skipper, as sole occupant, had requested assistance. The Lifeboat was launched at 2.58 a.m. and headed to the reported position. On nearing it Coxswain Kinnin asked the SANS PEUR to flash a light as nothing could be seen of her. Eventually the casualty was found some two miles East of the Point of Ayre and at 3.55 a.m. a tow line was passed and the return to Ramsey commenced. An hour-and-a-half later the cruiser anchored off the port to await the tide and the Skipper was satisfied that he was in no further danger. The *James Ball Ritchie* was rehoused at 6.30 a.m. It was later found that the engine of the SANS PEUR had severely overheated causing the smoke but it had not caught fire.

Another night-time call-out took place on the 6th June. At 00.20 a.m. the Liverpool Coastguards telephoned Capt. Brew to inform him that the cabin craft WINDRISE, with five people on board, had engine failure 12 miles North of Peel. It was agreed to page the Crew and this was done successfully two minutes later. At 00.35 a.m. the *James Ball Ritchie* was launched and set a course for the Point of Ayre. Five minutes later the services of a small tug were offered by a friend of the owner of the WINDRISE. This vessel was moored in Bangor, Northern Ireland, which was the destination of the casualty. After consultation with the Coastguards it was agreed to accept this help and the Ramsey Lifeboat was recalled. She was beached at 1.00 a.m. ready for rehousing. The weather was calm with good visibility all night.

An aborted call-out took place four days later, on the 10th June. The Liverpool Coastguards telephoned the Hon. Secretary to inform him that the yacht THE FIFTIES, with a failed auxiliary engine, was anchored close to Ramsey Harbour and in difficulties. The sole occupant of the craft was attempting to weigh both his anchors but, with an ESE force 5 wind and moderate seas, he was having little success. As Capt. Brew was speaking to the Coastguards the yacht PIERIS passed the harbour office outward bound. Her Skipper was contacted and asked to assist THE FIFTIES if possible. In the meantime, at 7.10 a.m., the Lifeboat Crew was paged as a precaution. Twice the PIERIS managed to get THE FIFTIES under tow but each time the line parted. Just as the Lifeboat was about to launch word was received that the casualty had got a line ashore on to the harbour wall. The Shore Crew hurried to the scene and the yacht was manhandled to a safe berth in the port.

The attraction (sometimes fatal) of the cliffs at Maughold Head caused yet another Lifeboat call-out at 10.10 p.m. on the 3rd July. Boys will be boys and this time four of them were reported to be trapped on a ledge at the base of the cliffs. This information was passed by the Liverpool Coastguards to the Hon. Secretary and the *James Ball Ritchie* was waterborne at 10.22 p.m. Ten minutes later, however, the Crew was recalled as a nearby resident had used his own dinghy to rescue the youngsters and land them safely.

THE MFV FAY SERVICE

Later, during the first week of July, an escapade in aid of charity took place when two tin baths were paddled across the Irish Sea from Whitehaven to Ramsey. They were accompanied by the small commercial fishing vessel FAY. All went well and the destination was made without mishap. In the early morning of the 6th, the mfv FAY left Ramsey to return to her home port of Whitehaven with nine people aboard. At 4.47 a.m. the Hon. Secretary was telephoned by the Liverpool Coastguard Marine Rescue Centre stating that the FAY was sinking in a position five miles East of Ramsey. The *James Ball Ritchie*, with Coxswain Kinnin at the helm, was away at 5.00 a.m. and soon a full scale search was put into operation. The Ramsey Lifeboat was ordered to set a course for Whitehaven, presuming this would be the track taken by the FAY. Mfv BALCARY, fishing nearby, was the first to join the Lifeboat, then the Isle of Man Steam Packet Company ferries TYNWALD and PEVERIL. Next arrived the RAF Valley helicopter Rescue 122, the mfv's STAR OF PEACE and IRREE LAA and the Nimrod aircraft RESCUE 01. A Naval vessel berthed in Douglas left harbour to assist and the Douglas Lifeboat was also launched. At 5.50 a.m. the *James Ball Ritchie* had passed the original "five miles East of Ramsey" casualty position and requested the Liverpool MRSC for further search instructions. None came and at 07.00 a.m. the Lifeboat was only three-quarters-of-a-mile South of the King William Bank Buoy, some 15 miles from Ramsey. The Coxswain decided that this was too far out and stopped to again try and obtain further instructions. These

R. Oram

The Crew and their families, Summer 1987.
Back row: T. Gaines, J. Crowe (Asst. Mechanic), R. Stanfield, A. Clague, J. Clague, M. Matthews, A. Faragher, C. Jones, G. Evison, J. Kneale (Mechanic), A. Clague, P. Faragher, A. Kinnin,Front row: Mrs. S. Stanfield with Julie and James, Mrs. M. Clague, Mrs. D. Martin, D. Martin (2nd Coxswain), K. Christian, J. Kinnin (Coxswain), Mrs. D. Kinnin, Mrs. M. Gaines, Mrs. H. Kneale.

were received and requested him to steam West for five miles and then turn and search Northwards. At 8.00 a.m. the Nimrod aircraft sighted the survivors in the water clinging on to the tin baths not far from the Point of Ayre. The FAY had sunk. The Douglas Lifeboat soon picked up the survivors and the helicopter then took six of them direct to Noble's Hospital, Douglas, whilst the Lifeboat landed the remaining three people. Their position had been well North of the original search area -- in a position which one would have expected to find them taken on the ebb tide out of Ramsey. The *James Ball Ritchie* was recalled and rehoused at 10.30 a.m. The weather was good throughout with a slight E'ly breeze and calm seas. Fate had looked kindly on the scene that day.

The third service of July took place on the 10th. This time the Hon. Secretary was informed by the Liverpool Coastguard MRSC at 1.50 p.m. that two canoeists in a sponsored paddle around the Island and one occupant of their rescue launch, the SOLITAIRE of Castletown, were having problems at the Point of Ayre. The launch had a rope around her propeller and assistance was requested. The *James Ball Ritchie* was launched at 2.05 p.m. and reached the casualty at 2.55 p.m. Already the canoeists had scrambled ashore at Cranstal and the Auxiliary Coastguard Mobile Unit was informed. A tow for the SOLITAIRE was commenced at 2.53 p.m. and the boats reached the harbour 35 minutes later. The Lifeboat was rehoused at 4.12 p.m. The seas had been slight with a light WNW wind but poor visibility in drizzle.

The evening of the 15th July saw the Crew and Committee Members attending a pleasant Ladies' Guild annual barbecue on the outskirts of Ramsey. As Sod's Law would have it, the Hon. Secretary and Crew were paged in the middle of it at 9.00 p.m. Two canoeists were trapped under the Queen's Pier and assistance was required. The Auxiliary Coastguards were also in attendance. The Lifeboat was away at 9.12 p.m. and found two people clinging on to the Pier structure at water level; one was also holding on to a sail-board and the other a canoe! Apparently the sail-boarder had been blown offshore and managed to get a hold of the Pier structure. The canoeist had seen his plight and gone to assist and found that all he could do was to help the surf-boarder hold on to the Pier. A heaving line was thrown from the Lifeboat and the Coxswain then manoeuvered her close into the Pier in order to pluck the canoeist off the steel legs. The operation was repeated a second time to reach the surf-boarder and the two men and their craft were landed in Ramsey harbour entrance within 12 minutes. The Lifeboat was rehoused at 10.30 p.m. – well after the end of the barbeque! There was a fresh WNW force 5 wind during the service but only a slight sea close into the beach.

July was not finished yet but the last service of the month also turned out to be the last service of the year.

The Lifeboat launch took place at 4.15 p.m. on the 20th, after Capt. Brew had been informed that four girls were in difficulties on a homemade raft near The Carrick (Rock), SE of Ramsey harbour. The Auxiliary Coastguards were also on hand and at 4.25 p.m. it was reported that the girls had scrambled ashore by themselves at Port Lewaigue. The *James Ball Ritchie* was rehoused and refuelled at 5.34 p.m.

At a meeting of the RNLI Executive Committee of the Committee of Management held on the 28th June, 1989, at the Poole Headquarters, the decision was taken to allocate the Mersey Class Fast Carriage Lifeboat ON 1171 to Ramsey. This Lifeboat was to be of fibre-reinforced composite construction (FRC) and have a speed of about 17 knots. According to the building schedule the boat would be handed over to the RNLI in the autumn of 1990 and following trials and Crew training, be delivered to Ramsey early in 1991.

Later in the year, following discussions with Mrs. Ann Ritchie, it was announced that the new Lifeboat would be called *Ann and James Ritchie*. The Branch Committee and Crew expressed their delight that the contribution to the RNLI by Mrs. Ritchie and her late husband was to be recognised in this way.

The main consequence of the allocation of the new Lifeboat was that the Norbury Boathouse would have to be demolished to make way for a new one on the same site. The Norbury Boathouse would not provide the necessary internal height or floor strength to accommodate the new boat, its carriage and heavy tractor, without major alterations. As the cost of alterations would be a large percentage of the cost of a new boathouse the decision was taken to demolish and rebuild.

A Royal Visit

On the 8th August Coxswain James Kinnin and the other Crew and Committee Members were spoken to by Her Majesty the Queen and the Duke of Edinburgh when they paid a brief visit to Ramsey as a part of their day on the Isle of Man. The Royal Party landed from the Royal Yacht Britannia at Peel and boarded her again in the late afternoon in Douglas Bay. That evening produced a fine spectacle off Douglas. A fireworks display was held on the beach with a backcloth provided by Britannia, her Naval escort, HMS Amazon and the Northern Lighthouses Board tender, Fingal, dressed overall with white lights and floodlit. The Tower of Refuge was also well lit as usual and flying the RNLI ensign; Sir William Hillary would, no doubt, have been pleased with the attention paid to his Institution Crews and Members by the Monarch of the day in 1989 and on and by those same waters which, in tempest, brought the tragedies and unselfish heroism which led, through his efforts, to our RNLI.

Despite national and local opposition the Ramsey Coastguard Marine Rescue Sub-Centre ceased operations shortly after 9.00 a.m. on 17th January, 1989. Operational responsibility was transferred to the Liverpool Coastguard MRSC. At the A.G.M. the Branch Officers and Committee thanked all the Coastguards who had served Ramsey over the years and for their co-operation and friendship. The 17th January was a sad day for the Branch and the end of a long era of co-operation between the two Services. District Controller Appleton was to continue residing in Ramsey, however, and would remain a valued Committee Member.

On the 11th February Coxswain Kinnin and a Crew from Ramsey left Dumbarton to deliver the Port Erin Lifeboat to the Isle of Man at the end of an extensive refit. Severe weather prevented completion of this passage, however, and the boat was left in the care of the Troon Branch in order that Coxswain Kinnin and his men could return to Ramsey. The Lifeboat was eventually delivered by a Crew from Troon. The relief Lifeboat from Port Erin was then delivered to Holyhead by 2nd Cox Ray Stanfield and a Ramsey Crew on the 24th February, ready for her onward passage to Barmouth.

On the 6th May Commodore George Cooper, Chief of RNLI Operations, paid an informal visit to the Station whilst on a visit to Ramsey to speak at a very successful fund-raising dinner organised by the Ladies' Guild.

On Lifeboat Day, the 19th August, the Station's Administrative Officer, Sqn. Ldr. John Sands, was presented with the Institution's Silver Badge in recognition of his services to the Branch. The Annual Appeal that day was made by Mr. Paul Moulton of Manx Radio and raised £2519. The Ladies' Guild was congratulated as always; 1989 saw yet another record year for money raised. The annual total of £15,000 was remitted to RNLI Headquarters at Poole.

B. P. Grenfell

Launching the *James Ball Ritchie* into an approaching storm. March, 1986.

B. P. Grenfell

Launching the *James Ball Ritchie* - leaving the carriage. March, 1986.

2nd Cox Ray Stanfield received a serious injury to his foot whilst at work on the 10th August. This caused him to stand down temporarily from the Crew and Mr. Kevin Christian took his place.

1990

The *James Ball Ritchie* was launched for six services in 1990.

The first of these took place at 11.33 a.m. on the 20th March. The weather was good with a SW'ly force 3 breeze and a slight sea. At 11.20 a.m. the Hon. Secretary was telephoned by the Liverpool Coastguards and asked to launch the Lifeboat to assist a person who was thought to have fallen over the cliff at the Dhoon. The Lifeboat was at sea within 13 minutes and reached Cornaa at 12.18 p.m. A search Southwards commenced but at 12.57 p.m. the Auxiliary Coastguards, also at the scene on the shore, reported that they had not found anyone in difficulty. The *James Ball Ritchie* slowly retraced her track to Ramsey, searching on the way. Nothing was found and she was rehoused at 2.15 p.m. The Coastguards later reported that as they completed their return cliff climb they had met two people on the path. It was thought that perhaps these persons had been considered by the caller to be in trouble. 2nd Cox Ray Stanfield was back in the Crew for this service. Remarkably he had not missed any services during his incapacity.

Yet another cliff tragedy took place on the 12th April. The Crew was paged direct from Liverpool at 3.55 p.m. to attend a person who had fallen over a cliff edge near Maughold Head. The *James Ball Ritchie* was away at 4.05 p.m. and arrived at the scene near the Lighthouse in 20 minutes. The Coastguard Team descended the cliff and the Lifeboat dinghy was used by two of the Lifeboatmen who went ashore to give assistance. Sadly, the casualty, a young boy, was found to be dead. A Doctor arrived at 4.54 p.m. and the Police gave permission for the body to be returned to Ramsey aboard the *James Ball Ritchie* to a waiting ambulance. The Lifeboat was refuelled and ready for service again at 6.38 p.m. The funeral service was held a week later at Christ Church, the Dhoon, and Coxswain Jim Kinnin together with the Police Sergeant Ian Bradshaw, Coastguard Officer Philip Corlett and Ambulance Driver John Kaighen, representing some 40 people involved in the rescue attempt, acted as pall bearers. Mrs. Ann Ritchie, President of the Ramsey RNLI Branch and the Ladies' Lifeboat Guild and long-time benefactor of the RNLI, was cremated the same day in Douglas. Branch Chairman Dr. E.C.B. Corlett and Mrs. E. Corlett, Sqn. Ldr. and Mrs. J. Sands and many others represented the Ramsey Station at the funeral and Mr. A.K. Oliver, Head of the Fund Raising Committee and others represented the RNLI Headquarters, Poole.

The yacht JONIKA with a failed auxiliary engine called for assistance at 5.20 a.m. on the 30th April. She was off Maughold Head, becalmed in thick fog and concerned about being run down by another vessel. This was reported to Capt. Brew via Liverpool and the Lifeboat was launched at 5.38 a.m. Very soon afterwards Mechanic Martin established vhf contact with the yacht and a good vhf D/F bearing was obtained and used to find her. The two boats met at 6.51 a.m. and within four minutes a tow was established and a course set for Ramsey. The JONIKA had to anchor off the harbour at 7.35 a.m. owing to the tide but the *James Ball Ritchie* was released, recovered and ready for duty again at 8.55 a.m.

At 10.35 a.m. on the 5th August the Deputy Launching Authority was asked by the Liverpool Coastguards to authorise the launch of the *James Ball Ritchie* to join a search for a cabin cruiser with a crew of three overdue from Drummore in Southern Scotland. The Ramsey Lifeboat was away at 10.52 a.m. and headed for the Point of Ayre where Coxswain Kinnin was given an area to search to the North West by the Liverpool MRSC. Three other lifeboats and a helicopter made up the rescue team. Visibility was good in a force 6 - 7 NW'ly wind. The sea was rough. Six-and-a-half hours were spent searching without success and at 5.57 p.m. the *James Ball Ritchie* was released from the area and returned to her Station. It was 8.25 p.m. before she was rehoused. Coxswain Kinnin experienced difficulties with the radio communications on this service and all messages had to be relayed to the Clyde Coastguards via either Liverpool or Belfast. The casualty was found the next day at 7.40 a.m. by the mfv GOLDEN REAPER. She was off the Niarbyl on the Island's West Coast, South of Peel. All occupants were safe.

The Isle of Man registered cabin cruiser EMJAY suffered engine failure one-and-a-half miles North of the Point of Ayre at 3.46 p.m. on the 26th August. She had a crew of three. The weather was fresh with a moderate sea from the SSW wind, force 4 - 5. The Hon. Secretary was advised of the occurrence by the Liverpool Coastguards and the Lifeboat was launched at 4.01 p.m. with 2nd Cox Stanfield in charge. By the time the casualty was reached at 4.55 p.m. another yacht had taken up the required tow. The *James Ball Ritchie* took over the task and brought the EMJAY back to her own mooring in Ramsey harbour. The Lifeboat was back on station at 7.25 p.m.

A LONG SEARCH

A long search constituted the last service of 1990 for the *James Ball Ritchie*. At 11.10 p.m. on the 1st October the Hon. Secretary of the

B. P. Grenfell

Recovery. The relief lifeboat *Vincent Nesfield* being prepared for the carriage, March, 1987.

B. P. Grenfell

Recovery. The *Vincent Nesfield* being eased on to her carriage, March, 1987.

Peel RNLI Branch telephoned Capt. Brew to inform him that their inshore Lifeboat had launched to search for the small fishing vessel SERENITY which was overdue in Peel. Liverpool Coastguards were asked for an update on the incident and at that point a request was made for the *James Ball Ritchie* to be launched. This was done at 11.35 p.m. and 2nd Cox Stanfield as Acting Cox. was asked to search one-and-a-half miles offshore from the Point of Ayre to Peel. Peel Castle was reached at 2.34 a.m. and the 2nd coxswain asked permission to return on a reciprocal course, but this time two and a half miles offshore. At 4.40 a.m. the Lifeboat was off Ballaugh Cronk beach on the West Coast and it was agreed for her to return direct to Ramsey, refuel and resume the search later, in daylight.

The *James Ball Ritchie* departed Ramsey at 8.15 a.m. on the 2nd to search Ramsey Bay. Only 10 minutes later she was recalled as the casualty had been discovered ashore near Strangford Lough, Northern Ireland. As work was underway on rebuilding the Boathouse, the beach was not immediately clear for recovery and the Lifeboat remained on station in the harbour until 1.15 p.m. It was later reported that the owner of the SERENITY had had a heart attack and died whilst fishing and his boat had steamed out of control Westwards until she grounded in Northern Ireland.

The last Branch Committee Meeting to be held in the original Norbury Boathouse took place on the 1st March, 1990, just a few months under the 100 years of its existence. On the 20th March, the new era for the Ramsey RNLI Station began when demolition work commenced on the old Boathouse. It was the start of the major investment programme in Ramsey, promised by the RNLI. By the 10th May the site had been cleared and on the 2nd July an Isle of Man firm, Messrs. Parkinson Ltd., the main contractors, began work on the New Norbury Boathouse. It was completed early in 1991.

Prior to this demolition, Members of the Crew, Committee and Guild removed all useful items from the Boathouse. This included the timber floor of the Committee Room which was to be used as the floor to the new Crew Room. A temporary Crew Room was set up in a building formerly used by the Coastguards and taken over by the Royal Naval Auxiliary Service. A container was sited on the promenade to store various items of gear and the Lifeboat, its carriage and tractor, stood out the months on the slipway. All furniture, framed photographs, pictures, books and records were put into safe storage.

Between the 5th March and the 1st May an RNLI Mobile Training Unit and Instructor were on the Island and the Ramsey Crew, together with those from other Stations, took full advantage of this facility to improve their radar, navigation and radio skills.

On the 26th March, at very short notice, Coxswain Kinnin and a Crew took the *James Ball Ritchie* to Workington, Cumbria, to carry out a series of beaching, recovery and launching trials. The Ramsey Lifeboat was required as a result of a breakdown of a relief Mersey Class Lifeboat whilst on a passage to carry out this work. This resulted in no Lifeboat being stationed at Ramsey for three days but fortunately no call came for a service. The Coxswain and Crew later received a letter of thanks from Commodore George Cooper, Chief of RNLI Operations, for their contribution during two very busy days at Workington.

On the 12th May, Mr. Hugh Fogarty, Deputy Divisional Inspector, paid a brief visit to Ramsey to introduce Mr. George Rawlinson who was to succeed him on the 2nd June. Twelve days later a similar introductory visit was paid by the outgoing Inspector Michael Vlasto with his successor, Mr. Jeffery Mankertz. Mr. Vlasto was thanked by all concerned for his assistance and friendship during his service as District Inspector and he was wished well in his new post at Headquarters with responsibilities for all aspects of crew training.

Committee Meetings throughout the rest of 1990 were held in the Ocean Ranger Room at Shipdesine House, Ramsey, by kind permission of Burness Corlett and Partners, the naval architects.

A report was made on the progress of the Boathouse Appeal (or Building Fund) on the 7th June. To that date some £109,000 had been committed locally to the cost of the new Boathouse which was estimated to be £250,000. The opening ceremony was tentatively fixed for the first week of April, 1991, and Mrs. Helen Vlasto had agreed to perform the official duties on the day. It was hoped that HRH the Duke of Kent would consent to name the new Lifeboat during the summer of 1991 and that the Lord Bishop of Sodor and Man would dedicate it.

At the A.G.M. on the 6th December the Branch Treasurer, Mr. Steven Spencer, told the gathering that the year had been another record one for fund-raising by the Ladies' Guild and the figure was £16,230 overall. £12,500 had been committed to Branch Funds and £3730 to the Building Account. This latter Fund now stood at £137,416.

During the year the President of the Branch and President of the Ladies' Guild, Mrs. Ann Ritchie, died. It was sad to note that she had not lived to see the new Lifeboat *Ann and James Ritchie* with which she had been so closely associated. Similarly her husband had not lived to see the old *James Ball Ritchie* delivered to the Station in 1970.

Island Photographics Isle of Man Examiner

Trials of the new Talus MBH 200 hp tractor on her arrival at Ramsey on the 28th November, 1990.

Washing down the *James Ball Ritchie* before housing, 1988. B. P. Grenfell
L. to R: R. Crowe, K. Christian, K. Airey, J. Clague.

Ernest Collister, former Tractor Driver, Helper and Maintenance Mechanic and Jackie Corkish died in 1990.

THE BIGLAND TALUS TRACTOR

During the forenoon of Wednesday, 28th November, 1990, the huge 17-ton Bigland Talus tractor arrived in Ramsey on a low-loader trailer after her delivery journey from Knighton, in Powys, Wales, It was a cold, grey day but there were smiles on the faces of the Members of the Branch who had gathered for the occasion and who were eagerly waiting to put the monster through her paces. The manufacturers had their engineers on hand and RNLI Western Divisional Inspector J. Mankertz attended the trials.

The Isle of Man Examiner reporter Sue Wooley covered the event and headed her report;

"250,000 land giant takes to the sea at Ramsey with the greatest of ease." She continued:

"Thundering over the sands in a seventeen -and-a-half ton tractor, leaving behind a deep trail of catapillar tracks, is an exhilirating experience. But the adrenalin really begins to flow when you head straight for the sea and the water begins to lap around the sides. This is exciting enough for a reporter being giving a test drive by the Station Mechanic - but in true emergency, with rough seas breaking over the top of the cab, it would be a situation calling for supreme confidence and capability.

These are qualities which are fortunately possessed in great abundance by the Crew of the Ramsey Lifeboat, whose new custom-built, quarter-of-a-million-pound tractor represents just part of the RNLI's investment in the Ramsey Station. the Talus MBH 200hp tractor is a truly remarkable machine -- the first to be specifically designed for the task of launching carriage lifeboats. Lifeboat tractors were previously converted from commercial designs. The development of this machine took place in local quaries and on farm roads and the prototype was tested in the most arduous launching conditions. Trials were completed in 1982 and the Ramsey tractor is the 20th to go on station.

The arrival of the diesel-powered Talus on November 28th caused a stir in Ramsey. Tractor Driver Juan Sable, who is a member of the Shore Crew and Station Mechanic Jimmy Martin, who is part of the sea-going Crew, had been away to Knighton on a course and were keen to put the tractor through its paces for the rest of the Crew.

Jimmy, who took over as Station Mechanic in 1987, explained that the system of launching was exactly the same, but leaves the driver feeling much more confident, especially in rough seas, as this model has been specially designed for the job. Whereas its predecessor was completely open to the elements, the Talus has a totally enclosed, fully watertight cab and is capable of operating at a greater depth of water.

A low-water launch from Ramsey beach can present a particular problem, especially if there is an Easterly gale blowing, because the tractor has to negotiate two banks of sand before the boat can be launched. This is where the Talus comes into its own.

As it enters the water, bilge pumps begin to operate and the driver has the confidence of knowing that is cab is fully watertight and can operate efficiently in up to eight feet of water.

Once the lauch is completed, the driver simply turns his seat around and pushes the joy-stick forward. If the worst comes to the worst and heavy seas make it impossible to move, the driver can climb out of an escape hatch in the roof. With the hatches battened down, the tractor would remain safe until low tide allowed it to be recovered.

Other features include two quartz iodine headlights fitted at each end in glazed watertight boxes and two quartz iodine floodlights mounted at each end of the cab roof. Because the tractor has been specifically designed, it has been possible to build in a very efficient air cooling system for use on the beach. When the tractor enters the water, a pair of protected keel coolers take over automatically.

The RNLI's current investment programme in Ramsey amounts to close on three-quarters-of-a-million pounds and the local Branch is doing its utmost to make a significant contribution to that cost.

A new boathouse is currently under construction to house the new Mersey Class fast carriage boat, the *Ann and James Ritchie,* which is due on station in the spring and will replace the 21 years old *James Ball Ritchie.*

The days of man-handling or horse-drawing the lifeboat to the water's edge are long past, and with its powerful new tractor and state of the art vessel, the Ramsey Branch looks forward eargerly to a new era in its history".

In mid-February, 1991, the Isle of Man Post Office Authority paid tribute to the Island's RNLI Stations by issuing a set of five postage stamps which figured each of the five lifeboats currently guarding the local coasts. The 17p value stamp depicted the Tyne Class lifeboat of Douglas, *Sir William Hillary;* the 21p value, Port Erin's Rother Class, *Osman Gabriel;* the 31p stamp the Port St. Mary Arun Class *The Gough Ritchie,* the 37p value the Atlantic 21 Class, *John Batstone* of Peel; and the 26p stamp showed the Ramsey Mersey Class boat *Ann and James Ritchie* which arrived on station in July. The set was designed by Andie Peck and will undoubtedly become a collector's item.

The day of Saturday, 6th April, dawned with grey skies and a fresh SE'ly wind. By mid-morning heavy rain was being blown into Ramsey Bay before a force 6-7 near gale. The *James Ball Ritchie,* on her carriage, took the stand on the slipway with bunting streaming from her rigging and looking as smart as she did on her arrival at Ramsey in 1970. It was to be the official Opening of the Norbury Boathouse at 11.30 a.m. and the weather gave no consideration to that fact whatsover!

A large crowd braved the elements and

B. P. Grenfell

100 years old and looking her age! The Norbury Boathouse in 1990.

B. P. Grenfell

1990. Inside the Norbury Boathouse. Note some of the Service Boards on the right-hand wall.

B. P. Grenfell

The New Norbury Boathouse under construction December, 1990.

B. P. Grenfell

The New Norbury Boathouse, operational in March, 1991.
To the right of the main door is the RNLI shop, managed by the Ladies' Guild and above it the well fitted-out Crew Room.

A. Lowe

Station Committee Chairman Dr. E. C. B. Corlett addressing the guests at the Opening of the New Norbury Boathouse on Saturday, 6th April, 1991. Mr. G. R. Newman, a Vice-President of the RNLI Committee of Management, is sitting on the left.

A. Lowe

Mrs Edna Corlett receiving the RNLI Silver Badge at the Opening of the New Norbury Boathouse from Mr. G. R. Newman, for her 10 years service as Hon. Secretary and Chairman of the Ramsey Ladies' Lifeboat Guild.

gathered inside the Boathouse, well-clad in raincoats, hats and waterproof footwear. The scene was brightened by more bunting, flags and flowers and not least by the Ramsey Town Band resplendent in their red and gold uniforms. The music was very tuneful and vibrant and gave the occasion an atmosphere of celebration in contrast to the austere conditions outside.

After singing the National Anthem and the Manx National Anthem, the gathering sat down for Dr. Ewan Corlett, Branch Chairman, to open proceedings with an initial address. He said that the old Boathouse was built in 1890-91 and now, 100 years later, a new one was in place. He thanked everyone for all their hard work and sheer determination and stated that about £150,000 -- a large proportion of the cost of the Boathouse -- had been raised locally by special efforts, donations and legacies. Dr. Corlett said that he did wish to mention one special gift of £22,000 by Mr. Harney in memory of his late wife. This had been used to furnish and equip the new Crew Room. He then introduced the Chairman of the RNLI Search and Rescue Committee, Mr. Graham Newman, who was accompanied by his wife.

Next, posies were presented to the Chief Guest, Mrs. Helen Vlasto, and Mrs. Newman by Jemma Martin and Julie Stanfield, daughters of serving Lifeboatmen. Mrs. Vlasto is the wife of Michael Vlasto, the former Wester Divisional Inspector of Lifeboats and now in charge of crew training at the Poole Headquarters.

Mr. Newman then presented Mrs. Edna Corlett, the Chairman's wife, with the Institution's Silver Badge in recognition of her 14 years' service to the Ladies' Lifeboat Guild, 10 of which she spent as Honorary Secretary followed by four years as Chairman. Mr. Newman spoke of the work of the RNLI and the future programme of modernisation and he mentioned that he had just visited all the Island's five Lifeboat Stations and was very impressed with all that he had seen. He noted the cost of this new Boathouse and said that in 1890 the initial Norbury Boathouse had cost £1,733. The Mersey Class Lifeboat soon to be stationed at Ramsey had cost a further £500,000. Mr. Newman told his audience that soon Ramsey's Crew would be leaving for Poole for training before delivering the *Ann and James Ritchie* to her station.

Mr. George Rawlinson, Deputy Inspector of Lifeboats, Western Division, followed with a talk on the background of the New Norbury Boathouse and the new lifeboat and equipment.

Dr. Corlett next invited Mrs. Vlasto to officially declare the New Norbury Boathouse "Open" and this she did by unveiling a plaque in Manx Slate giving the date of the ceremony. The Rev. D. B. Foster, Honorary Chaplain to the Station, dedicated the Boathouse. All then joined in singing maritime hymns ending with the moving Manx Fishermen's Evening Hymn. Capt. Michael Brew, Honorary Branch Secretary and Harbour Master, closed the proceedings with a vote of thanks to the Guests and Officials. A buffet

A. Lowe

Opening the New Norbury Boathouse, 6th April, 1991, Mrs. Helen Vlasto, wife of the former Western Divisional Lifeboat Inspector, and Coxswain Jim Kinnin.

A. Lowe

Opening the New Norbury Boathouse, 1991.
Some of the guests, including the Chairman of the Ramsey Commissioners, Mr. W. Irving, and, standing left of centre, Mr. M. Vlasto, RNLI Staff Officer (Crew Training).

A. Lowe

Opening the New Norbury Boathouse, 1991. Captain M. Brew, Station Hon. Secretary, giving the closing address.

A. Lowe

Opening the New Norbury Boathouse, 1991. The Ramsey Town Band at full throttle.

lunch was next on the agenda and everyone made a dash, in the very persistent rain, to St. Paul's Hall..

(It was later confirmed that out of the £174,000 cost of the New Norbury Boathouse, £148,000 -- some 85% of the total -- had been raised in Ramsey.)

The demolition of the 100-years-old Norbury Boathouse took place in May 1990, and early in July Parkinsons Ltd., the Douglas builders, commenced work on the New Norbury Boathouse. This is a very different type of building to the old one and took seven months to complete. The foundations are of heavily reinforced concrete to take the 17 tonnes tractor, the carriage and the 14 tonnes of Lifeboat. The main Boathouse frames and beams are of galvanised steel and because of the very narrow space between its walls and the adjoining buildings, the roof was constructed first. The lower side walls were then built up of brick and masonry to two-thirds' height and these were topped by sheet steel cladding of "W" shaped section which was weatherproofed by an outer lining of plasticated material. On the inside are insulated plain steel panels. The completed building is 20.5 metres long, 9.3 metres wide and 7.3 metres high at the apex. Skylights let daylight into the Lifeboat area and the main door is steel with a concertina action. On the ground floor at the right is a fitted Lifeboat Shop which is manned by the Ladies' Lifeboat Guild. Above this an upper floor runs for about two-thirds of the length of the main structure and contains a well fitted-out Crew Room, drying room and toilet. The pitch pine floor of the old Committee Room was taken up and re-used for this area. The furniture was fitted by Coxswain Kinnin. Parkinsons' handed the new keys over to Hon. Secretary Capt. Mike Brew on the 31st January, 1991. It was, however, sad to lose the old Committee Room together with all the historical artifacts of the Station. They have no place in these modern times, so it seems.

The first service of the year took place eight days after the official opening of the Boathouse. At 1.30 p.m., 14th April, on a quiet Sunday afternoon, Capt. Ken Horsley was Duty Harbour Master and working at his desk in the Harbour Office. To his astonishment he suddenly saw through his window a small motor car plunge from the North Quay wall into the harbour. The Police were informed immediately and Capt. Horsley then ran to the South wall and found the car driver on the surface and shouting that his passenger was trapped in the vehicle. A lifebuoy was thrown to the survivor and he was assisted ashore with the help of two passers-by. Meanwhile the Isle of Man Coastguard Marine Rescue Unit was alerted and they informed the Liverpool Coastguards who in turn requested the Lifeboat to launch. Police Constable Steven Grainger was on the scene within minutes and he immediately stripped off his uniform and dived into the harbour. He did his utmost to get the passenger door open but was unable to do so. The cold waters forced him to retire and he came ashore. The *James Ball Ritchie* was afloat at 1.39 p.m. and made haste round the South pier into the harbour and helped an amateur diver to relocate the car, buoy its position and attatch a towline. Initially the Lifeboat towed the vehicle along the bottom towards the shingle beach near the Swing Bridge but the weight of the tow was so great that steering the *James Ball Ritchie* with any accuracy became impossible. This prevented her from getting the car completely clear of the water but it did enable the second occupant of the car to be recovered, although, sadly, too late. The Talus lifeboat tractor later completed the salvage with the aid of the Local Authorities and many helpers. Listed for this service were Coxswain J. Kinnin, 2nd Coxswain R. Stanfield, Station Mechanic J. Martin, Asst. Mechanic R. Crowe and Crew Members M. Kenyon, K. Airey and A. J. Clague. The Head Launcher was A. Faragher with Tractor Driver J. Sable, Assistant P. Faragher and Lightman J. Kneale. The Station Helpers included A. Midwood, D. Corlett, B. Killip, A. Gaines, A. Clague, K. Holland, I.Clague, N. Crowe, P. Cubberley and P. Faragher. Ramsey-based Police Constable Grainger later received the Chief Constable's Commendation for his attempted rescue.

On the 26th May, another Sunday, the Island was in the throes of the T.T. fortnight; the famous motor-cycle road-racing events. It was also the day of the Round the Island Yacht Race, organised annually by the Ramsey-based Manx Sailing and Cruising Club. Hundreds of motor cyclists and local residents were watching sand-racing on the Ramsey beach. At 3.55 p..m. the Deputy Launching Authority and Branch Administrative Officer, Sqn. Ldr. John Sands, overheard on his radio scanner the Liverpool Coastguards receiving a MAYDAY distress call from a dismasted yacht, although he was unaware of her location. Within minutes the U.K. Coastguards telephoned the DLA and requested the Lifeboat to be launched. Further paging signals were not received in Ramsey but several Crew Members who were near the Boathouse at the time, including 2nd Coxswain Stanfield, also heard the MAYDAY distress call on their scanners and realised that there was a strong possibility that a launch was in the offing. When the order came the maroons were fired and the response by the remainder of the Crew was immediate and the Lifeboat was away at 4.20 p.m., under Coxswain Kinnin. The weather was good with a calm sea and a light

Westerly breeze. The casualty turned out to be the auxiliary multi-hulled yacht DUBBLE TRUBBLE which was amongst the leaders of the race. She was sighted at 5.00 p.m. off the Dhoon Glen, just North of Laxey, and taken in tow. At 6.10p.m. she anchored off Ramsey to await the tide and was able to berth later using her own outboard motor. (This engine was of a small capacity and unsuitable for steaming any distance). The *James Ball Ritchie* was rehoused at 6.45 p..m..

So ended the long career of this noble Lifeboat at Ramsey. She was not called upon again for a service and on the 12th July, 1991, the new Mersey Class RNLB *Ann and James Ritchie* took over her tasks. The *James Ball Ritchie* is to remain in Ramsey Harbour until lifeboat Day on the 27th July and then two days later Coxswain Jim Kinnin and a crew are to sail the boat to the Clyde where she will undergo a special survey and if found fit, will pass into the rescue fleet of the RNLI for relief duties around the UK coasts.

During her 21 years at the port, she was launched some 140 times on services, saved 76 lives and recovered 21 vessels. (see the List of Services).

THE RNLI PRAYER

Merciful Father, all things in Heaven and Earth are held with your loving care, look with favour upon the Royal National Lifeboat Institution.
Protect and bless the crews of all their lifeboats and all those who risk their own safety to bring help to others.
Guide all who work for the Institution that they may be faithful to the vision of its founders, so that it may always be seen as a beacon of hope and light to those who find themselves in peril on the seas.
Through the same Jesus Christ, to whom with you and the Holy Spirit be Honour and Glory, now and forever. Amen.

CHAPTER 10

The Ramsey Ladies' Lifeboat Guild
1913 - 1991

THE present-day Ladies' Lifeboat Guild started out as the Ladies' Auxiliary in 1913. Unfortunately the early history of the Guild has had to be gleaned from the original Minutes Books of the Branch Committee, as the records of the Ladies' Committee are only avaialble from 1940.

It was at a Branch Committee Meeting in the Ramsey Court House on the 28th February, 1913, that it was resolved to set up the Ladies' Auxiliary. Elections were held and Mrs. Cruickshank took the Presidency with Mrs. Norbury, Vice-President, Mrs. M. W. Harrison, Chairman, Mrs. H. K. Callow, Treasurer, and Miss Paton and Miss Garrett, joint Honorary Secretaries. Mrs. Harrison was the wife of the Rev. M. W. Harrison, Vicar of South Ramsey from 1911 and a Member of the RNLI Committee. He later became a Canon and Chairman of the Ramsey Town Commissioners and was Chairman of the RNLI Branch Committee for 20 years. Mrs. Harrison was re-elected annually as Chairman of the Ladies' Committee until her death in 1954.

The main purpose of the Ladies' Auxiliary was to raise funds for the Ramsey Station and to assist in the events which took place connected with the running of the Lifeboat. The first income recorded was shown in the 1917 Annual Report of the Branch. It lists, amongst other monies received from various sources, " From Ramsey Palace...£7. 1s 0d and Y.M.C.A. Concert....£2. 10s. 0d." No doubt these events were arranged by the Ladies. Only two years later in 1919, with the same Ladies' Auxiliary Officers at the helm, the Annual Report included "Summer Effort...£100 1s. 4d." From that year until the 1940's the annual sum raised by the ladies and donated to the General Branch Funds appeared to range between £50 and £142. This latter sum was raised in 1920 and enabled the Branch to remit £100 to the RNLI Headquarters.

During 1926 the name of the Ladies' Auxiliary changed to the Ladies' Guild and a year later to the Ladies' Lifeboat Guild. In 1926 the Officers of their Committee had hardly changed and were listed as Mrs. Groves, President; Mrs. Harrison, Chairman; Mrs. Callow, Hon. Treasurer; Miss Garrett and Miss Paton, joint Hon. Secretaries, and Miss I. B. Clucas. Four years later the Committee list showed that Mrs. Harrison and Mrs. Chrystal had been elected to join the main body of gentlemen members and it later became accepted practice for the Chairman and Hon. Secretary of the Ladies' Committee to become members of the Branch Committee.

By 1933 the number of Ladies' Lifeboat Guild members had risen to 15 and two years later to 17. This gradually increased over the years to the large body of ladies now associated with lifeboat activities. The main fund-raising event of each year has always been Lifeboat Day (or Flag Day) which is held in the summer months. Apart from the Annual Appeal, which is often given by the Lt. Governor, an Island dignitary or a U.K. celebrity speaking from the Boathouse precincts, a house-to-house and street-to-street collection throughout the town and outlying Northern districts is made for funds. Numerous other events are also staged on Ramsey Lifeboat Day to raise money to maintain the Station and its Lifeboat. In modern times regular events are arranged by the Guild throughout the year with coffee mornings, barbecues, film shows, lectures, bridge and whist drives, rummage sales and buffet suppers -- all bringing in the necessary income.

At the Branch AGM in November, 1938, it was reported that Mrs. Groves had died. She had been the Guild President since 1923.

The 1940s

During the Second World War the Guild decided to concentrate the fund-raising annually on Lifeboat Day because so many other war charity events were being staged throughout the year in connection with the war effort. In 1946 the sum of £132 was raised on Flag Day and for many years this sum was only exceeded at the same event in 1949 when it was coupled with the naming ceremony of the new Lifeboat, the *Thomas Corbett*. On that occasion the record sum of £178 was reached. The ladies also paid a standard annual subscription to the Branch, in line with Members of the main Committee. From the Minutes Book records it seems that only one Ladies' Lifeboat Guild meeting was held each year during the 1940s.

1951 saw two members of the Ladies' Lifeboat Guild recognised by the Institution. Mrs. M. Quayle, Hon. Secretary, and Mrs. G. Teare,Hon. Treasurer, received an official Record of Thanks from the RNLI for their work for the Station. They had served as officers since 1940 and were Committee Members before that. Mrs. Quayle served for a further two years after which she resigned. Her position was taken by Mrs. E. Waters.

From 1953 more frequent Guild meetings were held and suggestions were made to increase the fund-raising events. It was also agreed to increase the membership of the Committee. It then stood at 19 but by 1955 had increased to 40. The annual memnership subscription was discontinued because of the success of the increased number of events then being organised.

On the 7th May, 1954, Mrs. M. W. Harrison, Chairman, died in hospital. She had held the post for 41 years. Mrs. R. Kneale was elected the new Chairman in her stead. Later in the summer a fete was held and the £125 profits were passed to the Branch Treasurer. The record sum of £196 was raised on Lifeboat Day and a whist drive and dance held at Andreas raised a further £36. In 1954 mention was also made of an impending visit of Her Majesty The Queen to Ramsey on the 9th August, but no other details were given in the records.

In 1958 Miss. R. Shaw was elected the Hon. Secretary and an Executive Committee of all the Guild Officers plus a further eight Committee Members was formed to run the day-to-day business. A year later changes in the rules for the election of the Chairmen were made. It was decided that the Chairman should stand for re-election annually for a period of three consecutive years but after that should stand down. It was further decided that after such a period the Chairman should automatically become a member of the Executive Committee.

The 1960s

A press cutting in one of the Minutes Books for 1961 states:

> "The Lifeboat Day collection in Ramsey and district have again beaten the record this year - by nearly £35 - and the Ramsey Ladies' Lifeboat Guild wish to express their warm thanks to all collectors and to those who contributed so generously, enabling the magnificent sum of £243 11s 5d to be raised."

These figures gradually increased throughout the 1960s and the annual coffee mornings became very popular and alone raised £134 in 1964 increasing to £241 in 1969. These were originally held in private houses, then in the Mooragh Park Cafe and eventually by 1973, in St. Paul's Hall, which was more central and easily available to the general public. Raffles and souvenir sales always took place.

At the end of 1961 the Executive Committee

Ladies' Guild collection

Mrs. Lily Harrison who was elected as the first Chairman, in 1913, of the Ladies' Auxiliary and continued as Chairman of the Ladies' Committee for the next 41 years. She was awarded the RNLI Gold Badge.

had increased to 12 and it was decided to keep it at that level. This included eight elected Members and four ex-officio and therefore two Members were asked to resign annually by rota. A year later Mrs. E. MacEwan completed her three years as Chairman and stood down and Mrs. G. Teare was elected in her place. Miss R. Shaw was elected Secretary and also Hon. Treasurer as a temporary measure.

In 1963 Her Majesty The Queen Mother visited Ramsey and although the records show that the Lifeboat Crew was invited to attend in Parliament Square for the occasion there was no mention of the Ladies' Guild or Branch Committee Members being present.

1965 proved a landmark year for fund-raising and Lifeboat Day produced £287. The Appeal was given by the well known entertainer Val Doonican. By the financial year-end the Guild had reached the £500 figure. Discussions took place at several meetings in the year on limiting the size of membership, It had currently grown to 42 members and although a further 46 non-members had assisted in the Flag Day collections, it was suggested that a limit should be set on the numbers and possibly a waiting list opened. This was not thought to be feasible by the majority and the matter dropped. However, it was decided to draw up a new set of rules for the Guild in due course.

This year was the last for Mrs. G. Teare, J.P., as Chairman, she had accrued 43 years of service to the Ladies' Guild and been on the Committee since 1922, In total, three new Committee Officers were elected on the 10th November, 1965, and the committee was led by the new Chairman, Miss F. Weldon, Hon. Secretary Mrs. T. Weldhen, and Hon. Treasurer Mrs. W. Corlett.

The first important event of 1966 took place when the Chairman of the RNLI, Captain the Hon. V. M. Wyndham-Quin, R.N., visited the Norbury Boathouse and had coffee with the Guild, Crew and Branch Committee Members. On the 8th June, 1966, Major Disley, the RNLI Area Organising Secretary, presented Mrs. G. Teare with the Institution's Silver Badge for her many years of service to the Branch. The ceremony was held at the Grand Island Hotel and was followed by a luncheon. With the usual coffee morning, Flag Day and attendance at the Manx Agricultural Show, five events were recorded for the year instead of the usual two.

The Ramsey Courier newspaper annually carried Christmas Appeals for Charity and the RNLI Branch regularly benefitted from these.

July 11th, 1967, was a red letter day for the Ladies' Guild. Chairman Miss F. Weldon accompanied Branch Chairman Major Keith Grimble Groves to a London reception in honour of H.R.H. Princess Marina's 25 years as President of the RNLI.

In November Mrs. W. Edwards was presented with a posthumous award on behalf of her late husband, W. R. Edwards, for his 33 years of service to the Ramsey RNLI. This took the form of a Vellum and the ceremony took place at the Norbury Boathouse.

On the 10th July, 1968, many Guild Members attended the funeral of Mrs. M. Quayle at St. Paul's Church. She had been the oldest Member of the Guild. This year saw further changes in Officers and Mrs. S. C. Callister became Chairman, Miss F. Weldon the Hon. Secretary, Mrs. J. Green the Asst. Secretary and Mrs. W. Corlett, Treasurer.

THE 1970s

This decade continued with the steady rise in the fund-raising totals and in 1970 the Ladies' Guild paid some £300 into Branch Funds plus the £343 they raised on Lifeboat Day in conjunction with general Branch events. Mrs. A. Ritchie became a Member of the Guild during this year, having moved to Ramsey from her previous home nearer Douglas. She very soon became the Guild President.

Early in 1974 the tragic death took place of Miss F. Weldon in a motor car accident. She had been a Guild Member for 17 years; five as Hon. Secretary and three as Chairman. Later that year the deaths occurred of Miss L. Shaw and her sister, Miss R. Shaw. Both had been ardent Guild Members and the latter had been Hon. Secretary for some seven years.

On a happier note, Mrs. G. Teare was selected to represent the Guild at a garden party at Buckingham Palace on the 16th June.

1974 was the RNLI 150th Anniversary Year and extra events were staged for fund-raising. These were very successful and the Chairman's Report in October referred to the figures which showed that £363 were raised at a wine and cheese party at the Beach Hotel; £449 were raised at the Mooragh Park coffee morning; £111 at a stamp auction; a good-as-new sale raised £449 and Lifeboat Day £462. The total of £1930 was certainly another annual record.

In January, 1975, it was decided to elect two addtional Executive Committee officers to assist with the increasing work load. The senior officers listed for that year were; President Mrs. A. Ritchie, Chairman Mrs. R. Teare, Vice-Chairman Mrs. M. Buckley, Hon. Secretary Mrs. K. Stidwill, Treasurer Mrs. G. Peake and Asst. Treasurer Mrs. R. Cannell. The annual subscription charge was re-introduced for all Members at 25p. A social Committee was also introduced with Mrs. J. Hill-Heaton as its Secretary and Sub-Committee Members Mrs. H. Sands, Miss G. Burns and Mrs. G. Peake. It was noted that more Crew wives now belonged to the Guild but it was difficult for many to attend morning meetings. It was therefore resolved to have monthly social meetings in the evening.

1976 saw Mrs. H. Sands being asked to act as Liason Officer between the Guild and the Branch Committee. During this year Mrs. Ritchie was presented with a signed photograph of the Crew (taken in 1974). Mrs. Stidwill announced the intention of having more frequent but smaller fund-raising events in the future and the Branch Press Officer, Mr. J. Podmore, agreed to publicise these occasions. From this year the Lifeboat Day funds raised were accredited to the Ladies' Guild only and not shown, as before, under general Branch activities. The Guild arranged a sponsored walk during the summer and the proceeds of £170 were used to purchase a two-way radio for use between the Boathouse and the Lifeboat at sea.

In 1977 Lady Sugden was elected Chairman; Mrs. K. Stidwill remained Hon. Secretary and Mrs. H. Sands became the Hon. Treasurer of the Guild. It was agreed to increase the number of regular Committee Meetings that year and they were set for February, April, July and November with Executive Meetings one week beforehand. It was also suggested that the Guild Annual Report should be read out at the Branch A.G.M.s.

Mrs. B. Green was re-elected Press Officer and Mrs. H. Sands, Liason Officer. At the financial year-end £2100 was handed over to general

J. Sands collection

Some Officers of the Ladies' Guild Committee c1980.
L to R: Mrs. J. Corlett, Hon. Treasurer Mrs. H. Sands, Chairman Mrs. B. Green, Mrs. M. Fraser-Casey, Regional Fund-Raising Manager Mr. D. Jones, Hon. Secretary Mrs. E. Corlett and President Mrs. A. Ritchie.

Branch Funds.

During 1978 Mrs. A. Ritchie was awarded an RNLI Vellum for her services to the RNLI. Later, Mrs. E. Corlett was elected to the Committee.

1979 was the 150th Anniversary of the founding of the Ramsey Station and the Duke of Atholl made the annual Appeal on Lifeboat Day. This raised £882 and the year's events another £1917. These included a Re-dedication Service held by the Lord Bishop and attended by the Lt. Governor; a champagne reception; a lecture on the work of the Trinity House by Capt. R. Watkin, R.N., and a Crew and Wives "Chicken and Chips" evening.

At the end of the year an RNLI NW Bulletin stated that in 1978 the total funds raised by the combined five Isle of Man RNLI Branches amounted to £19,997, of which Ramsey's share was a very creditable £4010. During the financial year September 1978-79 the Ladies' Guild handed over £2800 to Branch Funds.

The 1980s

The decade of the 1980s saw the biggest changes in local RNLI fund-raising. These were instigated over the period by the Ladies' Guild and the annual sums handed over to the Branch (and thence to Headquarters) increased dramatically. More annual events were staged and the selling of souvenirs, Christmas cards and calendars were stepped up and became very successful. It became Guild policy to rent a vacant shop in Ramsey at Christmastime to effect such sales.

1981 was a year of increased activity and two particularly interesting lectures were arranged. One was by the local yachtsman Nicky Keig who showed a film of the 1980 Observer Trans-Atlantic Yacht Race in which he participated and came second. That evening raised £574. Later in the year Robin Corlett gave a film show on the Lifeboat Service and also slides taken in Antarctica. Lifeboat Day was held on the 1st August and the Lt. Governor attended with Rear Admiral Graham of the RNLI. At the A.G.M. of £3271 was handed over to the Branch Treasurer.

During the following year, 1982, an evening supper with a fashion show proved popular. However, a special event took place on the 26th June and when a Summer Dance was held in Ramsey. All proceeds were given to the RNLI Widows and Orphans Pension Fund after the Penlee Lifeboat Disaster. A sum of £956 was raised. (This included donations of £500). Lifeboat Day raised £1408 during which Gerry Marsden of Gerry and the Pacemakers made the annual Appeal . On that day Station Mechanic Jimmy Kneale received the RNLI Long Service Certificate from Branch President, Mrs. A. Ritchie. With another £2150 from events throughout the 12 months, a sum of £3558 was handed to the Branch at the year's end.

Officers of the Guild for the 1981-83 period of service were; President Mrs. A. Ritchie, Vice-President Mrs. V. Nicholls, Chairman Mrs. B. Green, Hon. Secretary Mrs. E. Corlett and Hon. Treasurer Mrs. H. Sands.

In 1983 a Philips Antique Valuation Day was well attended and raised £230. At the year's A.G.M. Mrs. A. Ritchie was made Life President of the Branch and Guild. At this meeting it was announced that £4500 had been raised in the year for the Branch and this was over double the figure raised in 1977.

Further elections of officers took place and Mrs. K. Stidwell became the new Chairman; Mrs. P. Dearden, Vice-Chairman; Mrs. M. Fraser-Casey, Asst. Hon. Secretary and Mrs. F. Hyde, Asst. Treasurer, Mrs. E. Corlett and Mrs. H. Sands continued in their respective posts as Hon. Secretary and Treasurer. The new posts of Assistant Hon. Secretary and Asst. Treasurer were created as a result of the increased work-load and as a back-up system for the Executive Committee.

In 1984 there was yet another big increase in the funds raised when the total reached £6000.

A film entitled "s.s. Great Britain Born Again" was shown during the year and covered the salvaging of that remarkable vessel from her virtual grave in the Falkland Islands and the voyage to her original home in the Port of Bristol and subsequent restoration. Much of the responsibility for this work was on the shoulders of the local naval architect, Dr. Ewan Corlett, a Ramsey Branch Committee Member in 1984 and soon to become Branch Chairman.

On the 17th May, 1985, H.R.H. Princess Alexandra and her husband, the Honourable Angus Ogilvy, paid a brief visit to the Ramsey Station and were introduced to the Crew. The Guild arranged for a bouquet of flowers to be presented by the daughter of a Lifeboatman and they manned the Lifeboat shop and arranged light refreshments for those assembled.

This year's programme included a barbecue at the Maughold Venture Centre and a very successful coffee morning which alone raised £938. The annual total handed to the Branch Treasurer was £5400.

Very unexpectedly, Chairman Mrs. K. Stidwell died in 1985, and also Members Mrs. J. Grocott and Mrs. P. Parkes. Mrs. P. Dearden took over as Chairman with Mrs. H. Sands as Vice-Chairman. Hon. Secretary Mrs. E. Corlett was joined by Mrs. J. Cannan as Asst. Secretary, Mrs. F. Hyde was elected Treasurer but resigned shortly afterwards when her husband was transferred to the Channel Islands. The position remained vacant until Mrs. N. Pugh took over in 1986 with Asst. Hon. Treasurer, Mrs. J. Daniels, Mrs. B. Green was appointed Vice-President and elected to continue as Press Officer for the Ladies.

A film show arranged by the Guild in late October, 1986, proved a very popular one. This was an American one on the subject of perhaps the oldest iron sailing ship still afloat, the Star of India, owned by the San Diego Maritime Museum of California. This ship was built in Ramsey in 1863 as the full-rigged ship Euterpe. Only recently a Branch Committee Member, Capt. R. C. Watkin, C.B.E., M.N.I., R.N. (Retd.), had been entertained aboard her. Other residents of Ramsey were also due to visit her in due course. A second film on the RNLI was also shown during the evening.

At the year's A.G.M. on the 12th November, Mr. D. M. Jones, the RNLI North-West Regional Organiser, was present as he always attempted to be on this annual occasion. The Hon. Treasurer, Mrs. N. Pugh, listed the programme accomplished during the year and the monies raised:- film show £224; cheese and wine party £686; coffee morning with tombola £715; Lifeboat Day with the house-to-house and street collections £1550; barbecue £738; souvenir sales £1591 and general donations £864. A total of £6039 was handed over to the Branch , which was a considerable increase on 1985. It was noted the takings of the shop, which was taken over by the Guild in Parliament Street for one week in November for souvenir and Christmas sales, were £1100. Guild membership stood at 55 ladies in 1986.

At a Guild meeting early in 1987 congratulations were sent to Mr. T. E. Tregellis, the former Branch Treasurer, on receiving the RNLI Silver Badge for all his years of service to the Station. Congratulations were also sent to Coxswain James Kinnin and his crew for the Vellum award and Certificates they received after the Round the Island Yacht Race rescues of the previous year. The Lt. Governor, Major General Laurence New, attended the Boathouse on the 5th September to present these awards personally. The Guild Members were on hand, as usual upon such occassions, to offer light refreshments.

Earlier in the year, during April, Captain N. J. Barker, C.B.E., M.B.I.M., M.N.I., R.N., gave a unique talk to the Guild and their guests on his experiences in the Antartic survey vessel H.M.S. Endurance. He saw action off South Georgia when the Argentinians invaded the Falkland Islands and had some hair-raising stories to relate. Later in September another interesting lecture with films was given by British Telecom Marine Division (Southampton) Officers, whilst they were on the Island for the Nautical Institute. The talk was on the development of cable ships and submarine cable-laying. This was very opportune as a new fibre-optic telecommunications cable was soon to be laid from the

G. Cooke — Ladies' Guild collection

Some of the Ramsey Ladies' Lifeboat Guild Executive Committee at the Annual Barbeque, July, 1991. L to R: Vice-Chairman Hilary Sands, Hon. Secretary Mary Page, Hon. Asst. Treasurer Julie Daniels, Chairman Edna Corlett, Hon Press Officer Jane Forth, Vice-President Barbara Green, Shirley Steele, Hon. Treasurer Nora Pugh and Hon. Souvenir Secretary Joyce Wilson.

Isle of Man to the Cumbrian Coast.

The year was therefore a busy one but the rewards were even greater than before and the Guild raised the magnificent sum £9816 - a 50% increase on the previous year. At the end of 1987 Mrs. J. Forth, Committee Member, was asked to commission a water colour painting of the Ramsey Quayside to be presented, as a retirement gift, to Station Mechanic Jimmy Kneale at Christmastime. Another change took place amongst the officers of the Guild at the A.G.M. and Mrs. H. Sands was elected Chairman. The other officers remained in their posts but Souvenir Secretaries were elected for the first time with Mrs. J. Wilson and Mrs. M. Spencer taking on the work with a Sub-Committee of Members including Mrs. J. Forth, Mrs. E. Kendall, Mrs. J. Daniels and Mrs. R. Clague.

In 1988 all the Executive Officers were re-elected but it was decided to appoint two Assistant Hon. Secretaries in view of the ever-increasing work-load and responsibilities and to aid the ladies in learning the work of the Secretariat. Mrs. L. Smalley and Mrs. M. Page were elected. Mrs. J. Forth became the Guild Press Officer and a year later acted as the Branch Press Officer for a time.

Yet another increase in the funds raised was recorded and £10,543 were handed to the Branch Treasurer. The programme included all the usual functions and receipts were up on all events.

It was thought that the year 1989 would top all records for some time to come as the annual sum handed over by the Guild to the Branch was some £15,000. But not so, as 1990 was destined to become a year of extra effort in order to raise special funds towards the cost of the New Norbury Boathouse. In an RNLI Annual Newsletter it was reported that the Ramsey Ladies' Lifeboat Guild had raised the highest total of any North-West UK Branch, reaching the quite remarkable sum of £16,494.

The lily was even more gilded by the award of the RNLI Silver Badge to Mrs. B. Green, the Vice-President, and to Mrs. E. Corlett, Guild Chairman since 1990.

(Author's note. Ladies' initials. In the early part of this century ladies commonly used their husband's initials. From the 1960s this began to change and ladies began to use their own initials, and signatures with their own christian names. This has presented somewhat of a problem with this chapter. Even in the records, on one single page the same lady is shown with differing sets of initials. I have endeavoured to use the initials which I am assured are in the most common use. Please accept my apologies if I have got it wrong!).

CHAPTER 11

Ann and James Ritchie
On station 12th July, 1991

The new Mersey Class Lifeboat ON 1171 *Ann and James Ritchie* took over the Ramsey Station from the *James Ball Ritchie* on the 12th July, 1991. Her construction commenced in June, 1989, at FBM Ltd., in their Cowes Shipyard, Isle of Wight. She was the third Fibre Reinforced Composite Mersey Class lifeboat to be built by the company and the sixth Isle of Man RNLI lifeboat to be built there. The Liverpool Class ON 862 *Thomas Corbett* of the 1948-1970 era was the last Ramsey one to be built by this yard. A bequest of the late Mrs. Ann Ritchie met the half-a-million pounds cost of this very sophisticated craft.

An RNLI leaflet produced in 1990 gives a concise description of the new Class. The Mersey Class all-weather lifeboat has been designed by RNLI staff primarily for stations where the lifeboat has to be launched into the sea from a carriage, although she is capable of operating from slipways and may also lie afloat at berths. There are 22 tractor and carriage launched lifeboat stations around the coast. The Mersey has a speed of 17 knots - more than twice the speed of the Oakley and Rother Class Lifeboats which she replaces.

Early Mersey Class lifeboats are constructed of aluminium with the first of the Class being placed on station at Bridlington in November, 1988. Later Mersey Class lifeboats are constructed in fibre-reinforced composite (FRC). Both aluminium and FRC are new materials to the RNLI, combining strength with light weight.

The depth of the Mersey, 1.86 (6ft), is designed to provide access to machinery and a low freeboard for recovering survivors, whilst maintaining sufficient height in the bow for good seakeeping and to prevent taking aboard the lifeboat too much sea in rough weather. The hull is of round bilge, semi-displacement form incorporating a tunnel stern to give protection to the propellers. Should the lifeboat capsize, the inherent buoyancy of her watertight wheelhouse enables her to self-right in 5 seconds.

In the wheelhouse there is permanent seating for a crew of six with an additional jump seat provided for a doctor. The wheelhouse console incorporates engine controls, the hydraulic steering unit and wheel, tachometers, alarms, compass, helm indicator and controls for vhf Direction Finder unit, navigation lights, wipers, horn and searchlight.

At the navigator's position is the stabilised radar, a chart table and a Decca Navigator. At the mechanic's position is the main switchboard and a radio table with mf radio transmitter and receiver, vhf radio telephone and mf direction finder. A second vhf transceiver and echo sounder are fitted at the upper steering position.

The main details are:-

length 11.57m (38ft), beam 3.81m (12ft 6in), depth 1.86m (6ft), draught (typical) 0.98m F (3ft 2in) 0.92m A (3ft 0in), speed 17 knots, engines 2x Caterpillar 3208T turbo-charged marine diesels, fuel capacity 1100 litres (approx.245 gallons), crew of 6, range 145 nautical miles at full speed.

The new boat's operational number is "12-14". This is used as a visual identification number and is painted on her hull in threee locations. It is also used in radio communication work. The "12" signifies her approximate length in metres and the "14" the number in her order of building in the Class.

As a matter of local interest, the Ramsey Station Committee Chairman, the Rev. Dr. Ewan Corlett, has been involved to an appreciable extent in the development of these new Fast Carriage Boats, both aluminium and reinforced fibre composite. As a naval architect and as a member of the RNLI Boat and Technical Consultative Committees, he advised in detail on the structure of the aluminium series and on the hydrodynamics of both types.

The FCB is appreciably smaller than the Arun and Tyne Classes and yet has to have much the same sea-going capabilities and speed. The design team at Poole was faced with a very diffficult problem and it is much to its credit that the vessels are so satisfactory. Indeed, in head seas it is considered from measurements that the FCB is probably superior to either Arun or the Tyne.

That being said, a considerable amount of tuning of the hydrodynamics was necessary, minor changes to the shapes of the tunnels, of the spraychines and in particular of the trimming tabs, were all necessary and the Chairman was

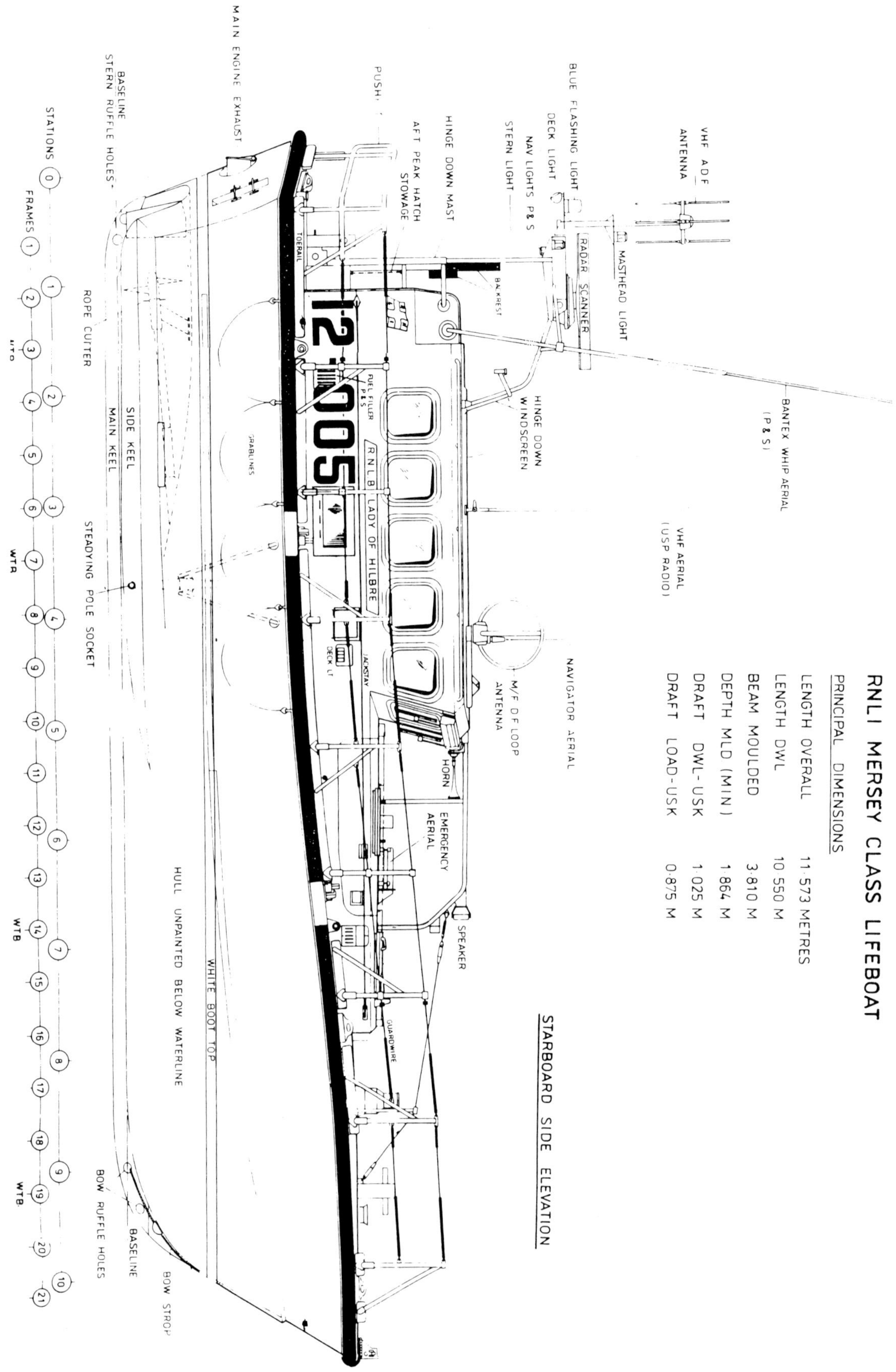
RNLI MERSEY CLASS LIFEBOAT
PRINCIPAL DIMENSIONS
LENGTH OVERALL 11·573 METRES
LENGTH DWL 10·550 M
BEAM MOULDED 3·810 M
DEPTH MLD (MIN) 1·864 M
DRAFT DWL-USK 1·025 M
DRAFT LOAD-USK 0·875 M
STARBOARD SIDE ELEVATION
VHF ADF ANTENNA
MASTHEAD LIGHT
RADAR SCANNER
BLUE FLASHING LIGHT
DECK LIGHT
NAV LIGHTS P& S
STERN LIGHT
BACKREST
BANTEX WHIP AERIAL (P & S)
HINGE DOWN WINDSCREEN
HINGE DOWN MAST
AFT PEAK HATCH STOWAGE
MAIN ENGINE EXHAUST
BASELINE
STERN RUFFLE HOLES
STATIONS
FRAMES
TOERAIL
ROPE CUTTER
SIDE KEEL
MAIN KEEL
STEADYING POLE SOCKET
12-005
RNLB LADY OF HILBRE
FUEL FILLER P&S
GRABLINES
JACKSTAY
DECK LT
VHF AERIAL (USP RADIO)
NAVIGATOR AERIAL
M/F D F LOOP ANTENNA
HORN
EMERGENCY AERIAL
SPEAKER
GUARDWIRE
HULL UNPAINTED BELOW WATERLINE
WHITE BOOT TOP
BOW RUFFLE HOLES
BASELINE
BOW STROP
WTB

RNLI Poole

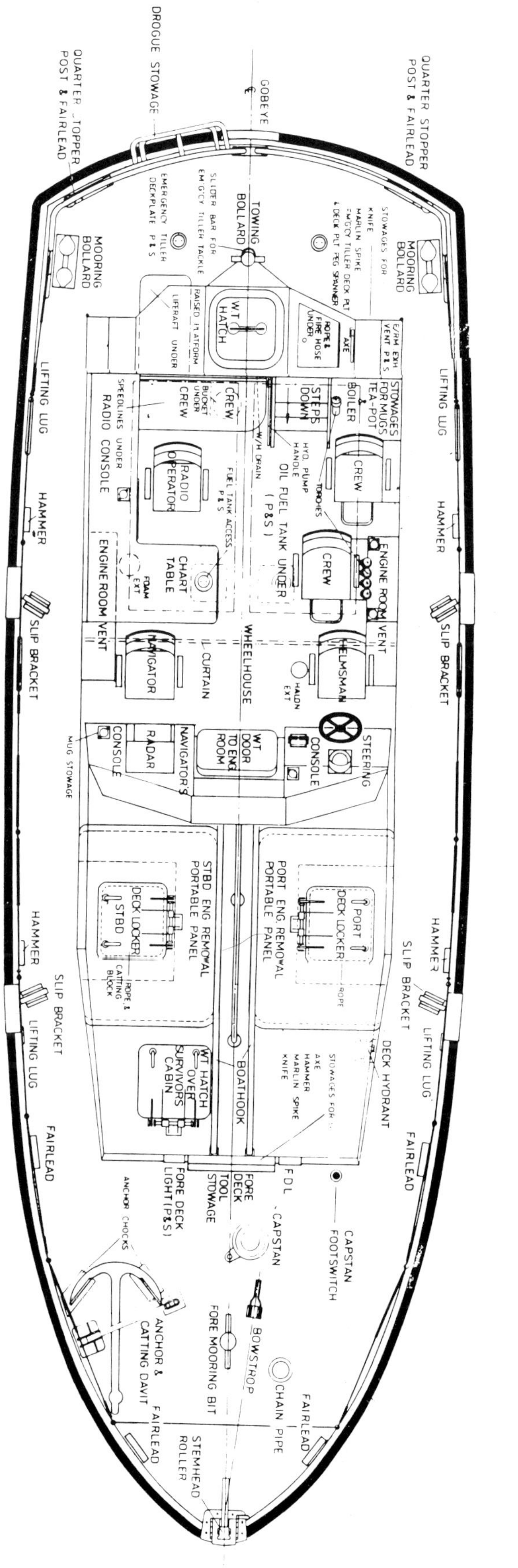

PLAN VIEW OF DECK AND WHEELHOUSE ARRANGEMENT

RNLI Poole

J. Morris

Work progressing on the Mersey Class RNLB O.N. 1171, destined for Ramsey, in the Cowes Shipyard of FBM Ltd., January, 1991.

J. Morris

Mersey Class Lifeboats under construction at FBM Ltd., September, 1990, L to R: North Sunderland, Filey, Ramsey and Newquay.

FBM Ltd.

Preparing to launch the *Ann and James Ritchie* February, 1991.

FBM Ltd.

The *Ann and James Ritchie* afloat for the first time at the Cowes, Isle of Wight, shipyard of FBM Ltd.

Gilbert Hampton Photography

1

FBM Ltd.

The *Ann and James Ritchie* undergoing self-righting trials.

"Over she goes".

Gilbert Hampton Photography

2

FBM Ltd.

Gilbert Hampton Photography — 3 — FBM Ltd.

Self-righting trials at Cowes, March 1991.

"Up she comes".

Gilbert Hampton Photography — 4 — FBM Ltd.

Gilbert Hampton Photography

The *Ann and James Ritchie* on builders' trials off the Isle of Wight May, 1991.

Gilbert Hampton Photography

The *Ann and James Ritchie* on sea trials.

FBM Ltd.

FBM Ltd.

Stern view of RNLB O.N. 1171 showing the deep propeller tunnels.

able to assist in optimising these features. This culminated in a week of trials, of both 1125 and 1148, the prototype aluminium and FRC boats, respectively. During these, some of the recommendations were tested and others suggested and these had marked effect on handling and speed. The Ramsey Station is glad to have been of some assistance in the development of this successful Class.

On the 22nd March, 1991, the Hon. Secretary, Capt. Michael Brew and Coxswain Jim Kinnin attended the self-righting trials of Ramsey's new boat at the FBM yard at Cowes. From the 1st to 3rd May, Station Mechanic Jim Martin attended a motor mechanics' course at the RNLI training school at Poole. Ten days later Jim Martin returned South with Coxswain Jim Kinnin and Assistant Mechanic designate, Mark Kenyon. This time they joined the *Ann and James Ritchie* for her 40-hour trials which included passages to Alderney, Salcombe, Falmouth, Plymouth and Weymouth.

The final five days of intensive training commenced in Poole on Monday, 24th June. Staff Coxswain Mike Storey took over the *James Ball Ritchie* in Ramsey and on Sunday 23rd, Hon. Secretary Capt. Michael Brew, Coxswain Jim Kinnin, 2nd Coxswain Ray Stanfield, Mechanic Jim Martin and Crewmen Kevin Christian, Alistair Clague and Kim Holland left by air for London and thence by coach to Poole.

Their first day was spent in the classroom with lectures on machinery, general boat operations, fault correction and a video was shown dealing with liferafts. Senior RNLI officers joined them for lunch and the Lifeboat berthed shortly after midday following her passage from the builders' yard at Cowes. The Crew were able to inspect her later in the afternoon; for some of them this was for the first time.

By 10.45 a.m. on the second day the Crew were aboard the *Ann and James Ritchie* and raring to go. Some hours were first spent within the Poole harbour area, testing the equipment and the communications systems and generally getting the feel of the craft. Later in the day they put to sea and were given an anchoring demonstration and taught how not to pick up lobster pots by RNLI's John Cauldwell!. The day was very wet with low cloud, rain and a WSW'ly wind, force 5-6.

More classroom work took up Wednesday morning with chartwork and instruction on the latest Decca Navigator systems. During the day the Crew were able to go aboard the very latest RNLI Fast Afloat Boat (FAB) 3 which was in the harbour. They were very impressed with her size and that she was capable of 26 knots. She had a survivor capacity of 20 persons. The afternoon was spent out in Poole Bay in another SSW force 6 wind with a considerable sea running. A simulated fire exercise was carried out and then a man overboard drill. It was good to get back to the digs in the evening and down a large steak. (£2.50 extra). Jimmy Martin was happy.

Thursday 27th was spent in a similar manner with classroom work in the morning and a sea passage in the afternoon. A sea passage with a difference, in fact. This time all the wheelhouse windows were covered over and the Crew was instructed to proceed blind to Chapman's Pool, some 12 miles down the coast. They made it and arrived within 12 feet of their destination. More man overboard drills, navigation tuition and then back to base. This time Hon. Secretary Michael Brew was at the wheel and so a 'special' man overboard drill was held for him on the way! As the boat docked, much to the surprise of the Crew, Ramsey Hon. Treasurer Steven Spencer and his wife Mary greeted them on the quayside. This was certainly a cause for celebration and, amongst other things, steak and kidney pie followed - except for Jimmy Martin - yet another steak!

The big day soon arrived. Friday 28th was a very busy one with more theoretical work ashore, lunch and then a visit to the Headquarters. A helicopter exercise had also been arranged for the forenoon but was cancelled when the aircraft became unavailable. Michael Brew and

J. Morris

The Ramsey Delivery Crew during training at Poole 26th June, 1991. L to R: Crewman Kevin Christian, 2nd Coxswain Ray Stanfield, Emergency Mechanic Alister Clague, Station Mechanic Jim Martin, Coxswain Jim Kinnin and Crewman Kim Holland.

J. Morris

The *Ann and James Ritchie* leaves the RNLI berth at Poole for an afternoon's training exercise 26th June, 1991.

P. Monekton

The motor tug Sea Viper aground at Gewnnap Head, near Land's End. The crew of this vessel was taken off by the *Ann and James Ritchie* at 2.00 a.m., Sunday 30th June, 1991, during the Lifeboat's delivery passage from Poole to Ramsey.

P. Monekton

RNLI Deputy Divisional Inspector George Rawlinson (sitting, port side), RNLI Engineer Jim Cowan (standing in stern sheets), Mechanic Jim Martin (standing centre), Coxswain Jim Kinnin and Crewman Kim Holland, all of the *Ann and James Ritchie*, with Penlee RNLI Hon. Secretary and a lifeboatman during the landing of the crew of the tug Sea Viper at Newlyn, Cornwall, during the early hours of Sunday, 30th June, 1991.

B. P. Grenfell

The Old and the New.
The *James Ball Ritchie* welcomes the new *Ann and James Ritchie* to Ramsey on Friday, 5th July, 1991.

B. P. Grenfell

Waiting for the tide.
The *James Ball Ritchie* and the *Ann and James Ritchie* off the harbour entrance at Ramsey, 5th July, 1991.

Alistair Clague had to return to the Island on the following day, so in order to give Alistair some extra "sea time", Kevin Christian travelled with Michael to Weymouth overland to meet the boat in the evening. At 4.20 p.m. the *Ann and James Ritchie* was set, with a well-informed Crew, to commence her delivery passage to Ramsey. RNLI Deputy Divisional Inspector George Rawlinson headed the party together with Staff Engineer Jimmy Cowan. Little did they know that this would be no ordinary delivery run!

The Delivery Passage

Crewman Kim Holland kept a terse diary of the events that followed and takes up the story from noon on the 28th:-

"Round HQ in the afternoon. Interesting but a bit rushed. Left with Lifeboat at 4.20 p.m. to get the 4.30 p.m. bridge. On the way home, at last! Across Weymouth Bay to find the Weymouth lifeboat using vhf/DF - relatively easy. (Got there at 6.30 p.m.) Tow practice with the Arun but only short due to Weymouth having had a call-out a bit earlier. Tied up near the Kaisei, a large Japanese vessel, at 7.20 p.m. Digs at the Oxford Hotel. O.K. but a bit of a rabbit warren. Difficult to locate the shower room etc. On the way down to the meal met Jimmy Martin - still trying to locate the shower room! Had a meal in the Old Brewery, all on a big table. Steak and other things good; a few beers later.

Saturday 29th/Sunday 30th. Left Weymouth shortly after 9.00 a.m. George (Dpty. D.I.) had been ashore to get a chart as one was missing for this next day's run. This was also to be our obligatory night passage as part of the return work-up. Put into Salcombe for lunch at the Yacht Club. The local crew were very friendly and glad to see a passage boat in. Left about 4.00 p.m. for Fowey to refuel. Misty with rain in Fowey. A meal was arranged by the Fowey crew in a local pub - only £2.50 including a sweet, steak-pie and chips. Excellent!

Left Fowey at 10.00 p.m., destination Padstow, (North Cornwall), via Lizard Head and Land's End in the dark. Mist and rain with moderate seas and wind SW force 4-5. Poor visibility forced us to concentrate hard on the nav. aids and radar to locate the Lizard. Approaching Lands End - about 4 miles South of it - picked up a MAYDAY call on vhf channel 16 from the tug Sea viper. Time 01.03 a.m. The tug is 90ft. long with a crew of three. Aground on rocks near Land's End; holed in her engine-room and taking in water. (In actual fact off Gwennap Head, inside the Runnel Stone Rock Buoy).

Coastguards at Falmouth take the call. We notify our position as soon as we can, having used the vhf/DF to gain a bearing of the tug. Pass the position to the Coastguards. They assume tug to be aground on Runnel Stone, treacherous rocks just South of Land's End. D.I. George knows the Stone but DF and our position indicate that the tug is ahore on the coast, not Runnel Stone.

We ask Coastguards to launch Penlee (Newlyn) lifeboat to back us up if we can't get in. It's their patch and they have the local knowledge.

Visibility down to 30 yards; using vhf/DF and radar to steer and Decca to plot as best we can. First we have to negotiate two targets (coasters?) inside our course. Too dangerous to cross their bows, so we reverse our course and pass close astern of them. D.I. takes the helm up top. Ray on the radar; Jim Martin, Kevin and Kim tog up for the foredeck after setting up and moving the searchlights. Ray and Jim (the Cox) take the searchlights and we locate the casualty. Jimmy, the Staff mechanic, mans the radios and the depth-finder and we go in for the tug.

Tug hard-on, surrounded by rocks. Fully lit. Liferaft inflated alongside her. Approx. 1.30 a.m., radio message from tug states that she is holed in the engine-room. On the second pass we get two men over our bow. Made a fourth pass to get the third and last man aboard us. Came astern very carefully. Only 8ft of water under centre of our keel! We kept the searchlights sweeping on the rocks all around. Proceeded to sea on a reciprocal course to the one used going in. Slow again with a bow lookout. Once clear we inform the Coastguards and then full steam ahead for Newlyn. The Arun was out off Newlyn and so we followed her in (nasty approach) and tied up alongside her. Landed the tug men and we also went ashore for tea. Refuelled and then set off again at 4.00 a.m. for Padstow. Arrived just after 8.00 a.m. - quite a trip and everyone very tired! Went to a local hotel for digs but the rooms were still occupied and not ready. Had breakfast with a bottle of "ships stores" and then up to rooms to sleep until 4.00 p.m. Down to the boat to clean her up. Had a look around Padstow - very small. Had an evening meal meal, a drink and then back to bed.

Monday 1st July. On the boat for 9.30 a.m. start. We collected local newspapers on the way which carried the story of our trip and the rescue on the front page. It appears that the tug's radar was out of action and also the local Coastguard Station's radar not working. Photo's of the tug and us in the Western News. Also a bit on the tele. showing the tug - stern now awash and rocks all around. We head off for Fishguard. Due to have a helicopter exercise in St. Brides Bay at 3.00 p.m. When 28 miles South of Milford Haven the alarm bells ring out - starboard engine overheating. Throttle off; water in the bilges, including fresh water from the cooling system. Looks serious. Engine shut down as there is too much smoke from the starboard one. Proceeding to Milford Haven on one engine at 7.2 knots as the drag on the starboard propeller is heating up the the gear box oil. Gloom and despair prevail!

Took four hours to reach the Marine Service berth. At 6.00 p.m. we await the arrival of the Fishguard crew to pick us up for the night. We leave the mechanics to investigate the problem. A Caterpillar engineer is due to arrive soon. At the Glendower Hotel, Fishguard. O.K. It's Bernie the landlord's birthday. Still doom and gloom by late evening as the news is not good. Maybe piston or the head

B. P. Grenfell

The End of an Era.
After 21 years of service at Ramsey the *James Ball Ritchie* leads her successor, the *Ann and James Ritchie,* into harbour on the 5th July, 1991.

gone. We may have to fly home without the boat.

Tuesday, 2nd. News from the boat. Spare parts ordered but they are not arriving until Wednesday, from Belgium. May be able to fix things. Have the day ashore but not very happy with the situation. Cox Kinnin goes lobster fishing with the Fishguard Cox. The mechanics come back to Fishguard with us to await the arrival of the parts.

Wednesday, 3rd. Still having to wait for news. Bernie lets us have use of the hotel's mini-bus. With Ritchie from the Fishguard crew, we go out to St. David's to see the boat there and meet the crew. Spend all the afternoon there and have a meal. Get back to the Fishguard Boathouse at 7.30 p.m. and receive a message to go to Milford. Lifeboat may be ready for trials soon. Arrive there about 8.15 p.m. but there are still putting things together. 9.00 p.m. engines are started up and all seems O.K. We go out out into the Haven for 30 minutes trials to make sure. All O.K. - phew, are we glad! We return to drop the Caterpillar engineer and at 10.30 p.m. head out to sea, bound Fishguard. Another night run and through Ramsey Sound - some place that - six knots tide against. We reach Fishguard at 1.30 a.m. and find the refuelling boys waiting. They also have hospitality awaiting us.

Thursday, 4th We leave Fishguard at 9.30 and first have a helicopter exercise in the Bay at 11.00 a.m. with an R.A.F. "Sea King". A lot of messing about and it seems that the "Sea King" needs more practice than we do! Away for Holyhead by noon. Extremely hot in full gear; we are glad to get it off.Another alarm trips on the way up so we shut down instantly and there are worried looks all round. It is only a bilge alarm in the tank space - caused by water splahing about, drawn in by the fans. We arrive on time in Holyhead at 6.15 p.m.; we refuel, tie-up in the fish dock and then off to the digs. The Llandudno Cox comes over to say "Hello" and has a meal with us. Early night and home tomorrow.

Friday, 5th July. Tynwald Day. Early breakfast and we are away by 9.00 a.m.; eta Port St. Mary 12.00 noon. An uneventful trip up; all eager to be going home - the boat very quiet. Refuel at Port St. Mary and away by 1.00 p.m. as we must be in Ramsey Bay by 3.00 p.m. Mood now quite happy and cheerful. Whilst passing Douglas we request a record on Manx Radio and have a look at a Polish sail training ship. We stop off Maughold Head to decorate the boat overall with bunting prepared in Port St. Mary. Very hot, but for the photos we don full gear plus helmets. Boy, its hot! Greeted by Ramsey Lifeboat *James Ball Ritchie* and then spent 20 minutes flashing up and down the Bay to then follow the Ramsey boat into the harbour to be greeted by wives, girl-friends and officials etc. SOME TRIP!"

THE SEA VIPER RESCUE

On the 1st July, 1991, the Plymouth Western Morning News gave front page coverage to the SEA VIPER rescue and a photograph of some of the *Ann and James Ritchie* Crew landing the three survivors of the tug in Newlyn harbour during the early hours of Sunday, 30th June. Also shown was a later shot of the tug high and dry on the rocks at low water. The Editor has kindly given permission to reprint the article.

The Press report was written by Colin Gregory and headed:-

"Westcountry MP angered by reasons for failure of equipment. Coastguard radar out as tug grounds.

The three-man crew of a tug were rescued by a passing lifeboat off the Cornish coast early yesterday morning after their vessel hit rocks near a Coastguard Station where the radar equipment is out of action.

The 72-tonne SEA VIPER, en route from Milford Haven to Torquay and with its own radar out of order, hit rocks near Gwennap Head early on Sunday morning when the visibility was almost zero because of dense fog.

Officers at the nearby Coastguard Station were unaware that the tug was near the rocks and the St. Ives M.P. David Harris said last night that if the radar had been working it may have prevented the shipwreck.

The lifeboat, which had lifeboat Inspector George Rawlinson on board as well as the Cox and four-man crew, took the tug crew off the stern of the vessel in shallow sea.

The Penlee lifeboat, under Cox Jimmy Madron, had also been alerted by Falmouth Coastguards who received the MAYDAY call, but stood-by as the Isle of Man lifeboat was nearer.

The tug crew, owner Chris Merrix, and her Skipper Graham Tiley, of Teignmouth, Geoff Yard, of Torquay, and engineer Mike Smith, from Portland, were taken to the Fishermen's Mission at Newlyn.

Mr. Tiley said last night: "There were three of us on the bridge when we went aground. Visibility was zero. We were very impressed by the performance of the lifeboat and her crew".

The tug GOLIATH went to the scene last night with the SEA VIPER'S crew in a bid to pull her off the rocks

St. Ives M.P. Davis Harris criticised the failure to repair the radar at Gwenapp Head, which had been put off because the Station is due to be closed down under an internal review.

It is one of the three manned Coastguard Stations in West Cornwall which the review recommends should lose its regular manning.

Mr. Harris has taken up the issue of the radar equipment with the Shipping Minister Patrick McLoughlin but was told it was old and not worth repairing.

He was also told that it was not owned by the Coastguards but on loan from the Ministry of Defence.

"This is dodging the issue. It is wrong not to have working radar at Gwennap Head", said Mr. Harris last night.

He is to see the Minister later this month on the question of manned watches.

A Coastguard spokesman at Falmouth said they could not comment on policy, and the regional controller was not avaialble last night.

Emergency services were in action again last night when the St. Ives lifeboat took a crewman with head injuries from a yacht off the Cornish coast."

In fact, Ramsey knows the feeling well. Their own Coastguard Station was shut down completely in January, 1989, by the UK Government.

Even in this modern age of high technology, it is just as well that we have the RNLI and the crews so willing to man their lifeboats. We still need them.

LETTERS, 1835 - 1845

In 1835 the Lt. Governor and Tynwald (the Manx Parliament) ordered the High Bailiff of Ramsey to reorganise the Committee and to raise subscriptions to support the Insular Shipwreck Institution. A strong Committee was appointed under the Chairmanship of the Ramsey High Bailiff, F. Tellett, J.P., with Deemster Christian and other influential members.

Two documents relating to this matter are set out hereunder plus a facsimile of Sir William Hillary's to Mr. Tellet. The original document was kindly loaned for reproduction by Mrs. Constance Radclifffe of Maughold, the local historian.

Castle Rushen. 25th June, 1835

Dear Sir,

As the time is approaching when the annual report of our Insular Shipwreck Institution must be prepared for the Tynwald Court, I am directed by His Excellency the Lt. Governor to aquaint you that a report is expected from you that the district of Ramsey has followed the example of Castletown in meeting for the purpose of filling up the vacancies which the lapse of time has caused in the Committee; and taking measures to place your district in an efficient state.

It is of much consequence that the formation of a Committee should take place, otherwise you may expect that the Stores at Ramsey will be withdrawn; and that in the event of any disaster occurring on your coast, you will not be in a condition to claim from the parent company any pecuniary assistance whatever.

The subject is one of great importance not only as it regards the Cause of Humanity but also the honour and interests of the Island.

The Bishop, Archeacon, Deemster Christian, Mr. Farrant, Mr. Hinds, Mr. Lamothe, Jnr., and other gentlemen have expressed their readiness to meet to effect the purpose desired.

The Lt. Governor has therefore directed me to request of you to take an early opportunity to call a meeting of the influential Inhabitants of Ramsey and its district to afford them an opportuniy, which the Lt. Governor has no doubt they will cordially embrace, of expressing themselves desirous to enter into the plan proposed to reorganise the Committee and to enter into subscriptions to support the great object of the Institution.

I am, Dear Sir,
Yours very faithfully,
Geo. Quirk, (Clerk to the Council)

High Bailiff of Ramsey.

A STATEMENT

In the year 1835 a Meeting was held in Ramsey for the purpose of reconstructing a local branch of the Isle of Man District Association of the National Institution for the Preservation of Life from Shipwreck; at which Meeting a Branch Association for the Port of Ramsey was accordingly instituted; and a Committee was appointed, consisting of the principal gentlemen of the Town and Neighbourhood. A subscription was subsequently raised, and after various negotiations between the Committee and the benevolent Sir William Hillary - the original Founder of the Society for the Preservation of Life from Shipwreck - a large and excellent Lifeboat was purchased by the Committee for the Port of Ramsey on very advantageous terms. Owing to the inadequacy of the original subscription to meet incidental expenses the lifeboat has since the time of her purchase been lying in the Harbour of Ramsey exposed to the injuries of the weather.

At a meeting lately held in the Court House, Ramsey, The High Bailiff in the Chair, it was resolved to raise an additional sum to build a shed for the protection of the Lifeboat and her stores from injury by weather, the expenses of which shed it is estimated will amount to £10 or thereabouts. The Liberality of the Public is therefore appealed to in order to raise the above sum.

List of Subscribers

The Lord Bishop	£1
The Venerable Archdeacon (additional)	£1
The Revd. Geo. Hambleton	10 shillings
A Friend (By Revd. G. Hambleton)	10 shillings

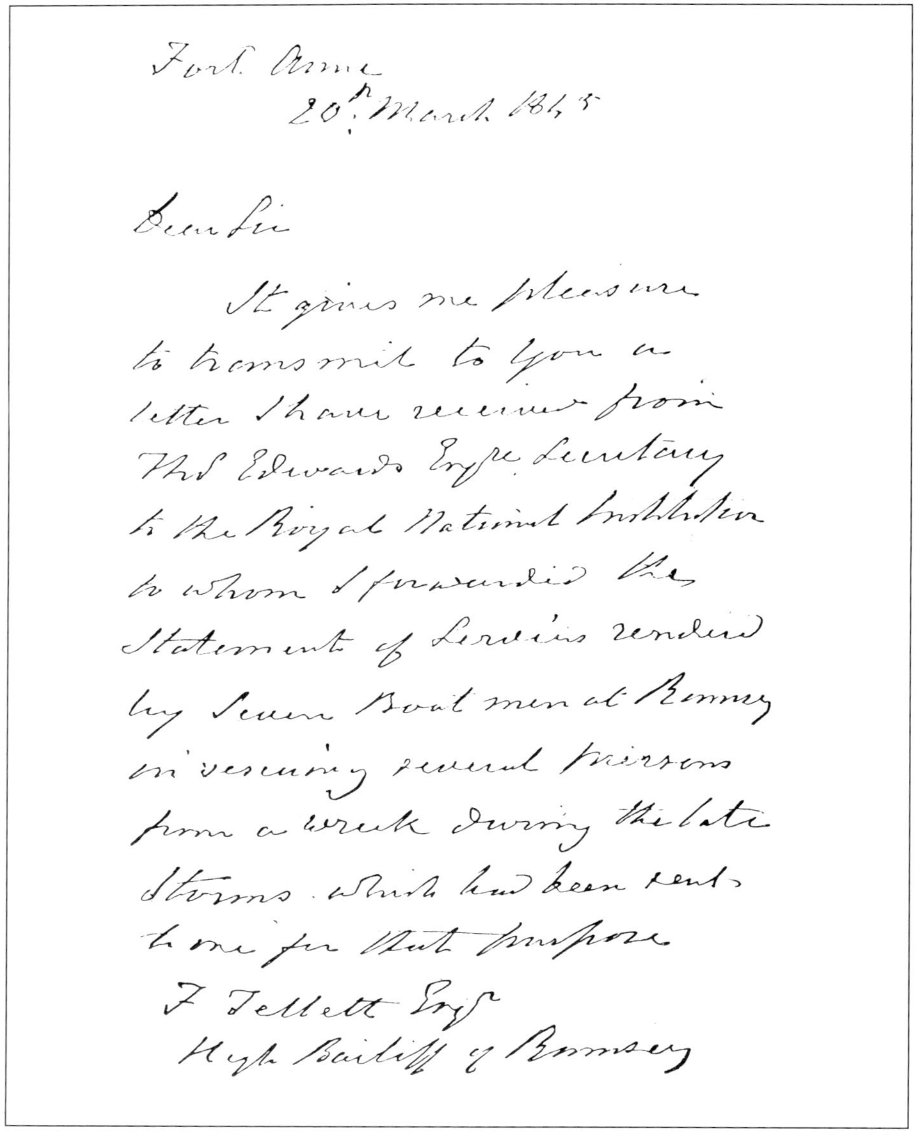

Fort Anne
20th March 1845

Dear Sir

It gives me pleasure to transmit to you a letter I have received from Thos Edwards Esqe. Secretary to the Royal National Institution to whom I forwarded the Statement of Services rendered by Seven Boat men at Romney in rescuing several persons from a wreck during the late Storms which had been sent to me for that purpose

F Tellett Esqr
High Bailiff of Romney

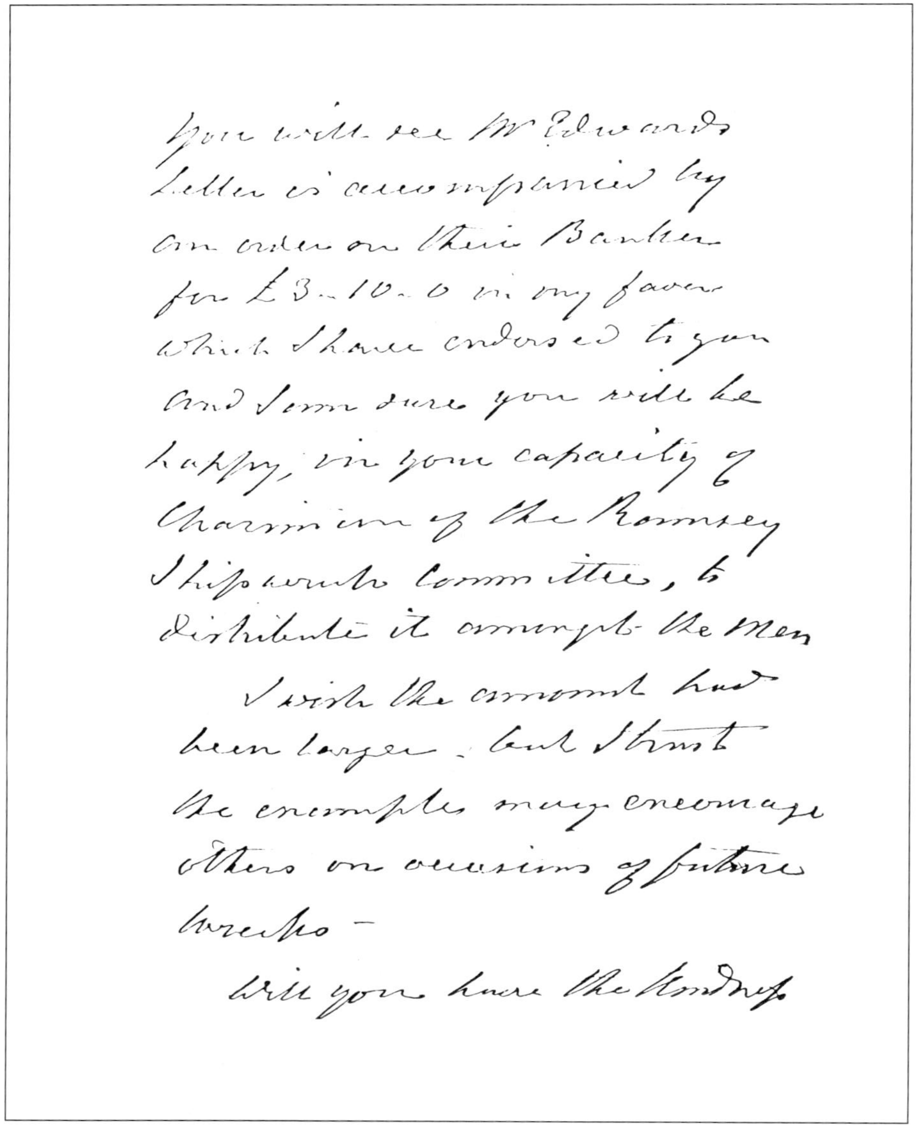

You will see Mr Edwards Letter is accompanied by an order on their Banker for £3-10-0 in my favor which I have endorsed to you and I am sure you will be happy, in your capacity of Chairman of the Romney Shipwreck Committee, to distribute it amongst the Men

I wish the amount had been larger, but I trust the example may encourage others on occasions of future wrecks –

Will you have the Kindness

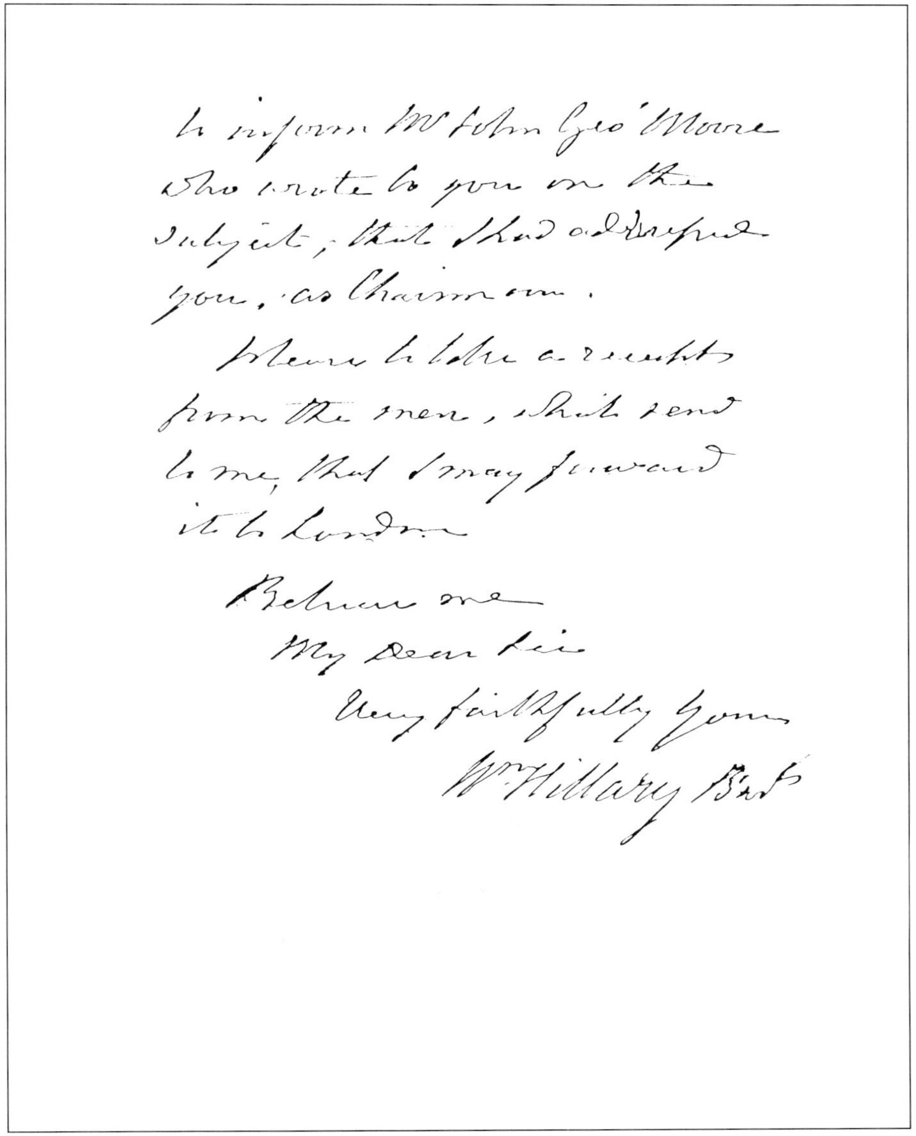
to inform Mr John Geo' Moore
who wrote to you on the
subject, that I had addressed
you, as Chairman.
Please to take a receipt
from the men, which send
to me, that I may forward
it to London
Believe me
My Dear Sir
Very faithfully Yours
Wm Hillary Bart

Fort Anne
20th March 1845

Dear Sir, It gives me great pleasure to transmit to you a letter I have received from Thos Edwards Esq., Secretary to the Royal National Institution to whom I forwarded the statement of services rendered by seven Boatmen at Ramsey in rescuing several persons from a wreck during the late storms, which had been sent to me for that purpose.

F. Tellet Esq.,
High Eailiff of Ramsey.

You will see Mr. Edwards letter is accompanied by an order on their Bankers for £3-10-0 in my favour which I have endorsed to you and I am sure you will be happy, in your capacity as Chairman of the Ramsey Shipwreck Committee, to distribute it amongst the Men.

I wish the amount had been larger, but I trust the example may encourage others on occasions of future wrecks -

Will you have the kindness to inform Mr. John Geo' Moore who wrote to you on the subject, that I have addressed you, as Chairman.

Please to take a receipt from the men, which send to me, that I may forward it to London.

Believe me
My Dear Sir
Very faithfully yours

Wm. Hillary Bart

MEDALS AND AWARDS

RNLI Medals

1845 SILVER MEDAL
Mr. John Cowin for the rescue of six persons from the schooner HAZLEWOOD. (See Sir William Hillary's letter, pages 208 and 209).

1883 SILVER MEDAL
Coxswain Robert Fell for gallant services in saving lives at sea during the past 14 years.

1890 SILVER MEDALS
Coxswain Robert Garrett and Hon. Secretary E. C. Kerr for the rescue of 18 persons from the dredger WALTER BIBBY and the schooner MARGARET on 7th November, 1890.

1941 BRONZE MEDAL
Coxswain John Comish for the rescue of 13 of the crew of the trawler STRATHAIRLIE on the 21st January, 1941.

RNLI Awards

1932 GOLD BADGE
Mrs. M. W. Harrison for services as Chairman of the Ladies' Lifeboat Guild for 20 years.

1964 GOLD BADGE
Mr. W. R. Edwards in recognition of 30 years' service as Honorary Secretary to the Branch.

1965 SILVER BADGE
Mrs. G. J. Teare, J.P., for services as Treasurer and Chairman to the Ladies' Guild.

1987 SILVER BADGE
Mr. T. E. Tregellis for 12 years' service as Branch Treasurer.

1989 SILVER BADGE
Sqn. Ldr. J. Sands, Branch Administrative Officer since 1975, for his services to the Branch.

1990 SILVER BADGE
Mrs. B. Green for her long services as Hon. Secretary and Chairman of the Ladies' Guild.

1990 SILVER BADGE
Mrs. E. Corlett for her long services as Hon. Secretary and Chairman of the Ladies' Guild.

In addition to the above awards, many Coxswains and Members of the Crew have received RNLI Long Service Certificates and Honorary Secretaries and Treasurers of both the Branch Committee and the Ladies' Guild have received Certificates of Thanks from the RNLI for their long years of loyal service.

In 1968, after 100 years of the Station serving under the auspices of the RNLI, the Chairman of the Committee of Management, Admiral Sir Wilfred Woods, G.B.E., K.B.E., D.S.O., sent a framed letter commemorating the fact that during this period 537 lives had been saved from Ramsey and five RNLI medals had been awarded to the Branch.

Of particular note are the recent thanks of the RNLI on Vellum to Coxswain Jim Kinnin and Certificates to each of his Crew of seven for their services to yachts in the 1986 Round the Island Race when 14 yachtsmen and three of their craft were brought to safety. (See page 156).

Other Awards

1918 SEA GALLANTRY AWARD to Bowman William Henry Sharpe for "Gallantry in saving life at sea" in rescuing the crew of ss TORBAY on the 15th March, 1918. (Presented at Buckingham Palace by H. M. King George V).

1937 The Finnish Government awarded a Silver Medal to Coxswain Lord and Bronze Medals to his Crew for services rendered to the ss ESBO of Helsingfors, on the 19th Oct. 1937.

1966 M.B.E. to Mr. W. R. Edwards for his services to the RNLI.

1968 The Royal Humane Society's Certificate on Vellum awarded to Mr. R. E. Wilkinson, a reserve Crew Member, for saving the life of a man in danger of drowning off the lifeboat slipway.

1971 B.E.M. to Coxswain W. F. Cottier for his services to the RNLI.

1986 B.E.M. to Station Mechanic J. Kneale for his services to the RNLI.

NOTE: After the rescue of the crew of Norwegian brig GIER, in 1893 (see page 32), the UK board of Trade awarded medals to two Ramsey businessmen, Mr. Frederick Brew (Silver) and Mr. John Brew (Bronze). Mr. John Brew was the grandfather of the present Branch Chairman, Rev. Dr. Ewan Corlett.

COXSWAINS, SECOND COXSWAINS, BOWMEN AND MECHANICS

COXSWAINS

1868 Thomas Kaighin (Father)
1873 Robert Fell
1883 Thomas Kaighin (Son)
1890 Robert Garrett (Father)
1903 Harry Corkish
1925 John Garrett (Son)
1930 J. T. Lord
1938 John Comish
1946 Ernest Starkey
1952 W. F. Cottier
1972 D. Walker
1973 L. W. Gawne
1985 J. Kinnin

BOWMEN

1897 W. F. Martin
1901 J. Crix
1917 W. H. Sharpe
1927 J. T. Lord
1930 J. Christian
1938 W. Crix
1945 F. Cottier
1950 F. W. Kinnin
1952 P. I. Crowe
1961 D. R. Walker
(Appointment of Bowman discontinued hereafter)

SECOND COXSWAINS

1868 Robert Fell
1873 Thomas Kaighin (Son)
1883 John Cowell
1886 Robert Garrett
1890 Oscar Corlett
1897 W. F. Martin
1916 John Garrett (Son)
1925 John Comish
1938 F. L. Ball
1950 W. F. Cottier
1952 F. W. Kinnin
1976 J. Kinnin
1985 D. Martin
1988 R. Stanfield

MECHANICS

1931 William Kennish
1941 T. A. Corlett
1941 Stanley Lindsay
1956 T. A. Corlett
1964 J. Kneale
1987 J. Martin

ENROLLED CREW LIST OF THE RNLB *Ann and James Ritchie* in JULY, 1991.

James Kinnin . . . . Coxswain
Raymond Stanfield . . . . 2nd Coxswain
James Martin . . . . Station Mechanic
Ronald Crowe . . . . .Asst. Mechanic
Kevin Crowe
Gerald Evison . . . . Emergency Mechanic
Kevin Christian
Alistair Clague . . . . . . Emergency Mechanic
Kim Holland
Anthony Gaines
Alan Clague
John Clague
Mark Matthews
Mark Kenyon . . . . . . Emergency Mechanic
Andrew Benson
Kevin Airey
Andre Midwood
Neil Crowe

(Note: Mark Kenyon is the Assistant Mechanic designate)

SHORE SIDE

Juan Sable . . . . Tractor Driver
Percy Faragher . . . . Assistant Driver
Albert Faragher . . . . Head Launcher
James Kneale . . . . Lightman

THE RAMSEY STATION COMMITTEE

CHAIRMEN

1835-1868 F. Tellet, J.P., High Bailiff of Ramsey

1868-1881 Rev. William Bell Christian, J.P., M.H.K.
Son of Deemster John Christian of Milntown.
Vicar of Lezayre 1845-1861. Member of the old "Self-Elected" House of Keys, but democratically elected as a Member for Ramsey in 1866, being one of only two clergymen Members. Receiver General, 1883-1886. Branch Chairman for 12 years.

1881-1900 Rev. George Paton
Curate of St. Paul's, Ramsey 1869. Chaplain 1871-1900
Branch Hon. Secretary 1868-1881, then Chairman for 19 years.

1900-1916 James Murray Cruickshank, J.P.
High Bailiff, Branch Committee Member for 4 years and then Chairman for 16 years.

1916-1927 Thomas Horsfall Midwood, J.P.
Chairman of Ramsey Town Commissioners 1908-1910
Branch Committee Member 1911-1916, then Chairman for 11 years.

1927-1946 Canon Mark Wilks Harrison, J.P., M.A.
Vicar of South Ramsey 1911-1946, Chairman of the Ramsey Town Commissioners 1932-1934; 1938-40; 1945-46 Branch Committee Member 1911-1927, then Chairman for 20 years.

1946-1958 Rev Halford William Young
Vicar of St. Olaves, Ramsey, 1930-1951, Branch Committee Member 1930-1946, then Chairman for 12 years.

1958-1971 Keith Grimble Groves, O.B.E., J.P., M.A., L.L.M.
Barrister-at-Law. Branch Committee Member from 1939. Vice-Chairman 1946-1958 and Chairman 1958-1971. Author of the first History of the Ramsey Station in 1968.

1971-1977 Major General Sir Henry H. C. Sugden, K.B.E., C.B., D.S.O., M.H.K., F.I.C.E.
Branch Committee Member 1962-1964; Vice-Chairman 1965-1971 and then Chairman for 6 years.

1977-1982 Mr. W. J. Corlett
Divisional Inspector of the Special Constabulary
Branch Hon. Treasurer 1966-1970; Vice-Chairman 1972-1977 and then Chairman for five years.

1982-1985 Mr. S. C. Callister
Chairman of the Diocesan Board of Finance
Branch Committee Member 1971-79; Vice-Chairman 1979-1982 and then Chairman for three years.

1985 Mr. B.T. Swales, F.C.I.S.
Manager & Secretary of the Ramsey Steamship Co.; Lloyds Agent; Branch Committee Member 1946-1950, Hon. Treasurer 1950-1965, Hon. Secretary 1967-1985, then Chairman until his sudden death.

1986 Dr. E. C. B. Corlett, O.B.E., M.A., Ph.D., F.Eng, F.R.I.N.A.
Branch Committee Member 1978-1985; Vice-Chairman 1985 and then Chairman from 1986

HONORARY SECRETARIES AND TREASURERS

1935-	John C. Stephen
1869-1881	Rev. George Paton
1881-1907	Mr. E. C. Kerr
1907-1910	Mr. W. L. Corlett
1910-1915	Mr. D. Vondy
1915-1927	Captain Evans and Mr. A. H. Teare
1927-1930	Mr. A. H. Teare
1930-1934	Mr. J. B. Kee
1934-1962	Mr. J. Ramsey F.I.C.S., and Mr. W. R. Edwards

HONORARY SECRETARIES

1962-1967	Mr. W. R. Edwards, M.B.E.
1967-1985	Mr. B. T. Swales, F.I.C.S.
1985-	Captain M. Brew, M.N.I.

HONORARY TREASURERS

1950-1965	Mr. B. T. Swales, F.I.C.S.
1965-1971	Mr. W. J. Corlett
1971-1984	Mr. T. E. Tregellis
1984-1989	Mr. A. B. Dailey, A.C.A.
1989-	Mr. J. S. Spencer

STATION ADMINISTRATIVE OFFICER

1975- Sqn. Ldr. J. Sands, R.A.F. (Retd.) (A new appointment from 1975)

RAMSEY STATION EXECUTIVE COMMITTEE, JULY, 1991

Chairman:	Rev. Dr. Ewan Corlett
Vice-Chairman:	Captain Neil Luck
Hon. Secretary:	Captain Michael Brew
Hon. Treasurer:	Mr. Steven Spencer
Hon. Administrative Officer:	Sqn. Ldr. John Sands, RAF (Retd.)

RAMSEY LADIES' LIFEBOAT GUILD EXECUTIVE COMMITTEE, JULY, 1991

Vice-President:	Mrs. Barbara Green
Chairman:	Mrs. Edna Corlett
Vice-Chairman:	Mrs. Hilary Sands
Hon. Secretary:	Mrs. Mary Page
Hon. Treasurer:	Mrs. Nora Pugh
Hon. Assistant Treasurer:	Mrs. Julie Daniels
Hon. Social Secretary:	Mrs. Lyn Smalley
Hon. Souvenir Secretary:	Mrs. Mary Spencer
Hon. Souvenir Secretary:	Mrs. Joyce Wilson
Hon. Press Officer:	Mrs. Jane Forth
	Mrs. Shirley Steele

LIST OF SERVICES

The Two Sisters 1868-1890 and 1894

DATE		VESSEL	TYPE	REGISTERED	SERVICE	SAVED VLS.	SAVED LIVES
1868	Dec 11	Jane	Brigantine	Workington	Crew rescued		4
		Prudence	Schooner	Aberystwyth	Crew rescued		4
1870	Feb 6	John Bell	Schooner	Barrow	Crew rescued		8
	Oct 8	Gipsy	Schooner	Liverpool	Crew rescued		10
	Dec 18	Pearl	Smack	Ramsey	Crew rescued		3
1871	Jan 16	Lady Huntley	Brigantine	Maryport	Crew rescued		4
	Feb 5	William	Schooner	Liverpool	Crew rescued	1	3
	Aug 20	Rapid	Schooner	Preston	Crew rescued	1	2
	Oct 29	Pausillippo	Schooner	Ramsey	Crew rescued		3
1873	Oct 22	Mary	Schooner	Douglas	Crew rescued		3
1874	May 15	Kilda	Yacht	Belfast	Took off 2 crew & L/Bmen brought yacht in.	1	5
	Sept 15	Venus	Smack	Douglas	Crew rescued	1	4
	Nov 26	Maria	Schooner/yacht	Preston	Crew rescued		6
		Laurel	Smack	Castletown	Crew rescued		3
1875	Dec 24	Thistle	Smack	Castletown	Crew rescued		3
1880	Feb 9	John Wesley	Schooner	Aberystwyth	Crew rescued		5
	Oct 25	Victoire	Brigantine	Irvine	Crew rescued	1	5
	Oct 27	William Hill	Brigantine	Dundalk	Crew rescued	1	5
	Nov 14	Ada	Schooner	Beaumaris	Crew rescued		4
1881	Oct 14	Eulala	Schooner	Dumfries	Crew rescued		4
	Nov 26	Wonder	Schooner	–	Not required on arrival		
		Shannon	Steamship	–	Not required on arrival		
1882	Mar 26	Countess of Caithness	Schooner	Gloucester		1	4
1883	Mar 6	Emerald Isle	Trawler	Whitehaven			4
	Apr 27	Flora	Flat	Runcorn		1	3
	Sept 27	Hereward	Barque	–	Rendered assistance		
1884	Oct 31	Daniel Yorke	Wherry	Dundalk	Crew rescued		4
1885	Oct 2	Professo	Brigantine	Tvedestrand (Norway)	Rendered assistance		
1886	Oct 5	Vulcan	Schooner	Douglas	Rendered assistance		
1887	Mar 11	Isabella Stuart	Schooner	Ardrossan	Towed into Ramsey	1	4
	Nov 1	Kattie Darling	Schooner	Chester	Crew rescued		3
		Prothesa	Brigantine	Teignmouth	Crew rescued		7
1889	Aug 16	Volunteer	Pleasure boat	Ramsey	Rendered assistance		
	Dec 24	James Williamson	Schooner	–	Not required on arrival		
1890	Jan 14	Zealot	Cutter	Peel	Crew rescued		1
		W.M.J.	Schooner	Swansea	Crew rescued		4
		Otter	Cutter	Port St. Mary	Crew rescued		4
		Hamilton	Cutter	Ramsey	Crew rescued		3
	Nov 7	Walter Bibby	Steam dredger	Preston	Crew rescued		15
		Margaret	Schooner	Belfast	Crew rescued		3
1894	Jan 30	Celestina	Barque	Fiume (Yugoslavia)	Rendered assistance		
					GRAND TOTALS – Services 41	9	147

O.N. 222 *Mary Isabella* (1) 1888-1896

DATE		VESSEL	TYPE	REGISTERED	SERVICE	SAVED VLS.	SAVED LIVES
1889	Feb 8	Patrick	Cutter	Peel	Crew rescued		4
	Feb 13	Brilliant	Schooner	Peel	Saved vessel after crew abandoned	1	
1891	Jan 31	Leona	Schooner	Belfast	Crew rescued		4
	Oct 9	Columba	Barque	Kristiansand (Norway)	Crew rescued		9
	Oct 9	Columba	Barque	"	Assisted to save vessel	1	
	Oct 13	Mary Agnes	Schooner	Dumfries	Took off crew/saved vessel	1	3
	Oct 14	Unity	Schooner	Chester	Took off crew/saved vessel	1	4
1892	July 2	Mary Jane	Schooner	Ramsey	Rescued crew		3
	Aug 12	Royal Fern	Cutter	Peel	Saved vessel and crew	1	3
1893	Apr 17	Annie	Schooner	Lancaster	Crew rescued		3
	Nov 22	Jean McCrae	Schooner	Ardrossan	Towed into Ramsey	1	4
	Nov 26	MacRae	Steamship	Glasgow	Assistance to save vessel	1	
	Dec 10	Sultana Reina	Brigantine	Liverpool	Crew rescued		6
		Cormorant	Brigantine	Norway	Rescue attempt failed		
	Dec 15	Not Forgot	Schooner	Chester	Took off crew		3
1894	Jan 30	Margaret Annie	Smack	Ramsey	Assistance not required		
	Feb 7	Annie Jane	Nicky	Peel	Assistance not required		
		Dolphin	Smack	Dublin	Took off crew		4
	Dec 22	Margaret Jones	Schooner	Caernafon	Took off crew		3
		Excelsior	Schooner	Chester	Took off crew		4
		Agnes	Schooner		Assistance not required		
1895	Feb 7	Margaret & Elizabeth	Schooner	Liverpool	Took off crew		2
	Nov 10	Ellen & Mary	Schooner	Wigtown	Took off crew		3
		Globe	Brigantine	Whitehaven	Took off crew		7
		Harvest Home	Schooner	Preston	Took off crew		4
	Nov 15	Somerset	Brigantine	Christiana (Norway)	Took off crew		9
	Nov 23	Gem	Schooner	Ramsey	Took off crew		4
					GRAND TOTALS – Services 27	7	86

O.N. 391 *Mary Isabella* (2) 1896-1915

DATE		VESSEL	TYPE	REGISTERED	SERVICE	SAVED VLS.	SAVED LIVES
1896	Sep 17	Grace Darling	Cutter	Ramsey	Took off crew		5
	Oct 8	Giovanni	Barque	Lilesand (Sweden)	Took off crew		13
1897	Mar 28	Uto	Brigantine	Lilesand	Landed crew of 6		
	June 16	Maid of Irvine	Schooner	Belfast	Took off crew		3
		Furness Abbey	Schooner	Lancaster	Took off crew		3
	Aug 17	Lucinda	Cutter/yacht	Beaumaris	Landed crew of 2		
		Belgian King	Steamship	Newcastle	Took telegram ashore		
	Nov 28	Nelson	Schooner	Belfast	Took off crew		5
	Dec 14	Glynaeron	Schooner	Beaumaris	Took off crew of 5		
1898	Apr 13	Newlands	Ketch	Newport	Landed 5		
	May 11	Parkside	Brigantine	Dundalk	Took off crew		5
	Nov 23	William Thompson	Schooner	Dumfries	Took off crew		4
		Bessie Arnold	Schooner	Whitehaven	Took off crew		5
		Manx Maid	Steamship	Ramsey	Took off crew		5
	Dec 27	Twin Sisters	Schooner	Stranraer	Took off crew		3
		Annie Warren	Schooner	Aberdovey	Took off crew		5
		Return	Schooner	Greenock	Took off crew		5
1899	Jan 12	Twin Sisters	Schooner	Stranraer	Landed crew of 3		
	Mar 28	Maxim	Brigantine	Drogheda	Took off crew		4
	Nov 1	Cordillera	Barque	Buenos Aires	Took off crew		11
	Nov 3	Cordillera	Barque	Buenos Aires	Took off crew		4
	Nov 9	Africa	Barque	Lisbon	Took off crew		16
	Dec 16	Ruby	Schooner	Aberystwyth	Took off crew		4
1900	Aug 3	Queen	Smack	Douglas	Rendered assistance		
	Oct 4	Topdal	Barque	Mandal (Norway)	Took off crew		8
	Dec 17	Rheidol Vale	Schooner	Aberystwyth	Took off crew		3
	Dec 22	Unknown			7 hour search, nothing found		
1902	Feb 8	Ellesmere	Schooner	Runcorn	Took off crew		3
	Nov 11	Aviles	Steamship	Aviles	Escorted two ships' boats ashore		
1904	Jan 29	Useful	Schooner	Barrow	Took off crew		4
	Nov 10	Elizabeth Ellen Fisher	Schooner	Fleetwood	Took off crew		4
1905	Jan 14	Conqueror	Steam tug	Liverpool	Attempted a rescue		
1907	Feb 20	Isabella	Schooner	Baow	Took off crew		4
1908	Jun 28	Guiding Star	Schooner	Runcorn	Took off crew		4
1910	Jan 8	Glide	Schooner	Belfast	Took off crew		4
		Glide	Schooner	Belfast	Put L/B crew aboard to man pumps	1	
	Aug 18	Sea Bird	Yacht	Caernafon	Took off crew		3
1911	Feb 21	Claggan	Schooner	Barrow	Landed crew of 3		
	Sept 1	Bahama Bank	Light Vessel		Landed crewman for medical attention		
	Oct 29	X.L.	Ketch	Castletown	Landed crew of 4		
	Nov 12	Faithful	Ketch/trawler	Ramsey	Landed crew of 3		
1912	Jul 17	Jessie Sinclair	Schooner	Port St. Mary	Assisted crew and ship		
	Nov 26	Princess Louise	Schooner	Barrow	Landed crew of 4		
1914	Nov 15	Coniston	Schooner	Barrow	Took off crew		4
	Dec 30	J.H. Barrow	Shooner	Lancaster	Took off crew		5
1915	Mar 18	New Leader	Ketch	Ramsey	Took off crew		4
	Oct 28	Holy Wath	Schooner	Whitehaven	Took off crew		3
	Nov 12	Sigrid	Barque	Brevik	No rescue: L/B damaged		
					GRAND TOTALS – Services 48	1	153

O.N. 402 *Anna Maria Lee* 1916-1927

DATE		VESSEL	TYPE	REGISTERED	SERVICE	SAVED VLS.	SAVED LIVES
1916	Apr 25	Malpas Belle	Brigantine	Truro	Took off crew		6
1917	Dec 16	Castlerock	Steamship	Belfast	Stood by the ship		
1918	Oct 5	Forest Deer	Schooner	Dublin	Took off crew		3
	Oct 7	Marie Edmond	Ketch	Ostend	Landed 1 crewman		
		Marie Edmond	Ketch	Ostend	Took off 3 crewmen		3
1919	Mar 20	Carronpark	Steamship	Greenock	Took 5 crewmen to vessel		
1921	Dec 30	Ianthe	Schooner	Bristol	Landed 7; assisted vessel		
1922	Feb 8	Brackenholm	Schooner	Bideford	Landed crew of 3		
1924	Jul 10	Marie Celine	Ketch	Drogheda	Landed crew of 3		
1925	Feb 8	Amis Reunis	Ketch	Falmouth	Assisted, saving vessel	1	5
	Apr 4	Elizabeth Hyam	Schooner	Chester	Took off crew		4
	Oct 9	Unknown			Searched NW coast after rocket sighting. Nothing found		
	Dec 19	Ben Gullion	Schooner	Dumfries	Landed crew of 3		
1926	Jan 26	Unknown			Searched for 6 hours after rocket sighting. Nothing found		
1927	Jan 26	Unknown			To Bahama Bank on a false alarm		
		Austrums	Barquentine	Riga, Latvia	Service abandoned after crew rescued by the Rocket Brigade.		
					GRAND TOTALS – Services 16	1	21

O.N. 512 *Matthew Simpson* 1927-1931

DATE		VESSEL	TYPE	REGISTERED	SERVICE	SAVED VLS.	SAVED LIVES
1927	Jun 26	Cevic	Steam Trawler	Fleetwood	Took off crew		6
1928	Aug 23	Cumberland Coast	Steamship		Stood by vessel on fire		
1929	Mar 20	Florence Brierley	Steam trawler		Launched but not required		
	Apr 1	Venus	Schooner	Castletown	Took off crew		4
1930	Nov 18	H.M.S. Doon	Steamship		Stood-by ashore		
					GRAND TOTALS – Services 5	–	10

O.N. 745 *Lady Harrison* 1931-1948

DATE		VESSEL	TYPE	REGISTERED	SERVICE	SAVED VLS.	SAVED LIVES
1931	Dec 3	Pasages	Steam trawler	Grimsby	Rescue made by Rocket Brigade at Jurby. Service aborted.		
1932	Jan 5	Hawthorn	Steamship	Liverpool	Landed injured man		
	Dec 21	Velia	Steam trawler	Fleetwood	Laid out a sea anchor		
1934	Jun 6	Jubilee	Yacht	Fleetwood	Towed vessel clear of beach	1	2
1935	Apr 10	Edith May	Motor schooner	Wexford	Landed crew of 3		
	Sept 8	Fanstona	Motor yacht	Fleetwood	Towed to Ramsey	1	4
	Oct 19	Esbo	Cargo vessel	Helsingfors (Finland)	Service aborted owing to weather		
1936	Oct 27	Goleta	Steamship	London	Landed injured man. Took out medicines and stores		
	Oct 27	Edith May	Schooner	Wexford	Landed crew of 3		
	Nov 11	Little Orme	Steamship		Stood-by vessel aground		
1937	Jul 21	Aircraft GAEIJ	Reported ditched		$11^{1}/_{2}$ hour search in severe gale for ditched plane. Nothing found.		
1938	Jan 21	Nora	Steamship	Liverpool	Landed Master injured. Rendered assistance		
1939	Mar 11	Unknown	Small boat		Service to Laxey for boat in trouble. Nothing found.		
	Sep 13	Greypoint	Steamship	Belfast	Launched but assistance not required.		
	Oct 26	B84	Drifter		Service to drifter in distress. Vessel made Douglas.		
	Dec 10	Duke of Lancaster	Steamship	Barrow	Rendered assistance after collision. Escorted. Landed		
		Fireking	Steamship	Liverpool	12 men from FIRE KING - one injured.		
1940	Jan 16	3 R.A.F. launches			Stood by one launch		
	Feb 16	Glendun	Steamship	Belfast	Rescued crew		10
	Feb 28	Ulster Queen	Motor vessel	Belfast	Transferred passengers to Duke of Lancaster. Landed crew.		60
	Jul 29	Aircraft	Reported missing		Two hour search off Burrow Head. Nothing bound.		
	Nov 9	Princess Irene	Motor vessel	Groningen	Service to vessel aground. Not required on arrival		
1941	April 17	Carita	Motor vessel		Service to assist. Vessel under tow upon arrival.		
	Sep 7	Unknown			Search off Isle of Whithorn for sinking ship. Nothing found.		
	Nov 20	Strathairlie	Steam trawler	Aberdeen	Rescued crew one at a time		13
1942	Mar 2	Aircraft	Crashed		Search for crashed aircraft. Aborted when aircraft found at Jurby.		
	Mar 27	Aircraft	Missing		Searched south to Douglas. Nothing found.		
	Sep 14	Caribou	Fishing boat	Ramsey	Towed boat to Ramsey		
1943	Mar 6	Unidentified aircraft			Six hour search of NW coast. Nothing found.		

Continued ...

DATE		VESSEL	TYPE	REGISTERED	SERVICE	SAVED VLS.	SAVED LIVES
1943	Jun 24	Unidentified boat			Service to Laxey but not required on arrival.		
	Dec 7	Glenmaroon	Steamship		On stand-by for ship hit by aircraft. Not required.		
	Dec 29	Cairngorn	Motor vessel		Vessel ashore at Point of Ayre but not required on arrival.		
1944	Jun 29	Unidentified			Red flares seen off Pier. Searched, but nothing found.		
1945	May 13	RAF	aerial L/B		In distress but service not required on arrival.		
	May 14	R.A.F.	Dinghy		Launched to assist. Rescue launch took distress over.		
	Sep 25	Empire Fathom	Motor vessel		Launch to put a pilot aboard aborted. Fouled propeller.		
1946	Feb 3	Rian	Motor vessel	Groningen	Landed 6 crewmen after vessel in collision.		
	Sep 10	Majestic	Fishing smack	Ramsey	Took off crew		4
	Oct 12	M.O.B. 7	Steamship		Stood by vessel under repair		
1947	Aug 14	Capella	Fishing vessel	Fishguard	Landed injured skipper. Towed vessel to Ramsey		
1948	Jan 6	Teazel	Motor vessel	Cardiff	Service aborted as L/B grounded. Nothing found.		
	Feb 5	Noreg	Steam trawler	Hull	Laid out anchor for grounded vessel.		
	Jun 11	Aircraft			Reported aircraft down. Search aborted - false alarm.		
	Jul 27	Northness	Steam trawler	Hull	Laid out kedge anchor and stood by until vessel refloated		
	Sep 8	Seamew	Yacht	Ramsey	Towed to Ramsey.		
	Sep 12	Warrior	Tug	Glasgow	Took doctor out to injured seaman		
				GRAND TOTALS	Services – 48	2	93

O.N. 862 *Thomas Corbett* 1948 - 1970

DATE		VESSEL	TYPE	REGISTERED	SERVICE	SAVED VLS.	SAVED LIVES
1948	Sep 28	Aircraft	Overdue		Stood-by ashore only.		
	Oct 21	Unknown	Flares seen		Two hour search for source of flares. Nothing found.		
	Dec 6	Saxton	Steamship	Middlesbrough	Stood-by vessel aground. No action taken.		
1949	Mar 4	Capella	Fishing vessel	Ramsey	Took off two seamen		2
	Jun 29	Sea Hornet	Aircraft	Ditched	Searched but aborted when pilot found by another plane.		
	Aug 24	Larus	Small dinghy		Searched for missing crew-man. Not found.		
1950	Feb 17	Ben Henshaw	Motor tanker	London	Took out doctor to deceased ex-Master. Brought body ashore.		
	Feb 24	St. Oran	Steamship		Took off doctor to vessel but found she only wanted stores.		
	Jul 24	Boy over cliffs	Maughold Head		Landed doctor and nurse on headland. Transferred to hospital.		
1951	May 22	Brighter Hope	Motor fishing vessel (MFV)	Belfast	Assistance given to vessel on fire and later beached.		
	Jul 10	Rapide	Aircraft	Missing	Searched and found small wreckage. No survivor.		
1952	Mar 16	Nabro	MFV	Dublin	Towed into Ramsey.		
	Oct 28	Second	Steamship	Belfast	Landed injured seaman.		
	Oct 29	Unknown			Distress flare reported. searched: nothing found.		
	Nov 7	Selford	Fish carrier	St. Helier	Stood-by ashore in gale conditions. Vessel's anchor fouled.		
	Nov 20	Ben Jee	Steamship	Ramsey	Stood-by grounded vessel at Point of Ayre.		
	Dec 12	Patricia Hague	Steam trawler	Fleetwood	Stood-by disabled ship then escorted her to Douglas.		
1954	Jul 22	Oxford	Aircraft	Missing	Searched for 7 hours. Nothing found.		
	Sep 19	Fulmar	Yacht	Douglas	Wreckage of yacht found - searched for crew but aborted.		
1955	Jan 2	Unknown	Flares seen		Searched area towards Seascales. Nothing found.		
	Sep 13	Unknown	Flare seen		Searched NE from Point of Ayre. Nothing found.		
	Dec 29	Red Lancer	Steam trawler	Fleetwood	Took out doctor to treat two seamen (2 trips).		
		Red Dragon	Steam trawler	Fleetwood	Landed sick man for hospital treatment.		
1956	Mar 8	Albert Fleetwood Lady	Rowing boat Trawler	Ramsey Fleetwood	Bodies reported from capsized boat (ex Fleetwood Lady). Searched Bay and only debris found.		
	July 27	Nimbus (R.A.F.)	Sailing dinghy	R.A.F. Jurby	Boat capsized. Crew stood-by but no launch.		
	Aug 25	Dreadnought	MFV	Peel	Engine failure. Towed vessel back to Ramsey.		
	Oct 2	Boston Valiant	Trawler	Fleetwood	Took doctor out to suspected case appendicitis.		

continued...

DATE		VESSEL	TYPE	REGISTERED	SERVICE	SAVED VLS.	SAVED LIVES
1957	Jan 28	Baron Ramsay	Steamship	Glasgow	Took out stores		
	May 29	Unknown	Parachute flare		Three hour search off Laxey Nothing found.		
	Jun 16	Pygmalion	MFV	Fleetwood	Vessel off Bahama Bank with fouled propeller. Towed to Ramsey.		
	Aug 23	Zulu	Yacht	Fleetwood	Trouble in heavy weather off Laxey. Escorted to Ramsey.		
1958	May 10	Sea Lion	MFV	Ramsey	Engine failure. Towed to Douglas.	1	2
	Jul 23	Un-named	Rubber dinghy		Drifting out to sea. When taken in tow, launch cancelled.		
	Nov 10	Lord Plender	Trawler	Fleetwood	Grounded on Whitestone Bank. L/B re-called when she re-floated.		
1959	Oct 1	Jet aircraft	Ditched		Searched off Point of Ayre. Nothing found.		
	Dec 30	Wyre Majestic	Motor trawler		Vessel grounded Mull of Galloway. Re-called an hour after launch.		
1961	Feb 20	Aircraft	Avro Anson	Overdue	Commenced search off Point of Ayre but re-called. Plane found crashed.		
	Aug 28	RAF Launch 1653		RAF Jurby	Launch suffered broken wind-screen and bilge pump. Escorted.		
	Nov 28	Auspicity	Coastal tanker	London	Vessel in collision and damaged. Escorted to Ramsey.		
1962	Aug 4	Playmate	Yacht	Lytham	Overdue. Possible sighting. Found yacht OK - returned.		
1963	Jul 30	Missing Boy			Searched northern coast for missing boy. Not found.		
1964	Oct 9	Children's Friend	MFV	Fleetwood	Engine trouble. Towed back to Ramsey.		
	Dec 26	Radio Caroline	Pirate Radio Ship		Landed wounded seaman.		
1965	Jan 27	Radio Caroline	Pirate Radio Ship		Landed bleeding seaman.		
	Jul 22	Aircraft	Lightning	Ditched	Searched but helicopter found survivors & did rescue.		
	Aug 4	Boat	Cruising sloop		Caught in heavy weather. Towed to Ramsey.	1	3
	Aug 27	Loch Lein			Vessel aground at Point of Ayre. Found vessel high and dry. Returned.		
	Oct 1	Radio Caroline	Pirate Radio Ship		Sustained hull damage. L/B crew on stand-by. No launch.		
	Dec 22	Radio Caroline	Pirate Radio Ship		Master sustained dog bite. Took out Doctor to stitch hand.		
1966	Mar 22	Radio Caroline	Pirate Radio Ship		Crew with gashed hand. Took out Doctor and landed seaman.		
	Aug 2	Master Frank	MFV	Ramsey	Sheared crankshaft. Towed vessel into port.		
	Aug 22	Cotick	Yacht	London	Failed engine. Towed to Ramsey.	1	3
	Nov 5	Unknown	Parachute flares sighted		Searched around Bahama Bank. Nothing found.		

continued...

Thomas Corbett 1948 - 1970 *(continued)*

DATE		VESSEL	TYPE	REGISTERED	SERVICE	SAVED VLS.	SAVED LIVES
1967	Apr 30	Bobbie	Catamaran		MFV picked up crew. L/B towed vessel to port.		
	July 30	Gamecock	Cabin cruiser		Vessel overdue but found by Barrow L/B. Re-called.		
	Sep 4	Radio Caroline	Pirate Radio Ship		To deliver message to stop an attempted swim in gales.		
1968	Jan 14	Yarvil	Motor vessel	London	Vessel had steering gear trouble. About to launch when cancelled.		
	Feb 4	Irene	Motor vessel	Helsingfors (Sweden)	Took out Doctor & Constable to dead man. Body ashore.		
	May 19	Lady Eleanor	MFV	Ramsey	Vessel with engine failure. Towed in from Whitestone Bank Bay.		
	Sep 14	Zineh	Yacht		Escorted in from Queen's Pier.		
	Dec 14	Robert Hewett	Trawler		Searched for 4 hours for man overboard. Nothing found.		
	Dec 19	Helmsman	Motor tanker	London	Ship reported aground Rue Point. Launched in gale. Not required.		
1969	May 18	Verbena	MFV		Put pump aboard grounded vessel. Held her up to tide.		
	Aug 18	Oursine	Yacht		Vessel badly anchored near Queen's Pier. Re-moored her and landed owner.		
	Oct 4	Unknown	Glass fibre dinghy		Searched for any survivors of empty dinghy. Found. nothing.		
	Dec 10	Two skin divers			Two skin divers missing. Launched and found them aboard MFV. Returned.		
					GRAND TOTALS Services – 63	3	10

Reserve Lifeboat No. 795 *Frank & William Oates* 1961

DATE		VESSEL	TYPE	REGISTERED	SERVICE	SAVED VLS.	SAVED LIVES
1961	Mar 26	Dolores	Aux. yacht		Dismasted yacht towed by M/V COLEBROOK. Took over tow at Maughold.		
	May 5	Boy fallen over cliff and injured			Towed dinghy to Maughold Head. Picked up and landed injured boy.		1
					GRAND TOTALS Services – 2	–	1

Reserve Lifeboat O.N. 792 *Annie Rowland & Isabella Forrest* 1964

DATE		VESSEL	TYPE	REGISTERED	SERVICE	SAVED VLS.	SAVED LIVES
1964	Apr 3	Unknown	Report of an explosion		Searched NW coast for 7 hours. Nothing found.		
	May 18	Wyndrush	Yacht		Attended vessel aground but crew already ashore.		
	May 19	Boy over cliff			Took dinghy and Doctor to injured boy at the Dhoon. Took boy to Laxey for transfer to hospital.		
	May 26	Pygmalion	M.F.V.		Launched to pick up survivors after vessel exploded and sank. Another MFV attended. Not needed.		
	Aug 24	Small boat and Dinghy		R.A.F.	Picked up 2 men from each boat and then towed boats back to Ramsey.	1	4
	Sep 8	Small boat			Took dinghy to Bulgham Bay and picked up woman and two children. Landed hem at Ramsey.		3
	Oct 22	Wanderboro Warrior	MFV	Castletown	Vessel run ut of fuel. Towed back from North of Point of Ayre.		
				GRAND TOTALS	Services – 7	1	7

Reserve Lifeboat O.N. 994 *Vincent Nesfield* 1974-1975, 1979, 1980, 1987

DATE		VESSEL	TYPE	REGISTERED	SERVICE	SAVED VLS.	SAVED LIVES
1974	Dec 19		Lady over cliff		Launched but not required.		
1975	Feb 7	Random Harvest	MFV		Engine failure. Towed from Point of Ayre to Ramsey.		
	Mar 1	Pern	MFV	Grimsby	Stood-by vessel until tow arranged.		
	Apr 9	Wyre Victory	Trawler	Fishguard	Took out Doctor and Constable. Landed injured deck hand.		
1979	Nov 4	Idena	Stern trawler	Fleetwood	Took out Doctor who confirmed death of the Skipper.		
	Nov 11	Boy Anthony	Small MFV		Took out Doctor to sick crewman.		
1980	Feb 14	Triton	Small MFV		Searched for vessel said to be in distress. Not found.		
	Mar 10	Eclipse	Yacht		Yacht in doubt of position in bad weather. Escorted to port.		
	May 7	Osprey	Small MFV	Maryport	Long search for overdue vessel. Nothing found.		
1987	Apr 28	Janmar	Trawler		Landed injured seaman.		
	Aug 15	Sea Follie	Cabin cruiser	Isle of Man	Fouled propeller. Towed to Ramsey.		
	Aug 23	Freedom of Mann	Yacht	Ramsey	Escorted to port.		
	Aug 31	Mochrum Scart	Yacht	Ramsey	Yacht crew transferred to Lifeboat. Yacht towed to Ramsey.	1	2
	Sept 1	Unknown	Red flares		Searched for a casualty. Nothing found.		
	Sept 3	Amanda Jane	Fishing vessel	Douglas	Launched but not required.		
	Oct 16	Spheroid	Ro-ro freight		Escorted partially disabled vessel to Ramsey Bay		
	Oct 25	Elmar	Cabin cruiser	Isle of Man	Engine failure. Towed to Ramsey.		
				GRAND TOTALS	Services – 17	1	2

O.N. 995 *James Ball Ritchie* 1970-1991

DATE		VESSEL	TYPE	REGISTERED	SERVICE	SAVED VLS.	SAVED LIVES
1970	May 24	Rhian	Yacht		Launched in reply to red flares. Towed yacht into port.		
	May 31	Solan Goose	Sailing dinghy		Attended capsized boat. Not required on arrival.		
	Aug 30	Varuna	Yacht		Yacht with engine trouble. Towed to port. Returned to assist others.		
	Sep 1	Charlie	Yacht		Yacht on Ballacash Bank making no headway. Towed her to Ramsey.	1	2
	Oct 5	Ellan Vannin	MFV		Towed disabled vessel to Ramsey.		
1971	Jan 22	Raylight	MV	Greenock	Escorted vessel under tow towards Peel.		
	May 26	Carina	Power Boat		Boat with damaged rudder. Towed to Ramsey.	1	2
	May 28	Unknown			Launched in answer to a 'Mayday' call. Possibly hoax.		
	June 3	Levitation Tri	Trimaran		Yacht with damaged float. Towed to Douglas.	1	3
	Aug 10	Starbank	MFV		Rescued crew and passengers from raft after MFV grounded.		6
1972	Jan 25	Lustre	MFV	Newry	Vessel lost rudder east of Ramsey. Towed to port.		
	Mar 27	Sea Kitten	Catamaran		Took aboard 2 crew of vessel in a water-logged state.		2
	May 21	Boy over cliff			Launched to assist rescue. Not required. Boy died.		
	June 3		Sailing Dinghy		Righted dinghy and towed to port. Crew otherwise landed.	1	
	June 21		Dinghy with outboard		Launched to give assistance but not required.		
	July 24	Wyre Defence	Motor trawler		Took out Doctor and landed injured Engineer.		
	Aug 5	Luneda	Trawler	Fleetwood	Searched for man overboard. Not found.		
1973	Jun 30	Ametustus	Yacht		Escorted to port.		
		Aphelion	Yacht		Escorted to port.		
	Sep 20	Escape	Yacht		Towed yacht to port. Landed crewman.	1	1
	Oct 27	Fiona	MFV		Vessel with engine trouble. Towed to Peel	1	4
1974	Feb 2	Ben Veg	Motor Vessel	Ramsey	Vessel anchored with engine trouble. Stood by her.		
	Feb 21	Wyre Conqueror	MFV	Fleetwood	Searched for man overboard. Picked up another crew member from the sea.		1
	May 6	Malcolm Miller	Sail training	Aberdeen	Landed sick cadet for hospital.		
	Aug 2	Bajo	Speedboat		Disabled with engine trouble. Towed to Ramsey.		
	Aug 4	Unknown	Motorboat		Answered distress flares. Peel L/B took tow.		
	Sep 15	Trident of Mann	Yacht		Thought to be in difficulty. Not required.		

continued...